S HALLE
"INDER".

# The
# Dressmaker's
# Dictionary

*A reference book of terms, processes and
stitches for all dressmakers.*

# The Dressmaker's Dictionary

ANN LADBURY

Illustrations by Jil Shipley and others

B. T. Batsford Ltd   London

## Dedication

Friends have told me I should dedicate my books. So,
as I hope this dictionary will provide answers to lots
of dressmakers' questions, let me dedicate this one to
all the people who write to me with their queries.
'What is meant by . . . ?' 'What is the best way to . . . ?'
'How do I set about . . . ?' 'What exactly is . . . ?'
etc, etc.

© Ann Ladbury 1982
First published 1982

ISBN 0 7134 1823 0

Typeset and designed by Tek Art Ltd
Printed in Great Britain by
Butler & Tanner Ltd
Frome, Somerset
for the Publishers B.T. Batsford Ltd
4 Fitzhardinge St, London W1H 0AH

# Preface

Everyone engaged in learning needs, at some time, to look things up. The reasons vary; it may be to refresh the memory, perhaps a decision between two methods has to be made; or it may be necessary to distinguish between similar terms. Whatever the reason, one can look it up in this dictionary. It contains the traditional terms of stitches, processes and equipment in common use in dressmaking as well as new ideas and new aids. It is arranged in alphabetical order for rapid reference and if there is a need for details of how to go about a process in order to be sure of good results, they will also be found here. In addition, where things have become known by two names, both are listed, with the definition appearing under the one that is most often used.

# Acknowledgment

My thanks are due to Selectus Limited, Vilene Limited and to J & P Coats Ltd for their help, and thanks to McCalls and Burda for permission to use their sizing charts. Also to the Sewing Machine Trade Association for allowing me to quote from their booklet *Choosing a Sewing Machine* and to Lightning Fasteners for permission to reproduce text and illustrations from their Zip Fitting Folder. My thanks also to Barbara Wain and Sylvia Cowham for the typing.

## ADJUSTABLE MARKER

A very useful piece of measuring equipment consisting of a 15 cm (6 in.) metal strip with a moveable arrow. It is more rigid than a tape measure and quicker to use, especially where a measurement has to be repeated. Set the arrow for a hem, buttonholes, width of crossway strip, etc., and quickly cut or chalk at intervals beside the arrow. It is worth having two markers for occasions when two measurements are needed and one marked can be left for any length of time. Use two markers also for marking both the length of buttonholes and the space between.

## ADJUSTABLE ZIP FOOT

This is one of the most useful of the additional feet provided with a sewing machine. If not part of the standard equipment it is worth buying. The construction of the foot varies with the make of machine but the principle is that it can be adjusted so that the machine needle stitches very close beside the zip teeth. A small part is hollowed to take the needle point but as the foot can be adjusted to sew to the right or left it is best gently to check that the needle is not going to hit the foot and break, and adjust it a little more if necessary.

Most zip feet are constructed so that they clamp well to the fabric to prevent movement of fabric or zip tape. Some zip feet have a section at the back which lowers on to the zip teeth to keep them flat and prevent puckering.

The zip foot can be used for sewing in the con-

cealed type zip as well as the conventional zips with visible teeth. Some zip feet have a central channel, specially constructed for sewing in concealed zips by clamping over the zip teeth forming a bridge.

## A-LINE

The original term came from Christian Dior and indicated a sharp A shape in the form of fullness below the knee. We now use the term to describe any dress or skirt which shapes out from waist to hips and where the seams continue at a slight outward angle, giving a skirt that is wider at the hem than the hips but not full enough to fall into folds.

## ALTERATIONS

If alterations, such as replacing zips, have to be made to a completed garment it helps to remember the following:

Unpick only the essential area. Do not rush ahead taking out a zip or taking off a whole waistband. As you release the first stitches see if there is another layer of possibly interfacing or lining that is going to be freed. If so, stop and put in a row of tacking to hold it in place.

If possible try on the alteration before actually finishing it off. It is easy to take in too much or too little.

Do not press out all the creases until it is re-assembled. Stitching lines are a guide either to be re-used or you can stitch parallel to them.

Often it will be easier to finish off the alteration by hand stitching on the right side if the area is small or difficult to reach. Sometimes it is difficult to line up a row of machining on the inside with the remains of previous stitching so it solves this to work slip stitch or something similar on the right side to finish.

With ready-made clothes take note of the construction, as you unpick, and if any edges fray or weak areas appear, reinforce them before attempting to make the alteration.

## ANCHOR MACHINE EMBROIDERY THREAD

A fine mercerised thread used for all types of machine embroidery. No. 30 or 50 may be used depending on the result required and the thickness of the fabric. This thread is also best used for making machine-made buttonholes on fine fabrics, working round the buttonhole twice if necessary. Machine Embroidery Thread has not sufficient strength for seam construction in garments but it can be used effectively for light decorative embroidery work on baby clothes. It is also a good idea to use it for tacking when working on very fine silks such as chiffon.

# ANORAK

Once a purely practical walking and camping jacket in drab colours but now developed into a useful warm garment for children; part of school uniform; and as a fashion garment. The main features that have been retained are the ribbed or elastic cuffs and waistband and centre front opening with open-ended zip. Collar styles vary, including the addition of hoods. Fabrics include proofed popl'n, nylon ciré, all quilted and padded fabrics, woollens, knits and any suitable fashion fabrics such as combinations of cord and knitting.

# APPLIED SHELL-GATHERS

A decorative strip of fabric gathered up before being applied to the right side of a garment. It works especially well in fabrics that are fine but do not crush easily. Decide on the finished width of the strip according to the position on the garment and cut a length of fabric on the cross and a little more than twice the finished width. Fold the strip right side inside and stitch near the raw edges with a slight zig-zag stitch or a stretch stitch. Turn the tube right side out, work the join to the centre and press. On the upper side work a row of running stitches to zig-zag across the tube. Pull up the thread slightly until the tube forms shells. Fasten off the thread. Place the strip on the right side of the garment and machine down the centre with a small straight or zig-zag stitch. Do not press.

The stitches used to attach the motifs may be unobtrusive, such as slip hemming, or they may be planned to the design and therefore embroidery stitches and appropriate threads would be used.

## Hand appliqué

Use either entirely non-fraying fabrics such as jersey, plastic, felt, Colourphelt and other non-woven materials so that the shapes may be applied by sticking in place using pieces of Bondaweb or Wundaweb, and then stitched round the edge using one of the close embroidery stitches such as loop stitch. If finer fraying fabrics are used there is a choice of two methods, depending on the type of material being used. The first is to press Bondaweb on to the wrong side of a piece of fabric, larger than the motif, or large enough to cut all motifs. Peel off the paper and cut out the motifs, marking them with pencil first or use a cardboard template if several are to be the same. Household articles are also quite useful, such as saucers, coins and match boxes. Place the motif in position, slipping a small piece of Wundaweb underneath and pressing, then stitching round the edge with an embroidery stitch.

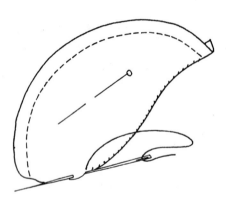

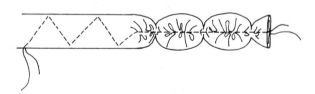

# APPLIQUE

A decorative effect produced by applying additional pieces of fabric of various sizes and shapes to an existing garment or household article. The applied fabrics may be contrasting in texture as well as colour, they may be applied singly or in an overlapping sequence to form a picture. However, if the article is to be washed frequently, all fabrics should be similar in fibre content.

The second method must be used with soft or fine fraying fabrics. Mark out the shape of the motif on the fabric and machine on the line. Trim away the surplus fabric leaving 3 mm ($\frac{1}{8}$ in.) outside the machining. Pin motif in position, turn under the 3 mm ($\frac{1}{8}$ in.) so that the machining just disappears and neatly slip stitch the edge using normal sewing thread. Embroidery stitches can be added afterwards if you wish.

**Machine appliqué**
Decide on the design. Keep the outline as simple as
possible, with very few additional rows of stitching
which will require careful finishing of threads at the
end. Most outlines, even initials, can be simplified.
Trace a motif or draw your own design on soft sew-
in Vilene and cut out. Pin this to the garment and
adjust it until it looks right. Unpin the Vilene but
mark its position on the garment with a chalk cross.

Decide on the fabric for the motif and on the
thread colour. This can match either of the fabrics or
you can introduce a new colour. Use Anchor Machine
Embroidery no. 30 or 50, or, for a heavier result, use
normal sewing thread such as Drima.

Set the machine to satin stitch. Stitch length: $\frac{3}{4}$;
zig-zag: $1\frac{1}{2}$. Attach the satin stitch foot.

Pin the Vilene template to the fabric and mark
round it with a dotted pencil line. Trim away some of
the surplus fabric but leave at least 2 cm ($\frac{3}{4}$ in.) extending beyond the pencil line. Place the fabric on the
right side of the garment. Slip a piece of Wundaweb
between the two and press until it adheres.

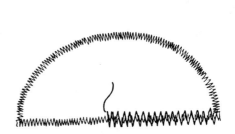

## ARMHOLE

This can be one of the most difficult areas to fit
partly because flesh does not accumulate uniformly
but also because the armhole is affected by the slope
of the shoulder and the width of the back and chest.
However, it helps to understand the main principles
of the shape of the armhole for a standard set-in
sleeve. It is the shape of the armhole that is important,
not necessarily its depth. A low armhole is not only
uncomfortable but it means the whole dress lifts
when you raise your arms. The underarm should
follow the curve of the body with just a little ease
for comfort. Study your pattern carefully; place
the back and front together at the side seam. There
should be a slight scoop at the back but much more
at the front. Below, you can see a poor armhole with
a better shape drawn in. It is worth making this small
alteration; it is invariably more comfortable to wear
and if it isn't right you can scoop it away again.

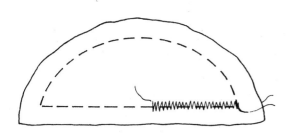

Put paper underneath the work and work satin
stitch round the design following the line. Try to start
and finish at a point convenient for fastening off or
for moving on to the next part of the design. If the
design has two sections that will partly overlap, work
on the underneath one first but avoid a ridge by satin
stitching only round that part that will not be covered
by the upper part.

Remove the garment from the machine. Tear off
the paper. Trim the thread ends and carefully trim
away the excess fabric close to the satin stich. Adjust
the stitch to work a zig-zag width of 2, still keeping
to a stitch length of $\frac{3}{4}$. Work round the motif again,
stitching exactly over the first row. The slightly wider
stitch will cover the first stitching. Remember to put
a fresh piece of paper underneath.

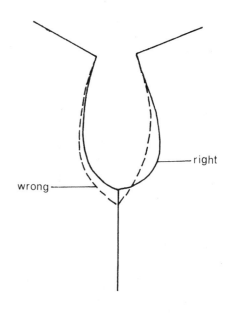

Check the depth of your armhole by placing a ruler under your arm and across your back. Get someone to measure from your back neck or shoulder to the ruler. Check your pattern. Most people need a shallower armhole so fill it in as shown. If you have a pad of flesh at the front of your arm and armholes cut across it uncomfortably, raise the armhole line so that the sleeve join is above the flesh — do not lower it or it will be loose and uncomfortable.

Pin the back and front patterns together at underarm and measure. If the armhole on the pattern is too deep, move the back pattern down, so shortening the distance between neck and underarm point. Fill in back armhole curve to make a good line with the front armhole. If the armhole is too shallow, move the back pattern up and cut out the back armhole curve.

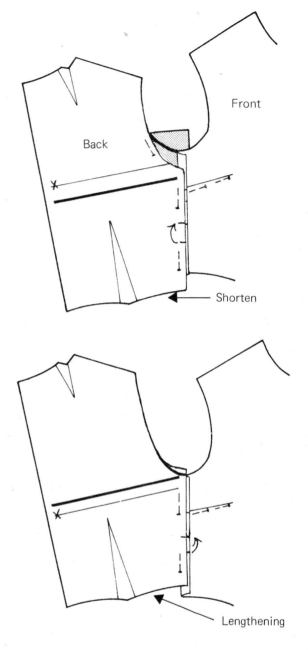

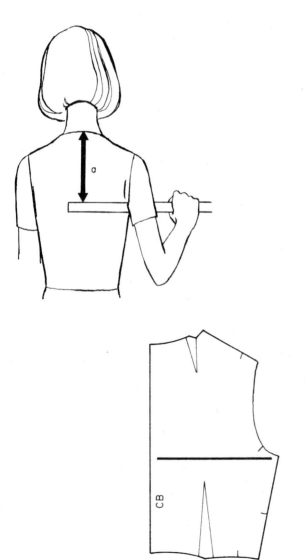

Mark a new balance mark across the two patterns, at the side seam, before unpinning. Having altered the back armhole, be prepared, at the fitting stage, to raise or lower the front shoulder seam a little. It is best not to do this on the pattern because it is by no means always correct on every figure. The sleeve remains unaltered; you would only need to enlarge or reduce the sleeve head if you made a massive alteration to the depth of armhole.

(See also *Waist Fitting*, page 123.)

# ARROWHEADS

A decorative triangle of thread (also known as sprats' heads), usually quite small, that can be worked at the tops of pleats and slit openings, and sometimes featured at the ends of piped pockets. It is a useful method of neatening these places and the arrowhead also strengthens and prevents seams splitting under strain.

Use sharp tailor's chalk and a ruler and mark an equilateral triangle on the right side of the fabric making sure the chalk lines cross at the corners to provide a clear point for stitching.

Use a thick thread such as buttonhole twist, Drima Bold or Anchor Soft and thread a fairly long piece into a Between needle big enough to take the thread but not so thick that you have difficulty in penetrating the fabric. Use the thread singly and put a knot in the end. Use matching thread unless you are very expert in working arrowheads.

Bring the thread up at point A but do not pull the knot close to the underside of the fabric. After working a few stitches the knotted end will be held in place so you can then cut off the knot.

Follow the sequence shown in the diagrams using stab stitch and making sure the tension is even on each stitch. Do not crowd the stitches, they should be sufficiently close to allow the threads to lie comfortably side by side. When the central diamond is full fasten off on the wrong side by running the needle under and over a few threads. Press on the wrong side.

If you have to make several the same size make sure you note the size of the chalked triangle because the finished arrowhead tends to be smaller.

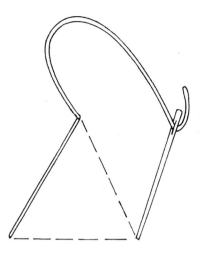

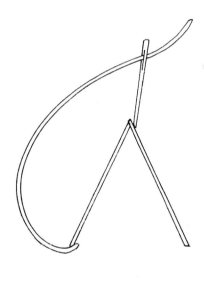

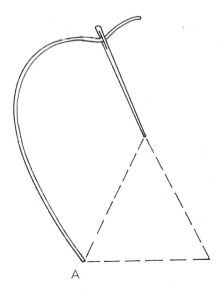

A

If you work arrowheads at the tops of inverted pleats stitch only through the top layers of fabric, not through to the pleat backing or the pleats will pucker.

Arrowheads can be worked very easily in an embroidery hoop provided the fabric is not too thick.

## ATTACHED FACING

If a garment edge is perfectly straight and needs finishing with a facing there is no necessity for cutting an additional piece of fabric and simply re-joining it. Even if the pattern provides a separate piece it is worth pinning it to the main piece to see if it can be cut in one — there may be insufficient material for instance. The pattern may already be cut to include a facing edge to be turned back. In either case, cut out with the grain of the fabric following the grain of the main piece, mark the fold line, that is the point where the facing is to fold back, and press a length of Fold-a-Band in position with the central holes exactly over the fold line. You may need to add an additional interfacing but often the Fold-a-Band will provide the necessary support as well as an accurate and crisp edge. The illustration shows an attached facing on a blouse front.

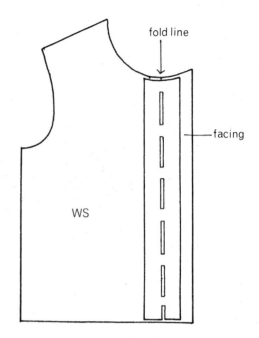

fold line

facing

WS

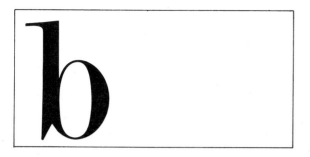

## BACK STITCH

This term has two meanings. In hand sewing it is a stitch that is mainly used for repair in places where a seam has split and it is not worth getting out the machine to re-stitch. Sometimes it may be used for very short rows of stitching that may be awkward to reach by machine, although in the majority of such cases the half back stitch is probably more effective.

To replace or imitate machining, thread a small needle with a short piece of thread. Use a knot and start to overlap the machining by at least 1 cm ($\frac{3}{8}$ in.). Bring the needle out, pull the thread fairly tight, pass the needle back to the previous stitch, or into a hole made by the machine needle, pass the needle under far enough to leave room for the next backward movement and so on. Fasten off firmly. One of the disadvantages of the stitch is that it looks untidy on the wrong side, but this is not important when repairing an open seam.

Back stitch is a much used embroidery stitch especially effective on even weave linens and canvas where geometric designs are used.

(See also *Half Back Stitch*.)

## BACKING

An entire section or part of a section of garment may be backed. The two main reasons for backing are to add strength, as in the case of pockets or for a repetitive process such as decoration, or to make sure the fabric cannot be seen through, as in the case of lace.

The choice of backing material depends on the task it has to perform. A piece of tape folded into two or three is a strong backing for a button on a working garment; a piece of cotton lawn or light Vilene would be adequate for a yoke; thin taffeta or even chiffon would be a suitable backing for lace. When backing a limited area so that a process can be worked make sure the backing fabric extends well beyond the area the process will occupy. Place the fabrics together and baste, or in the case of iron-on Vilene, press in position.

If an entire garment is to be backed or mounted great care must be taken with the choice of backing fabric. In general it should be lighter in weight and softer but of a similar nature. For example, mount jersey fabrics onto nylon jersey backing.

Cut out the whole garment and cut out the backing, place each piece of fabric wrong side down on to the wrong side of the mounting and with the whole piece flat on the table work basting stitches all over each piece. Begin in the centre to eliminate any movement to one side. Keep the stitches fairly loose.

Make up the garment treating all pieces as one layer. If the correct weight of backing has been used there will be no problem with excess bulk in seams and darts.

In embroidery this is a flat outline stitch. Work from right to left. Take a stitch through the fabric, then a back stitch, half the length of the first stitch, to where the needle was first inserted. Take the next stitch to bring the needle in front of the first stitch so that when the next back stitch is taken it is the same length as the previous one.

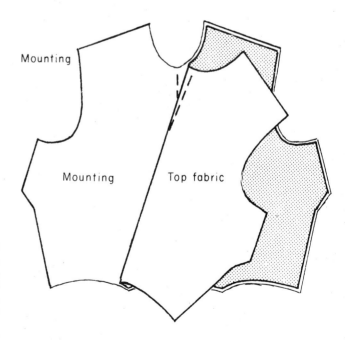

Mounting

Mounting    Top fabric

It is sometimes desirable to make up a garment that is partly backed or mounted and partly loose-lined. (See also *Lining*.)

**Reasons for backing or mounting an entire garment**
Providing support for the top fabric will considerably reduce creasing in wear, and in the case of fitted skirts and dresses it will also prevent seating. The heavier the person the more strain is placed on the fabric in wear, so mounting is a great advantage. A very slim person who always buys top quality very expensive material does not have to mount for reasons of strain or fabric support, but she may nevertheless like to do it because the whole silhouette is crisper and more shapely and the outfit remains looking fresh and new for much longer. Mounted fabric is much easier to sew, slippage of seams is less likely, puckering is eliminated, and pressing is easier because seam imprints are less likely. Also hems never show because the stitching is taken only through the mounting.

Mounted garments travel better because they crease less, both in the suitcase and being worn.

There are two things to consider in garments which need mounting. First, if you are using a fabric which will not perform as you want it to as a single layer, then you must mount it, whatever the garment. Secondly, if you are making a garment which by its style puts a strain on the fabric, you should mount it. Examples of this include close fitting articles such as straight dresses and skirts.

**Fabrics for mounting**
The success of mounting depends on the correct choice of the supporting fabric and this may be a further deciding factor. If you are unable to buy a suitable mounting, or you are not sure what to use, then it is better not to do it.

Occasionally people complain that mounted clothes are hot, which surprises me until I see the variety of underwear they are still wearing. Mounting can replace a slip and clothes stand away from the body. It is, of course, more expensive to mount, although you eliminate the cost of lining in most cases.

Suggestions for mounting fabrics are: cotton lawn, Vincel/cotton or any soft, thin cotton, voile, chiffon, viscose, polyester/cotton. Only use conventional lining fabric if you want a slippery effect.

**Buy the fabric first**
Buy your fabric and have it with you when you buy the mounting, placing it on top of various mountings to feel the effect. The top material should be supported, but it should not have its character eliminated by a strong or opposite mounting.

Buy the same amount of mounting material unless you are omitting some part such as sleeves, in which case buy 50 cm ($\frac{1}{2}$ yd) less for short or $\frac{3}{4}$ sleeves and 70 cm ($\frac{3}{4}$ yd) less for long sleeves.

If you locate a supply of the most used mounting fabrics it is useful to buy a large amount for future use.

If the fabric is sheer or open, then a suitable colour of mounting must be found, but with solid fabrics white can be used for most things which is more economical than buying short lengths.

Most reasonably priced material is now pre-shrunk as part of the finishing, but if you are doubtful wash and iron the whole length before cutting out.

It helps to eliminate static electricity if the length of nylon jersey and also the length of synthetic top fabric is washed through in a fabric softener before cutting out. After making up, continue to rinse synthetic garments in one of these softeners.

## BAG OUT

A term and a method of construction used mainly in the ready-to-wear industry. It is a quick way of lining by which you make the garment or part of it and make the lining. Place the two right sides together, stitch round the outside leaving a good-sized gap for turning through, turn through and press. The gap is then stitched by hand.

The disadvantages of this method of lining are that the lining is always liable to part from the garment and bag away from it because it is not fixed and also the edges of the lining will always tend to show at the edge of the garment.

The only cases where bagging out can be used successfully are where two layers of fabric are being used, for example in making straps, belts or bibs for dungarees.

(See also *Lining*.)

## BALANCE

Balance refers to the hang and the proportion of a garment, and this is dependent on the posture of the person as well as the shape. Someone with a forward-tilted posture will need the front length of the garment from neck to hem considerably shorter than that provided by a pattern. Someone with a large or prominent bust will find the balance of a pattern incorrect because she will need more length in the front. There are many other instances where the balance of front and back of any garment have to be adjusted to produce a properly fitting garment and this is of course in addition to fitting.

(See also *Fitting*.)

## BALANCE MARKS

Marks on a pattern, usually triangles, to show where one piece matches another. To distinguish various similar pieces different numbers of balance marks are used, for example one on the front of a sleeve and also on the corresponding armhole, and two at the back. Sometimes balance marks are also numbered so that for instance the balance marks on both parts of a skirt seam to be joined will bear the same number. For beginners and those who seldom sew these numbers are helpful as they ensure that the correct, and perhaps fairly similar, pieces are being joined. However, to make full use of them the pattern pieces must be kept laid out beside the fabric pieces until the whole thing is assembled.

I think experienced sewers should make very limited use of balance marks. In a few places — gathered areas, tucks, pleats, pocket positions, and other style features — they must be used, but in the construction of basic seams it is far better to observe the grain of the fabric and make a smooth seam than to force balance marks to meet. Even in more involved processes such as setting in sleeves and attaching a collar, provided the obvious points match, such as underarm or centre back and front, it is far better to manipulate the layers of fabric and ease to produce a correctly fitting result than it is to rely on balance marks. Also, of course, any slight adjustment at fitting means the balance marks no longer match anyway.

When cutting out, cut a smooth edge to every pattern piece, never cut the triangles outwards or, worse still, inwards. Then any that will be needed should be marked with tailor tacks (page 304), carbon paper and tracing wheel (page 311), or if there are only one or two and you will be doing the appropriate stitching immediately make a mark with tailor's chalk or a chalk pencil.

The balance marks that are really useful are the ones you add yourself. The occasions when you might do this include times when you have made a fitting adjustment, but you need to undo the seam and re-assemble it to the new marks; marking the position of a seam pocket, perhaps at the correct level; and also when making pattern adaptations. For this last use of a balance mark draw a style line such as a yoke on a paper pattern, then make balance marks across it before cutting the pattern to ensure correct matching when re-joining in fabric.

## BALL BUTTONS

These are buttons made by knotting a cord. They are often combined with frog fastenings or rouleau loops but they are effective purely as decoration. They are not very successful if used with any of the conventional slit buttonholes because if you lengthen the shank sufficiently to allow the buttonhole to close under it, the button wobbles. Loops simply wind round the button loosely. Not a strong fastening, so it should not be used at points of strain.

Use lengths of rouleau or thin cord to make the buttons. The thicker the cord the larger the button will be, so try to keep them in proportion on the garment. Fine rouleau will make very small buttons but it can be filled with cord to produce larger ones.

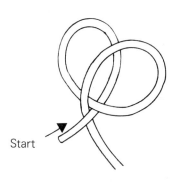

Start

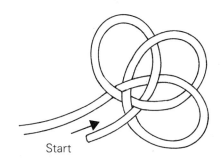

Start

Fine cord can be used double with good effect; two colours can be used. In order to tie the knot you need quite a long length of cord so buy or make plenty and cut into the number of pieces required plus a few extra ones to practise on. Allow about 15 to 25 cm (6 to 8 in.) for each button depending on thickness. It is difficult to describe in words which way to wind the cord, but if you follow the illustrations it should work correctly. Form it quite loosely and then gently ease the knot into a ball. Make sure the cord loops in the direction indicated.

## BAND COLLAR

A narrow strip of fabric attached to a basic neckline. It looks better and is easier to attach if the fabric is cut on the cross but sometimes fashion dictates that it is straight and therefore stands away from the neck. The neck fastening may be at the centre front or the centre back. Always interface with medium to firm interfacing depending on the fabric. For details of attaching see *Stand Collars*, page 70.

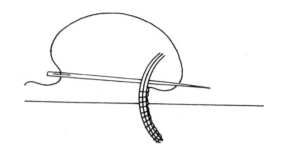

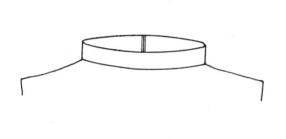

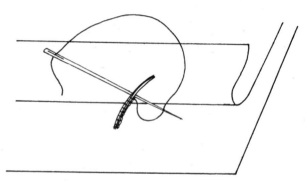

## BAR TACKS

There are two kinds of bar tacks, those that strengthen and those that loosely attach. The latter are also called French tacks.

A strengthening bar tack may be needed at the base of a zip, the end of a pocket, buttonhole, the step of a lapel, or any point where regular strain is applied. To work them by machine, set the stitch width to $3\frac{1}{2}$ or 4 and satin stitch for about four or five stitches.

To work by hand make four or five stab stitches on top of each other about 3 to 5 mm ($\frac{1}{8}$ to $\frac{1}{4}$ in.) long, pulling the thread tight. The threads may then be tightened and drawn together by working close loop stitch over them. Depending on the position of the tack the loop stitches may be taken through the fabric underneath as well for extra strength, but this does make the tack more obvious.

Bar tacks may be worked on the wrong side or the right side but they must be very small and neat wherever they are.

Loose longer tacks are used to keep linings in place. Make several threads about 5 mm to 1 cm ($\frac{1}{4}$ to $\frac{3}{8}$ in.) long between the lining and the garment, trying to confine the stitching to the seam allowances so that they are not visible from the right side. Work close loop stitch over the threads. Alternatively, a less strong tack can be made by working chain stitch for 1 cm ($\frac{3}{8}$ in.) between lining and garment.

The tacks may be placed at intervals round a hem or down seams but do not use too many or they restrict the hang of the garment.

## BASTING

The word has come to have two meanings. First, it is the description tailors use for tacking, i.e. all temporary constructional stitching. Secondly, it can be used to describe tacking worked in diagonal rows, to cover a fairly large area or to hold several thicknesses securely. This can also be described as diagonal tacking.

A slightly larger needle than for permanent hand sewing is used, and the basting stitches vary in size according to the area, type of fabric, and how long it will be before the permanent stitch is inserted.

Use a number 5 or 6 Between needle, a fairly long piece of tacking thread, e.g. Atlas, and put a knot in the end. Arrange the area or layers flat or, if introducing shaping, over the curve of the hand. Insert the needle horizontally and take a stitch, insert it again directly below the first stitch and so on. Stitches are usually about 1 cm ($\frac{3}{8}$ in.) wide and the diagonals are about 3 to 4 cm ($1\frac{1}{4}$ to $1\frac{1}{2}$ in.) long, but smaller if the work needs to be held more closely together. When covering a large area work up and down in parallel rows. Do not pull stitches tight or ridges will be formed. Do not fasten off ends of thread tightly, a loose end may be left or one single back stitch can be made. The reason for not finishing basting too firmly is to enable it to be easily removed later, either by

pulling on the knot or with the use of a bodkin slipped under the thread. Never use normal sewing thread for basting. It is strong and its removal may harm the fabric.

The illustrations show the use of basting for covering an entire area and making two diagonal stitches in one place to hold several layers, e.g. pleat.

A 'baste' in tailoring is the term used to describe a coat or jacket ensemble (with basting or tacking stitches) ready for fitting and adjusting.

(See also *Tacking*.)

## BATEAU

A bateau or boat neckline is one that is shallow at the centre front and back, but cut wide to the shoulders producing a curved edge like a boat hull. This is not a particularly flattering neckline; necklaces cannot be added so the edge is often decorated in some way. Often used in evening wear but in crisp fabrics since any movements make the front neck droop.

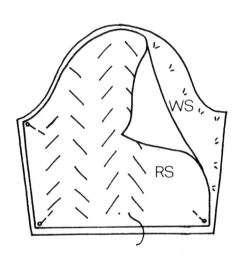

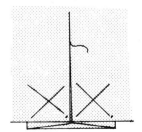

## BATTING

An American term for wadding (see *page 323*).

## BATTLE

The name battle-jacket derives from the casual hard-wearing battle dress of wartime. The jacket is waist length pleated or gathered into a band, which may be wide elastic or ribbing as may be the cuffs. Correctly a battle jacket has a fly-front buttoned opening but this is now often changed to a zip. The jacket has four roomy patch pockets, often with box pleats in them exactly like army dress.

## BATWING

A style of sleeve where the sleeve is cut in one with the bodice but the underarm is low enough to provide sufficient room for movement. When the arm is raised the general shape is rather similar to a bat's wing — a gentle curve from waist round to wrist.

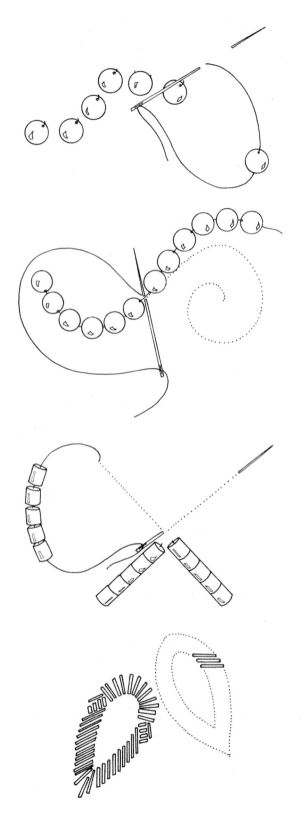

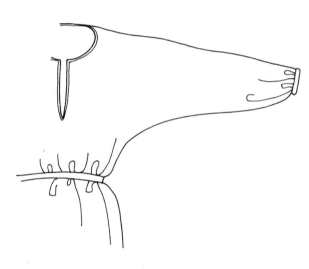

## BEADS

Many types of wooden, glass and plastic beads in a variety of shapes and colours are available for decoration.

Use synthetic thread, such as Drima, for strength and run it through beeswax. Use a beading needle. These are specially long in order that several beads may be threaded on at one time. Attach in a design either singly, working a back stitch to attach each, or thread several on to the needle and lay them down in a straight line as part of the design. Scroll or curved designs are best worked with long rod or baguette type beads threaded first on to a length of thread and then couched in position by working a stitch between each bead. Rod shaped beads too can be effective when sewn close together but slanting, to give a dense outline to a design.

Always back the area of fabric to be beaded and where possible use an embroidery frame.

## BEESWAX

Cakes of hard wax used for coating threads for sewing on buttons and other jobs needing strength. The wax serves two purposes; it adds a layer of wax which takes wear and therefore prevents the thread wearing through too quickly, and for extra strength thread it is used double and to run it through wax will bind the two threads together and make them easier to sew with. In addition when hand sewing with some synthetic threads the thread may twist and snarl, a light coating of wax will straighten it out.

Beads and sequins tend to have sharp edges which wear through thread; run the thread through beeswax and this is less likely to happen.

Very few dry-cleaning firms bother to re-lubricate the teeth of zips after cleaning. You can do it yourself by running the beeswax along the teeth.

Buy beeswax in small round or square cakes or in plastic holders (though the holder has to be removed to use the wax for some things).

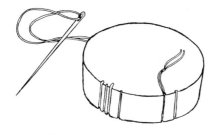

## BELL SLEEVE

A style of sleeve that is fitted smoothly into a plain armhole but from about elbow level it is flared. The shape is achieved by cutting a straight sleeve pattern into four pieces and opening up at the bottom. The sleeve may be short or long.

(See also *Trumpet Sleeve*, page 314.)

## BELT LOOPS

Belt loops, often called carriers, may be attached at the side seams of a garment either to hold the belt in position in wear or to prevent it becoming separated, for instance on dressing gowns, robes, wrap-over coats and jackets. Alternatively, a belt may be added to a waistline as decoration or as a further fastening and fitting device such as on trousers and jeans. Loops may be made of fabric, thread or in some cases a tape such as petersham ribbon can be used.

Measure the width and thickness of the belt and then allow 3 to 5 mm ($\frac{1}{8}$ to $\frac{1}{4}$ in.) ease depending on the thickness of the fabric being used. Do not allow too much ease or the belt will move in wear.

**Fabric loops**

Firm loops are made from fabric cut on the straight grain. Cut the piece 1.5 to 2 cm ($\frac{5}{8}$ to $\frac{3}{4}$ in.) wide and long enough to make all loops plus seam allowances. Turn in and press 5 mm ($\frac{1}{4}$ in.) along each side. Fold so that the edges meet and tack. Either slip stitch the folds together or machine along both sides of the strip.

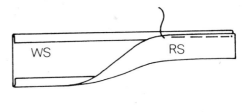

Soft loops can be made from a length of crossway fabric made into a tube of rouleau. Make it as narrow as possible, cutting the fabric as little as 1 cm ($\frac{3}{8}$ in.) wide in very fine fabrics. Less ease may be allowed on each loop as there is plenty of ease in the rouleau.

**Thread loops**

Always work these at a seam or through a double layer of fabric or the strain on the loop may tear the fabric. The loops themselves are strong but the point of attachment is not. If necessary place a narrow length of fabric, seam binding, or Vilene behind the loop position to add strength.

Use a long piece of thread, doubled and waxed. Use normal thread such as Drima unless working on heavy fabric in which case use buttonhole twist or Drima Bold.

Begin on the wrong side with a back stitch, and a knot on the end of the thread which can be cut off later if fabric is lightweight. Place the belt in position and bring the needle up beside it. As the ease is difficult to calculate with this type of loop it is best to work it over the belt.

Put four strands of thread in place across the belt, stabbing the needle back and forth. Make a back stitch at one side then remove the belt. Work close loop stitch over the strands of thread. Pass the needle to the wrong side and fasten off firmly.

### Position of belt loops

Mark the position of decorative loops with chalk marks on the right side of the fabric, spacing them as you wish.

If the loops are specifically to hold the belt at the waist, put on the garment and add the belt. Arrange any gathers or fullness, making sure the side seams are actually at the side. Using pins or tailor's chalk mark the garment above and below the belt at one side seam only. Take off the garment and check the distance between the pins to ensure that it is correct for the belt including the ease. Fold the garment to put the side seams together and match the underarm points exactly. Using the first side as a guide, mark the position of the other loop.

### Methods of attaching fabric loops

Cut the length of fabric into the required number of pieces allowing ease plus 1 cm ($\frac{3}{8}$ in.) seam allowance at each end of each loop.

### Flat loops

Turn in 5 mm ($\frac{1}{4}$ in.) at each end and press. Place loop in position and hold by inserting a pin across the centre. Hem round the end and back stitch across the loop 5 cm (2 in.) from the end. It may be necessary to stab stitch through all layers to do this successfully. Repeat at the far end.

If you wish to machine the loops make sure they are tacked in position first, then stitch in a square, adding a cross in addition if the design and fabric call for it.

Loops made from rouleau look best if the ends are inserted in the seam. Unpick a few seam stitches and push the end of the loop in. Turn garment to the wrong side and re-stitch the seam.

### Folded loops

These can look neater than flat loops but their main use is where the position of the belt may need to be varied or where a rigid belt position puts undue strain on the garment; for example a stretch towelling robe or any garment where the sleeve is cut in one with the main part and therefore the whole thing lifts when arms are raised.

Cut the loops allowing 5 mm ($\frac{1}{4}$ in.) each end for seam allowance. Fold loop in half and insert in a seam. If the fabric is bulky place the two ends side by side but otherwise they can be left together. Re-stitch the seam to hold. The loop in use can be varied in position to the extent of its length. If there is no convenient seam make a circle of the loop and stitch across it to attach to the garment.

When putting loops on the waistband of a skirt or trousers, slip the ends under the waistband before joining band to trousers. Press the loops up so that they lie over the band. You can leave them loose for the belt or work a bar tack through the top to hold. The most conventional method is to make the waistband with a join along the top, make and position all the loops machining across the ends to hold them, before attaching the waistband to the garment.

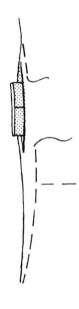

Inserting belt

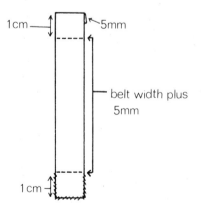

1cm — 5mm

belt width plus 5mm

1cm

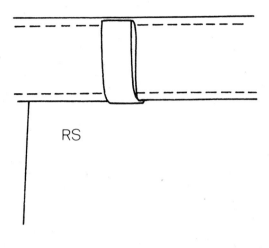

RS

RS

RS

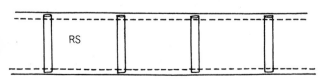

RS

## BELTING

Any stiffening manufactured especially for inserting in belts and waistbands. Some varieties are intended to be concealed, some are stitched on the back of a length of fabric, the edges of which have been turned in. One type, Fusabelta, has an additional adhesive flap on it and the raw edges of the fabric are simply tucked under the flap and pressed. No sewing is necessary. Most belting, including petersham, which can also be used, is available in a variety of widths. Fold-a-Band even has a row of central perforations to make it easy to keep the belt or waistband even in width.

## BELTS

The style and width of belt should complement the garment. Choose the type and also decide on the type of fastening. Straight belts will ride above the waist and if too tight will be uncomfortable. If a buckle, ring or clasp is to be used make sure you have it before making the belt.

Curved belts are comfortable to wear because they settle below the actual waistline. Curved petersham is used to obtain the correct curve and this may then be used to stiffen the belt, or a wider stiffening can be made using pelmet weight Vilene. Other stiffenings may be manufactured in specific widths and so the preferred width must be purchased.

Calculate the length required by measuring round the waist over the garment. A wide belt will have to be longer than the basic waist measurement. If the belt is to overlap and fasten the precise length is not vital; make it plenty long enough and trim later. Tie belts should be long enough to produce a tie to suit the fabric.

If the fabric has to be joined make the join on the cross and press it open.

## Belt fastenings

Choose the method most suitable for the garment and for the type of belt. If a buckle is used it may have a prong and therefore you will have to insert metal or worked eyelets. If no prong is used sew a piece of Velcro to the end of the belt with the corresponding piece on the belt itself. Make the second piece larger to allow for adjustment. A clasp may also be fastened with Velcro. If both sides of the clasp are attached with Velcro it enables the same clasp to be used on several belts. Allow at least 6 cm (2⅜ in.) extra on the belt to thread through each part of the clasp. Sew Velcro to each end, with corresponding pieces on the inside of the belt.

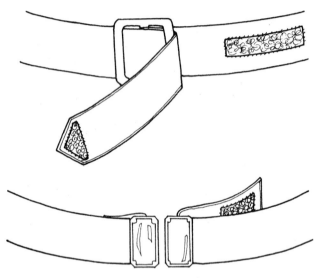

## Bias sash

Cut two pieces of fabric on the bias, long enough to tie and fairly wide. Place the pieces wrong sides together and tack, then bind all outer edges. Although this type of sash can simply be stitched and turned through, it is always likely to curl in wear.

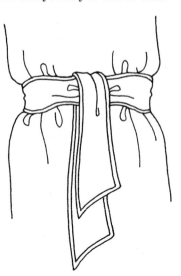

## Conventional straight belt

Select a belt backing or petersham of suitable width. Trim it to length plus sufficient for the type of fastening to be used. Cut a strip of fabric on the straight grain the same size but allowing a small turning all round. Tack the backing to the wrong side of the fabric. If this proves difficult due to the stiffness of the backing try pressing it in place using

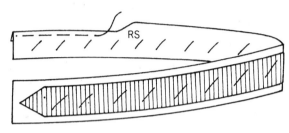

Wundaweb. From the right side turn under the raw edge of the fabric so that it only just covers the edge of the backing. Tack. Press and machine round the outer edge.

Alternatively the backing may be enclosed between two pieces of fabric. Tack the backing to one piece and machine along each edge. Place the second piece of fabric to this, right sides together. Machine together along one edge, off the edge of the backing. Finish the end, possibly mitred, and the second side by stitching the edges together. Turn right side out and machine round the belt for decoration if desired.

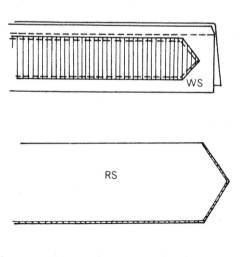

## Curved belt

A curved belt may be made in one piece in plain fabric but if the weave or the pattern are visible there will have to be a join to prevent the grain from being too distorted at the ends of the belt. Measure and cut curved petersham to size for a curved belt, allowing more overlap than usual as the belt settles below the waist in wear. Place it on double fabric and cut out allowing a small seam allowance all round. If joins are to be made divide the petersham into two, or three, disregarding the overlap. Cut curved fabric pieces the correct length but allow for the joins. Seam the pieces together and press open, then place the petersham on the wrong side of one piece. Tack the two together and attach the petersham either by machining along each edge — a straight or decorative stitch may be used — or work herringbone stitch. Place the second shaped piece of fabric to this, right sides together and machine along the concave edge just off the edge of the petersham. Trim the turnings but do not snip.

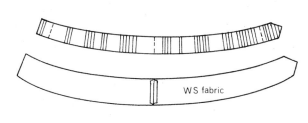

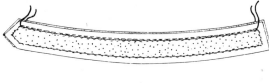

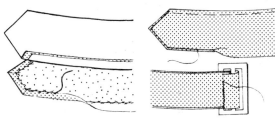

Roll the fabric over to cover the petersham, tack the edge. Fold the raw edge over the edge of the petersham and tack down. If the fabric is springy work herringbone stitch over the edge. Turn in the second raw edge to meet it and slip stitch together. Attach buckle or other fastening.

## Plaited belt

A soft decorative belt fastened with a clasp. Make three long tubes of fabric and machine along each side of each one. Place all three together and machine across the ends to hold. Pin to the ironing surface and plait. Machine the other end. Neaten by overcasting. Attach clasp.

## Quick belt

Fusabelta may be used to stiffen and back a belt in one go. Cut the length required plus fastening. Cut a strip of fabric on the straight grain the same size but add 5 mm ($\frac{1}{4}$ in.) turnings all round. Place this wrong side up on the pressing surface, place the Fusabelta adhesive side down and then tuck the raw edges of the fabric between the two layers of backing. Press carefully with the toe of the iron. Turn the belt over and press again. Neaten the ends. The belt may have stitching added all round.

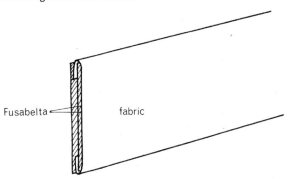

## Shirred belt

A simple elasticated belt fastened with a clasp can be made from a single strip of practically any fabric, including plastic, georgette, wool or jersey. Cut a length of fabric the width required. The length is difficult to specify because the amount by which it is drawn up varies with the fabric. A short measured piece could be worked and re-measured for an accurate calculation. Neaten each raw edge of the fabric by a method suitable for the garment and the fabric. Work parallel rows of shirring along the length, fairly close together. Stitch across each end twice to anchor the elastic and trim and neaten each raw end. Pass through a clasp and stitch back. As with all shirring, hold the belt in the steam from boiling water to shrink it up to provide more grip.

## Single sash

This is very successful if made in jersey fabric but it is also a good way of treating transparent fabrics. Cut the fabric 10 cm (4 in.) wide or wider, on the bias if possible. Work a close zig-zag machine stitch all round the edge. With jersey fabric or a sash cut on the cross, turn the edge under and stretch it as you machine. This will flute it. Trim off the raw edge on the wrong side.

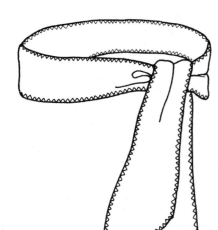

## Tie belt

Suitable in almost any fabric the tie can be made between 2 and 6 to 8 cm ($\frac{3}{4}$ and $2\frac{3}{8}$ to $3\frac{1}{8}$ in.) wide when finished. It may be passed twice round the waist. It may be knotted or tied in a bow. Calculate the approximate length needed, trimming it if necessary after cutting. It is easier to determine the precise length with a piece of fabric actually tied and in place.

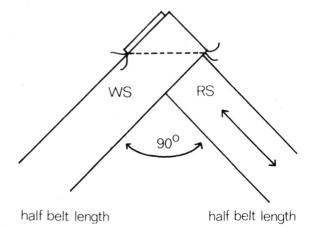

WS RS

90°

half belt length half belt length

## Soft belt with buckle

This is particularly successful when made in jersey fabric. Cut a strip of fabric on the straight grain, wide enough to fold double and stitch, and when finished to be wider than the buckle. Roll and press the belt when turned through and machine round the edge. This produces a raised edge which helps to keep the belt fastened in addition to the wrinkled fabric of the belt. The end of the belt may be fastened down but it looks attractive if left to hang loose.

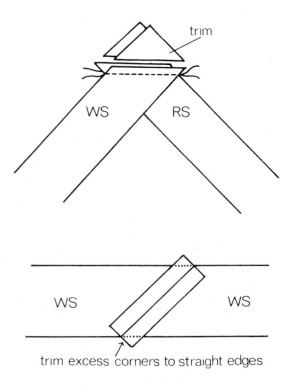

trim

WS RS

WS WS

trim excess corners to straight edges

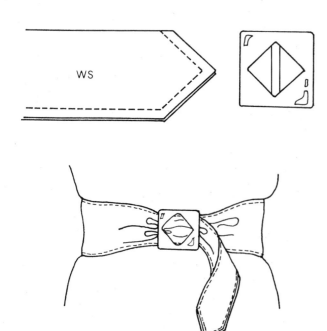

WS

Cut a length of fabric on the straight grain twice the width required plus two turnings, allowing as much length as you want for tying in a knot or a box. Soft fabrics can be interfaced with soft Vilene. Alternatively cut a length of Fold-a-Band, press to fabric and cut round. If the fabric has to be joined, make the join on the cross as it 'gives' and is less bulky and less obvious.

Fold the fabric with right sides together and tack. Angle the ends of the belt if you wish. Chalk a line on which to stitch or use Fold-a-Band as a guide. Machine across each end and almost to the centre, leaving a gap for turning through. Do not have the gap where there is a join. Press the stitching flat. Trim all edges and cut off corners.

Turn through with a ruler or a knitting needle. Pull out the corners well and roll the edge and tack. Turn in the raw edges at the gap and tack. Press well. Slip stitch the gap. Remove tacks. The edges may be stitched for a firmer finish or to tie in with other top-stitching.

If the tie belt is to be knotted it may look better in wear if it is simply looped over and then a small piece of Velcro attached just below to hold it to waist size. This is a particularly useful tip if the belt is for a coat or raincoat, in a fabric that looks ugly when knotted.

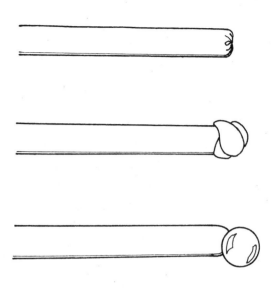

### Tube belt

Cut a long bias strip of fabric and make up as rouleau, inserting piping cord in it if it is needed to make it more substantial. Finish the ends by tying a knot or by gathering it up with the raw edge tucked inside. Beads may be attached to the ends. An alternative belt is made in the same way but longer, and knotted at regular intervals.

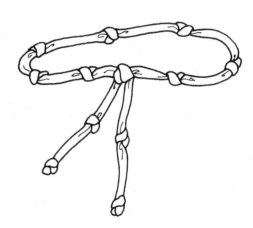

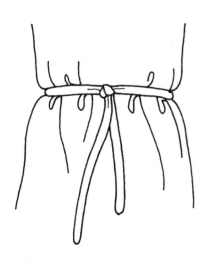

### Wide shaped belt

Best made in crisp fabric or suede, leather, PVC, etc. Cut two wide pieces of fabric, shaping the ends narrower to pass through a wooden or plastic ring. Attach firm Vilene to the wrong side of one piece. Put both pieces right sides together and machine round the outside, leaving a short gap in the stitching. Trim the edges and turn the belt right side out. Press, slip stitch the gap. Pass the ends through the ring and stitch one end back in place. The other end is held back with a hook or with Velcro.

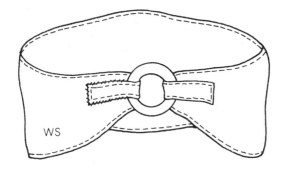

WS

## BERMUDA

The term which is used to describe close-fitting plain or patterned shorts reaching almost to the knee and which can be unflattering on many people.

## BERTHA

A design of wide soft collar with a rounded outer edge reaching to the shoulders or hanging over the shoulders. It often has a narrow contrasting bow at the centre front.

## BETWEENS

The name given to a type of sewing needle used in dressmaking and tailoring. The needles are short so hand sewing is easy because your fingers are nearer to the point as you make the stitch and you have more control. They are thus quicker to use than the alternative sewing needle, the much longer Sharps. Betweens were once referred to as Egg-eyed but in fact the eyes of both Betweens and Sharps needles are the same shape and size.

The most useful sizes of Betweens are from 5 for tacking and sewing on buttons, to 7 or 8 for normal hand sewing and it is useful to have a few size 9 or 10 for working on fine fabric. Always select the correct size for the job — it makes it easier and more pleasant to sew, the needle penetrates the fabric without difficulty and it forms a hole of the right size to take the thread. Never use a needle for too long. Like machine needles they become blunt or bent quite quickly. When hand sewing on synthetics such as nylon and polyester you will need a new needle quite frequently.

Throw the used needle away. Do not put it back in your basket.

## BIAS

The term refers to any direction on woven fabric that is not on the line of the warp or weft thread. It is also used in reference to pieces of knit fabric that are at an angle to the wale but it is not really correct to use the word 'bias' in this context.

The advantage of bias is that it has 'give' and this can be used to provide style and comfort by cutting garment sections on the bias; it can provide a decorative effect and, used in narrow strips, it can be persuaded to go round curves.

If you pull a piece of woven fabric at an angle of 45° to the edge it will stretch a lot which, is maximum bias; if you do the same at any other angle the fabric will stretch less. Bias at all angles is useful for various purposes but sometimes because of the pattern or weave it is necessary to use it only at its maximum, i.e. 45°, even though this amount of stretch may not be required.

## BIAS BINDING

Purchased by the length or on a pre-pack card, bindings are strips of woven material cut from wide fabric at an angle of 45° to the selvedge. All bias bindings have the ability to 'give', and do not fray, and they are pre-shrunk and pressed. They are folded, that is folded in from each side, so that the edges meet, or nearly meet, in the centre. Widths range from 10 to 22 mm ($\frac{3}{8}$ to $\frac{7}{8}$ in.), occasionally wider. Bindings are now made from synthetic fibres and blends as well as from cotton. A wide range is made in plain colours, a few from printed fabrics, and some from plain coloured satin. Apart from their use in enclosing edges, bindings have many decorative uses, including being used folded double, as a piping.

## BIAS CUT

A garment such as a dress or skirt with each section cut with the bias of the fabric hanging vertically. It is most effective when soft clinging fabrics are used, such as crepe and voile and some very interesting designs can be created. The number of paper patterns on sale for entirely bias cut garments is limited, probably because the pieces are more difficult to fit and handle, but also because substantial amounts of fabric are usually required.

## BIAS INSERTION SEAM

(See *Piped Seam*, page 281.)

## BIAS SEAM

A seam the edges of which are on the bias or cross. Skirt seams are the most important because they affect the appearance of the entire garment, but all seams should be treated like this.

Begin by cutting out all pieces, remove the pattern

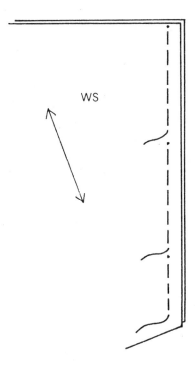

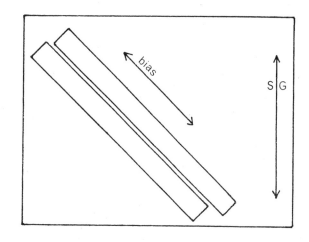

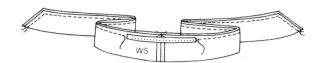

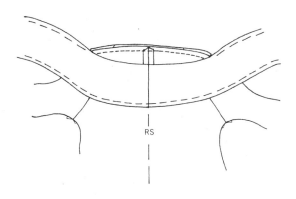

and hang up the pieces of fabric. Pin loops of tape to the waist edges and put on a coat hanger. Leave for a few days to allow the seam edges to drop.

Join the seam by placing the two layers right sides together on the table with the hem to the right. Begin tacking the seam and on reaching the end of the thread leave the end loose. Tack the entire seam. Take hold of the waist and hem ends of the fabric and pull to loosen the tacking stitches. Set your machine to a medium stitch and a slight zig-zag. Stitch from hem to waist, pulling the fabric very slightly as it goes under the foot. Use synthetic thread such as Coats' Drima, which will also stretch with the seam.

Remove tackings and press the seam from hem to waist, stretching slightly. The more excess stretch that can be removed from the seam during construction the less it will drop during wear. However, allow the whole skirt to hang for a few days before turning up the hem and also be prepared to re-level the hem at intervals during the life of the skirt.

## BIAS TIE NECK

A neckline finish made from a wide piece of fabric cut on the true cross. The strip is attached to the neckline to neaten it and the extended ends tie in a bow or as a tie. If the collar is to fold over round the neck, cut the strips at least four times the finished

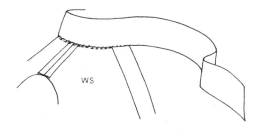

width plus turnings; if it is to stand up at the back of the neck allow twice the width plus turnings. Another way of calculating the fabric is to decide on the width you want the tie part. The ends may be straight or angled. As a long piece of fabric will be needed it is more economical to join two pieces on the straight grain at the centre back.

With all except very soft fabrics insert a narrow strip of soft Iron-on Vilene along one edge of the bias tie, at the centre, to reinforce the part that will be joined to the garment neckline.

Fold the fabric right sides together and stitch across the ends and towards the centre, leaving a gap for the neck of 11cm ($4\frac{3}{8}$ in.) across the centre. Trim the seam allowance and the corners, turn tie right side out, roll edges, tack and press.

Place the tie right side to right side of the blouse neck, matching centre back yoke to the seam in the tie. Pin and tack one edge of the tie to the blouse neck edge. Machine the tie to neck.

Trim the turnings and press up into the bias tie. Turn under the raw edge round inside of the neck. Tack and hem into the machining.

## BIAS TUBING

This is made in the same way as rouleau but is usually called tubing if it is fairly wide and to be used for plaiting or to make a belt.

## BINDINGS

### Bias binding
Commercially produced bias strip already joined and with edges pressed over. All bias bindings have the ability to 'give' and do not fray, and they are pre-shrunk. The binding is made from cotton, and the softer type is made from a mixture of cotton and viscose fibres. Widths range from 10 to 22 mm ($\frac{3}{8}$ to

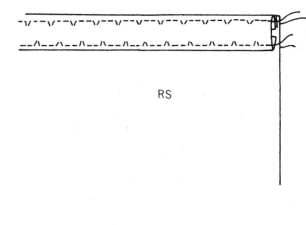

RS

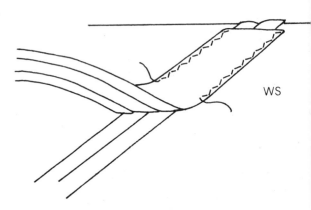

WS

$\frac{7}{8}$ in.), occasionally wider. Narrow and medium width binding may be used for clothes and furnishings but the wider ones are of coarser texture and usually confined to use on heavier domestic repairs. Most types are sold in cut lengths on cards and also from larger rolls by the metre. There is a wide variety of colours available in the narrow width including a few printed fabrics which produce interesting results when applied to plain fabrics.

Bias binding may be applied flat and stitched along both edges either as decoration or as a seam finish, for example on the right side of quilted seams; it may be applied over a raw edge so that equal amounts of binding are visible on each side; it may be applied to an edge so that it is only visible on one side or the other.

Attach by machine, machine embroidery stitches, by hand, or hand embroidery.

### Bias strips
Strips of material cut on the cross to use for binding edges to neaten or for decoration. The fabric from which the strips are cut will vary according to its

WS

eventual use but it may be lining, cotton lawn, self-fabric or a contrasting plain or print. If the fabric has a pattern printed or woven in lines such as checks or stripes the bias strips must be cut at an angle of 45°, otherwise they need not be fully at that angle.

Take a warp thread and fold the fabric until it lies over a weft thread, so producing a fold on the cross. Cut carefully along this fold and then cut strips parallel with the cut edge. Press the strips, stretching them slightly to stop them bubbling when they are used.

Bias strips can be cut slightly off the 45° angle and this can be useful if you are short of fabric. Some fabrics stretch less than others so test a small piece first to make sure there will be enough 'give' for the particular position for which it is needed. Do not stretch the strips as you will need all the 'give' there is in them.

If you have a rectangle of fabric to spare and you need a long piece of crossway fabric, you can make it by joining the piece first and then cutting. First mark out the strips at 45° in the width required.

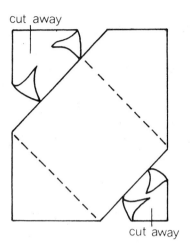

Mark with chalk or tacking. Trim off the triangles left at each end.

Fold the fabric with right sides together to join the shorter edges together, but leave the width of one strip extending as you start to tack. Machine a seam and press open. Cut the strip by cutting round and round following the chalk line.

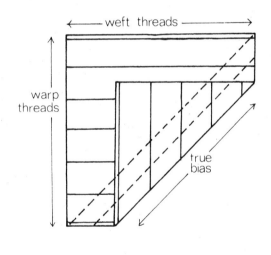

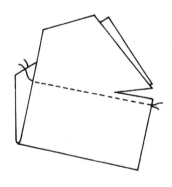

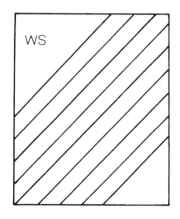

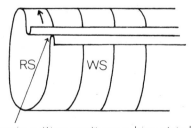

begin cutting continuous bias strip here

To join short lengths of crossway strip, place the strips, end to end, wrong side up, and trim off on the straight grain. Using the iron, press over a small turning on each strip. Lift these ends and place the creases together; pin or tack. Open each join out and look at it from the right side to make sure the long edges are level. Stitch by machine or hand. Press the joins open and trim off the edges.

These open joins are sometimes difficult to make in fine fabrics. An easier way is to trim the ends of the strips to allow only 3 mm ($\frac{1}{8}$ in.) seam allowance, set your machine to the overlock or blind hem stitch, stitch the join and press it to one side.

(See also *Bias* and *Bias Binding*.)

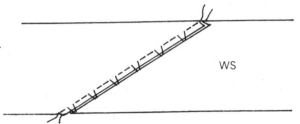

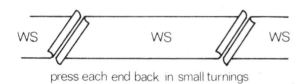

trim ends of strips on straight of grain

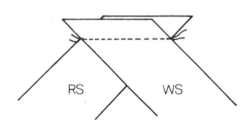

press each end back in small turnings

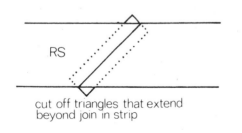

cut off triangles that extend beyond join in strip

### Bound edge

A bound edge is one finished with bias strips of fabric or with purchased bias binding. Equal amounts of the binding are visible on both sides of the edge. It is a useful finish if facings cannot be applied; it gives an opportunity for adding an edging in contrasting fabric; it can be applied easily to shaped edges due to the 'give' in the bias strip. Equally it can be used on straight edges but in this case the bias strip should be slightly stretched when applied, or it may wrinkle. It is also the best way of enclosing bulky edges such as quilting.

The crossways strips to be used should be made twice the width of the amount intended to be visible plus two seam allowances of 5 mm ($\frac{1}{4}$ in.) Prepare stretch and join sufficient bias strip. (See *Bias strips*, above.) The finished width is partly a matter of choice, although binding looks best if it is made as narrow as the fabric will allow. Very fine fabrics, such as voile and chiffon, can be as narrow as 3 mm ($\frac{1}{8}$ in.) when finished but cottons and thicker fabrics may have to be from 5 to 7 mm ($\frac{1}{4}$ in.), with pile fabrics finished at possibly 1 cm ($\frac{3}{8}$ in.). It is best to experiment with a small piece before cutting the strip, rather than trying to adjust the width after starting to attach it because it is very difficult to trim bias strip evenly with it in any position other than flat on the table.

If you wish the edge of the binding when finished to be in a precise position either for fit (neckline) or for accuracy (if it has to be joined to another edge later) then begin by trimming some fabric from the edge of the garment. The amount to be trimmed should equal the finished width of the binding. If the addition of the binding will not substantially affect the garment, for instance adding 5 mm ($\frac{1}{4}$ in.) to the hem of a flared skirt, a low neckline, an armhole or a sleeve edge, then there is no need to trim the edge.

In fact in many cases where a concave edge is being handled it is liable to stretch and may even have already stretched, the addition of the binding will then tighten the edge and help to raise it to give a neater finish.

*Attaching to the right side*    Place the bias strip right side down to the right side of the garment. Align the edges so that you take the full seam allowance on the garment, despite any previous markings there may be, but taking only 5 mm ($\frac{1}{4}$ in.) on the strip. Tack. It helps when removing tackings later if you stitch to one side of the 5 mm ($\frac{1}{4}$ in.) line. Slightly stretch the binding as you tack. If when applying to a straight edge you can control your machining accurately, you can omit the tacking stage.

Set the machine to a slight zig-zag stitch with the dial only fractionally off '0' and machine. Remove tackings and with the garment right side up run the toe of the iron between the garment and the binding to push the binding over so that it is right side up. Do not press too heavily at this stage.

On the wrong side trim both the turnings to 5 mm ($\frac{1}{4}$ in.) or if the finished width of bindings is to be 5 mm ($\frac{1}{4}$ in.) or less, trim off a little more. Never cut off too much or the finished edge will be limp.

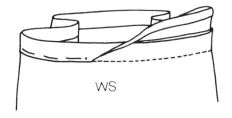

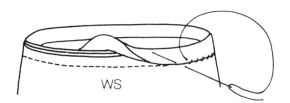

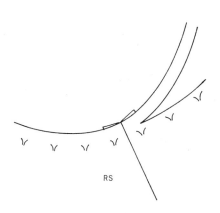

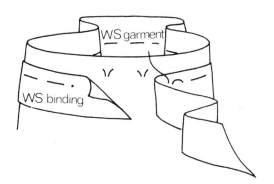

With the wrong side towards you fold the raw edge of the binding down 5 mm ($\frac{1}{4}$ in.) or almost to meet the trimmed edges, fold it again to bring the binding edge to the line of machining and tack. Tack fairly near the edge of the binding and use small stitches or the binding will spring away. Press lightly on the binding. Finish by working hemming stitch, picking up each machine stitch on the needle and passing it into the folded edge of the binding, picking up as little as possible of the fabric. It may sound laborious, especially to beginners, to pick up every stitch, but it is worth it. It is easy because the stitches act as a guide and you do not have to control the size of your stitch. It is very quick and produces a firm finish. If you are tempted to try hemming into alternate stitches only, the binding will have a tendency to move in wear and it may be caught and pulled down, as with a badly stitched hem.

Remove the tackings and press both sides of the garment.

*Attaching to the wrong side*    This method produces visible stitching on the right side of the garment so its use is more limited.

Attach the binding exactly as described under the previous instructions above but stitching it with the right side of the binding to the wrong side of the garment. Press and trim the raw edges.

With the right side of the garment towards you, fold over 4 mm ($\frac{1}{4}$ in.) of the binding, that is a little less than the amount allowed when cutting the strips. Fold again bringing the edge of the binding to a position where it just covers the machine stitches. Tack. Again it will be necessary to tack on the edge and with small stitches. Press lightly. Finish the edge by machine. You can use a medium length straight stitch but it is difficult to produce a perfectly accurate row of machining due to the varying thickness between binding and garment. A small zig-zag can be used, or the blind hem stitch or another stitch that makes one zig-zag at intervals which can go over the fold of the binding. Alternatively, use a contrasting thread and work a machine embroidery stitch. Remove tacking stitches and press.

*Binding a heavy fabric*    This can be a useful way of finishing a bulky edge such as blanket cloth. It is used on coat hems and can also be decorative. Use a suitable lightweight fabric: the choice will depend upon the garment and the effect you want, e.g. lining, cotton, silk. Alternatively, you can use the same fabric as the garment.

Cut and prepare the binding and apply it to the right side as described in the instructions for attaching to the right side. Trim and press the binding. With the right side of the garment towards you roll the binding away from you to produce an edge of even width. Tack through the garment and the binding just below the join. You will only be able to insert one tacking stitch at a time; roll and tack, roll and tack, and so on, otherwise the binding can pull out of position and wrinkle.

Finish by working hand prick stitch invisibly exactly in the join, working from the right side. Press lightly after removing tackings. When using this finish decoratively, possibly adding a contrasting textured binding to a neckline or sleeve, it will be necessary to hold down the raw edge on the binding on the inside with herringbone stitch.

An alternative finish to prick stitch is machining exactly in the join from the right side, but this slightly stiffens the edge and it is, of course, visible.

(See also *Double bind*, next page.)

*Making joins*    If the edge is circular, that is, all seams have been completed, start to tack the binding in place at a point where the joining will not be visible, such as the underarm or the back of the neck. Start and end the tacking 4 cm ($1\frac{1}{2}$ in.) from the position of the proposed join. Use the toe of the iron and press over both ends of the binding so that the folds meet. If there are other joins in the binding and they were made on the straight grain then this join too should be on the straight grain, that is at an angle. However, since this is not easy to do, it is excusable to decide to make a straight join, especially if there is a seam to line up with.

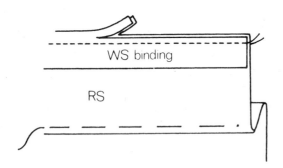

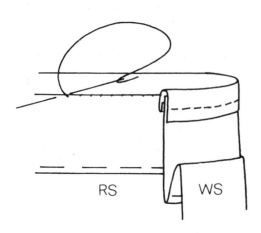

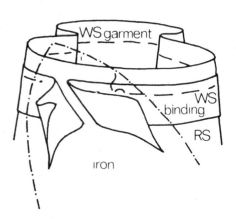

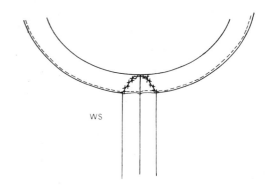

Lift the ends and join, holding the two pressed creases together. It is often easier to back stitch this by hand than machine it. Trim the surplus ends of bias, press the join and machine the binding to the garment.

An easier way of making a join which may appeal to those less experienced is as follows. Leave one seam of the garment unstitched. This should preferably be one that will not be too obvious in wear. Attach the binding and trim and press the turnings. Join the garment seam making sure the binding seams meet exactly. Press open. Trim and finish the seam. Trim the turnings to 3 mm ($\frac{1}{8}$ in.) within the binding. Fold over and finish the binding in the usual way.

A further alternative suitable for non-fraying fabrics is to complete the binding and then join the seam. Press the seam open and finish the edges but trim back the edges of the binding and hold them down with herringbone stitch.

### Double bind

This produced a finish double the thickness of a normal bound edge, so it can be used to add weight to improve hang. It is also the easiest method to employ when using very fine fabrics or those difficult to control, such as chiffon and crêpe and stretchy jersey. This method should also be used if a contrasting fabric much lighter in weight than the garment is being used.

It is possible to produce an exceptionally narrow finish, without having to overcome the problem of handling the raw edge of the binding.

The width of the strip to be cut must be calculated accurately and the strip cut precisely as no adjustment can be made later. Practise first on a small piece to obtain a suitable width. Cut and join crossway strips four times the desired finished width, plus two seam allowances of 5 mm ($\frac{1}{4}$ in.). Time the edge of the garment if necessary by the amount of the binding width when finished.

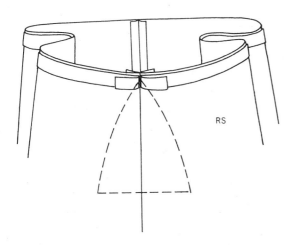

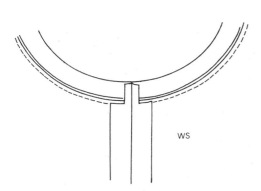

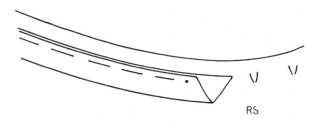

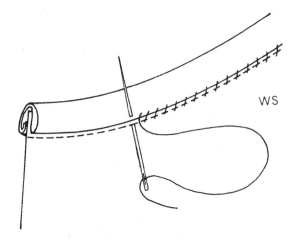

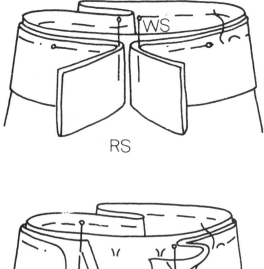

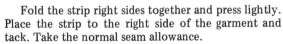

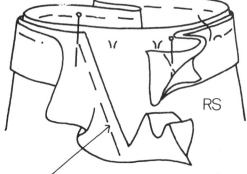

denotes seam line on straight of grain

Fold the strip right sides together and press lightly. Place the strip to the right side of the garment and tack. Take the normal seam allowance.

On the garment you may or may not have trimmed the edge but still take the full allowance. Take only 5 mm ($\frac{1}{4}$ in.) on the binding. Tack, keeping the stitches slightly to one side for ease of removal later. Machine. Trim the seam allowance of the garment and also trim a fraction from the two edges of binding.

With the wrong side of the garment towards you roll the binding over and tack it with its folded edge just on the machine stitching. Do not press either before folding it over or at this stage because the folded edge is liable to stretch easily,

Finish by working hemming stitches into every machine stitch. As you hem keep the binding pushed well forward with the thumb of your other hand to prevent it stretching. Remove tackings and press.

*Joins*    To make a join on the straight grain when double binding a finished circular edge is difficult.

Tack the strip in place but leave 6 cm ($2\frac{3}{8}$ in.) free where the join is to be. Open out the binding and mark the straight grain on each end of the binding. These two marks when joined must form a binding of exactly the right size. It helps to mark the straight grain on one end with a few tacking stitches and then experiment by pinning together and adjusting until you find the position for the other end of the binding. Join the marks, trim the turnings, re-fold the binding wrong sides together and complete the tacking before machining to the garment.

An easier alternative to this fiddly join is to double bind the edge before stitching the final seam of the garment. Choose an inconspicuous seam and trim the seam and binding edges and hold down with herringbone stitch.

## BISHOP

A full length sleeve usually gathered into the wrist. It is very full and therefore often confined to light fabrics, most of the fullness appearing below the elbow.

## BLANKET STITCH

(See *Loop Stitch*, an embroidery stitch.)

## BLIND STITCH

The stitch used for catching the fabric of a hem to the garment. Probably called 'blind' because the essential point it that is must not be visible on the right side of the garment. It is a slightly misleading name; preferable is the more common 'catch stitch' which indicates the lightness of touch necessary and also, catch stitch can be used in places other than the hem.

(See also *Catch Stitch*.)

## BLOCK

(See *Pressing Block*.)

## BLOUSON

A style of top, jacket or bodice of a dress, cut loose to below the waist then using a drawstring or elastic to pull it in to the hips. The actual line of blouson may be at any level from the waist to the hips depending on the design and the figure.

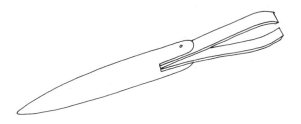

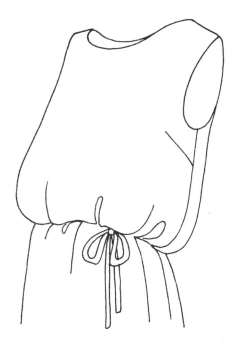

points of scissors and other implements can damage the fabric. A modern version is the 'Tweezerbodkin'. This is made with a plastic pointed end for removing tacks and the opposite end consists of tweezers for pulling out thread ends and for unpicking. The plastic end is also very useful for re-shaping the round end of hand-worked buttonholes, and for unpicking hand-sewing. The 'Tweezerbodkin' also has other uses in embroidery and general craft work.

(See also *Stiletto*.)

## BODY RULERS

These are flexible jointed rulers in the 'Fantastic Fit' product range. The straight one can be used for all length measurements on the body. The two curved

## BOBBIN

The round metal device which holds the thread forming the underneath part of a machine stitch. Also called a spool.

·Always fill the spool or bobbin with the same type of thread as the machine is using. Most machines stop automatically when the spool is full; never try to put more thread on. Always fill the spool using the mechanism provided on the machine to ensure that it is evenly wound and therefore when stitching it will be evenly released.

## BODKIN

An old pointed tool used for removing tacking and basting  threads. They were originally made of bone and a few of ivory. The slightly rounded end slides easily between the thread and the fabric, whereas

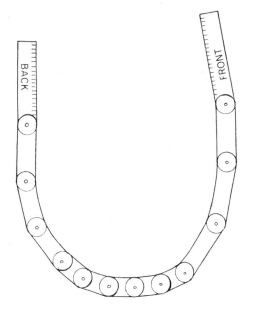

rulers, one for armhole and one for crutch, are pressed onto the body to fit. The ruler is carefully removed and placed on the pattern. The deviation between figure and pattern shape will be evident and a new line is drawn. All rulers are marked and graded.

## BOILER SUIT

An all-in-one trousers, top and sleeves, usually made in casual woven or knitted fabrics such as denim, poplin, sailcloth. It is often of shirtwaister style with patch pockets and top stitching.

(See also *Jump Suit*.)

## BOKHARA COUCHING

An embroidery filling stitch similar to Romanian couching. Lay thread from left to right by taking a stitch, then take small stitches under the thread into the fabric. Insert the needle slightly behind each time and make the crossing stitches quite close together.

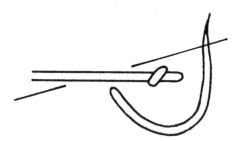

## BOLD

The name that J & P Coats give to their thick top-stitching thread. It can also be used for hand-worked buttonholes made on medium to thick fabrics. It is available in a fairly wide range of colours on spools containing 30 metres. It is a spun polyester thread.

## BOLERO

A sleeveless or cap-sleeved jacket cut straight and finishing above the waist. The style is taken from the Spanish bullfighter outfit so it should have no fastening and the armholes should allow for a full-sleeved blouse underneath. Any fabric may be used

including felt, quilting, suede, velvet and rich embroidery. An easy garment to make but the inside can often be seen so the corners are usually rounded, the bolero lined and the edges all bound with braid or binding.

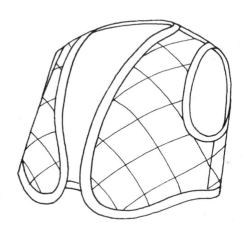

## BOMBER

The name given to a slightly military style waist length jacket with wrist and hip bands often of a different material. Can be zipped or buttoned and made from any fabric from waterproof types and blanket cloth to suede and fur.

(See also *Battle Jacket*.)

## BONDAWEB

A fine non-woven web backed with transparent paper, it is pressed on to fabric, adhesive side down, using a medium hot iron and a damp pressing muslin. Press with sharp movements until the paper appears speckled. Leave until cool, then peel off the paper backing. The web is in position but dry so you can now work on that area. Later when re-pressed the web will become sticky so it must be covered by another layer of fabric.

It has a number of uses including the application of appliqué; holding any piece of fabric in position while stitched, for example patches; to prevent fraying at the ends of cut openings and in button-holes, particularly piped or bound varieties and in many other areas where a small piece will also lessen or completely prevent fraying.

Bondaweb is sold in sheets folded into a poly-thene pre-pack.

(See also *Wundaweb*.)

## BORDER FABRICS

Some fabrics have a decorative border along one selvedge. This may be printed, woven or embroidered. It may be geometric or floral, contrasting or subtly self-coloured or shaded. Beyond the border the fabric might be plain or patterned evenly, or the border may continue in a modified design across the width of the fabric. When buying these materials remember that their use is limited, but to balance this the interest is entirely in the design and so a simple style is called for. Look at the fabric and decide how it can be used to good effect. The simplest way is to make a dress or skirt in one piece with the border at the hemline. Consider also the possibility of using the border on sleeves or cuffs, collar, belt, pockets, or on a jacket but not the skirt or dress. It might also be possible to cut off the border and rejoin it where it is wanted. With imagination you will find scope for interesting use of these fabrics.

Always adjust the pattern to fit before placing it on the fabric, especially if the hemline falls on the border. Also, either fold the fabric carefully and pin it together, or cut out on single fabric. Remember that borders will not match exactly on sloping seams, and on curved hemlines the border will run off the bottom. On all except very general floral borders these features should not be exaggerated.

## BOW

Knotted ends of fabric, often a belt or neck finish. A bow will drape better if the fabric is on the cross with ends cut at an angle. The fabric is always double, either one straight piece folded, and possibly neatening an edge at the same time as on a neckline, or made from two pieces in order to introduce shape.

If part of the fabric forms a feature on the garment such as neck band or cuff, interface that part only but not the ends that will form the bow.

## BOW TIE

A stiff bow, usually quite small. It can be made from firm ribbon or from fabric, the latter may need stiffening with Vilene or Fold-a-Band.

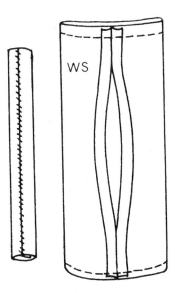

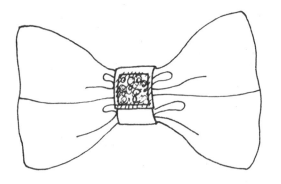

The easiest way to make a bow tie is to construct it so that it doesn't have to be tied at all when worn. Cut a rectangle of fabric, fold it right sides together and stitch down the side, leaving a gap for turning through at the centre. Stitch across the ends of the tube and turn it right side out. Press. Make a narrow strip about 1 cm ($\frac{3}{8}$ in.) wide by turning in the edges of a 3 cm ($1\frac{1}{4}$ in.) wide piece of fabric and hemming or machining along each edge. Wrap this round the centre of the rectangle, and stitch at the back.

If you want the bow to have really open ends make the tube just over twice the finished length of the bow and fold the ends to meet each other at the back.

Attach to the neck of a shirt by sewing a small square of Velcro to the back of the bow and a corresponding piece to the neck. Alternatively, make a narrow neckband of fabric or ribbon to fasten at the back with Velcro and sew the bow at the front.

## BOX

The word used to describe any garment, usually a coat or jacket, that is cut straight with straight sleeves, presenting a square or rectangular box outline. The look is often emphasised with shoulder pads and by adding a straight skirt to a jacket.

## BRAID

Braid may be woven, plaited or knitted in a wide variety of colours and designs often in mix and match designs or with matching single motifs. There are also different types designed to put together, one for the edge, perhaps fringed, another to apply within the edge of the article. Choice of fibre and washability is as important as colour and design.

The decision to use hand or machine stitching will depend entirely on the type of braid and the effect wanted. Hand sewing, such as hemming or prick stitch, should be worked in thread to match the part of the braid being sewn; decorative stitching by hand or machine can be matching or contrasting; interesting effects can be achieved by adding a machine embroidery stitch to the edge of the braid in a perfectly matching thread.

If you have a finished edge to guide you there is often no need to tack the braid down, nor to keep measuring to get it straight. If you do need a line then draw a chalk line where one edge of the braid will be, so that it is clearly visible as you tack. With very open or complicated braids it is safest to tack with small stitches in a perfectly matching thread and leave them in to avoid the possibility of harming the braid in removing them.

When attaching braid by machine it may help you to use the quilting foot on the machine which gives a clearer view of the needle.

**Flat braid, e.g. ric-rac**
Lay the braid on the fabric and hold it while stitching. Work a tiny prick stitch in each point of the braid criss-crossing the thread on the wrong side as you move from one point to the next. The alternative is to work a row of back stitching or machining down the centre of the braid, but with this method the points of the braid may tend to curl up.

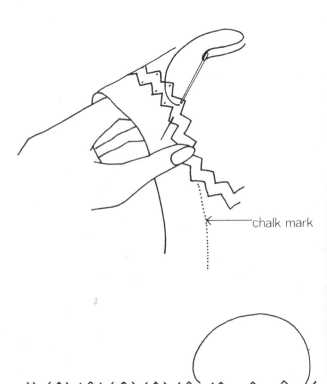

chalk mark

Ric-rac can be attached decoratively by working herringbone stitch across the braid, using a contrasting embroidery thread.

### Edging

This produces a picot edge. Place the ric-rac to the right side of the garment with the centre of the braid over the fitting line. Tack down the centre. Place facing right side down onto the braid. Turn the work over and tack, following the fitting line exactly.

Machine on this line. Trim the turnings, but do not cut the ric-rac. Roll and finish the facings in the usual way.

### Raised braid

Most raised braids look best attached by hand. Before turning up the hem tack and catch down lightly with one prick stitch or fell stitch (depending on the design of the braid) in each extending bead along the edge of the braid.

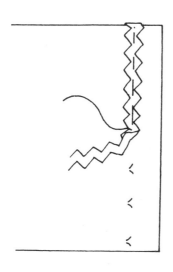

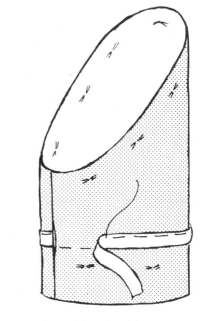

Attaching braid to sleeve

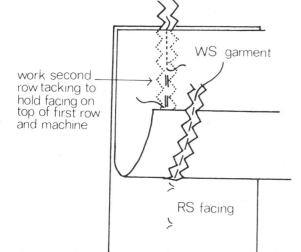

work second row tacking to hold facing on top of first row and machine

WS garment

RS facing

### Soutache

This is a narrow two-cord silky braid designed to be sewn down the centre. This is best done with a hand prick stitch but it can be done by machine using the zip foot.

### Fancy braid

This is the kind of braid which is used on men's dinner suit trousers. Attach it by hand using felling down each edge. Do not pull the thread tightly.

Joins should be placed where they are not obvious. Either lap one end over the other, turn under the hem, or turn in both ends to meet each other and oversew. If the ends can be brought to a seam in the garment make a small slit in the seam, push the ends of the braid through, turn garment to the wrong side and re-stitch the seam.

Do not flatten raised braids by pressing. Use the toe of the iron to press up to the edge of the braid. Arrange a thick towel on the pressing surface and press the stitching lightly on the wrong side.

## BRIDLE

A stay used in tailored collars and lapels to help to keep the shape. The bridle is usually a piece of tailor's stay-tape or it may a piece of tailor's linen tape, or even, on lightweight fabrics it can be the selvedge cut from a piece of lining. The bridle is placed along the roll line of the lapel and extended into the collar to stabilise that part of a tailored coat or jacket.

(For details of attaching see *Tailored Collar*, page 71.)

## BUCKLE

Kits to cover a metal base with fabric are obtainable, or covered buckles can be made professionally. Purchased buckles are usually metal, wood or plastic and may be with or without a prong. There is a wide variety of clasps too, although often the most interesting type of buckle can be found on old clothes or in second-hand collections.

The easiest way to use a buckle is to remove the prong and fasten the belt by sewing a small piece of Velcro to the end of the belt and a corresponding piece to the belt. The fastening is slightly adjustable. Clasps may be made adjustable in the same way.

## BULK

The term bulk used in dressmaking refers to unnecessary layers of material that have built up inside the garment usually as a result of seaming several pieces of fabric together. If these layers form a ridge that is visible on the outside or if they cause an edge to balloon rather than lie flat they become bulk and must be trimmed, layered and pressed.

## BULLION STITCH

A coiled and knotted embroidery stitch. Take a small back stitch but do not pull the needle right through. Then twist the thread round the needle to cover the back stitch. Pull the needle through, holding the twisted threads with the thumb, then re-insert the needle, in the same place, pulling the thread through until the stitch lies flat. (See diagrams next column.)

## BUST

Obviously a part of the body but also the name used to describe a dress form or dummy.

(See *Dummy*.)

Twist the thread around the needle

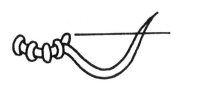

## BUST POINT

An important figure position to establish when fitting a top. The bust point is that part of the bust prominence that comes out furthest. In some figures especially small ones it is often well defined but on larger, more generally shaped busts, it may be difficult to determine. Foundation garments of different makes and styles can alter the position of the bust point and fashion changes will decree that sometimes busts are conical and well defined, at others they are rounded.

When bust shaping is provided by darts it is essential to establish precisely where the bust point is so that the darts may be fitted accordingly. (See *Darts*.)

Less defined shaping, such as gathers, may be easier to fit as the exact bust point position need not be established but nevertheless you should be aware of its importance. If, for instance, you have an unusually low bust point and you choose a pattern with gathers in a high yoke seam, the provision of shaping by gathering may be lost down at bust level making the garment tight or at least uncomfortable. Similarly a figure with a sharply prominent bust will find the prominence very much emphasised by a very low yoke seam.

On some styles and certainly when fitting a basic pattern establish the bust point level by measuring from mid-shoulder down onto the fullest point of the bust and make a note of the measurement. Remember that it may vary with different foundation garments.

It is interesting to note that an average bust point depth is about 20 to 23 cm (8 to 9 in.).

The width of the button stand should equal the diameter of the button to ensure that the button does not hang over the edge when fastened. In pattern drafting this distance is determined in conjunction with a decision about the size of the button. On a single breasted garment the button must be on the centre front so the stand is the amount beyond that point. It is obviously a wider piece for large buttons than for small ones. Sometimes there is a vertical band with buttons in vertical buttonholes in which case the button stand equals half the width of the band.

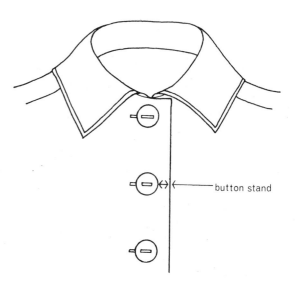

button stand

## BUTTOCKS

The buttocks obviously vary in shape and size and the width of fabric must be sufficient not to emhasise them if they are large. Large buttocks combined with a small waist can present a difficult fitting problem. Another point to consider in fitting, especially with trousers, is the position. Small, high buttocks are easier to fit than low or large ones. If the buttocks drop below crutch level, trouser fitting is extremely difficult.

## BUTTON SNAPS

These are press studs, but included in the pack is a metal button cap which you cover with fabric, and a metal disc to clip on to the back. The press stud fits into this disc, the holes being aligned, and the stitching is worked through both pieces together. Instructions for use are included and so is a circular pattern showing exactly what size piece of fabric must be cut to cover the button. Various sizes are available.

## BUTTON STAND

The term used to describe the amount of material (double or faced) that extends beyond the button-hole at the fastening edge of the garment. The expression is more often used in connection with pattern drafting than sewing.

## BUTTON THREAD

A strong thick thread for sewing buttons on coats, etc. Linen thread may be bought in skeins from tailors' trimming shops in limited colours, a wider range is available in haberdashery departments and this may be cotton with a glacé finish such as Coats' Extra Strong Button Thread, or an alternative is Coats' Heavy Duty thread which can be used for buttons but is also recommended for other jobs such as rucksack and tent repairs. It is strong, rot-proof and made from polyester.

## BUTTONHOLE STITCH

A dressmaking or embroidery stitch worked over an edge, often to prevent it from fraying. If you propose using it for embroidery first look at *Loop Stitch* (page 178), as this is also used and the two are often confused.

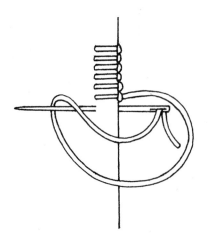

If used for worked buttonholes, the choice of thread depends on the fabric, but the stitch can be used simply as a neatening stitch over a raw edge, where only a short distance has to be covered and the raw edge has to be caught without adding bulk to a layer beneath.

Use single thread, insert the needle horizontally across the body and work towards you, except in the case of hand-worked tailored buttonholes. Take the shortest possible stitch that will control the fraying edge, wind the thread round the needle, towards you under the point of the needle, pull the needle through, then take hold of the thread nearer to the fabric and pull again, gently easing the knot that has formed onto the raw edge. Do not cram the stitches together, the knots should be close, the stitches should have slight gaps between.

## BUTTONHOLE TWIST

A thick, loosely twisted silk thread, with an attractive sheen. A soft twist for hand-tailored buttonholes can be bought in skeins at tailors' trimming shops, a wider range of fashion colours can be bought on spools on haberdashery counters, but this has a higher twist and can also be used for hand or machine decorative stitching. Drima Bold is also a buttonhole thread and a top stitching thread. It is polyester and very strong but has less sheen than silk. May be used by hand or in the machine. When using these thicker threads in the machine use a size 110 (18) machine needle or the stitch will not form correctly because a smaller needle does not make a hole large enough for the thread to pull through without shredding or twisting.

Silk twist becomes creased when stored. Always run a cool iron along it before threading through the needle.

## BUTTONS AND BUTTONHOLES

A form of fastening that has been in use for a very long time and still as strong and appropriate as ever.

A cut is made in the fabric to make the buttonhole and the cut edges are processed to prevent fraying and stretching and to add strength to take the strain of constant use. Types of buttonhole include piped, bound, hand-worked, machine-made and tailored, and the decision as to type depends on the type and thickness of fabric, the style of garment and the position on that garment. Another consideration should be the quantity that have to be made.

For those who prefer an easy way out, ready-made buttonholes can be bought in sets in pre-packs. The pack contains several machined buttonholes worked on a gauze-like fabric. The buttonholes are pressed into position, the heat of the iron melting the gauze and the buttonholes and garment fabric is slit in the usual way.

The size and type of button should be chosen before the buttonhole is decided upon, and the size depends upon the fabric, the garment and the position. Where there is strain and the garment very tight, for example jeans waistband, the button should be saucer shaped and be attached with a high shank or else it is difficult to fasten.

In general a blouse button should be small and flat because the fabric is probably lightweight. Coat buttons should be larger, dress and suit buttons medium-sized. If few buttons are used to form a style feature such as on a wrap-over skirt or blouse, or on a shoulder-fastened dress, they may be larger and more decorative.

Remember that buttons draw attention to the buttonholes and both should be inconspicuous unless the latter are perfect. If in doubt about the type of button to use have them covered in self-fabric, or buy a pack of moulds and cover them yourself. If the fabric is dull-surfaced, thick, or has a pile, use covered buttons with metal rims for easier fastening.

### Button and buttonhole positions

The buttonhole should lie in the direction of the strain on a close fastening such as cuff, waistband, fitted bodice. In all these positions the buttonhole should be horizontal with the button settled in the end and the same rule applies to decorative features such as tabs. On straps, etc., the buttonhole might be vertical but it still takes the strain of movement.

Vertical buttonholes are often used on the front fastening of men's shirts and always used on a strap opening because the buttonhole must be exactly in the centre and not allow any movement of the button but it is essential to make sure the garment is fairly loose fitting because they tend to come undone easily. Vertical buttonholes are also used under a flap or fly opening because there would be a danger of horizontal ones being visible.

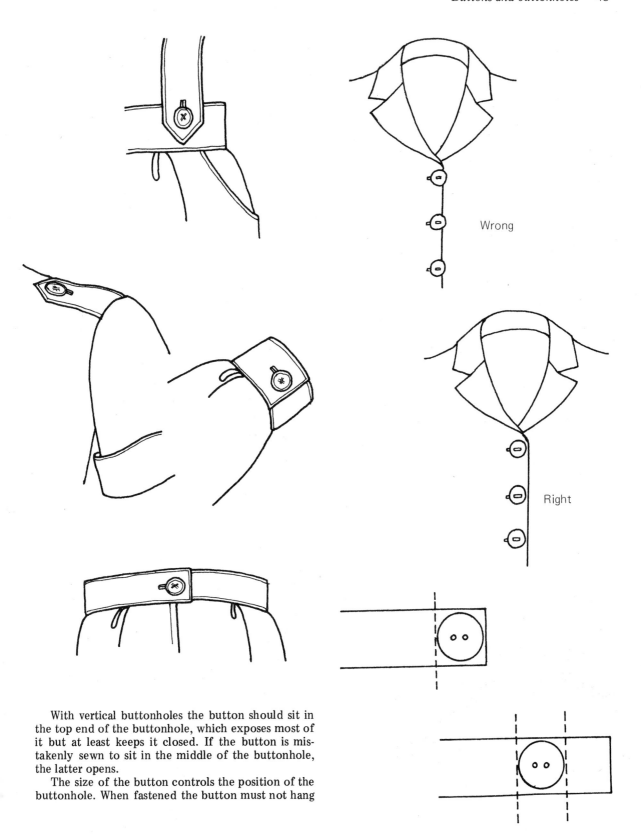

Wrong

Right

With vertical buttonholes the button should sit in the top end of the buttonhole, which exposes most of it but at least keeps it closed. If the button is mistakenly sewn to sit in the middle of the buttonhole, the latter opens.

The size of the button controls the position of the buttonhole. When fastened the button must not hang over the edge of the garment and in fact there should be a distance equal to half the diameter of the button between the edge of the garment and the edge of the button. At a centre front or centre back fastening the holes of the button should lie exactly on the central line of the garment. If there seems to be insufficient material to position the button there, then use a smaller button. Be guided by the size of button referred to on the pattern guide because it indicates that sufficient allowance for that size has been included in the pattern.

To find the correct position for the buttonhole, use the button. Place it against the edge (it may be finished or it may be a line of tacking depending upon the type of buttonhole being made) and make a chalk mark on its far side. Remove the button. That line marks the start of the buttonhole. Replace the button the other side of the line and chalk again on the far side. Remove the button and that marks the width of the buttonhole. Mark the position of the buttonhole itself between these lines. When marking several buttonholes use continuous lines of chalk or tacking. Use an adjustable marker set to size for absolute accuracy. Use a ruler for marking chalk lines. Ease is needed in the buttonhole to avoid strain and undue wear and a lumpy surface. For amounts of ease see entries under the various types of buttonhole.

### Machine-made buttonholes

Modern machines have a built-in mechanism for making buttonholes. It is often for this one facility that women want to change an old machine for a new one and if the type of sewing done involves a lot of buttonholes then it is a matter of necessity.

The degree of automation with the buttonhole varies with the type of machine but is mainly related to the price. However, it is not necessarily the most expensive model that will also produce the most perfect, close satin stitch, buttonhole. The easiest buttonhole to produce is obviously one that requires only the tap of an electronic button to work it, and another to make the machine memorise the length of the buttonhole so that it goes on making them the same size. Also easy, but less expensive, is the machine with dial settings or a set of button slots, each of which, when set, causes the machine to work one section of the buttonhole automatically until stopped. Less expensive than this is one where the stitch is easily altered from satin stitch to bar tack etc., but where you are required to turn the work round. There are also varying degrees of automation within these types according to the make and model of the machine. However, a good buttonhole foot which has some kind of guide or measuring device, or a slot for the button to rest, is invaluable, as it lessens the possibility of errors in size.

If the machine in use produces only a straight stitch, a buttonhole attachment may be available for it. This involves the fabric being gripped firmly and moved from side to side to form a type of satin stitch. If a lot of buttonholes are continually made, and there is no chance of obtaining a machine with a built-in mechanism, then it is worth having an attchment.

When making machine-made buttonholes, it is only the stitching that is quicker and easier; the initial preparation of fabric and marking of positions is the same as for other types of buttonhole. The method of working the buttonholes varies considerably and the instructions in the machine manual must be followed. However, the following will help to achieve good results with all types of machine and all fabrics.

There will be a tendency to fray as the buttonhole is cut after stitching, so insert a length of Wundaweb, in addition to the interfacing, between the layers of fabric. Press well. Mark the buttonholes exactly on the straight grain. The grain will be obscured when under the machine but the marks will be visible. If possible use a chalk pencil or tailor's chalk for marking as tacks can be difficult to remove later. Make all marks very clearly, extending the lines so that they can be seen beyond the buttonhole foot when working.

Work only with the right side up. On heavy or medium fabrics use normal sewing thread, on light fabrics use machine embroidery thread. If your test buttonhole looks heavy with normal thread, change to machine embroidery thread but work round the buttonhole twice.

If machine-made buttonholes are stretched in use they will buckle, so make the buttonhole 2 mm ($\frac{1}{8}$ in.) longer than the diameter of the button, more on thick fabrics.

After stitching, pierce only the centre between the rows with an unpicker or seam ripper, then use small scissors to snip to the ends.

If the fabric does fray after cutting apply a few drops of Fray-Check liquid to the edges. Clear nail varnish will also help.

An additional thread (gimp) should be inserted in buttonholes made in heavy fabrics or those where a raised stitch is required. Instructions for inserting will be found in the machine manual.

### Hand-sewn buttonholes

These are often neater than the buttonholes involving adding fabric, especially on fine fabric. Machine-made buttonholes are the alternative on these fabrics but on pure silk, voile, chiffon, georgette, these may be rather hard and even clumsy.

However, it is essential to be able to work them perfectly and this comes only with practice. Try to arrange that you have time to work all the buttonholes at one sitting because you will improve as you work. Start with the buttonholes that will show least. Use the same sized needle as you have used on the remainder of the garment and use normal sewing thread.

Use thicker thread, such as Drima Bold or buttonhole twist, only on thick fabrics and then you should make tailored buttonholes.

Hand buttonholes are usually the final process to be worked when all edges have been completed.

Mark the buttonhole positions with small tackings or with tailor's chalk. Allow only 1 to 2 mm ($\frac{1}{8}$ in.) ease on the diameter of the button as there is a fair amount of 'give' in this type of buttonhole.

Push a pin in at one end of the tacking and out at the other, and fold the fabric flat.

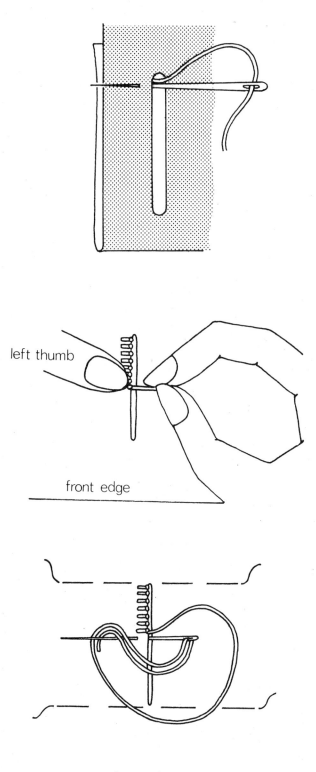

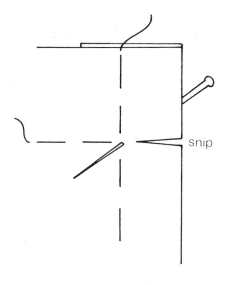

Make a small snip at the fold, remove the pin, and snip carefully into the holes by the pin. Remove the remains of the tacks. Chalk will disappear.

Use single thread and start with a knot. Place the knot on the wrong side a little way from the buttonhole, to be cut off later. Begin at the end farthest from the centre front or finished edge, and hold the work with the edge away from you. Work up the left side first.

Bring the thread up level with the end of the cut. Take a small stitch under the raw edge and with the needle still in the fabric, take the double part of the thread near the eye of the needle, winding it first away, then round the needle towards you.

Pull the needle through until the knot forms on the cut edge, then take hold of the thread near to the knot and tug it gently to settle it into position.

Take the next stitch the width of the thread you are using away from the first. Do not work the stitches too close or they will look crowded and uneven, because there will not be enough room for the knots. The knots should just touch, but the uprights should have slight spaces between them. Continue down the first side to the end.

Work round the end of the buttonhole with five stitches arranged evenly, turning the fabric. Keep these stitches shorter than the others for neatness. To prevent the knots from being crowded, lift the thread when settling the knots so that they appear on the top rather than round the raw edge. Work down the second side.

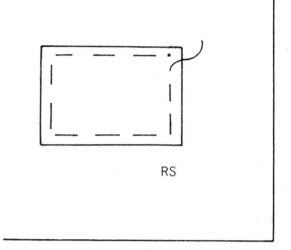

RS

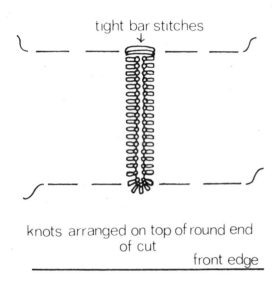

tight bar stitches

knots arranged on top of round end of cut

front edge

At the end of the buttonhole take your needle through the first stitch worked so that first and last stitches are joined. Finish the end by making a bar of four stitches, not quite the width of the button-hole. Pull the thread tight to embed it in the fabric. It is important to keep this end neat as it is always visible. Do not make more buttonhole stitches as it looks ugly.

Pass the thread to the wrong side and work loop stitch over the bar stitches to fasten off. Cut off the knot.

Oversew the buttonhole immediately to draw the edges together. Press on both sides when all the buttonholes are complete.

### Bound buttonholes

Sometimes called patch or one-piece buttonholes these are never as satisfactory or as professional-looking as piped buttonholes although they are similar in appearance. However, on fine or light-weight fabrics they may have to be used if machine-made or hand-worked buttonholes cannot be done.

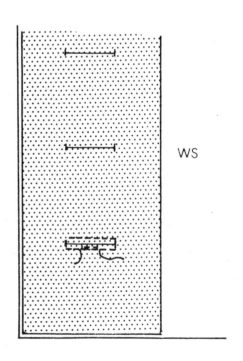

WS

Cut rectangles of fabric on the straight grain at least 2 cm ($\frac{3}{4}$ in.) wide and longer than the proposed buttonhole. Tack these pieces right side down onto the right side of the garment. As with all buttonholes the accuracy of the stitching is very important but the patches now cover the buttonhole markings. It is easiest therefore to mark the wrong side of the garment, where there is a layer of interfacing, using a tracing wheel and carbon paper, or a pencil.

Use a small stitch on the machine and stitch rectangles from this under side. Overlap the stitching to avoid having to sew in ends. The width of the rectangle should be twice the finished effect wanted on each edge. The finer as 2 mm ($\frac{1}{8}$ in.) on fine fabrics on something like baby clothes.

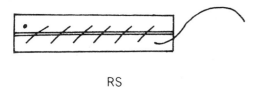

RS

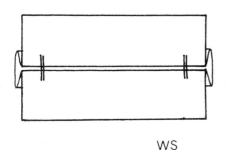

WS

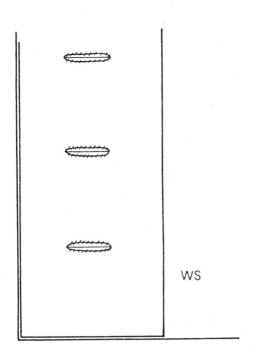

WS

Cut the centre of the buttonhole and carefully snip out the corners. Push the patch through the slit and work at the fabric with the fingers to roll and then fold two even edges. Oversew the folds together with tacking. Turn to the wrong side and press. Work a bar tack exactly at each end of the buttonhole. On the right side prick stitch may be worked in the join if the fabric is springy and will not remain flat. Complete the backs of the buttonholes by cutting a slit in the facing and turning in and hemming in an oval shape.

### Buttonholes in fur
If the conventional fastening of large wire hooks is unsuitable make piped or jetted buttonholes in fur, using pieces of leather or suede.

### Corded buttonholes
The construction of the buttonhole is similar to the piped version but cord is inserted in the edge. This not only produces a raised effect but encourages longer wear. There is almost no 'give' in this type of buttonhole so the amount of ease must be calculated carefully. The cord tends to prevent stretching so it is a useful buttonhole to use on stretchy fabrics and on leather and suede. Purchased piping may be used but if making it from fabric make a long strip cutting the fabric on the bias or on the straight depending on the effect required. Insert piping cord and machine, using the piping foot. Use a straight machine stitch.

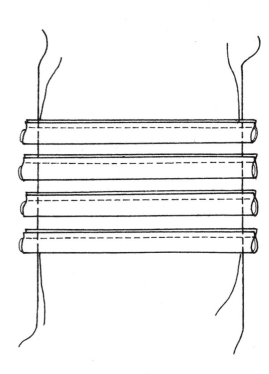

Cut the piping into equal lengths, cutting two pieces for each buttonhole. Machine across the ends of all pipings to prevent the cord from pulling out in wear. The pipings can be laid together for ease of stitching.

Construct the buttonholes as for piped buttonholes.

### Jetted buttonholes

These produce an effect that is very similar to piped buttonholes. They are made in exactly the same way as the first stage of a jetted pocket. This buttonhole is more difficult to do than the piped variety because it is small and fiddly and care has to be taken to ensure that the edges are exactly the same width. The

jetted buttonhole is normally the best one to select for thick fabrics such as coatings, reversible cloth, leather etc., where a prepared piping of double fabric might be difficult to stitch accurately. The other advantage of them is that on such fabrics as suede, leather, plastic, the jettings can be stuck in place with adhesive on the wrong side of the garment.

It often gives a good finish to the buttonhole to machine round in a rectangle from the right side.

### Piped buttonholes

These are made by applying a narrow, doubled piece of fabric to each side of the buttonhole. This piping is applied and stitched before the buttonholes are cut. Piped buttonholes are suitable for all heavy and medium weight fabrics and are easy to make. They are not suitable for fine or light fabrics such as voile or chiffon.

It helps in construction and in the finished result if Bondaweb is used in the piping and on the facing before the final stage is worked.

Mark the position of the buttonhole with chalk or tacking, putting one line to indicate the start of the buttonhole and another to show the end of it. Mark across between the lines to show the horizontal position of the buttonhole. Allow a little ease, about 2 to 3 mm ($\frac{1}{8}$ in.) on thick fabrics.

To prepare the piping cut a strip of fabric on the straight grain 2.5 cm (1 in.) wide, and long enough to make strips for each side of each buttonhole plus turnings at each end. Iron Bondaweb paper-backed

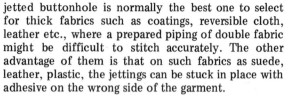

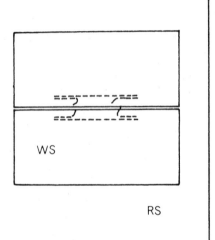

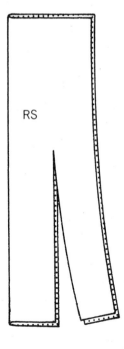

adhesive to the wrong side. Tear off the paper when cool. Fold strip in half down the middle and press to melt the adhesive and so stick the strip together.

Trim the piping down as narrow as you can for the fabric. The width will be about 7 mm ($\frac{1}{4}$ in.) for fine fabrics but wider on thicker fabrics. The finished piping on the buttonholes will be half the width you cut it at this stage.

An alternative method of making the piping is to cut the strip and attach the Bondaweb as described, but then fold each raw edge to the centre and press. The strip is then used like this, you have two pipings joined at the centre. This eliminates having to put raw edges close together and keep them together while stitching (*see below*), but the disadvantage is that the width cannot be adjusted at any stage.

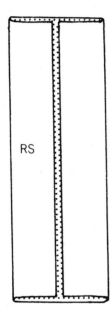

RS

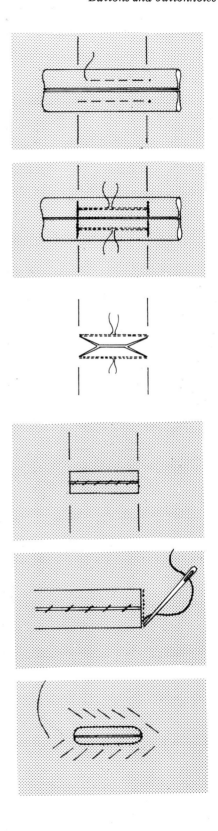

To attach the pipings cut pipings into equal lengths and place with cut edges meeting over the buttonhole mark. Tack. Re-mark the exact length of the button-hole with chalk, across the pipings.

Machine each piping. Use a small stitch, start in the middle and work to one end, turn, stitch to far end, turn and stitch back to the middle. This gives you extra strength but it also means that you don't have to sew in all the ends of thread to fasten them off. Remove tackings.

On the wrong side cut the centre of the button-hole between the rows of stitching and then cut out to the corners. Cut only the garment fabric unless you are using one folded piece, in which case snip along the centre of the piece first.

Push the pipings through to wrong side. On right side oversew folded edges together and press.

Tuck the end triangles back into position and hold in place by working a stab stitch through all layers across the end of the buttonhole. On some fabric you could machine all round the buttonhole.

Fold facing or backing fabric into position at the back of the buttonhole and tack. Mark the exact size of the buttonhole with pins and cut between. Turn in the raw edges and quickly hem round to finish. Remember to press a length of Bondaweb in position first if the fabric frays. Press well with a folded towel underneath to avoid imprints of piping.

### Seam buttonholes

If a slit is left in a seam this can be used as a buttonhole. It can be an integral part of the design or a pattern can be adapted to include a seam at the position where buttonholes are required. A pocket may be made in the same way. For anyone who is inexperienced or who prefers not to do conventional buttonholes, this is an excellent substitute.

Mark the seam line and mark out the buttonhole spaces on the line. Allow only the minimum of ease on the diameter of the button. Attach a strip of iron-on Vilene to the wrong side of both pieces of fabric in the same way as interfacing is inserted in other types of buttonhole. Fold-a-Band can be used as an aid instead of, or in addition to, the interfacing.

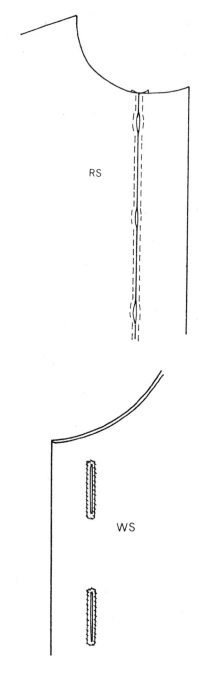

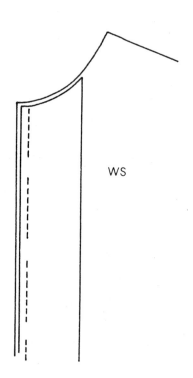

Centre the Fold-a-Band over the seam line and press. Mark out the buttonholes along the perforations, using them as a guide to keep them exact in size.

Stitch the seam, leaving the gaps, reversing at each end of each section of stitching. Press open the whole seam. Trim down the raw edges to 5 mm ($\frac{1}{4}$ in.) A row of machining may be worked on each side of the join, or work herringbone stitch over the raw edges. When the garment is complete mark the exact length of each buttonhole on the facing or backing behind the buttonholes. Cut slits and then rectangles. On fine light fabrics turn under the raw edge and hem. On thicker or non-fraying fabrics hem or loop-stitch closely over the edges.

### Tailored buttonholes

These are used on coats and jackets, and it is worth practising until you can do them well as they are a mark of a professional coat. Wundaweb will help prevent fraying.

Gimp is inserted into the edge of the buttonhole for strength and to prevent stretching, and also to produce a raised edge more in keeping with the thickness of the cloth. If you cannot obtain gimp, twist and wax several strands of embroidery thread — though it will not wear as well as tailor's gimp.

Make the buttonholes with silk buttonhole twist or a top-stitching thread such as Drima Bold.

Mark the buttonhole position with sharp chalk, and use a punch to make a hole in the cloth to form the round end. This is to take the thickness of the button shank needed on the heavier fabric. Cut from here to the other end.

Thread the gimp into a gimp needle, or, if this is unobtainable, into a darning needle. Put a knot in the end and bring the gimp out at the end of the buttonhole, starting at the end farthest from the centre front or finished edge. Leave the knot a little way from the buttonhole on the wrong side.

Thread the buttonhole twist into a large Between needle (no. 5 will take the twist) and knot the end. Bring the thread up to the left of the buttonhole holding it with the front edge away from you.

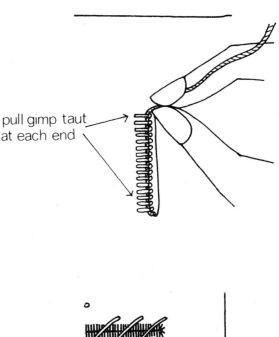

pull gimp taut at each end

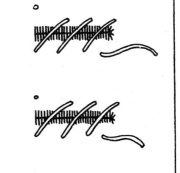

oversewn button hole edges

Work buttonhole stitch up the left side, round the end and down the other side. Make the stitches over the gimp, holding the gimp down with the thumb. At the end of each side pull the gimp taut to tighten the buttonhole. Do not crowd the stitches together. The knots should touch, but not the uprights.

Remember to lift the knots on to the top of the fabric when working the round end and make the stitches very short. Note that the stitch is worked away from you, winding the thread round the needle in the opposite direction from the previous method. This is so that the gimp can be held with the thumb. Pass the gimp through to the wrong side, and slide the needle between the layers of fabric for a little way. Bring the gimp out and cut off. Cut off the knot.

On the right side work a bar tack across the end of the buttonhole, making four stitches and then stab stitching neatly over them. Cut off the knot. Oversew the edges and press.

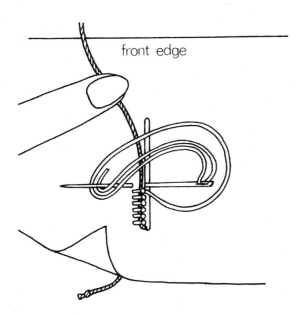

front edge

### Sewing on buttons

Use a slightly larger needle than for other hand sewing and thread with a fairly long piece of thread pulled double and knotted. Wax and twist the thread. One needle of thread prepared in this way will be sufficient to sew two large buttons or three small ones. Prepare more needles before you start so that you have plenty of thread ready. This will eliminate the tendency to sew the final button with too little thread and too few stitches to ensure it will wear well.

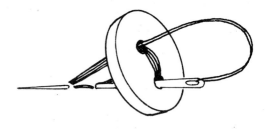

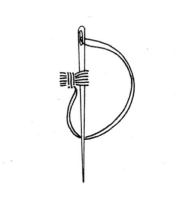

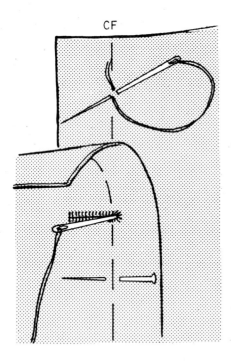

Locate the position of the button either by pinning up the opening and inserting the needle into the round end of the buttonhole, or by marking chalk crosses on the fabric. Insert the needle right through the fabric from the right side; bring it up to the top again and then repeat this to form two strong stitches. Cut off the knot in the thread. Slip the button on to the needle and insert the needle into the other hole and right into the fabric and out again in one movement. The button lies on its side while stitching which is the best way of allowing sufficient thread between the button and the fabric for the buttonhole to go over it and still lie flat.

If the button is decorative then it may be sewn flat to the fabric with stabbing stitches. Make sure the length of shank left is sufficient to take the thick-ness of the other edge of the garment. Work several stitches, three or four will be enough, and then bring the needle up under the button. If the button has four holes work three stitches in each pair of holes. If the button has its own looped shank underneath sew it flat to the fabric but using the same movement as before with the button on its side.

Complete the shank by winding the thread round the vertical threads, pull the thread tight and wind again, three times more, finishing with the thread down on the fabric. For special strength, for example on a waistband, pass the needle to the wrong side and work loop stitch over the threads found there. Fasten off with a back stitch and cut off the thread.

In all other cases, including buttons without a thread shank, pass the needle a couple of times through the fabric, across the base of the button then cut the thread close to the fabric.

When all buttons are sewn on, if any further pressing is absolutely necessary do it with the toe of the iron covered with a damp muslin, pushing round the button.

## CABLE CHAIN STITCH

A chain stitch worked towards you or from right to left, in the same way as chain stitch, but the thread is twisted round the needle once between each loop. (See *Chain Stitch*.)

## CABLE STITCH

A thick outline embroidery stitch, worked from left to right. The needle comes through on the outline of the design and is inserted a little to the right to be pulled through half-way along the length of the stitch, with the thread below the needle. The next stitch is taken in the same way, but with thread kept above the needle.

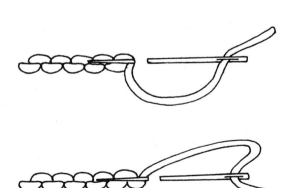

## CAFTAN/KAFTAN

A long loose casual garment derived from the East but adapted to be a fashion garment. It is usually full length, often based on a rectangular shape, even cut without shoulder seams — the fold of the fabric forming the shoulder and making a wide droopy sleeve. The style lends itself to elegant fabrics as well as casual cottons and border prints. Worn by men and women.

## CALYX EYED NEEDLES

These are a Sharps needle with a double eye, the top part of which is open. This type of needle is a great help to anyone handicapped or who has difficulty in threading a needle. The thread is held taut across the open top and pulled sharply down until it settles in the lower eye. Not available in small sizes.

## CAMISOLE

Once an obligatory women's under-garment for warmth it is now a fashion garment which can be an item of underwear, nightwear, evening or beach wear and made in the appropriate fabric with trimming. It has a straight top edge at underarm level with narrow straps. The sides are cut straight to below the waist and sometimes elastic or shirring is added to define the waistline.

## CANVAS

Canvas is used for interfacing coats and jackets. It is generally made of flax. Various weights are available to suit different fabrics. Collar canvas is very stiff and usually made of cotton. Shrink before use by sprinkling with water and pressing.

Canvas for embroidery is made in a wide variety of types and weights. The number of holes to the inch varies. Double canvas has two threads in each direction separating the holes for stitching.

## CAP SLEEVE

A small extension at shoulder level on a sleeveless bodice. The extension is usually just sufficient to cover the shoulder bone and the top of the arm. This alters the shape of the armhole which may be almost a straight line to the underarm.

Sometimes the cap is cut separately, made of double fabric and interfacing and attached to the armhole but only over the shoulder bone. It does not extend very far down the armhole.

## CAPE SLEEVE

A short, full, possibly circular sleeve that is loose and flowing. Very popular with Twenties style clothes.

## CARBON PAPER

Dressmakers' carbon paper is specially made to use for transferring pattern markings to fabric. It is often called tracing paper which is misleading.

A packet of carbon paper contains several sheets coloured, usually, white, orange or blue on one side. It is the coloured side that is placed facing the fabric. Although it is quick to use, it should first be tested on a scrap of fabric and pressed, to make sure the colour does not penetrate right through the fabric. The colour may come out in washing. it may even come off as you handle the fabric, but it may not come out at all.

It is a very quick and accurate way of marking interfacing and it is quite safe to use on it, even if it cannot be used on the fabric.

Use white carbon wherever possible, it is surprising how often it can be seen even on light fabric. Use dark blue only when essential. Use the carbon only on the wrong side of the fabric.

To use, cut the paper into strips about 6 cm ($2\frac{3}{8}$ in.) wide and fold with coloured side out. After cutting the fabric do not remove the pattern and slip the folded carbon paper between the fabric layers. Use a tracing wheel and run it along the seam lines, darts, etc.

If the pattern has no seam edges run the wheel beside the paper. Re-use the paper as often as possible. A smooth tracing wheel produces a better line than a spiked one and it does not harm the table surface. Use a ruler when marking straight lines.

## CASING

A casing is a section of double fabric, either an edge folded over or an applied piece of fabric, through which cord, elastic, etc., can be threaded. For strength the casing should always be sewn by machine using a straight or decorative stitch.

**Hem casing**
If the edge of the garment is straight, extra fabric can be allowed when cutting out to fold over. Allow sufficient to take the elastic or cord plus 2 mm ($\frac{1}{8}$ in.) ease or a little more if it is something thicker like a pyjama cord. Press and machine the top edge first, then turn under the raw edge and tack to form an even hem. Machine.

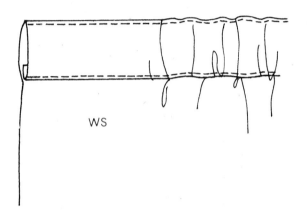

WS

If the casing itself is to be situated below the edge of the garment then twice this depth of heading should be allowed in addition when cutting out. If the fabric is too bulky turn under, remembering that it will be wrinkled when drawn up, neaten the raw edge and machine flat rather than turn it under.

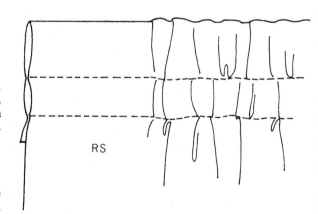

RS

## Applied casing — edges

If the edge of the garment is shaped, cut a crossway strip of self fabric or lining material, or use purchased bias binding if it is suitable.

Allow sufficient width to take the drawstring plus two small seam allowances. Tack and machine the crossway strip to the right side of the garment if a deliberate contrast is required or to the wrong side. Trim the turnings and run the iron along the edge under them. Fold the casing completely to one side making sure the join along the edge is not visible from the right side of the garment. Tack, press and machine with a straight or embroidery stitch. Turn under the other edge, tack and machine. If the edge is very shaped it may be necessary to snip the casing fabric at the edge to make it lie flat. Press well.

## Applied casing — waistline

Use self fabric, lining or nylon jersey cut on the cross, 2 mm ($\frac{1}{8}$ in.) wider than the elastic or cord, plus 1 cm ($\frac{3}{8}$ in.). Neaten both edges of the strip with zig-zag stitch or similar to prevent it curling up. On the garment, mark the waistline position with pins or chalk marks then run a row of tacking stitches round the waist just above this. The exact distance should be half the width of the prepared casing. Remove pins. On the wrong side place one edge of the casing against the tacking line; tack. Tack the other side. If these stitches are placed 5 mm ($\frac{1}{4}$ in.) inside the casing edge and exactly parallel they act as an accurate stitching guide. With the garment right side out work two rows of zig-zag or embroidery stitch, one on each row of tacking. Remove tacking and press.

## Slots for threading in edge casings

The slot should be on the wrong side for elastic, but the right side for drawstrings. If there is an opening in a seam make the opening before the casing and there will be an open slot at the end for threading. If the casing is continuous unpick the stitching of a seam between the casing stitching.

If there is no seam work a vertical buttonhole before making the casing; calculate the position carefully by folding and tacking the casing and then releasing sufficient tacking to make the buttonhole.

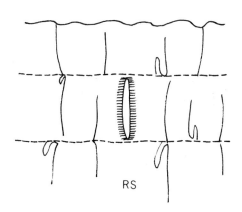

RS

## Slots for threading in applied casings

For threading elastic leave a gap of about $1\frac{1}{2}$ cm ($\frac{5}{8}$ in.) in one of the rows of machining. The least obtrusive position is at the side seam. Alternatively, the two ends of casing may be turned in to meet each other before stitching to the garment, so leaving a slot for threading.

If a cord is to be inserted and pulled to the right side and tied, the slots must be on the outside of the garment. Make two vertical buttonholes 1 to 2 cm ($\frac{3}{8}$ to $\frac{3}{4}$ in.) apart where the cord is to emerge. For a flat braid or thin cord a bound or hand made buttonhole will be satisfactory, but if the drawstring is bulky or firm the slot must be wide enough to allow the cord to emerge without wrinkling the fabric. This also applies if you are threading a wide, flat tie belt through the casing. Make two vertical slots as follows before attaching casing: calculate and mark the position with great accuracy; the slot must be long enough to take the cord but not too big otherwise the inside of the garment will be visible in wear. Cut two rectangles of fabric on the cross 2 cm ($\frac{3}{4}$ in.) longer than the planned slot and 2 cm ($\frac{3}{4}$ in.) wider. Press Bondaweb to the

RS

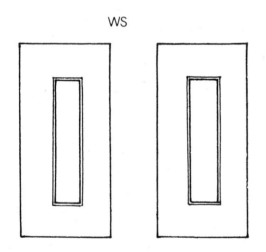

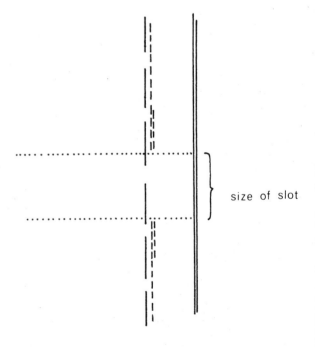

**Slot-in seam**

If it can be arranged to leave a gap in a seam through which to thread elastic or for drawstring ends to emerge it looks neat. Determine the position of the slot and mark sufficient to be left open. Do not make it too wide. Stitch the seam, reversing at each marked position. Remove tackings, press seam open and neaten the raw edges. Cut narrow strips of Wundaweb long enough to extend from 1 cm ($\frac{3}{8}$ in.) above to 1 cm ($\frac{3}{8}$ in.) below the slot. Slip them under the turnings and press.

size of slot

wrong side and peel off the paper. Place each piece right side down to the right side of the garment. Tack round the edges. Mark the length and width of the slot with pencil dots and machine. Count the machine stitches as you would for a buttonhole to enable you to make both slots identical.

Cut through the centre and out to the four corners of the stitching. Push the piece of fabric through to the wrong side, rolling the edges with your fingers to make sure nothing of the piece of fabric shows. Press the edges very carefully with the toe of the iron, then press the whole area on both sides. The patch will be stuck in position by the Bondaweb. Attach the casing making sure that the rows of machining pass across the ends of the slots accurately.

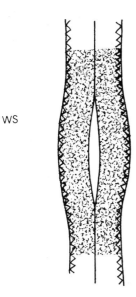

WS

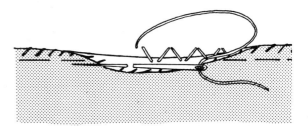

## CAT SUIT

An all-in-one garment including legs and long sleeves, usually made tight fitting in a stretch fabric, but often adapted to a fashion garment and including decorative features.

## CATCH STITCH

A stitch for loosely joining two layers of fabric. It should be worked between the layers so that no stitch is visible on either side. It is used for hems and also in other positions where it may be necessary to hold an inside layer in place to prevent it from moving in wear, e.g. facings.

Tack layers in position and neaten any raw edges. Press. Use a short length of thread with a knot in. Hold the garment with the hem facing uppermost, flat, not folded over your hand, and lift up the edge. Start the thread in this edge and if the fabric is very fine work a back stitch and then cut off the knot. Work from right to left unless you are left-handed picking up one thread of fabric from the fold and another from the garment 5 mm ($\frac{1}{4}$ in.) further along. Take each stitch carefully so as not to disturb the weave of the fabric and do not pull the thread tight. In fact merely because you have lifted the edge to work the stitch you will be leaving a little excess thread. It is a slow stitch to work but if hurried a line will eventually be visible on the garment. If the catch stitch is worked too far below the edge it will easily become caught and pulled away by a heel, etc., so work the stitch only just below the neatened edge.

On soft or jersey fabrics leave a small loop of extra thread that can be used up if the fabric is stretched in wear. Begin and end all lengths of thread in the hem or facing, not on the garment.

## CENTRE BACK/CENTRE FRONT

The centre front and centre back of a pattern represent the vertical line running the length of the garment exactly at the centre of the body. When drafting patterns these lines are established at the start and are always transferred to the next pattern stage during cutting. The straight grain of the fabric may run on the centre front and centre back lines. The lines are always marked on a pattern with a line. There may be buttons or some other feature at that point. If a pattern piece is to be cut to a fold it is the pattern edge that represents the centre front or centre back.

The lines are marked on main pattern pieces and correspondingly on any other pieces, such as a collar or facing, that crosses that line. When written the terms may be abbreviated to CF and CB.

## CHAIN STITCH

A firm outline stitch worked vertically towards you. Work rows close together as a filling stitch. The thread is brought out at the top of the line to be worked, held down by the thumb, while the needle

is inserted a little to the right of where it was brought through, and brought out again a short distance below. Pull the thread through gently, taking care to keep it under the needle, and to keep the chains regular in shape.

## CHAINED FEATHER STITCH

A looped embroidery stitch that is a combination of the angles of feather stitch and the loops of chain stitch. Closed chain stitches are worked at a diagonal slant, joined by small straight stitches which form a regualr zig-zag pattern at the same slant as the chain stitches.

(See also *Detached Chain Stitch/Daisy Stitch*.)

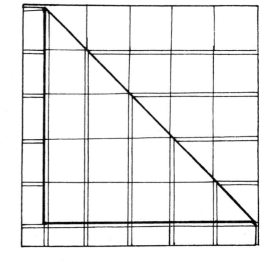

## CHALK PENCIL

A white pencil used for marking fabric. Only small marks such as dots and crosses are satisfactory as fabric often wrinkles if the pencil is dragged along in a line. The pencil has a brush on the end which is useful for removing marks but otherwise the pencil has no particular advantage over tailor's chalk.

## CHANEL

Coco Chanel's once new line in jackets has become the generic term for a straight cardigan style, collarless and edge-to-edge reaching to just below the waist. The edges of the front, the neck and the sleeves are usually edged with braid.

## CHECK FABRIC

Determine whether the check design is even or uneven, that is, whether it should be treated as one-way fabric and whether the pattern is the same across the weft as the warp. Very few checks are completely even, except small simple designs such as check gingham. Woven checks, especially in heavy fabrics are often uneven in size simply because the warp and weft threads are of different thickness. To discover whether the checks are even, fold over a corner of the fabric. If the checks do not match they are uneven and the fabric must be handled accordingly. Many are rectangular and not quite square and this limits their use, many are simply uneven in design.

Cutting out must be done with great care and then there should be few problems in making the garment.

**Remember the following**

Fold the fabric carefully right side out, pinning at intervals along the fold and then matching the checks along the edge in addition to making sure they lie on top of each other over the entire piece. After pinning on the pattern, remove these pins to avoid accidentally catching them with the scissors. Note that the fabric may have to be folded unevenly in order to find a good point on the design for the fold, and to match the checks.

Adjust the pattern to fit, including the skirt length and sleeve length, before putting it on the fabric. Alterations later may throw out the matching. With checks of even size or roughly equal amounts of colour visible, hold up the entire length of fabric and look in a mirror. You will find that whichever colour is placed at the centre front, or centre back, will become the dominant colour of the garment.

Put the pattern pieces in position one at a time, starting with the main ones. Trace the main lines of the checks onto the first piece at a point where

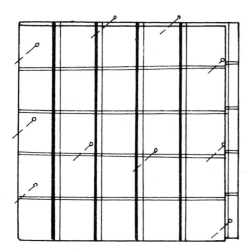

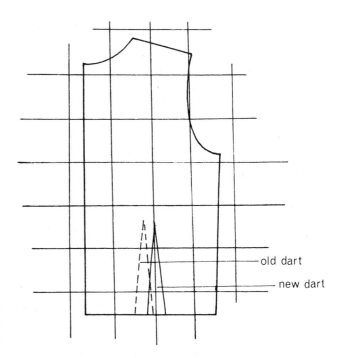

seams must match, e.g. side seams and armhole. Pin
the first piece then put the matching piece of pattern
against it and continue the lines onto it. Remember
to fold under the seam allowance so that the fitting
lines meet. Pin that piece of pattern in position,
match the next one and so on. Remember that the
facing pieces and possibly the collar must also match.
The latter may be cut on the cross but if on the
straight grain the checks should correspond with
those at the centre back of the bodice.

If the fabric is a one-way check place all pattern
pieces lying in the same direction.

Look at the darts; they should be centrally on a
main check. The dart can be moved slightly in order
to do this.

Do not cut small decorative pieces such as pockets,
wait until fitting stage and then place a piece of fabric
in position on the garment, with checks matching,
and pin the pattern to it. Remove and cut out.

When cutting out uneven checks do not fold the
fabric for pieces to be cut on the cross. Lay it out
singly and, for safety, make another copy of the
pattern piece and mark each 'right side', as it is very
easy to cut one wrongly. Work in the same way as

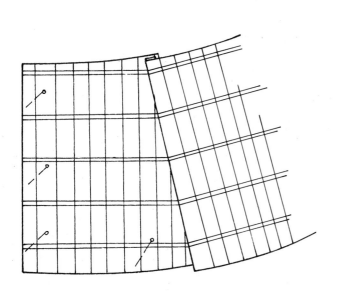

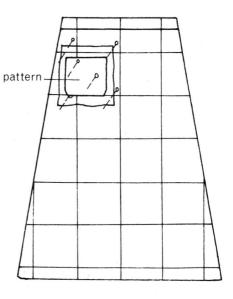

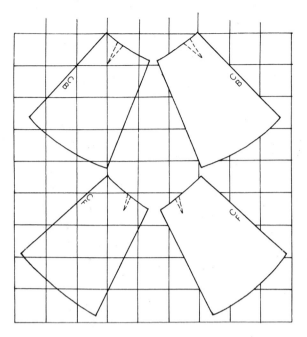

described above, placing one piece in position and tracing the checks onto the pattern before placing the matching piece, right side up.

It is usually possible to match checks on straight seams but it may not work on curved seams. Adjust the pattern, perhaps adding a little to one edge and subtacting it from another, to achieve a match, or straighten the seam and then adjust the garment to fit when it has been put together.

Finally always leave extra seam allowance on bias edges. This will allow for any adjustment at fitting without throwing out the matching; also, with skirts, the sections will be liable to drop and reduce the seam allowance width. Mark the seams, tack them and leave the skirt to hang by pinning tape loops to the waist. After a couple of days, fit the skirt, adjusting the seams if necessary. Make sure the centres are marked to ensure the skirt still hangs correctly after dropping. Some fabrics are liable to drop unevenly.

If the care and preparation described is daunting, or if there is a shortage of fabric which prevents correct matching, remember that checks and plain fabric can be used together. Even a quite narrow strip of plain fabric inserted in a garment will eliminate the problems, although if the checks are large they must still be balanced on the body. The same point can be applied if part of the design includes shaped bands. It will not be possible to keep the checks matching so cut bands from plain fabric.

Square checks can be used on the true cross but not on the bias.

With all check fabrics remember to fold under the seam allowances of the paper pattern when tracing the checks through to make them meet on the fitting line.

## CHEONGSAM

The traditional dress worn in some Far-Eastern countries, it is straight and tight-fitting with a stand or mandarin collar. The fastening is often asymmetrical running from the neckline to the armhole and piping, frog fastenings and ball buttons are usually added.

## CHEVRON STITCH

A double line embroidery stitch worked from left to right. The stitch is begun at the bottom left hand edge, a small stitch taken to the right, and another smaller to the left, with the needle coming out half way along the stitch just made. A diagonal stitch to the right brings the thread to the top line. A small stitch to the left is followed by a longer stitch to

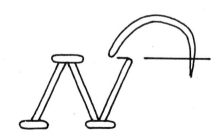

the right, bringing the needle through where the diagonal stitch ended. A diagonal stitch down to the bottom line brings the thread into place for the next stitch.

## CLAPPER

(See *Pressing Block*.)

## CLASSIC

The term used to describe any basic feature that has been accepted for its long-lasting simplicity, indicating that it never really goes completely out of fashion. Use it as a prefix to almost any term and it has meaning. For example to precede shirt collar; shirtwaister; pleated skirt; winter coat; jacket.

## CLEAN FINISH

A term sometimes used to describe neatening a raw edge. The term is not self explanatory but the implication is that the raw edges are to be treated by some means to prevent any fraying which would be untidy.

## CLEAN IRON

The trade mark of the iron cleaning stick marketed by Vilene.
(See *Iron Cleaner*.)

## CLIP

A small snip or cut made in the seam allowance after stitching a curved seam. The clipping is done only as often as necessary, the clips being about 1 cm ($\frac{3}{8}$ in.) apart. When pressed the seam will lie open and will easily press to shape while still keeping the seam allowance.

## CLOSED FEATHER STITCH

A stitch worked as for feather stitch, but the needle is slanted at a 45° angle to produce a closed rail effect.
(See *Feather Stitch*, page 115.)

## CLOSED HERRINGBONE STITCH

Worked in a similar way to herringbone stitch but the horizontal stitches touch. Use on sheer fabrics to create shadow effects. Work on the right side of the fabric. Called double back stitch if worked on the wrong side.

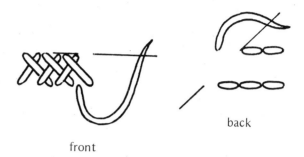

back

front

## CLOSED LOOP STITCH

A fancy variation on loop stitch with stitches being worked in pairs, their upright stitches becoming diagonal and joining at a top centre point to form triangles.
(See also *Loop Stitch*.)

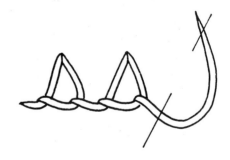

## CLOTH

Now regarded as a slightly old-fashioned term, but still used in the trade to describe all types of fabric except those that are lightweight.

## COAT DRESS

A dress, often button-through and possibly including other coat detail, but made in a medium-to-heavy fabric. Its usefulness is limited by the fact that if it is warm enough to wear outside as a coat during intermediate seasons, then it must be too warm as you step indoors and there is no part of it that can be removed!

## COAT HANGERS

(See *Hanging Loops*.)

## COAT LOOPS

(See *Hanging Loops*.)

## COLLARS

A collar is a double piece of fabric attached to a neck edge. Not only can the neck edge be almost any shape and depth — from high and round, V at front or back or both, square, boat shaped — but the collar too can be one of a variety of shapes and of any width. The shape of the outer edge of the collar gives it its style, and the shape of the inner or neck edge determines how it will look when worn. For instance some collars lie flat down on the garment, some stand upright to hug the neck or frame the face, some like shirt collars do both; they stand up for a little way and then they fall over. If in addition the garment has a front opening left as a rever style then the collar is really a 'stand and fall' at the back of the neck but a flat collar at the front.

Whatever the shape of the collar remember which is the neck edge and which is the outer edge, always mark its centre (back or front or both) to match accurately to the markings on the garment. Also remember that you can adjust the width of the collar at will, and also the shape of its outer edge including the ends, but do not alter the neck edge or it will not fit the neckline of the garment. The exception to this is of course if the neckline has been altered at fitting in which case the length of the collar must also be adjusted.

It is wise not to cut out a collar when the main garment pieces are being cut, just in case adjustments are required. Fit the garment then cut out an experimental collar in Vilene, pinning it to the garment to check its effect and then cutting out the fabric. If patterns have to be matched then cut on single fabric. A pattern may provide only half the collar pattern so that it has to be placed to a fold but if thick fabric is used this can be very inaccurate and it is worth cutting a whole pattern piece.

The straight grain of a collar is either precisely at the centre and vertical, or the collar may be cut on the bias for effect. A tailored coat collar combines both, the under collar being on the cross in order to roll it correctly, the top collar on the straight for correct appearance.

Main methods of attaching collars are stitching one edge and hemming the other, attaching then covering the join with lining (coats), sandwiching the collar between the garment and a facing (adds bulk — only use if inside neck edge is likely to show as it might on low necklines), binding (usually only on flat collars); or a combination of methods to suit the style of the collar.

Always interface collars either over the entire width or possibly only part of it, depending on the effect required. Always attach the interfacing to the under collar i.e., the piece that is the extension of the neck of the garment.

Always pin collars to necklines starting at the centre and arranging any ease near the shoulder seams. Insert the pins across the neck join not along it, and if it is at all difficult to handle snip and trim down the collar and neckline seam allowances.

Where possible machine the collar in place from the garment side for accuracy.

**Collar in lined neckline**
If there is to be a double layer of fabric at the neckline, either as lining or another piece of fabric as in a yoke that is double, the collar can be neatly inserted between the two layers. However, for accuracy and to retain the set of the collar it should not simply be sandwiched between and stitched.

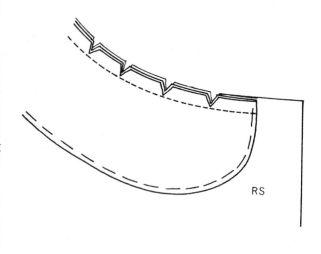

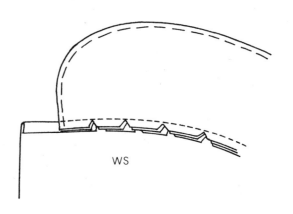

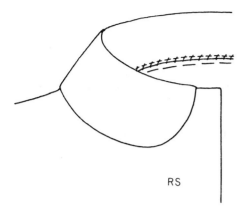

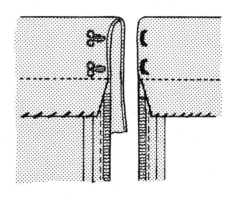

RS

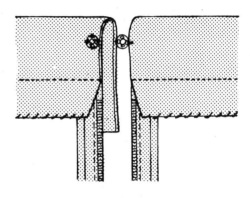

Place the made collar to the right side of the
neckline, matching centres etc. Tack. Snip the edge of
both neckline and collar and machine on the seam
line. Trim the turnings, hold the collar so that it
extends beyond the neckline and press all turnings
back onto the garment. Tack if the fabric is springy.
Bring the other layer of fabric up into position and
tack round the neck but below the join. Trim the raw
edge a little and snip, then turn in the edges, tack and
hem into the machining.

**Collar or neck edge fastening**
A stand collar, bound edge or any finish that extends
above a neckline zip needs a fastening. Even if the zip
is taken into the collar it is difficult to make it extend
quite to the top edge. Three neat methods follow;
select according to the depth of collar or binding. All
methods ensure that the edges meet edge-to-edge to
eliminate the bulk of overlapping.

*With hooks and loops*    Use two hooks size 0 or 00
and attach with buttonhole stitch to the inside of the
stand collar. Begin by anchoring the head of the hook
slightly back from the edge, then sew with close
stitches all round the two loop sections.

Work two small thread loops just inside the other
edge making a bar with four or five strands of thread
before covering them with loop stitch.

On a roll collar the hooks should go on the inside
part of the collar but it is often also necessary to put
at least one on the outer section as well. Alternatively
the zip may extend into the collar, leaving the outer
section to be fastened.

*Press stud*    If the fabric is very fine use a size 00
press stud, sewing the knob section under the edge of
the right side of the collar, using buttonhole stitch
but sewing the well section to the left edge just by

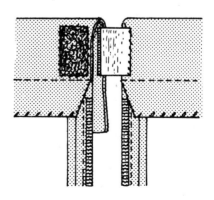

firmly sewing through one hole, the remainder of the press stud being left to extend. When it is fastened the collar falls edge to edge. This is a useful way of using a press stud in a variety of positions, e.g. a slit opening.

*Velcro*   This method is satisfactory for all collars that meet edge to edge and has the additional advantage of holding the collar upright. When using this on the roll collar note that the Velcro is stitched on the outer section, one piece extending.

### Collar with rever

With this type of collar it is still unnecessary to use a facing except from the front opening round to the shoulder seam. Even if the paper pattern provides a facing for the back of the neck it is best not to use it as it adds bulk and often does not lie flat.

Interface and make up the collar; open it at the neck edge and attach the neck edge of the under collar to the neck edge of the garment. This is quite

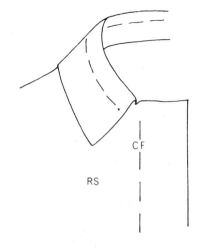

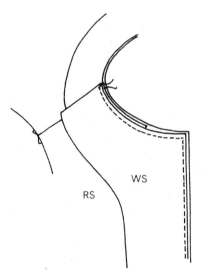

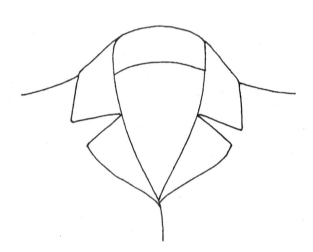

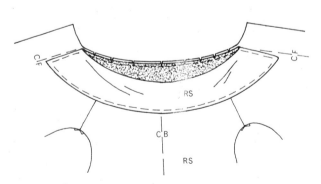

tricky to do and it will help to trim and snip the seam allowances. Match the centre back and front edges carefully. Machine. Press the join open first and then up into the collar.

Hold both layers of collar together as they will be in wear, i.e stand up and roll over at the back of the neck but flat at the front, and insert a row of tacking just below the neck join. Next join on the front facing (or it may be a fold-back type) and fold it back onto the right side of the garment, covering the collar at the neck edge. It is essential to keep the facing flat and the centre front and fold line correct so work at least two rows of tacking. At the neck edge tack and machine from fold of facing round to shoulder seam. On light fabrics the end of the facing may be folded over to neaten it.

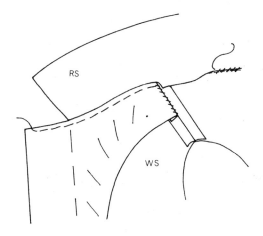

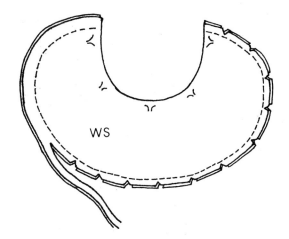

Trim, layer and snip all raw edges. Roll facing to wrong side of garment. Smooth down the facing, holding collar up. Tack through all layers just below the join. Also tack down the centre front fold and baste the entire facing flat. Hold it in place later with a row of basting stitches. Hem the end of the facing to the shoulder seam, or if it is a raw edge, work herringbone stitch over it.

Across the back of the neck turn under the collar raw edge and tack and hem into the machining. The edge will have to be snipped exactly where the end of the facing comes. Press well.

### Flat collars

These include Peter Pan collars and they may be in one or two pieces. The resulting collar lies flat because the neck edge is the same shape as the garment neck edge. This type of collar may be used on children's clothes and night wear. For adult clothes a better appearance results from slightly straightening the collar neck edge. This has the effect of making the collar stand up a little at the back of the neck before it rolls over.

Although this collar can be attached with a facing a narrow bias strip is easier to handle due to the concave curve on the neck edge.

The collar may be in one or two pieces. The illustrations show two but the method is the same for all flat collars. Cut four collar pieces and interface two of them. Place them together in pairs right sides together and tack and machine round the outer edge. Trim the edges and snip well. Roll collars right side out. Tack the outer edges with the join slightly hidden to the under side i.e. towards the interfaced piece. Press. Place the two collars together at the centre front (or back) and work a bar tack on the fitting line to hold them together. This is now one collar and easier to attach to the neckline.

Place collar to right side of neckline, matching centres and tack. Machine collar to neckline 1 mm ($\frac{1}{16}$ in.) outside the fitting line. Cut a piece of crossway fabric about 1.5 cm ($\frac{5}{8}$ in.) wide. If the fabric of the garment is bulky use lining fabric or purchased bias binding. Tack the strip on top of the machining. Turn the work over and machine using the last line of tacking as a guide, stitching 1 mm ($\frac{1}{16}$ in.) further into the garment. Trim and snip all raw edges.

Extend the collar beyond the garment, push the binding down flat on to the garment, and press. Turn under the raw edge of the binding, and also the ends. Tack and hem.

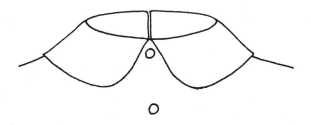

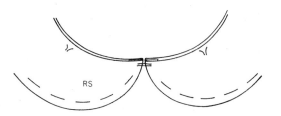

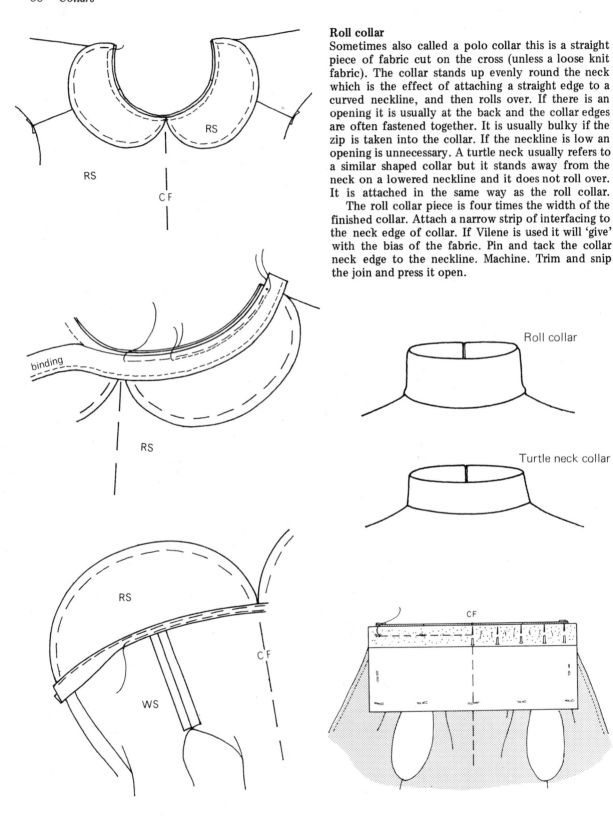

## Roll collar

Sometimes also called a polo collar this is a straight piece of fabric cut on the cross (unless a loose knit fabric). The collar stands up evenly round the neck which is the effect of attaching a straight edge to a curved neckline, and then rolls over. If there is an opening it is usually at the back and the collar edges are often fastened together. It is usually bulky if the zip is taken into the collar. If the neckline is low an opening is unnecessary. A turtle neck usually refers to a similar shaped collar but it stands away from the neck on a lowered neckline and it does not roll over. It is attached in the same way as the roll collar.

The roll collar piece is four times the width of the finished collar. Attach a narrow strip of interfacing to the neck edge of collar. If Vilene is used it will 'give' with the bias of the fabric. Pin and tack the collar neck edge to the neckline. Machine. Trim and snip the join and press it open.

Roll collar

Turtle neck collar

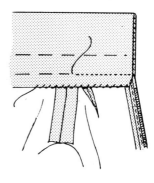

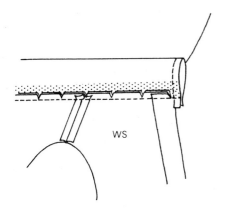

There are two methods of completing the collar and the choice depends on the fabric.

On fine fabrics, press all turnings up into the collar. Fold the collar ends right sides together and stitch across, lining up accurately with any zip, centre front edge etc. Trim ends and turn collar right side out. Press ends. Roll collar into wearing position and baste along the roll. Inside the neck turn under the raw edge and hem into the machine stitching.

On thicker fabrics turn in the ends of the collar level with any opening or zip. Press and if springy hold the edges down with herringbone stitch. Fold the raw edge to the inside, tack the ends together and slip stitch the folds together. Roll the collar into its wearing position and baste along the roll line. Work a row of tacking inside the neck but above the join.

With the right side of the garment towards you, work prick stitch in the neckline join making sure you penetrate the collar. Neaten the remaining raw edge of the collar, trimming it neatly first.

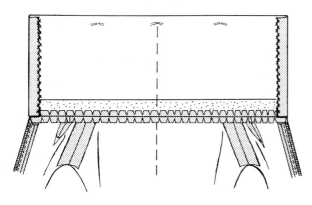

### Shawl collar

This is so called because one piece of fabric folds and wraps round the neck and shoulders, wrapping over at the front. It may literally be a wrap-over style like a dressing gown or coat, or it may button. There is usually a seam at the centre back and often the collar is cut as an extension of the front of the garment. Men's dinner jackets often have shawl collars, faced in silks as distinct from a notched collar and revere style although on women's clothes the collar may be notched.

Interface the garment front and collar extension. Use a soft interfacing in order not to spoil the roll that is so essential to this style of collar. There may be a dart or seam in the pattern running from the shoulder and it will be necessary to snip the edge later in order to wrap the collar extension round the back of the neck. It will help to prevent fraying if a small piece of Bondaweb is attached to this point before stitching the dart or snipping the fabric.

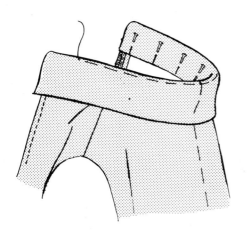

After stitching and snipping, join the front and back of the garment at the shoulder seams and press.

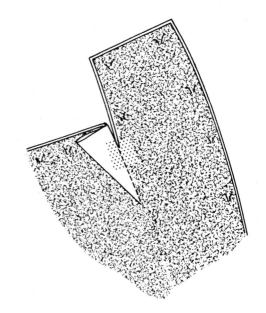

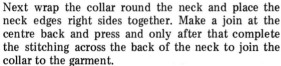

Next wrap the collar round the neck and place the neck edges right sides together. Make a join at the centre back and press and only after that complete the stitching across the back of the neck to join the collar to the garment.

There will be two facing pieces to be joined at the centre back and pressed. Place this to the garment collar, right sides together, matching centre backs. Tack and machine the outer edge. Trim and snip the edges. Roll facing to the inside and tack the edges. Press well. Roll collar into wearing position and baste the roll line. Finish at the back of the neck by working prick stitch through the join from shoulder seam to shoulder seam.

Neaten the remainder of the facing edge. It can be held in place with pieces of Wundaweb.

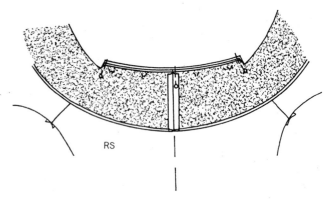

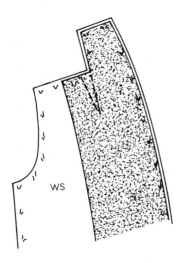

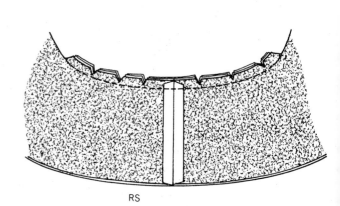

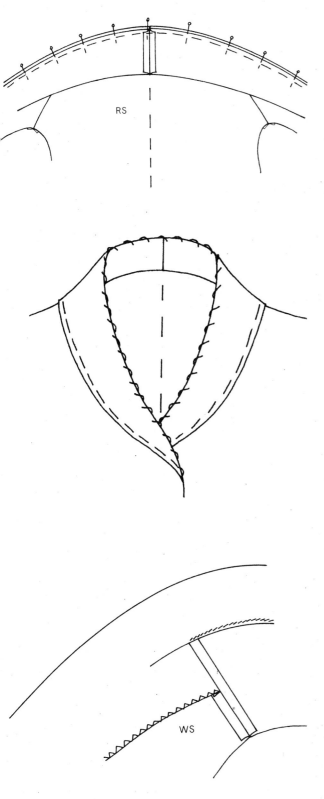

### Shirt collar

A conventional stiffened collar as found on manufactured shirts involves careful, neat construction. The bigger problem, however, lies in getting a stiff enough result since in manufacture special processes are used which cannot be performed in the home. Use the interfacings available for home sewing as you know what the results will be like, but build up several layers of varying weights. Try out several combinations on the fabric to see which is most suitable; it is wise to wash and iron it. It also helps to add small pieces to those areas such as the band and the collar points to stiffen them even further, vary the type and weight of interfacing, and the number of layers. For instance on silk or voile reduce them to the minimum but on denim build up several layers. The interfacings chosen must be washable. Interface pieces right to the edges so that all layers are included in seams.

Interface the top collar with a fine interfacing such as light iron-on Vilene Supershape. Interface the undercollar with the same Vilene but in medium weight but before attaching, cut out a 3 mm ($\frac{1}{8}$ in.) wide slit exactly on the roll line. Press it in position.

Using a firm iron-on interfacing, such as Heavy Supershape, cut shapes to fit the neckband and the collar points, and iron into position.

Cut off the corners to prevent too much bulk.

To make the collar place the two collar pieces right side together and machine round the outside on the fitting line. Trim the turnings very narrow,

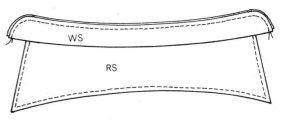

and also layer them. Cut the corners right away. If the band is cut all in one with the collar, snip well round the curved section. Turn to the right side, roll the edge, tack, and press well. If there is a separate neck band, work edge stitching round the collar first and then sandwich the collar between the band sections. Trim the edges and turn the band pieces to the right side; tack and press.

To attach the collar place the right side of the top collar to the wrong side of the neck edge; line up the centre fronts and the centre back accurately, and tack. It may help to snip the turnings. Machine from the collar side from the collar stitching one end to exactly the same spot on the other end. Trim the turnings and press into the collar. Turn under the raw edge of the under collar and bring it down onto the machining. Tack. Machine along this edge. If the band is separate, machine round all sides of the band. If the collar and band are cut in one, machine all round the outer edges of the collar and across the back of the neck.

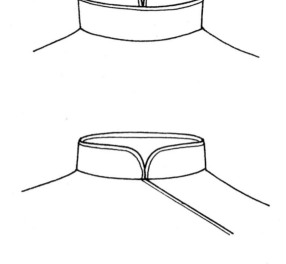

An alternative method of attaching which is easier on springy fabrics is to turn under and press the lower, open, edges of the neckband and place the under collar edge onto the neck edge of the right side of the shirt. Machine. Trim the turnings well. Trim down the turning on the remaining free edge of the neckband and lay this onto the wrong side of the neckline, on top of the edge beneath. Tack and machine.

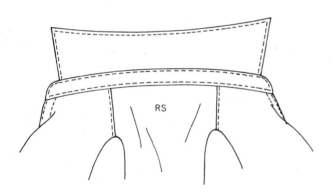

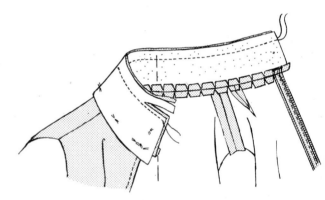

### Stand collar

Also called a band collar, this is a slightly shaped narrow piece of fabric standing up at the neck. It is usually open at the front or back, sometimes with a zip or a slit opening. If it has rounded corners at the front it is a mandarin collar.

Cut two pieces of collar and attach interfacing to one of them. Join the neck edge of the interfaced collar to the neck of the garment. Stitch, trim the seam, snip and press open. Place the second piece of collar against the first and tack. Machine across the ends and along the outer edge. Trim and turn collar right side out. Roll and tack the edges and press. Tack the two layers of collar together. Finish according to the fabric. With thick fabric neaten the raw edge then prick stitch through the neck join from the outside of

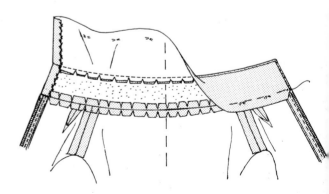

the garment. With fine fabrics press the turnings up into the collar, turn under the raw edge and hem.

If there is a facing or an extension for a fastening the easiest way to deal with it is to turn in the raw edge to form a neat corner and slip stitch around the neck edge from the end of the collar, round to the shoulder seam turn in and hem the edge of the facing.

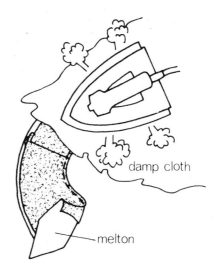

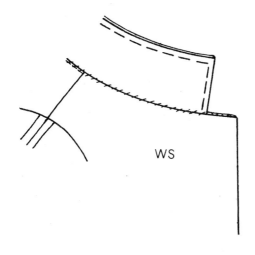

### Tailored collar

The collar and lapels of a tailored coat or jacket must be carefully handled. The aim is to create the correct shape during construction so that the collar retains its shape for the life of the garment. The instructions and illustrations refer to a collar with lapel that is open but the same method applies to a coat fastened right up to the neck. The difference would lie in the position of the roll line on the collar and the omission of a roll on the lapel.

The illustrations show canvas being applied to the collar and lapels. If Vilene is used as the interfacing the padding is omitted. On men's coats, and if possible on women's too, the under collar should be cut from melton cloth, as it does not fray and its use reduces bulk at the collar edge. However, if a good enough colour match is not available the fabric has to be used; melton is normally only available in men's clothing colours.

Prepare the coat fronts as described under *Interfacing*, page 162. Cut the canvas on the cross (it is often sold like this). It may need a centre back seam in which case lap one piece over the other and zig-zag stitch together. Seam the melton at the centre back with an open seam trimmed down very narrow. Baste both the melton and the collar canvas together. Mark the roll line with basting. It may be marked on the pattern but if not, find it by putting on the collar and creasing it.

*Padding*  Fold the collar, canvas outwards, along the roll line and press the crease with the iron, pulling the collar round into a curved shape. With the melton side towards you, work a row of back stitches along the roll line, pulling the thread tight and taking the stitches through to the canvas; pass the needle through to the other side, and work a row of padding stitches over the back stitching.

Working with the collar folded on the roll line and holding the stand part of the collar in your left hand (if right handed), continue padding from the roll line to the neck edge. There will be space for about three rows of padding. Do not work too near the edge of the canvas.

Turn the collar round and hold the outer edge. Work rows of padding from the roll line almost to the edge. Holding the collar like this makes it roll under as you stitch; the melton also becomes taut on the canvas, which gives a good shape to the under collar. Trim the canvas back 5 mm ($\frac{1}{4}$ in.) from the edge of the melton.

Press the under collar with a hot iron and damp cloth. Press up to the roll line on each edge on both the wrong side and the right side of the collar. Stretch

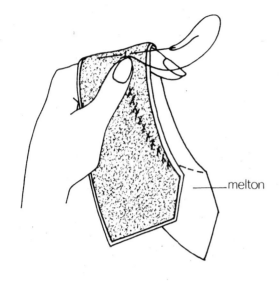

melton

the outer edge at the centre back, and the inner edge at the centre back, under the iron to curve the collar. If you are not sure of the correct shape for the collar, it can be put round the neck of a dummy and pressed. Try not to stretch the step of the collar up to the shoulder line at this stage.

Trim the turnings off the under collar pattern, and place it on the collar. Trim the outer edge of the canvas about 2 cm ($\frac{3}{4}$ in.) shorter than the melton. This checking is vital because the collar easily becomes distorted while padding and pressing, but it must now be accurately shaped as it forms the base of the top collar.

*Attaching the under collar*    Place the neck edge of the melton exactly onto the fitting line on the outside of the jacket neck. Match up the centre back lines and roll lines and bring the front corners of the melton exactly to the snip at the gorge. Hem the edge of the melton with very small, close, deep stitches. The stitches should catch the canvas along the gorge line. Attach front facings, trim and roll to wrong side.

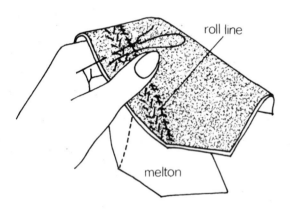

roll line

melton

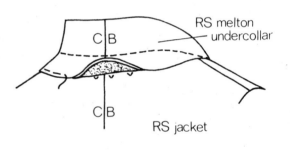

RS melton
undercollar

C B

C B

RS jacket

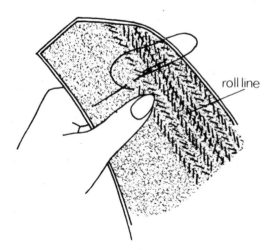

roll line

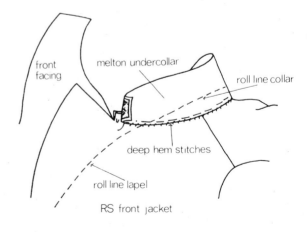

front facing

melton undercollar

roll line collar

deep hem stitches

roll line lapel

RS front jacket

Hem the jacket turnings to the under collar across the back of the neck. Herringbone over the edge of the canvas along the gorge line. Continue the bridle that is left at the top of the lapel roll round the collar. Baste, then hem firmly to the canvas. Press the neck seam, taking care not to pull the collar out of shape. Roll back, and work several rows of basting to hold it in a slightly rolled shape.

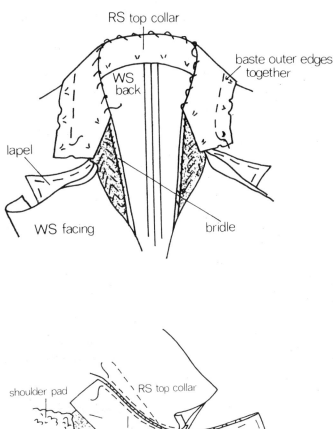

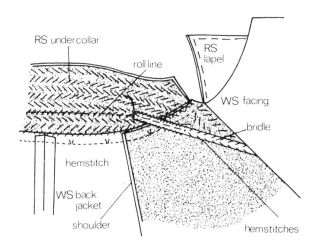

*Top collar*  Placing the top collar in position is easier to do with the jacket on a dummy. Place the top collar wrong side down onto the under collar, matching the centre backs.

Pin at the centre back, the corners, and at the point where the collar meets the lapel. There will be some ease between the pins. Work a row of basting at least 2 cm ($\frac{3}{4}$ in.) inside the collar edge, easing in the fullness. With the collar still in its rolled position, work another row of stitches along the roll line.

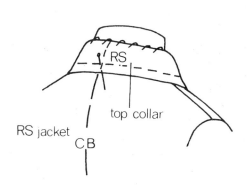

Trim the turnings on the collar and facing to 6 mm ($\frac{1}{4}$ in.) along the gorge line and also along the step of the lapel, and turn them both in to meet each other. Baste in position. Press. Slip stitch or ladder stitch together with tiny deep firm stitches, slightly drawing the two folds together. Slip stitch the step of the lapel. Trim the top edge of the collar to 6 mm ($\frac{1}{4}$ in.) beyond the edge of the melton.

Fold over the ends of the top collar, turning the edge in approximately 2 mm ($\frac{1}{8}$ in.) wider than the under collar: mitre the corners, cutting away the surplus bulk. Turn in and tack the outer edge of the collar in the same way. Tack the melton down flat to cover the raw edge. Press well.

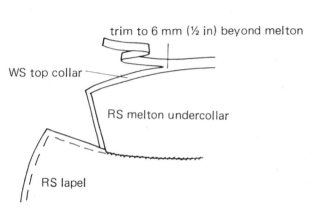

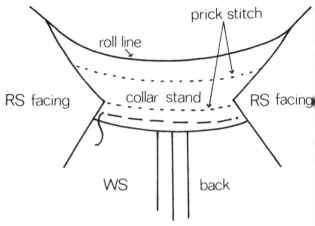

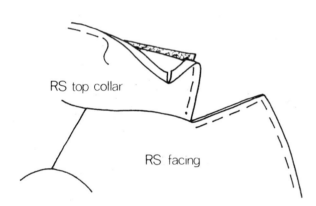

If the melton is not a good match for the colour of the cloth, it is better to finish the end of the collar in the following way. Turn in the outer edge of the collar, but not the ends. Finish by hemming the edge of the melton. Trim the melton at the collar ends and hem down. Fold the end of the collar over the melton and baste. Hem with tiny stitches along the sides and work over the raw edge with small herringbone stitches. Press well.

This method ensures that the edge of the melton never shows, but in addition it is slightly easier to achieve a well shaped collar end.

Work a bar tack on the underside where the collar and lapel form an angle and hem with tiny, close, deep stitches all round the outer edge of the collar.

*Finishing the back neck*  Tack down the raw edge of the collar below the roll line, then work a row of back stitching from the end of the facing through the top collar and into the melton beneath.

With the collar in its rolled position work another row of back stitching 5 mm ($\frac{1}{4}$ in.) below the roll line from the seam of the gorge right across the back of the neck. There is a slight amount of ease to be held in place. Complete the back neck of the lining.

If correctly held and padded, the lapel will automatically adopt the correct rolled position. Never press in a crease down the lapel, but press the wrong side and right side and, while still damp and warm, roll and fold it back with your fingers, smoothing it until cool.

**Semi-tailored collar**

If it proves to be impossible to obtain a melton cloth to blend with the fabric, or if you are making a dress or coat where melton would be too heavy, you can compromise and use a method which combines the careful handling and shaping and reduction of bulk of a tailored collar with the necessity of using ordinary fabric for the under collar.

*Under collar*  Cut the under collar on the cross (there may be a separate pattern piece) and join if necessary at the centre back. Interface. Pad and shape if using canvas: baste or press if using other interfacing such as Vilene.

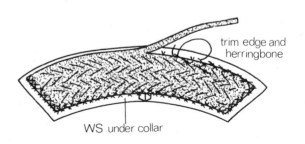

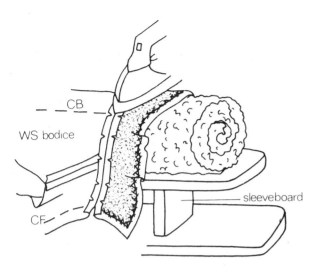

CB

WS bodice

sleeveboard

CF

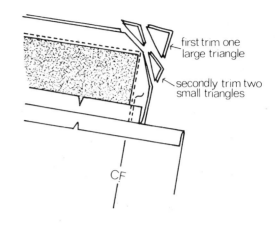

first trim one
large triangle

secondly trim two
small triangles

CF

Trim off the edge of the interfacing as for a tailored collar. If using sew-in interfacing the edge must be herringboned to the under collar round all edges.

Attach the neck edge to the garment, right sides together, making sure that the ends of the collar come to the correct points at the front. Snip the edges of the collar and of the neckline to make the join easier to do. Tack and machine or back stitch, but only stitch from the centre front mark, do not include the end turnings of the collar. Remove the tacks, and press the join open, laying it over a pressing pad or rolled up towel.

*Top collar*    Place the top collar to the under collar right sides together, and tack round the outer edge. Machine round the collar just off the edge of the interfacing. Trim and layer the turnings and cut off the corners.

Turn the collar through, roll and tack the edges, with the join well concealed on the under side, and press the edge well.

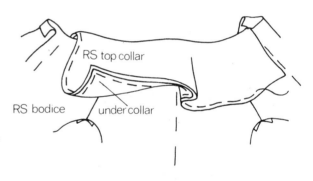

RS top collar

RS bodice    under collar

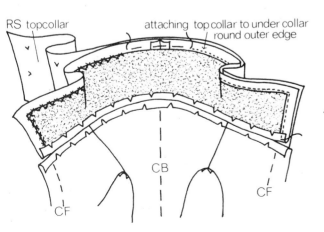

RS topcollar

attaching top collar to under collar
round outer edge

CB

CF

CF

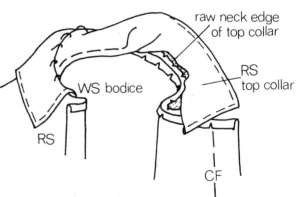

raw neck edge
of top collar

WS bodice

RS
top collar

RS

CF

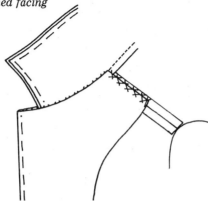

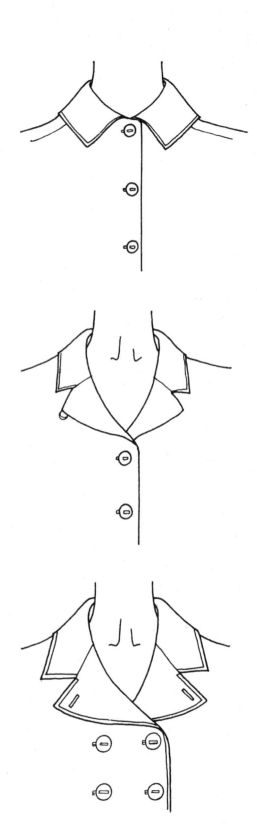

Roll the collar into the position it will adopt in wear, and work a row of basting along the roll. Bring the raw edge of the top collar down at the back of the neck and tack.

Turn the work over and, from the under collar side, work a row of back stitches in the neck join, taking the needle through to the top collar layer. If the garment is not to be lined, neaten the raw edge with overcasting and binding.

With a shirt-style collar in a soft fabric, work a row of back stitch across the back of the neck 1 cm ($\frac{3}{8}$ in.) below the roll line. Do not do this on cottons or lightweight fabrics.

*Finishing*   To finish the revers, open out the front facing, trim the turnings down to 5 mm ($\frac{1}{4}$ in.) and turn in the raw edge and tack. Turn in the raw edge round as far as the shoulder seam and tack. Press. Finish by slip stitching the step of the rever and round to the shoulder with very tiny invisible stitches. Attach the raw edge of the facing at the shoulder with herringbone stitch.

The raw edge of the facing from shoulder to hem can be neatened and left loose on blouses, etc., held down with herringbone stitch on heavy fabrics, or held down with pieces of fabric adhesive such as Wundaweb.

Note that this method of applying the under collar first and pressing the neck join open can be used on any fabric and any style of collar. It is easy to manipulate and produces good results. It is better not to use a back neck facing as it adds bulk.

## COMBINED FACING

(See *All-in-One Facing*, page 111, for definition.) See *Neck and Armhole Facing*, page 113, for attaching.)

## CONVERTIBLE COLLAR

A collar used on coats, shirt style blouses, dresses and jackets incorporating a traditional collar but with revers that can be worn open or closed up to the neck. The advantage is that a shirt can be worn with a tie or open, a coat can be opened or buttoned up. If you do not want a button and buttonhole to be visible when it is worn open then fasten it at the neck with a thread loop on the corner of the lapel and a small button under the collar. On a double breasted coat the under layer also has a button and buttonhole so that when it is worn open there is a buttonhole in each lapel.

## CORAL STITCH

An outline stitch using a single thread but with knots evenly spaced. Work towards you or from right to left. Allow thread to hang down and to the left then take a very small horizontal stitch under it. Move along and work another stitch.

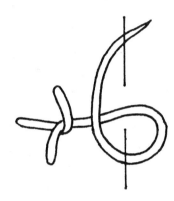

## CORD

Cord can be purchased by the metre in a variety of colours and several thicknesses. It is usually viscose or acetate fibre and therefore shiny.

Wherever possible insert the ends in a seam when using cord as ties. The other end may be finished by winding thread round and round 6 to 10 cm ($2\frac{3}{8}$ to 4 in.) from the end and then fraying out the fibres of the cord, or finer cord can have a wooden bead attached.

When using it flat on the fabric as decoration mark the position with a row of tacking, hold the fabric wrong side up but hold the cord underneath and back stitch through the fabric and into the cord.

To make your own very fine cord in a perfectly matching colour use buttonhole twist, Coton à Broder, Anchor Soft Embroidery thread or crochet cotton. Experiment to see how many strands are needed for the required thickness. Cut strands at least five times the length of the finished cord. Attach all strands firmly to a convenient point such as a coat hook or door handle and twist very tightly over the entire length.

Thread the end through something reasonably heavy, such as the handles of a pair of scissors, pull through to the half-way point and attach the free end to the door handle. The cord will twist. Wrap Sellotape (Scotch tape) or thread round each end before cutting the cord from its anchors.

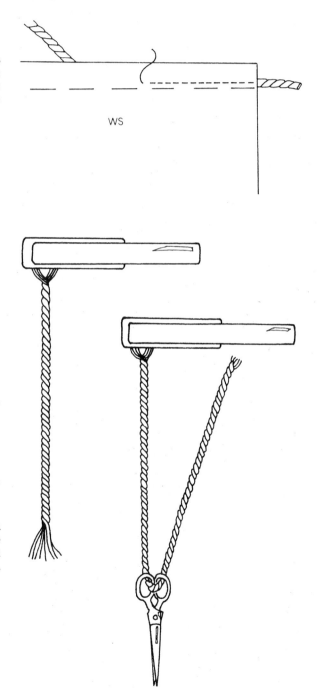

WS

## CORD GATHERING

Cord gathering is decorative gathering using a pearl-cord or crochet cotton and a zig-zag stitch.

Fix the embroidery foot on the machine and thread the cord through the hole in the foot or under the centre. Set the machine to a medium zig-zag and a fairly long stitch. Machine on the right side and work two rows or more of stitching 2 cm ($\frac{3}{4}$ in.) apart. Take hold of all the ends of the cord together and pull up to size. If the gathers extend for the full width of a garment section the ends of the thread will be caught and held in a seam later, but if not, then the ends of the thread and the cord must be passed to the wrong side and sewn in.

## CORNERS

Decide which edge of the finished corner will be least visible when the garment is worn and leave that side until last. Begin by turning a narrow hem on the other edge, tack and machine. Remove tackings, press well. Trim any fraying ends of fabric from the other edge and turn a hem of equal depth or, if possible, make it wider as it will be easier to handle. Tack and press, then using the points of small scissors snip away a little of the raw edge inside the corner. Machine. As the number of thicknesses now varies the machining may tend to wobble or even have difficulty in getting started as you have to begin right on the edge. It helps to lower the needle into the edge, lower the foot, take hold of the threads behind the foot and as you start machining gently pull the threads to help the machine over the bulk of the corner. Take extra care as you leave the corner and start stitching through only half the thickness. Remove tackings and press.

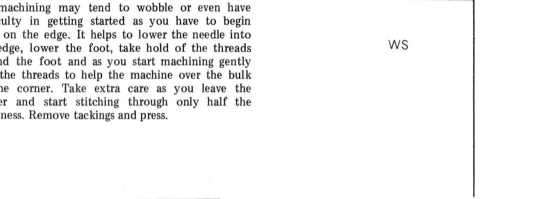

Thread the ends of machining into a needle and sew them in invisibly to fasten off. If it is unsuitable to leave the end of the hem open, the thread can be used to slip-stitch the folded edges together.

## COSSACK

A style of coat, jacket or top that has a stand collar, often made of fur, and with an asymmetric fastening from neck to hem. A close-fitting tailored effect.

## COUCHING

A common outline embroidery stitch. One thread is laid along the outline of the design. It is held to the fabric at intervals by small stitches worked in another thread, which may be of contrasting colour. The laid thread may also be thicker or of different texture.

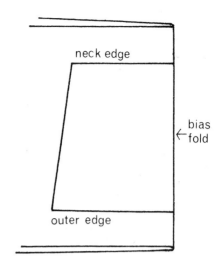

neck edge

bias
← fold

outer edge

## COUTURE HEM

The method of finishing a hemline invisibly by hand that was always used in couture dressmaking but rarely in home dressmaking. Now, however, it is the standard method used on dresses, skirts and coats, because it does not show. It is finished with catch stitch (see page 57).

## COWL

A style of draped collar that comes and goes in fashion. The neckline of the garment is lower than the basic line, often very low, to eliminate the need for an opening in the collar which could spoil the drape. When made in knit fabrics there is sufficient 'give' if the neckline is cut only 1 to 2 cm ($\frac{3}{8}$ to $\frac{3}{4}$ in.) lower at the front and left at its basic position at the back and shoulders.

The collar itself is a wide strip of fabric cut on the cross. It can be straight or it may be shallower at the back to avoid too much bulk at the back of the neck. The piece of fabric is joined at the centre back and then the piece folded wrong sides together and attached as for a roll collar (see page 66). However, this can be bulky and as it is difficult to keep the cowl arranged neatly or put a coat over the top a better shape and method of attaching is as follows.

Keep the outer edge straight but reduce the depth at the centre back by shaping the neckline edge. The length of the neckline edge must equal or be slightly shorter than the length of the neckline on the garment. The outer edge of the cowl should be longer to ensure that the neckline join is covered when the cowl is worn, so slope the centre back edge as shown. It is easy to cut this cowl for yourself if it

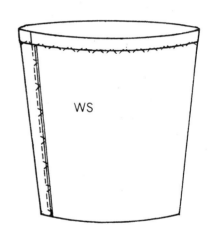

WS

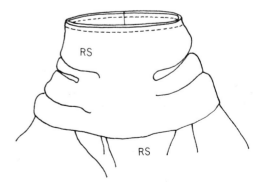

RS

RS

is not part of the pattern you are using, placing the shape shown to a crossway fold or by cutting the entire pattern and laying it on single fabric but on the cross. Cut out.

Fold right sides together and join at the centre back. The most unobtrusive join is a one-step narrow seam using the overlock or blind hem stitch. Press join to one side. Finish the outer, longer edge of the cowl by turning a narrow hem. This can be decorative, worked by hand or machine, or an excellent way of stabilising this edge is to first neaten it and then slip a narrow strip of Wundaweb under it. Press with a medium hot iron and damp cloth. If the fabric is of knit or jersey construction, stretch as you press and this makes the edge longer so that it has even more chance of covering the neck join.

Find the centre front point of the neckline edge and pin it to the centre front of the garment, placing the right side of the cowl to the wrong side of the neckline. Pin the cowl seam to the centre back of the neckline. Pin the remainder of the cowl edge and neckline edge together at intervals inserting all pins across the seam. Tack. Remove pins. Machine round the neck. Trim turnings off to 5 mm ($\frac{1}{4}$ in.) or less and neaten.

## CRETAN STITCH

A wide looped embroidery stitch worked in lines or to fill outlines. The effect can be varied by the closeness and length of stitches, working from left to right. A small stitch is worked at the lower edge of the area to be covered, with the thread under the needle point, then another small stitch at the top edge, with the needle to the centre and thread again under the needle.

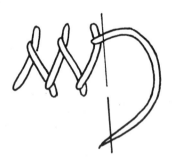

## CREW

This describes a normal neckline with no opening so it usually implies a ribbed edging of some 2 cm ($\frac{3}{4}$ in.). Garments made with a crew neck would, in addition to knitted ones, include tops, blousons, etc., with ribbed fabric or hand knitting added.

## CRUTCH DEPTH

The distance between the waist and the crutch or fork on women's trousers, culottes, etc. The measurement can be taken while sitting down, measuring straight down from waist to chair seat.

(See also *Crutch Seam*, page 272.)

## CRUTCH POINT

The position on women's trousers, culottes or shorts where the two inside leg seams and the crutch seam meet.

## CRYSTAL PLEATING

Continuous permanent pleating. The pleats are close together and very narrow.

## CUFFS

**Fold-a-Band cuff**
Cut a length of Fold-a-Band the length of the cuff when finished plus overlap, and press it to the wrong side of a piece of fabric with one edge exactly on the straight grain. Cut out round the outside of the Fold-a-Band allowing turnings. Place this to the sleeve right sides together arranging the overlap where it is required. Machine just off the edge of the Fold-a-Band. Trim the turnings into the cuff. Stitch the ends of the cuffs. Either fold right sides together and machine, just off the end of the Fold-a-Band, trimming and turning cuffs right side out, or turn in the cuff ends and slip stitch.

On the inside of the cuff you can turn under the raw edge and hem into the machine, the Fold-a-Band will keep the edge level. Alternatively on thick fabrics trim the edge almost to the Fold-a-Band and neaten. Tack it flat and either prick stitch through the seam, or machine round the cuff decoratively to hold the edge down.

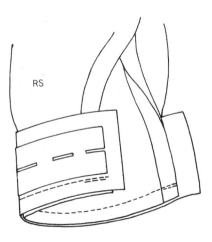

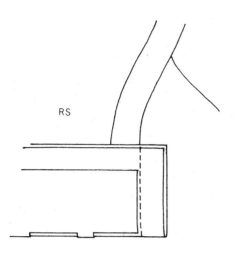

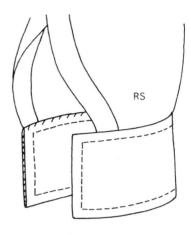

## Jersey cuff

When using jersey or stretch fabrics a cuff may be attached to a long sleeve without making an opening in the sleeve. The 'give' in the fabric is used to allow expansion for the hand to pass through. It is a useful way of avoiding bulk in bulky jersey fabrics.

If the jersey is stable, interfacing may be dispensed with. If interfacing is attached to the cuff it must be Superdrape which is the type that stretches. Make sure the stretch direction runs the length of the cuff.

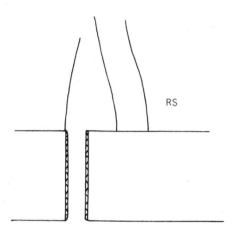

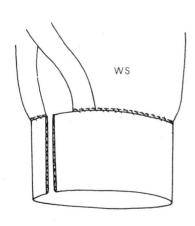

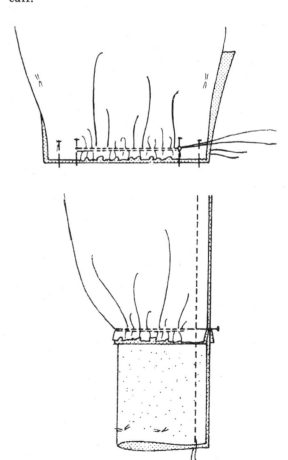

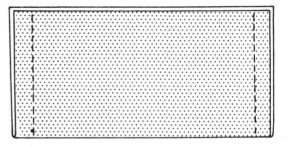

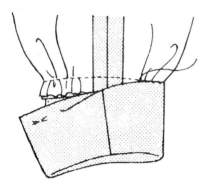

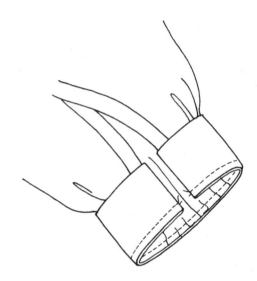

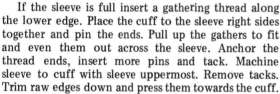

If the sleeve is full insert a gathering thread along the lower edge. Place the cuff to the sleeve right sides together and pin the ends. Pull up the gathers to fit and even them out across the sleeve. Anchor the thread ends, insert more pins and tack. Machine sleeve to cuff with sleeve uppermost. Remove tacks. Trim raw edges down and press them towards the cuff.

Fold the sleeve right sides together, insert a pin across the seam to hold the cuff seams together, tack and machine the seam. Remove tacks, press open and neaten the seam. Trim the seam allowances down where they fall in the cuff.

Fold cuff in half, turn in the raw edge and hem into the machining. Alternatively it can be machined but use a zig-zag or stretch stitch and work from the right side just inside the cuff edge. (See also *Quick Cuff*.)

### Quick cuff

This is a quick method of attaching a cuff to a long sleeve with an overlapping opening. Attach interfacing to the wrong side of the cuff either up to the fold line or across the entire cuff. Fold cuff right side inside and machine across the ends. Trim the corners and raw edges, turn cuff right side out and press.

Place against the sleeve on the outside, with the raw edges level and the ends level with the ends of the opening so that the overlap is formed. Gather or pleat the surplus of sleeve into the cuff. Tack and machine. Trim and neaten all raw edges together. Pull the cuff down so that it extends into the wearing position and press.

### Shaped turn-back cuff

If the sleeve and lower edge of the sleeve are shaped, the cuff has to be cut separately and joined to the sleeve. A pattern may be made simply by tracing off the lower edge of the sleeve and making it as deep as required.

Cut two pieces for each cuff and attach interfacing to one of them. Join the ends of both pieces and press open the joins. Trim edges. Place one inside the other, right sides together and machine round the top edge. Trim and snip if it is very curved. Turn cuff right side out and fold it along the stitched edge. Roll, tack and press this edge. Tack along the raw edges 2 cm ($\frac{3}{4}$ in.) in to hold them together.

Slip the cuff on to the right side of the sleeve and attach in one of two ways. The quickest method is to tack and machine through both cuff edges, and the sleeve, then trim and neaten. Roll the cuff on to the right side of the sleeve and press but making sure the neatened edge and join are hidden inside the cuff.

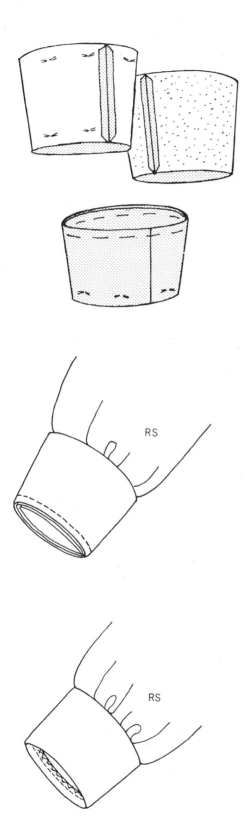

To use the other method, tack one edge of the cuff, the interfaced one, to the sleeve, holding the other layer back. Machine, trim and snip the seam and press open. To avoid creasing the sleeve push a rolled towel into the sleeve.

Fold the cuff into its finished position, turn the sleeve inside out and bring the raw edge of the cuff over to cover the seam. Back stitch or prick stitch through the cuff into the seam. Neaten the raw edge.

If the fabric is very lightweight the edges of the seam may be pressed into the cuff and then the raw edge turned under and hemmed to finish.

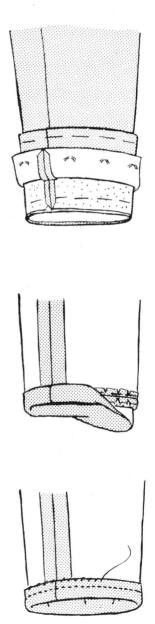

## Shirt cuff

Use firm interfacing, or as suggested for a stiff shirt collar, use two, or even three, layers of light interfacing until the required stiffness is achieved. Interface half the cuff only. Place cuff pieces right sides together. Tack and machine round outer edge. If the corners are rounded make sure stitching is accurate. This is done most easily by marking the interfacing with carbon paper and tracing wheel. Use the palest colour carbon paper, especially on pale fabric. Trim and layer the turnings.

Turn cuffs right side out, roll the edges, tack and press. Tack the tucks in the lower edge of the sleeve making sure the cuff is going to fit exactly. A shirt sleeve opening is of the overlapping type so no extension is left on the cuff.

Place the right side of the inner cuff piece (the one without interfacing) to the wrong side of the sleeve. Make sure the ends of the cuff coincide exactly with the ends of the opening. Tack and machine.

Trim turnings, pull cuff down to extend beyond the sleeve. Holding sleeve right side out, pull the second side of the cuff flat so that the raw edge lies over the join just made. Trim the seam edge a little then turn under and tack down, making sure that the edge covers the machining on the sleeve. With the right side out, machine all round the edge of the cuff, working a second row if required. Work the buttonholes.

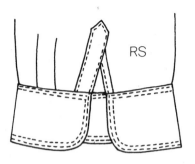

Sometimes double cuffs are made on men's shirts. Interface the entire cuff which is twice the depth it will be in wear. Then add another layer of light interfacing to the half of the cuff that will fold over on to the right side. Make and attach the cuff and work four buttonholes to take cuff links.

## Tailored cuff

Often called a hole-and-button cuff because there is a complete overlapping opening at the wrist, in the back seam, and worked buttonholes and buttons are added. It is the traditional cuff on men's jackets and sometimes on women's coats although it is acceptable to sew buttons through the sleeve without buttonholes. Use a suitable interfacing and hem reinforcement; this will be the same as used on the rest of the garment.

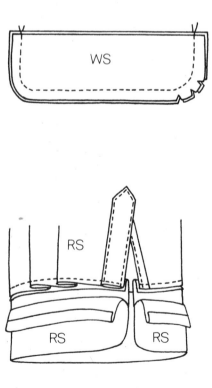

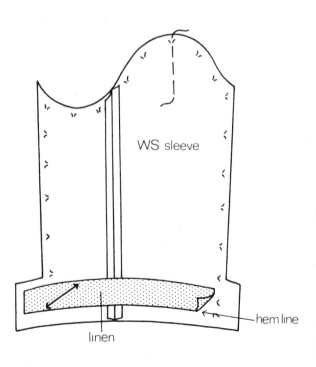

Join the top sleeve to the under sleeve at the underarm seam, and press open. On soft fabric reinforce the hem by herringboning a crossway strip of linen or a strip of interfacing. The lower edge must be exactly on the hemline. On the top sleeve, the reinforcement should reach the seam line; on the under sleeve it stops short of the edge by the width of a turning. If Vilene is used it should be cut to shape.

Fold over and tack the raw edge on the under sleeve and fold and tack the extension edge on the top sleeve.

Finish by turning up the hem and trimming the corner.

Reinforce a man's cuff to make the button and buttonholes. Baste a piece of linen 5 x 4 cm (2 x 1$\frac{5}{8}$ in.) into each end of the cuff, with the raw edges exactly on the hemline and fold lines.

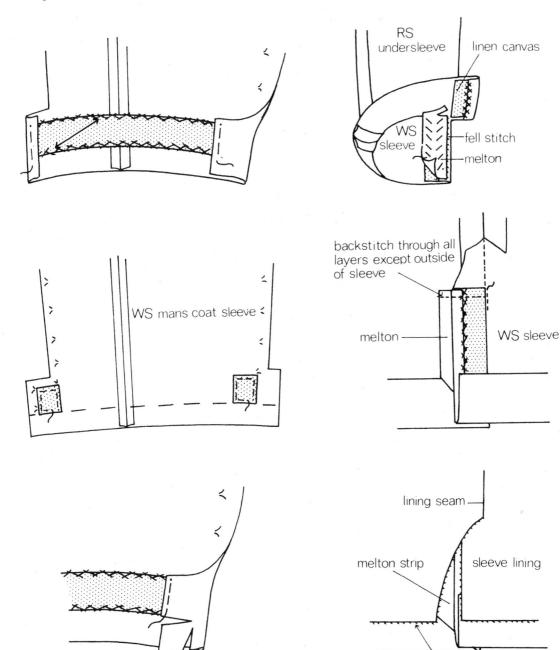

Baste on all cuffs pieces of linen 12 cm ($4\frac{3}{4}$ in.) long and 5 cm (2 in.) wide to the wrong side of each of the sleeve. Stitch the sleeve seam. The depth of the opening depends upon how many buttons are to be used, this can vary from 1 to 4. Press the seam open from the armhole, but towards the front of the sleeve, for about 14 cm ($5\frac{1}{2}$ in.) above the opening. On the underneath or extension side, fold over a single turning, and press. Herringbone to hold.

On the front side, fold back and press a turning. Cut a piece of melton cloth 6 cm ($2\frac{3}{8}$ in.) wide and baste it with its edge to the cuff edge. Fell along this edge. Trim the melton slightly at the top of the opening.

Turn up and finish the sleeve hems; mitre the corners over the melton and fell in place. Lap the opening, and baste it close from the right side.

On the wrong side back stitch across the top of the opening through all layers except the sleeve itself. Bring the sleeve lining down. Turn in, and fell close to the edge of the extension piece.

On the upper side where the buttonholes will go, slope the lining out to reveal the melton, so that the buttonholes will be worked through the non-fraying melton cloth and not through the lining. Fell all lining edges.

On a man's coat, and on a woman's if you wish, work buttonholes and attach buttons. These are not actually undone or used so the buttonholes need not necessarily be cut. Work the rows of buttonhole stitches very close together, so forming a well. Sew the buttons in the well at the round end.

If, on a woman's coat, no buttonholes are worked, sew the buttons right through the opening; omit a shank under the button.

### Turn-back cuff

The simplest type of turn-back cuff is an extension of the fabric. It is, however, confined to short sleeves and to long sleeves that are very wide at the wrist as the sleeve edge must be straight.

If the allowance for cuff is not part of the paper pattern it can easily be calculated and added. Work out the depth of cuff required by folding a piece of paper and trimming the long edges until it is the right size. Crease the paper along the folds. Do not cut the sides yet. Open out the sleeve pattern and place the paper cuff, folded on top, checking that the total length is correct. Use a ruler and draw the sleeve seam on the cuff. Cut on the line, open out the cuff and the correctly shaped edge will be visible. Pin or stick the cuff pattern to the bottom of the sleeve pattern and cut out in fabric. Mark the fold lines of the cuff. Note that on a short sleeve the shape will be less angled.

Stitch the sleeve seam following the shaped edge. Snip at the fold lines and press the seam open. Neaten the edges and neaten the lower edge of the sleeve. On

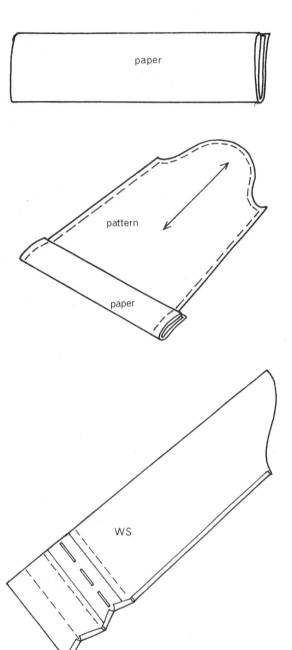

the wrong side place a length of Fold-a-Band with the central perforations over the crease line that will be the upper edge of the cuff, and press. Fold the cuff completely into the finished position and turn wrong side out. Slip a length of Wundaweb under the neatened edge and press. Do this lightly with the cuff still in the folded position, then open out the sleeve to avoid ridges caused by pressing and press again. Fold cuff up and press lightly.

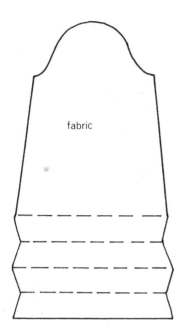

fabric

sleeve. The entire cuff is attached and the surplus forms a fold arranged at the outside of the arm where a cuff would normally overlap and fasten. Use a flat fastening such as Velcro or press studs to avoid adding more bulk. This cuff is not suitable for heavy fabrics.

Interface the cuff in the usual way and mark seam allowances or use Fold-a-Band. Insert a gathering thread (two if preferred) round the lower edge of the sleeve. Set the machine to the largest stitch that it will do, start well inside the edge to keep away from the underarm seam and reverse for a few stitches, then machine to the same point at the other side of the sleeve. Do not reverse or fasten off. Work with right side of work uppermost.

Place cuff to sleeve right sides together, pin at each end, pull up gathers to fit. Pull up only the spool thread, i.e. the one on the wrong side of fabric and wind the end round a pin to hold. Even out the gathers. Flatten the gathers for 2 cm ($\frac{3}{4}$ in.) where the sleeve opening would normally be. This is where the cuff will wrap over and it avoids too much bulk. Tack. Machine.

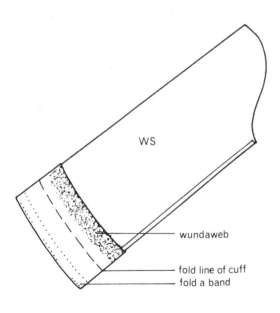

WS

wundaweb

fold line of cuff
fold a band

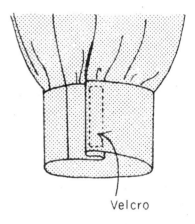

Velcro

If the fabric is floppy, or the cuff is particularly wide, work a series of bar tacks round the sleeve between the cuff and the sleeve 1 cm ($\frac{3}{8}$ in.) below the top edge of the cuff so that they are concealed.

### Wrap cuff

A unique method of having a fitted cuff on a long sleeve but without having to make an opening in the

Trim turnings and press down into cuff. Fold sleeve right sides together and tack and machine the seam through the sleeve and through the cuff. Keep the cuff joins level by inserting a pin and stitching over it. Turn in raw edge of cuff and tack to row of machining. Hem.

To attach fastening try a sleeve on and mark wrap over in line with your little finger. Cut a narrow strip of Velcro and hem the pieces in place so that when fastened it fits the wrist. Alternatively attach two press studs. Attach the fastening to the second sleeve in the same position.

## CULOTTES

A combination of skirt and trousers originally developed as a cycling garment for women. It is basically a skirt shape, long or short or mid-calf and A-line in outline. The centre front and centre back seam of the skirt is extended into the curve of a crutch seam and there is an inside leg seam, usually slightly angled, to the hem. There is often an inverted pleat at centre front and back making them slightly more flattering in wear, expecially when seen from the back.

## CUMMERBUND

A wide tightly fitting belt. It can be made by pleating the fabric and then backing it with stiff interfacing and lining the back, or it can be a wide piece of fairly soft fabric such as suede that wrinkles when put round the waist. Usually made in a contrasting colour or texture to emphasise the waist. For comfort in wear it can be made narrower at the back and fastened either with long ties that cross and fasten at the front, or with a piece of Velcro. This last method of fastening can be used on a full width belt as well as on a narrowed one.

The cummerbund should not be worn by women with prominent busts or by those who are short waisted unless only part of it is visible, as it is, for example, when worn by men under a dinner jacket.

The edge may be faced although this too adds weight and there is the problem of the free edge of the facing; the answer lies in using pieces of Wundaweb to hold this down, or in working a decorative stitch parallel with the curved edge of the garment.

Alternative finishes for curved edges include working satin stitch or a machine scalloped edge and trimming away the surplus fabric. If the curve is not too pronounced the edge of the fabric could be turned under before stitching and the raw edge trimmed off afterwards.

A further solution for a small area such as a sleeve is to make it double, the inside sleeve acting as a facing to the curved edge. Never try to make a conventional hem on a curved or shaped edge.

(See *Circular Hems*, page 144, for details of shaped skirt hems.)

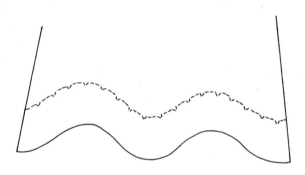

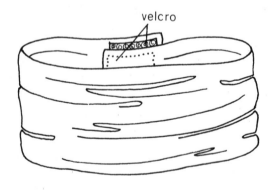

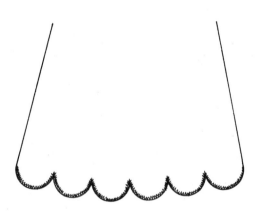

## CURVED EDGES

There are many places on a garment where there may be a curved edge to finish and the more pronounced the curve the more difficult it is to cope with. The edge can be bound without too much difficulty, although it is a visible finish and it adds weight, possibly restricting any drape or movement.

## CUTTING BOARD

A lightweight pin-board about 2 metres (2 yds) long and 1 metre (1 yd) wide, folded for ease of storage, but to be opened out to provide a surface for cutting out. A useful piece of equipment if a table is not available as it can be placed on a bed or on the floor.

The board is marked out in 2 cm ($\frac{3}{4}$ in.) squares so it can be used for making diagram patterns by pinning transparent paper on top. Most boards have other markings such as curves and diagonals to assist in cutting accurately. A further use is to lay out patterns on it in order to calculate the amount of fabric required.

## CUTTING LINE

The position for cutting the fabric which then becomes the raw edge of the pieces of garments. This is distinct from the fitting line or stitching line, which is some distance within. On a one-size fully printed pattern both fitting and cutting lines are marked. On a multi-size pattern only the cutting line is marked. On paper patterns without seam allowances, including those you draft and cut yourself, the edge of the pattern is the stitching line and you decide how far outside this to make the cutting line. The standard allowance on commercial patterns is 1.5 cm ($\frac{5}{8}$ in.) on seams, with varying amounts for hem edges. When fixing your own cutting line the distance can be varied according to the position on the garment and the fabric.

(See also *Seam Allowance*.)

## CUTTING OUT

Inexperienced sewers are usually more worried about cutting out than about any other sewing process, no doubt because they think mistakes cannot be rectified. Also, the process of sewing is fairly slow and allows time to think, whereas the cutting happens quickly. This nervousness is overcome only with experience so there is no point in delaying cutting out or getting someone else to do it. It is worth asking someone with only a little experience to look at the pattern pinned to the fabric before you cut, and to go through your list of pieces with you.

Remember that if a mistake is made it is usually possible to retrieve something, if only a smaller article, short sleeves, knitted or contrasting sections etc. Remember too that other processes could be used, e.g. a low neck instead of a high neck with a roll collar that uses a lot of fabric. One of the important points to bear in mind is that you need to concentrate and preferably to be quietly alone if you are nervous.

Another important factor which undoubtedly contributes to some people's dislike of cutting out is lack of space or equipment. The whole thing is so much easier if you use the correct scissors, good sharp pins, sharp tailor's chalk and a ruler. A large table which you can walk all round is ideal. The most irritating working area is the floor, it's a tiring position to be in and your body is in quite the wrong position. It is worth investing in a folding table such as decorators use, or use a large piece of hardboard or a

cutting out board and placing it on a bed, rather than using the floor. If space is limited pin and cut out one piece of pattern at a time. This is quite safe provided you have roughly marked the position of each piece with tailor's chalk. Cutting out is quite tiring anyway and it helps to do only that, or to cut out a couple of things and put them away, rather than to rush on to start the sewing immediately. Also cut out only the main pieces needed to start the garment, leaving small things like collars and facings until later. This speeds up the cutting out and is a good way of giving a beginner confidence. All pieces will have spaces marked out with chalk but do not pin the pieces to the fabric. Place the pieces in position. Follow the diagram on the pattern sheet if you need to, but it is better experience if you learn to work out how pieces fit onto fabric. If a pattern edge says 'fold' it must be placed to a fold of fabric on the straight grain. If there is a straight grain arrow on the piece it must lie on a straight thread or line of knitting or print. The only other point to remember is to check that the correct number of pieces will result from your cutting, e.g. two layers of collar, four pockets etc. Having done this you might as well go ahead and cut out; there is nothing else to check and no amount of delaying the moment is going to make any difference. It is highly unlikely that you will make a mistake.

Anchor each pattern piece with something like a pin box to make sure it all fits correctly on the fabric. With thick fabric place one or two more objects on to hold the first piece then take the tailor's chalk and a ruler and chalk round the outer edge of the paper. Remove the pattern. Place the next piece in position and mark in the same way. With lighter fabrics, place a few pins in. Insert them at an angle across the fabric, well inside the edge of the paper to avoid distortion. Do not use too many, it does not help to prevent mistakes and creates wobbly edges.

When cutting out, stand up and cut alongside the paper, or on the chalk line. If cutting beside paper, have the pattern on the right. This is easier and you can see the edge more clearly. Open the scissors wide but comfortably and cut confidently to the points. Do not close the scissors too slowly. With the other hand lift away the surplus fabric. This helps to put the scissors accurately into the cut as you move forward. Do not reach too far. Either walk round the table or carefully slide the fabric towards you. At corners cut slightly beyond the pattern, turn and cut the second edge accurately. If small curves are difficult to reach, cut straight across, then after cutting the entire piece return to the curve and cut it accurately.

If the pattern is pinned to the fabric do not lift the pieces after cutting but roll them up to move them. Fold spare fabric neatly, but not in small pieces, ready to cut the other pieces of pattern later.

## CUTTING-OUT SCISSORS

(See *Scissors*.)

## CUTWORK

Also called richelieu work. Cutwork is exactly what it says, fabric cut away in a pattern. Obviously the fabric edges would fray so they have to be stitched. Loop stitch is used when done by hand, satin stitch when worked by machine. The stitches are very close together and may be worked over initial rows of stitching or an extra thread, to produce a raised edge.

Mark the design on the fabric, work the stitching, even or varied in depth. Afterwards carefully cut away the areas in between to form the design.

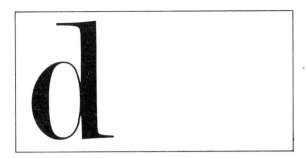

## DAISY STITCH

Also called detached chain stitch, this is a chain embroidery stitch, worked in the same way as chain stitch, but each loop is fastened by a small stitch at the base to enable single ovals to be made.

(See *Chain Stitch.*)

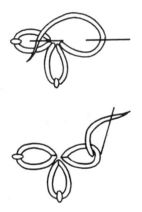

## DART TUCKS

A fold of fabric stitched on the inside of a garment forming a small pleat at the end. These tucks can provide shaping and fullness in a garment and may

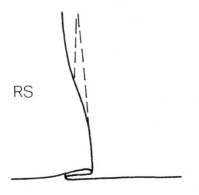

RS

sometimes be used instead of darts. The shaping is softer than that provided by a dart but dart tucks are suitable in certain positions, including the waists of bodices and skirts. Tack or pin the dart as usual and stitch on the wrong side, but stop the machine stitching before reaching the point of the dart.

## DARTS

A dart is a fold of fabric stitched to a point on the inside of a garment. The purpose of a dart is to provide shaping. The fact that the stitching runs to a point means that a bulge of fabric is formed at the point and this bulge can be fitted over the bulge of the figure.

The width and length of darts varies according to the position it occupies on the garment and what size of fabric bulge is needed. Darts must be fitted carefully to ensure that they are in the right place, are the right length and the right width.

Mark the fabric, making sure the base and the point are clearly visible. Fold the fabric wrong side out and match up the markings. It will be easier to do this if you have used tailor tacks as you can roll the two layers of fabric between your fingers until you can feel that the two sets of tailor tacks are together. If you need to hold it with pins before tacking, use no more than three, putting one across the end, one below the point and one half way.

Start tacking at the raw edges and work towards the point. Finish with one back stitch just short of the end of the dart. Leave the last pin in place, it will

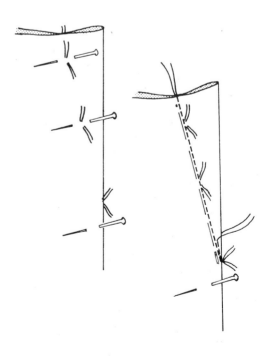

help to keep the fabric flat while you machine. Some people prefer to remove tailor tacks at this stage but I prefer to use them as a guide, ending my row of machining exactly on the last tailor tack instead of trampling tacking into the fabric. It helps, in addition, to measure off pairs of darts putting a chalk mark at the exact point of the dart, to ensure that they are the same length. You can also draw a straight line to stitch on if the dart is completely straight.

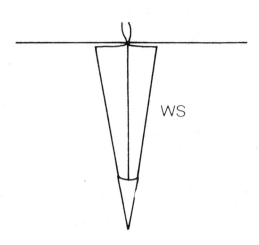

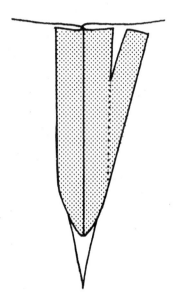

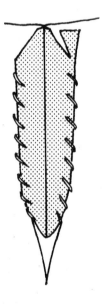

Put the work under the machine with the bulk of it to the left and starting at the raw edge, lower the foot at an angle so that it is pointing towards the end of the dart. Reverse and then machine carefully to the point. If you reverse to fasten off make sure you stitch in the fold of the dart.

Remove tacks by pulling the knot. Remove tailor tacks and the pin. Snip ends of threads close to the fabric. Place dart flat on sleeve board and press the stitching to smooth it.

If the fabric is thin, open out the work and place it on the sleeve board so that the point is level with the end of the board and the fabric of the dart is standing upright. Press dart over so that it is flat. Having pressed it in the correct direction, which is so that the bulk of the fabric is towards the centre of the garment, or in the case of horizontal bust darts, downwards to the waist, press it again really well, pressing only up to the end of the stitching. By arranging the dart on the sleeve board you can ensure that the shaping which the dart is providing in the fabric is not flattened.

Turn the work over and press again on the right side. In all medium and heavy weight fabrics the dart should be split open and trimmed to reduce bulk, but remember that all fitting must have been completed before any cutting away is done.

After pressing the stitching, split the dart along the fold nearly to the end. Trim away a little of the fabric. Open the work and press the dart open instead of to one side, taking great care with the point, which should be flattened. If using a damp muslin to press drape a corner of it over the toe of the iron and work carefully, continually looking under the cloth to make quite certain the dart is flat. You may have some additional pressing to do on the right side with this type of dart.

After the fabric is cool, neaten the raw edges of woven fabrics.

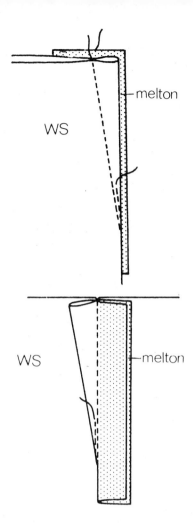

WS

melton

WS

melton

Small darts in bulky fabrics cannot be split and opened, and if pressed to one side a ridge will show on the right side. To overcome this place a narrow piece of soft cloth, such as melton, under the dart before stitching, making sure the melton is on the opposite side from the direction in which the dart will be pressed. Machine through the dart and the cloth. Press the dart to one side and the melton falls into a fold facing the other way.

## DECORATION

Any addition to an already wearable garment. Decoration often takes the form of embroidery or appliqué, but it can simply be the addition of braid, ribbon, beads, sequins, bows, ties, etc. For greatest effect and subtlety decoration should be kept to a basic minimum and if in doubt left off altogether.

## DECOUPE

The term refers to cutting but the technique is applied to the type of appliqué where a fabric is put on the back of the main fabric, and then the top or main fabric is cut away to reveal the contrast beneath.

## DENIER

A unit of measurement used to describe the weight per standard length of yarn. Denier is a useful way of describing the fineness of knit fabrics.

## DETACHED CHAIN STITCH

(See *Daisy Stitch*.)

## DIAGONAL BASTING

(See *Basting*.)

## DIOR

The fashion house of Christian Dior was the originator of many lines and fashions but the term that survives is the Dior pleat. This is a rather unsatisfactory imitation inverted pleat. In order to save fabric and reduce bulk leave a short slit in the skirt seam at the centre back.

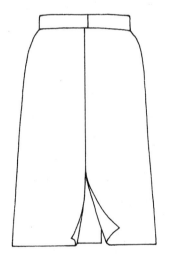

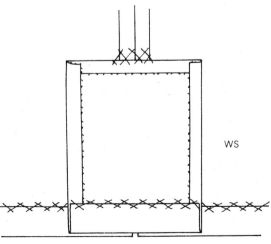

WS

Cut a rectangular piece of fabric and turn in the edges all round, even line it, then place it behind the slit, attaching it to the skirt only along the top edge so that the slit opens independently, yet gives the effect of a pleat.

## DIRECTION OF STITCHING

There are occasions when it is an advantage to machine, and also tack, in a specified direction. With a few fabrics it will make little difference but with most, especially velvet and all pile fabrics, jersey and all knit fabrics, voile, chiffon, crêpe, and any with movement in them, puckering and wrinkling can be eliminated.

Most seams run at an angle and on those that do, stitching is best worked from the wide part to the narrow, i.e. neck to armhole, underarm to waist, waist to hem. With woven fabrics this ensures stitching 'with' the direction of the weave which reduces puckering and fraying. With knitted fabrics you can slightly pull the fabric and stretch the seam to eliminate puckering. Pile fabrics are cut with the pile running up and so obviously the seam must be stitched in that direction, otherwise pushing against the pile will cause severe puckering. This rule must be applied to all sections of the garment, regardless of shape. With pile fabrics and velvet, if, in addition, you tack in that direction and leave the ends of tacking loose, this too will help to eliminate puckering.

## DIRNDL

A full skirt gathered or pleated into the waist; part of many national costumes. They do not often come into fashion as full and straight as they are worn in costume, but the style can be adapted to be less bulky and is normally referred to as 'peasant'.

## DOLMAN SLEEVE

A wide sleeve starting at the waist line, cut in one with the bodice. This type of sleeve, short or long, often narrows towards the hem, so lifting the arms causes a strain at the underarm. The solution is to insert a gusset which not only adds fabric but the gusset is cut on the bias giving more stretch.

## DOMETTE

A soft, fluffy, open-weave fabric, domette is used for padding the chest area of coats and jackets.

## DONKEY

A donkey is a large padded sleeveboard for tailoring. It has two arms of different sizes; both arms may be padded to give four different sized ends for pressing, or the small side may be of plain wood to provide a hard surface for some of the pressing involved in tailoring with good quality worsted cloth.

(See also *Sleeve Board*.)

## DOUBLE BACK STITCH

(See *Closed Herringbone Stitch*.)

## DOUBLE BREASTED

A man's or woman's jacket or coat with a fastening that wraps further over than the centre front line. It creates a broader squarer outline. Only the fastening edge has buttonholes, the opposite buttons are sewn on the outside of the coat, although an inside or jigger button will be needed to hold it in place.

Although it is a style feature, a double breasted winter coat is warmer than single breasted.

## DOUBLE FEATHER STITCH

Covering twice the area of feather stitch, this is worked in the same way, but two stitches are taken to each side alternately.

(See *Feather Stitch*.)

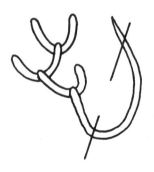

## DOUBLE KNOT STITCH

A thick outline embroidery stitch. Working to the outline of the design take a small vertical stitch, then a small horizontal stitch to the left. Pass the thread over the first stitch, under this stitch from right to

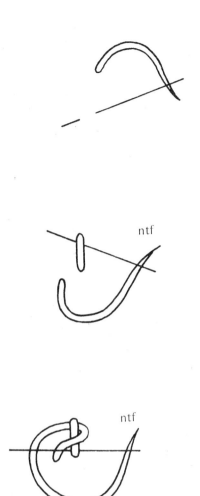

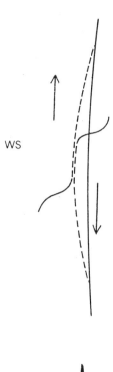

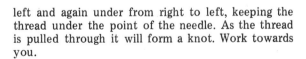

left and again under from right to left, keeping the thread under the point of the needle. As the thread is pulled through it will form a knot. Work towards you.

## DOUBLE POINTED DARTS

These produce shaping at both ends and are used mainly on dresses and coats without waist joins in order to shape the garment in to the waist and at the same time provide shaping for, at the front the bust and stomach and, at the back, the shoulder blades and bottom.

Tack and fit most carefully to keep the bulge at each end no bigger than necessary. It is better to increase waist shaping at the side seams rather than make this type of dart too wide at the centre.

Tack the dart in a slight curve and draw a line with tailor's chalk in addition if necessary. Make sure pairs of darts are identical in size and length. Begin machining at the centre and stitch to the point. Turn the work over and stitch from the centre to the other point. Fasten off all stitching. Remove tackings. Press on a sleeve board or pressing pad. With lightweight fabrics press the dart to one side, with heavy fabrics press flat with an equal amount of folded fabric each side of the central line of stitching. On heavy non-fraying fabrics cut the dart at the centre and along the fold and press open.

## DOUBLE THREAD STITCHING

A machine stitch worked with two normal sewing threads on the top of the machine which produce a slightly heavier line effective for decoration. Use on the right side of the garment where top stitching is required. Use the normal size machine needle for the fabric. Place one reel of thread on each spindle on top of the machine and thread each separately to the needle eye and thread the needle. Make sure one goes either side of the tension control disc. If you have only one spindle then wind the thread on to two machine spools and place one on top of the other. Insert the spool underneath in the usual way. Set the stitch length slightly longer than has been used in construction, but test the stitch to obtain the best effect. A zig-zag stitch may also be used but keep it fairly narrow.

(See also *Top Stitching.*)

## DRAFTING

Cutting a paper pattern. This may be from your own design or a copy of an illustration. Learning pattern drafting begins with the construction of basic bodice, skirt and sleeve outlines and then progresses to adapting these to various style features. There are a number of specialist books on pattern drafting.

## DRAPING

A method of obtaining a pattern for a garment by folding and pinning fabric to a dress form or dummy until the desired effect is obtained. As it is an experimental method usually a cheap fabric such as muslin, calico, etc., is used, pinning and cutting, and starting again if necessary. The resulting pieces are used to cut out the actual fabric.

## DRAW STITCH

A very small, close ladder stitch worked between two meeting folds to hold them together. The main use of draw stitch occurs when completing a collar and lapel by the hand-tailored method. The edges of the facing and top collar are turned in to meet each other from the end of the step to the end of the facing. (The line is called the gorge.) After tacking and pressing the folds are joined with draw stitch.

Use a small needle and a short piece of thread and take a small stitch alternately along each fold. Work from right to left and when crossing from one fold to the other insert the needle slightly back rather than opposite the point of emergence on the other fold. Pull the thread after each stitch to close the folds together but do not pull it tight or the fabric will wrinkle. Press well after removing tackings. There should be no evidence of the stitching on the outside of the garment.

## DRAWN THREADS

This decorative work can be done on a variety of plain weave fabric of all weights. Pull out the threads gently in sets of four, five, six etc., depending on the thickness of the yarns and the effect required. If you have not tried this form of decoration before, a thick coarse loosely woven fabric is easiest to start with.

At first withdraw yarns across the entire section, e.g. yoke, but latter you will see the possibilities of snipping and lifting out threads over a short distance. Retain the ends and weave them into the back of the fabric to prevent further unravelling.

The act of withdrawing the threads leaves a loose unstable area, so some stitching is necessary to hold it in shape. This stitching can be extended to form additional decoration.

The thread used can be matching or contrast, thick or thin, even the withdrawn yarns, depending on the effect required.

## DRAWSTRING

A cord inserted in a hem or casing to pull up an area of fullness. The cord may be purchased braid, cord, piping cord or rouleau made from crossway fabric or, if jersey, on the straight. Areas where drawstrings are used include wrists, ankles of casual track-suit type trousers, hems of blousons, necklines. The hem must always be narrow and the drawstring thin to be effective.

## DRAWSTRING NECK

Often part of a peasant style blouse or dress, the neckline is cut low and large enough to eliminate the necessity for an opening. An additional piece of fabric may be added to form a casing through which a cord or rouleau can be threaded. Alternatively on jersey fabric a narrow casing can be formed by folding over the edge of the fabric and working a

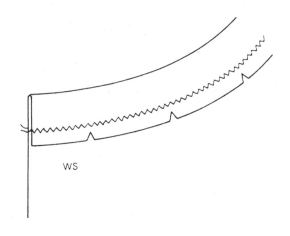

WS

small zig-zag stitch to hold it. It will be necessary to make a few small snips in the edge as it is turned over, especially on the more pronounced curved section of the neckline.

## DRAWSTRING WAIST

A dress or skirt the waist of which is made to fit by threading a cord or rouleau through a casing and drawing it up to tie in a bow or knot.

(See also *Casings.*)

## DRESSMAKERS' CARBON PAPER

(See *Carbon Paper.*)

## DRIMA

The two-spun polyester sewing thread made by J & P Coats. It is available in a wide range of colours in 100 metre spools, 200 metres in a more limited range and 500 metres in black, white and basic colours. The virtues of Drima are that it is very strong but fine and therefore beds well into the fabric; but also it has sufficient 'give' to ensure that it does not break in seams in stretch fabrics. Drima can be used on fabrics made from all fibres, a point worth remembering when you consider that fabrics can be blends or mixtures of as many as five or six fibres.

## DROPPED SHOULDER

As this term seems to imply an error in fitting it is probably best to describe this particular style feature as an extended shoulder.

(See *Extended Shoulder.*)

## DUAL FEED

Many machines are fitted with this device which, in effect, feeds the top layer of fabric at the same rate as the teeth in the base plate feed the lower layer. It is not used when stitching on a single layer but it is invaluable on seams, especially where a pattern has to be matched, or where the fabric is liable to creep, e.g. velvet.

## DUFFLE

A short or full length casual coat of thick, closely woven cloth, often unlined and with a hood or collar. It usually has welt seams, large patch pockets and toggle fastenings.

## DUMMY

There is a wide range of dummies or dress-forms available both solid and light construction. The main purpose of one is to check the hang and general appearance of a garment, to set and press a collar, to experiment with pocket positions and other decorative additions. Too many people think that a dummy will solve all fitting problems. This may be true once those problems have been identified and solved both at pattern and at body-fitting stage, but the dummy should still be used only to check balance; it is not intended that trying-on should be eliminated.

Inexpensive wire or similar dummies in self-construction kits are available and are ostensibly adjustable, so are some of the sectional types. However, unless the dummy adjusts at precisely the point where you have the problem it will be of no use in fitting. The wire variety tend to go out of shape when used, and additionally you must allow for the fact that if you squeeze the wire over you to obtain the shape then it is slightly bigger than you are.

Undoubtedly, the best kind are solid. They are available in a range of sizes and combinations of lengths and bust sizes, are comparatively expensive, but they are well made and last indefinitely. If you buy the size nearest to your measurements, or slightly smaller, you can pad it out with wadding to your measurements where necessary. It you have exaggerated problems, dress the dummy up with an old bra or girdle and carefully pad out. If its appearance is too basic then make a jersey cover from a thin fabric.

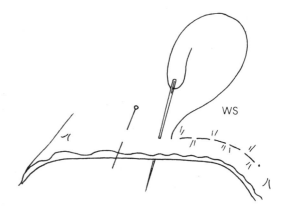

## EASE

Ease is the amount of room for movement allowed in a pattern and therefore in a garment. The amount of ease allowed by a designer varies according to fashion and style. When fitted clothes are in fashion the ease allowed is reduced. On the whole more ease is allowed in paper patterns than in ready-made clothes because the latter are tried on so it is possible to observe the ease before purchasing. Pattern companies have a standard amount of ease that they each work to but this is often concealed amongst style features, such as gathers, blousing, etc.

The amount of ease needed varies in different parts of the body and is determined by movement. When taking your measurements ease should be added after taking a firm measurement, but remember when checking a pattern piece that ease is already there. Examples of how ease varies include:

*wrist* — only 5 mm ($\frac{1}{4}$ in.) for comfort, nothing for movement
*waist* — about 2 to 3 cm ($\frac{3}{4}$ to $1\frac{1}{4}$ in.) for breathing and bending
*elbow* — whatever is required
across the *shoulder blades* from 2 to 5 cm ($\frac{3}{4}$ to 2 in.)
across *chest* — very little
*bust* — 4 to 10 cm ($1\frac{5}{8}$ to 4 in.)
*hips* — 4 to 6 cm ($1\frac{5}{8}$ to $2\frac{3}{8}$ in.)
*buttocks* — 6 to 10 cm ($2\frac{3}{4}$ to 4 in.)

The amounts in each position vary too because they are dependent on individual size. On the whole the fleshy person will need more ease than a bony person. Both fat and muscle need room to move. A large person needs more ease for sitting down than a small person.

The fabric used may provide some ease in which case less is required in the garment. This is why it is essential to be guided by any instructions on the pattern regarding choice of fabric.

## EASING

Easing refers to the manipulation of joining two fabric edges of different lengths. This occurs on a sleeve seam, a sleevehead being fitted to an armhole, and also where a dart is omitted and replaced by extra length in one edge.

There are usually marks on the pattern to indicate where the ease is to lie. These should be marked. Put the two pieces of fabric together and tack as far as these marks, then lift the fabric over the hand so that the longer of the two edges is on top and curving over the underneath one. Tack, but with small stitches, using the point of the needle to draw the ease back into position before making each stitch. The seam should be machined with this side uppermost to prevent the ease from being pressed into little tucks.

## EDGE STITCHING

Machine stitching worked on a fold on the right side. The stitch has a variety of uses from seam neatening and facing neatening, to decorative stitching on collars or pockets. It is important that the stitch should be adjusted until it is exactly the right length for the fabric — try it until it looks right and does not pucker. Edge stitching looks best in matching thread. Tack the edge if necessary but certainly press it. Work the machining with the fabric right side up. If a narrow edge has been turned under, make sure it is underneath and not on top where it can spring up. Stitch exactly beside the fold — so close to it that there would not be room for another row of stitching, and watch the needle as it penetrates the fabric. Do not watch the foot. Stitch slowly, press afterwards.

## EMBROIDERY STITCHES

(See under name of stitch for description and instructions.)

Back stitch — outline stitch
Blanket stitch — loop stitch
Bokhara couching — filling stitch
Bullion stitch — knotted stitch
Cable chain stitch — outline stitch
Cable stitch — outline stitch

Chain stitch — outline stitch or filling stitch
Chained feather stitch — loop stitch
Chevron stitch — flat stitch
Closed feather stitch — flat stitch
Closed herringbone stitch — flat stitch
Closed loop stitch — loop stitch
Coral stitch — outline stitch
Couching — outline stitch
Cretan stitch — loop stitch
Daisy stitch — filling stitch
Detached chain stitch — filling stitch
Double back stitch — flat stitch
Double feather stitch — loop stitch
Double knot stitch — knotted stitch
Feather stitch — loop stitch
Fishbone stitch — flat stitch
Flat stitch
Fly stitch — loop stitch
French knots — knotted stitch
Herringbone stitch — flat stitch
Insertion stitches
Knotted cable chain stitch — outline stitch
Knotted loop stitch — loop stitch
Leaf stitch — flat stitch
Long and short stitch — filling stitch
Loop stitch
Loop stitch with picot — edging stitch
Open chain stitch — outline or filling stitch
Overcast stitch — outline stitch
Raised chain band — composite stitch
Romanian couching — filling stitch
Romanian stitch — filling stitch
Rosette chain stitch — loop stitch
Satin stitch — outline or filling stitch
Seeding — filling stitch
Sheaf stitch — filling stitch
Single satin stitch — outline or filling stitch
Spanish knotted feather stitch — knotted stitch
Spider's web filling — filling stitch
Split stitch — outline stitch
Stem stitch — flat stitch, outline stitch
Straight stitch — filling stitch
Trailing stitch — outline stitch
Trellis couching — filling stitch
Twisted chain stitch — outline stitch or filling stitch
Vandyke stitch — looped stitch
Wheatear stitch — looped stitch
Zig-zag cable chain stitch — outline stitch

## EMBROIDERY THREADS

Some embroidery threads are made specifically for machine embroidery.

Others from thin stranded threads to wide wools can be selected entirely at the sewer's whim. The effect created is all important and unless there will be strain or wear she can select anything. If the article is to be washed the threads must be washable but

amongst those that can be used are wools, silk; Coton à Broder; Anchor stranded cotton (probably the one most used); Anchor pearl cottons in different thicknesses; crochet cotton.

The selection is made according to the background fabric and the particular embroidery technique being employed.

## EMPIRE LINE

The term now refers to any high-waisted style. The bodice is fitted and the attached skirt is usually fairly straight and containing a little fullness gathered or darted into the waist join. The line is continually fashionable in long dresses but it only looks well-balanced in a short dress when hemlines are on the knee or above.

## EVEN BASTING

Basting or tacking stitches that are even in length on the upper side, as opposed to uneven basting and tacking where a smaller stitch, even a back stitch, is used at intervals. Stitches should not be measured, but continued practice using the correct length of thread and with the fingers in the correct position will automatically result in even stitches.

(See *Tacking* for method of working.)

## EXTENDED SHOULDER

A style shoulder line where the armhole seam slopes off the normal set-in line. This seam may be only slightly beyond the shoulder bone and in this case it probably follows a normal line at the underarm.

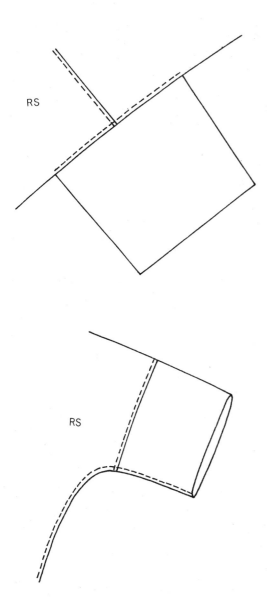

Alternatively the shoulder line may be extended further down the arm, possibly by as much as 10 to 15 cm (4 to 6 in.) and in this case the underarm will probably be low and roomy. In both cases the shape of the top of the sleeve has been adjusted accordingly. In the second style the sleeve would have little or no sleeve head shape.

Stitch the shoulder seams, often a welt or top-stitched seam is suitable, and then join the sleeve head to the armhole, possibly with the same type of seam, and then finally join the underarm seam of the sleeve and garment in one go. This method of adding the sleeve will ensure that you do not insert any

shaping in the sleeve head, shaping that is essential over the shoulder bone with a normal set-in sleeve but which would cause a bulge or bubble in an extended shoulder line.

## EXTENSION FACING

(See *Fold-back Facings*, page 112.)

## EYELET HOLES

Holes made in fabric and stitched. They may be used for the prongs of buckles, for lacing, for threading ribbon, or arranged in patterns for decoration on fine fabrics. If eyelet holes are worked by machine, the instructions in the machine manual should be followed.

To work eyelet holes by hand use a small needle with either sewing thread or embroidery thread in matching or contrasting colour, depending on the effect required.

If they are for decoration through a single or double layer of woven fabric, eyelet holes can be made by pushing a stiletto into the fabric, twisting it, and then quickly working a close neat oversewing stitch all round. Stop half-way round and reshape the hole with the stiletto.

If the eyelets are in a belt, then an actual hole must be punched with a buttonhole punch, or snip the fabric and cut a hole with scissors. Work buttonhole stitch round the hole to neaten the raw edge and take the wear of the prong. The knots of thread must be on the inner edge of the hole.

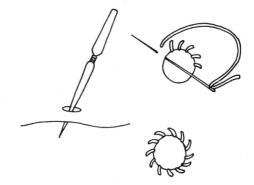

## EYELETS

Metal eyelets in various sizes and colours in addition to brass make a professional finish on any article to be laced. Each eyelet has two pieces, one for the outside of the garment and one for the back that fits into it. The easiest ones to apply are those with a little metal tool included. The tool is hammered into the eyelet to attach.

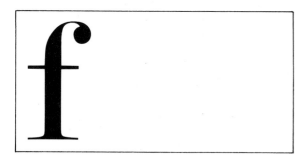

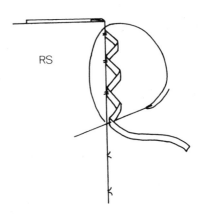

## FABRIC LOOPS

Often called rouleau loops because they are usually
made from a piece of rouleau. These are decorative
and fasten over dome or ball buttons. They can be
used singly at the top of slit openings, spaced down
an overlapping opening, or close together down a
sleeve, front or back bodice opening as a special
feature. Loops do not provide a firm opening unless
they are set in a continuous row. When a single one is
used it will fasten more firmly over the button if the
ends of rouleau are placed on top of each other. Make
trial loops to fit the buttons until the exact length
required is established.

It is best if the loops can be inserted in a seam. If
this is not possible the rouleau may be stitched by
hand to the garment edge, but this method should
not be used where there will be excessive strain in
wear.

To insert a row of loops in a seam it helps to tack
the rouleau to paper that has been marked out in
equal sections. Arrange the rouleau carefully and pin,
then tack straight down each edge of the paper. Place
the paper on the garment edge with the part of the
loop intended for the button facing into the garment.
Tack and then machine through loops, paper and

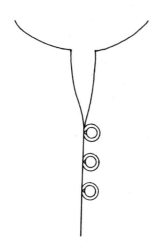

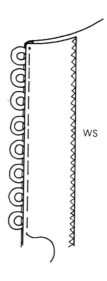

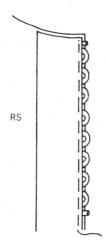

garment. Make sure the machining falls on the seam line of the garment. This may be the centre front or centre back line. Gently tear away the paper and remove all tackings. Place the garment facing right side down on top of the loops. Tack and machine again exactly on the seam allowance. Remove tackings and trim fabric edges but not the loops. Roll the facing to the wrong side so that the loops extend and tack the edge. Finish the edge of the facing.

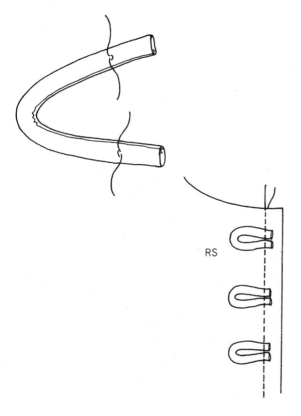

If spaced loops are to be made, cut lengths of rouleau and mark each one carefully with the amount needed to fasten over the button. Place them in position on the right side of the garment, with the loop extending away from the edge and with the 'legs' of the loop together. Machine or back stitch in place and finish with the facing as described for continuous loops.

## FABRIC PREPARATION

Before laying on pattern pieces to cut out, fabric should be pressed to remove fold lines and creases. The centre fold must be pressed out. This is especially important with printed fabrics where the existing lengthwise crease is unlikely to be exactly in the centre of a check, stripe or motif. Often the length will have to be refolded, slightly off-centre, in order to level up the design. With knits and jersey the centre crease is sometimes very difficult to press out. On pale colours a dirty line may remain. If this happens cut out with the fabric completely re-folded, avoiding the centre crease or mark. This may even necessitate cutting one or two pieces of garment with a centre seam instead of a fold.

Woven fabrics made of cotton, silk, viscose, acetate, etc., may be torn off the roll when bought. This ensures that the end of the piece is exactly on the straight grain and this helps when folding it ready to cut out. However, if the fabric is printed in stripes or checks or any other design involving lines of pattern, it is the pattern which must be lined up level when folding the fabric and not the torn end. Although it is important to align the fabric grain to the grain line on each pattern piece, it is more important to have horizontal and vertical lines of design correctly placed on the garment. It often helps to cut these off-grain prints one piece at a time because the error seems to become exaggerated if one long piece if folded in this way. Fold enough for one pattern piece and cut out, refold and cut the next and so on. Sometimes a print goes off grain towards one edge of the fabric only. Try to refold and cut main pieces without including that part, then use it for collars, sleeves, facings or belts.

If the end of the fabric has not been torn it must be straightened. With woven checks, cut the end by the check. With plain fabric and all-over or Jacquard designs the crosswise grain must be found.

Although the warp threads, which run the length of the fabric, are parallel with the selvedge and are therefore straight, the weft threads running across the width may not necessarily be at right angles to them. Sometimes, in finishing, the material is pulled and is then folded and rolled up, holding the weft threads crooked. Sometimes, too, it is cut crookedly in the shop. Straighten the end by lifting up one thread with a pin and easing it out. There is no need to pull the

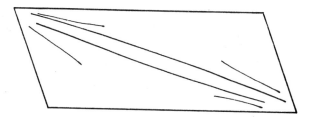

thread right out, if you simply disturb it a little right across it will leave a mark as you will know only too well from accidental snagging.

If the material is badly off grain don't cut off the triangle that appears, you may need it for cutting out a small piece of the garment. Alternatively this piece can be incorporated in the hem. Fold the fabric so that the marker thread is lying level and put in a few pins.

Smooth out the rest of the fabric to see if it will lie flat with the selvedges together. If not, then the weft threads are off-true and you should get someone to help you pull them straight. Open out the fabric and take the two shorter corners opposite. Pull in opposition until the fabric lies flat on the table. Delicate fabrics should be gently pulled.

Pin the end, pin the selvedges and press, to settle the threads in their new position. You will need to use a damp cloth or a steam iron to smooth out the bubbles. Do no use moisture on silk. Do not move fabric while damp.

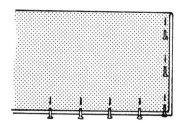

When using jersey or knit fabrics, draw a line across the fabric following a line of knitting using tailor's chalk and a ruler. This can be difficult to see but the fabric is of similar construction to hand knitting. Fold and pin to check that it will lie flat. Some synthetic jersey is almost impossible to straighten by pulling but you can usually ensure a straight grain on each piece of garment by folding the end level and smoothing a small area, lay on a pattern piece and cut, re-line the grain, smooth out and cut another piece, and so on.

## FACINGS

A faced edge is one that is double fabric; the piece of fabric used is the facing. Although the facing may be used on the outside of the edge as a style feature, it is more usual to have it on the wrong side and not visible from the outside.

The edge may need facing in order to attach fastenings or a raw edge may be faced in preference to other methods of finishing such as a hem, binding. If the edge is perfectly straight, e.g. front edge of a blouse, it is more convenient to allow extra fabric when cutting out and simply fold it back to form a facing. This can be referred to as a fold-back facing, joined-on facing, extension facing, etc. When it is folded back the facing edge at top and bottom must follow the garment edge. Facings may be cut separately for a straight edge in order to economise on fabric or because a seam is needed. For example rouleau loops may be inserted; in a coat it may help to stay the edge to have a seam and it also means the interfacing can be held firmly.

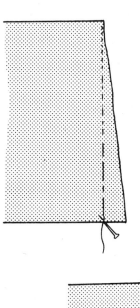

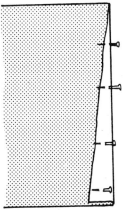

If the edge is shaped, for example neckline or arm-hole, a separate piece of fabric is used, with one edge cut to the same shape as the garment edge. This is referred to as a shaped facing. This usually has to be cut in more than one piece in order to make sure the grain is running in the same direction as on the garment. If this is not done it may bubble when applied and it can easily work its way out in wear and become visible at the edge.

The width of a facing is determined by the position on the garment. It should be wide enough to ensure that it lies flat inside the garment — narrow facings easily roll out of position. The loose edge of the facing may run parallel with the garment edge or it may be better to extend it at some point so that it can be caught in a seam, or even so that it combines with another facing nearby. (See *Neck and Armhole Facings*, page 113.) The facing on a blouse may have to be wide enough to take buttons and buttonholes at one point but wider than that at the neckline if it is to be worn open or turned back. Here the facing edge is shaped outwards and then continued so that it reaches as far as the shoulder seam. Avoid points and corners on the outer edges; they will curl up in wear. If the garment edge consists of several separate shapes it is best to cut the edge of the facing straight. The outer edge of the facing should be neatened by the method being used on the seam edges. If the fabric is bulky a lighter fabric such as lining, fine cotton, nylon jersey, can be used for the facings to reduce bulk.

In many instances interfacing will be required between the garment and the facing. Choose the correct type for the fabric and the position. Inter-facing pieces should be narrower than the facings so that they are covered. See *Interfacing*.)

### Cutting facings

A facing piece can be cut to fit any edge, even after garment seams have been made. It is not necessary to cut a paper pattern, the facing shape can be marked directly onto folded fabric, using tailor's chalk. A neckline is used as an illustration but the instructions apply to all facings.

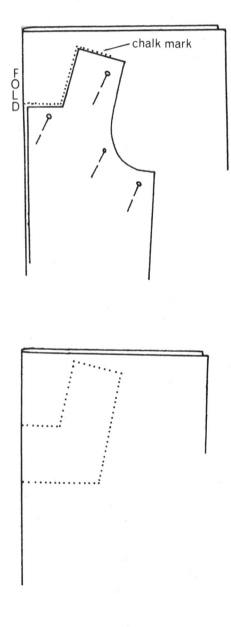

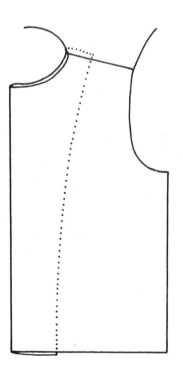

When cutting a facing using the main pattern pieces, lay each pattern on fabric, following grain lines, and fold instructions. Pin. Use tailor's chalk to mark round the neckline, and for a short distance down the centre front and centre back edge, and along the shoulder edges. Remove the pattern. Chalk lines to complete the facing shape, parallel with the neckline edge, making the facing between 4 and 6 cm ($1\frac{5}{8}$ to $2\frac{3}{8}$ in.) in width. Check that folds, seam positions, etc., are correct, then cut out.

When using a joined up garment as a guide to cutting facings, fold it in half at the centre front, pinning together round to the shoulder seam. Place this on to folded fabric making sure the straight grain of the garment lies on the straight grain of the fabric. Place the fold against the fabric fold. Pin down, holding the remainder of the garment out of the way. Chalk round the neckline of the garment and also draw a line level with the shoulder seam. Unpin the garment. Draw in the missing facing edge making the width between 4 and 6 cm ($1\frac{5}{8}$ to $2\frac{3}{8}$ in.). Add a seam allowance at the shoulder — the original chalk line was taken from the garment seamline in this case. Repeat with the back and front garment then cut out.

### Attaching and finishing facings

Most faced edges require to be kept in shape in wear and will need reinforcing.

Begin by attatching a suitable type of iron-on or sew-in interfacing to the garment edge. The facing pattern may be used to cut the correct shape of interfacing pieces but remember to trim at least 5 mm ($\frac{1}{4}$ in.) from the outer edge to ensure that the interfacing will be covered by the facing when it is in place. Also, if the facing pattern is in several pieces in order to preserve the correct grain line on the pattern, but non-woven interfacing such as Vilene is being used, it will be possible to combine the pattern pieces and cut the interfacing in one piece without any joins. Never attach interfacing to a facing, it makes it stiff and inclined to pop out of the garment in wear. It is the garment edge that needs stabilising.

Make sure the seam line is marked on the garment. It is not necessary to mark the facing pieces. Join and finish garment seams but do not join the facing pieces. Sometimes one seam will be left open, for example where zip is to be fitted.

Arrange the garment edge on the table, right side up, as flat as possible but without stretching it. Take each facing piece and place it right side down on top, matching the shaped edges, matching centres etc. Very shaped areas such as necklines and armholes are easier to handle if they are lifted onto the sleeve board.

The illustrations that follow show a neckline but the method is the same for all edges.

Insert a few pins across the seam line to hold the facing to the garment, use them also on a long or complicated edge. Tack from the facing side approxi-

mately on the seam line but stop the tacking well short of the ends of the facings. Fold back the meeting ends of the facings where joins are to be made, and press. The joins in a facing will often correspond with a seam in the garment so make sure they are pressed to meet exactly over the seam beneath. Use the toe of the iron to press and take care not to press on any pins or on the right side of the garment. There are two methods of dealing with these joins. The first is for firm woven fabrics: lift the two facing ends and, holding them together and upright, pin exactly on the crease. Repeat with all facing joins. Stitch the joins. This can usually be done by putting the join under the machine, lowering the foot and the needle,

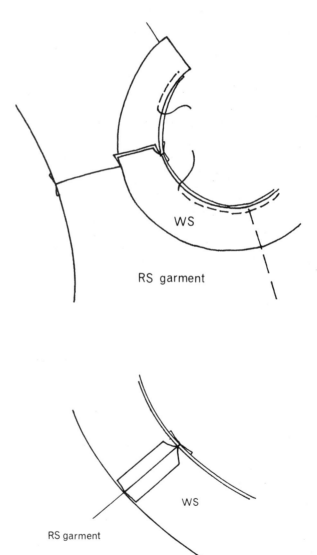

then removing the pins and stitching the seam in the crease mark. If the fabric is slippery or difficult to handle, tack the joins and remove the pins before machining. For total accuracy stitch the joins starting from the garment edge and working to the outer edge of the facing.

Use the next method if the facing ends are on the cross or if the fabric is jersey, lacy knit, twill weave, or if it is a different material from the garment, e.g. lining fabric.

After pressing the creases so that they meet trim the edges to 3 mm ($\frac{1}{8}$ in.) and angle the ends. Insert a couple of pins across the facing, into the garment. Keep them well clear of the seam line. Continue with attaching the facing as described in the following paragraphs. Remove the pins after the facing has been rolled into position on the wrong side of the garment, slip stitch the folded edges of facing together to finish.

Remove tacking and press the joins open. Trim the raw edges down to 3 mm ($\frac{1}{8}$ in.). On bulky fabrics trim the ends at an angle.

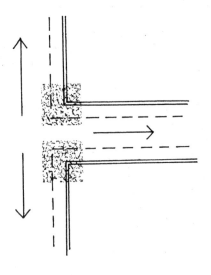

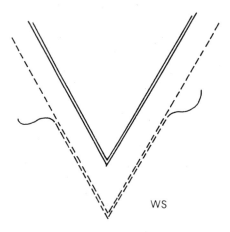

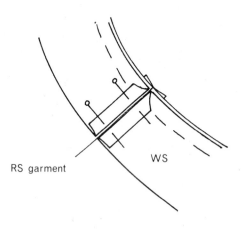

RS garment                    WS

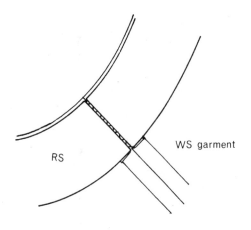

RS                    WS garment

Note that if there is an opening, either zipped, bound, or faced, it is usually best to complete that before attaching the facing, including putting in the zip.

Attach the facing to the garment by machining with the garment uppermost so that the marked fitting line may be followed.

The following points should be noted when working on shaped edges that are not simply smooth continuous lines.

If there is an angle to be stitched and therefore trimmed close to the stitching later, press a small square of Bondaweb over the corner on the garment before stitching. This will prevent fraying. Also, begin stitching at the angle, lowering the needle precisely into the corner, and stitching outwards. To complete, return to the angle and stitch outwards again. Do not overlap the stitching lines, but if the two rows do not meet accurately when completed, stitch round the whole angle again for a few centimetres.

If the fabric frays badly, or if it is a very open lacy fabric, use a smaller stitch at the angles.

If the faced edge also incorporates a slit opening cut the facing to include it and continue the stitching up both sides of the slit. An accurate slit can be made by pressing a piece of Fold-a-Band to the wrong side of the garment then the edges can be used as a stitching guide. The Fold-a-Band is also an interfacing for the slit.

If the slit opening comes at the top of a seam do not join the facing pieces at the bottom of the slit but attach with two separate rows of stitching. Start at the base of the opening on each side and make sure the first machine stitch exactly meets the last stitch

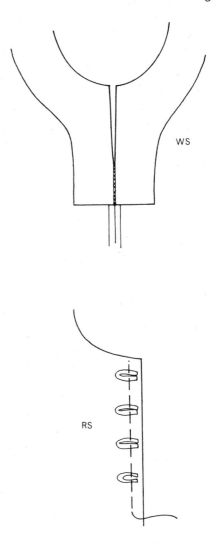

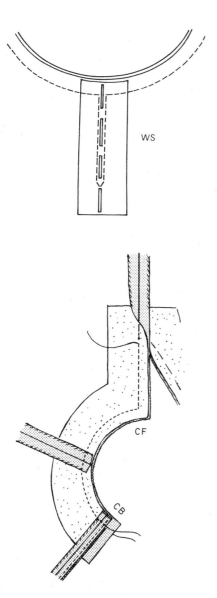

of the seam of the garment. The interfacing or Fold-a-Band should extend slightly below the base of the opening so that it remains firm in wear. The easiest way to complete the facing join is to press the edges under and slip stitch them together by hand, after the facing is completely attached.

If any ties, loops, braid, piping etc., are to be attached to a faced edge see if they can be tacked in place on the right side of the garment before the facing is attached then the facing will hold them firmly and neatly in position. Note that the additional feature must be placed facing inwards from the shaped edge and the interfacing must be in position on the under side. If the fabric or the additional feature is either springy, slippery or particularly thick, it is safest to machine it in place on the right side of the garment and then attach the facing as usual.

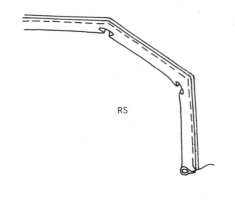

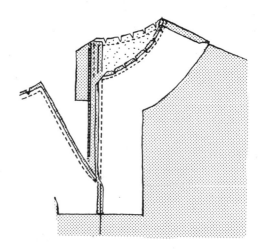

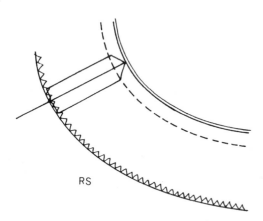

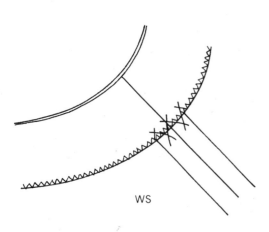

After machining the facing to the garment, trim the outer edge neatly so that it is a regular width all round and fraying fibres are removed. Neaten the edge by a method suitable for the fabric. This will probably be the method used on the garment seams. Press the neatening and also the facing stitching previously done.

Trim down the turnings. The precise amount of trimming will depend on the type and thickness of the fabric but cut away as much as possible. Leave the garment edge slightly wider than the facing edge to avoid a ridge. Snip these trimmed and layered turnings.

Make angled snips at intervals of 5 mm ($\frac{1}{4}$ in.) or less to within 1 mm ($\frac{1}{16}$ in.) of the machine stitching. The more acute the shape of the edge the closer the snips must be. It should not be necessary to clip out any fabric if the trimming and layering has been properly done, except at outward angled corners.

Place the work on the sleeve board and run the toe of the iron under the facing between the facing and the garment. Use either a steam iron or cover the toe of a dry iron with a damp muslin. Push the iron against the join all round.

Next, holding the garment with wrong side towards you, roll the facing over and keep rolling the edge with the fingers of both hands until the join appears at the edge. Roll the join so that it is very slightly to the inside of the garment and insert a couple of small tacking stitches. Roll the next part, tack, and so on. The stitches should penetrate the layered turnings otherwise the edge will bulge out and the join will move out of position. Do not, however, stitch too close to the edge or the facing will not stay in place. Press this edge well from the wrong side until the edge is flat and thin. As with all pressing use a damp cloth and have the iron hotter than usual.

Press sharply, otherwise both tacking and iron imprints may result.

Do not understitch the edge. This is the process where the facing is extended beyond the garment and a row of machining is worked through facing and turnings to keep them flat. This can only result in the facing becoming rigid from this extra stitching, it is then heavier than the garment and so it will spring out of place in wear. Correct manipulation, tacking and pressing of all edges produces the best results.

Arrange the entire facing in position and work a row of diagonal basting all round to hold it to the garment. Leave this area until the garment is complete then return to it and finish by working two or three herringbone stitches over the edge wherever the facing crosses a seam or a double area of fabric. Also slip a few small pieces of Wundaweb between facing and garment and press. This will hold the facing down out of sight.

If top stitching is required, possibly to match up other stitching on the garment, it is worked after the edge is complete. The stitching should not be regarded as a way of holding the facing in place instead of tacking and pressing.

Remove all the tackings before the final press.

### All-in-one facing

A facing is usually quite a narrow piece of fabric, just wide enough to settle inside the garment and remain there. Sometimes there may be two areas fairly close together requiring a facing and in this case one facing can be cut to cover the entire area. It must not cover any shaped areas of the garment or restrict movement in any way. The outer edge will as usual follow the shape of the edges to be faced, the free area should be curved so that edges are on the bias and therefore less likely to show a ridge through to the right side. The illustration shows an example of a design requiring this type of facing with the area shaded.

The best way of finishing this type is to sew the last edge by hand, rather than to try to sew it as a tube and turn it through.

(See *Neck and Armhole Facings.*)

### Decorative facing

A shaped facing may be attached so that it is visible on the outside of the garment. Contrasting fabric may be used. When finished the faced area may have braid applied to emphasise it as a style feature or it may be decorated in some other way, for example quilting.

Attach the interfacing to the outside of the garment. Apply the facing in the same way as for a wrong-side finish but place the facing pieces right side down on the inside of the garment. After stitching and trimming, the edge should be rolled so that the join is not visible from the outside. Tack, and press well, then work basting along the centre of the facing to hold it to the garment. The outer edge of the facing has to be stitched to the garment so an accurate even width must be marked. Use an adjustable marker and tack or chalk, with tailor's chalk or chalk pencil,

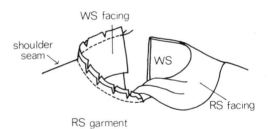

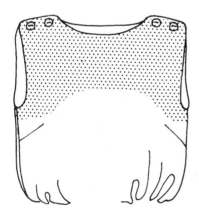

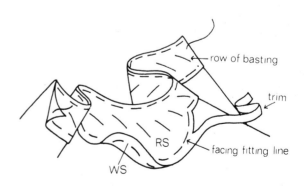

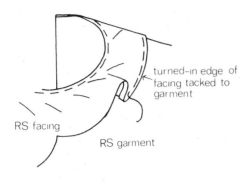

turned-in edge of
facing tacked to
garment

RS facing

RS garment

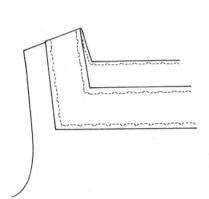

to include loops, interfacing, etc, or to introduce a different fabric for the facing. The garment is interfaced to the cut edge of the opening. The seam at this edge can be eliminated provided there is sufficient fabric, by pinning the pattern pieces together, matching the seam lines, but overlapping the seam allowances. The facing is then referred to as the fold-back type. The interfacing is still attached to the garment.

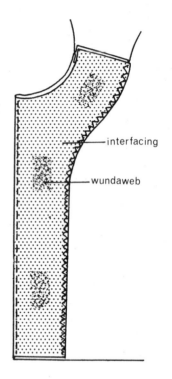

interfacing

wundaweb

on the facing, measuring evenly from the finished edge. If the edge is to be turned under trim it down to 5 mm ($\frac{1}{4}$ in.) beyond the marked line, turn it under and tack and press carefully. Then trim off a little more of the raw edge before tacking it to the garment.

Choose a method of finishing that is suitable for the garment and the fabric. Use a straight or zig-zag or decorative machine stitch. Use a large straight stitch in double thread or top stitching thread, or even slip-stitch it by hand working just under the edge. If braid is applied or if a satin stitch is used, the facing edge can be trimmed and tacked flat and the finish will cover the raw edge.

### Fold-back facings

A straight edge requiring a facing may have a separate piece of fabric joined on. The reasons for this include economy of fabric, the necessity for a seam in order

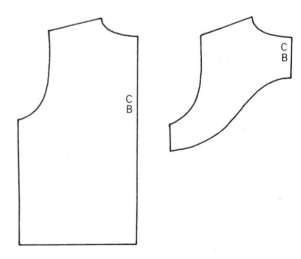

C
B

C
B

In medium and heavy fabrics it should stop at the fold line or a little beyond; in fine fabrics it may be extended to cover the facing section but only if this does not result in that area of garment being altered too much in handling or appearance.

(See *Interfacing*, page 162, for more detail.)

The free edge of a fold-back facing should be neatened in the usual way, or, in a lined garment, the lining overlaps the edge. The facing may be held in place against the garment by inserting a few pieces of Wundaweb beneath and pressing. The outer, folded, edge of the facing may be edge-stitched when complete in the same way as an attached facing.

### Neck-and-armhole facing

Also called a combined facing this is used to finish a garment with a collarless neckline and sleeveless arm-hole. The following method of attaching produces a good result with no risk of the facing becoming visible in wear. It also provides for the shoulder seams to be fitted and finished correctly before the facing is attached.

The illustration shows the pattern piece of the garment back bodice and the corresponding shape of the one-piece neck and armhole facing for it. If this shape of facing is not provided in the paper pattern it can easily be cut by following the outline of the main pieces. Place on double fabric and cut, treating back and front alike.

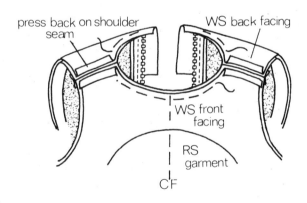

Interface the neckline of the garment in the usual way, or, if the entire neck and shoulder area requires interfacing in order to support it, then interface to the same shape as the facing but slightly smaller so that it will not be visible.

Join garment shoulder seams and press but do not neaten. Insert zip, if there is one — an alternative is a short slit opening made using the centre back edges of the facing.

Place the front facing to the neckline, right sides together; tack round the neck from shoulder to shoulder. Place the back neck facings in position and tack.

Make shoulder joins in the facing by pressing the turnings back so that the creases meet then lift the two edges and join the creases. Press open, and trim the raw edges.

Machine round the neck on the fitting line.. Trim, snip and roll the facing to the wrong side, then tack the edge and press. Smooth the facing out on the

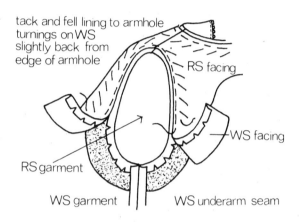

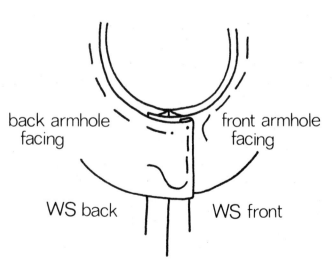

dress on the wrong side and baste all round the neck and armholes. Do not bring the basting too near the armhole edges.

Working from the right side, turn in the armhole edges and tack, snipping as you tack to enable the turnings to lie flat. Trim the edge down a little, then press.

Trim a little of the raw edge of the facing. Turn in the edge of the facing, snipping where necessary, so that the edge is 2 mm ($\frac{1}{8}$ in.) back from the armhole edge. At the underarm, let the front part lie flat, and turn under the back section and tack; then press.

Finish by felling all round, taking the needle through the turnings and interfacing only, not through to the garment layer. Neaten the outer edge of the facing. Hold this loose edge of facing down by hemming where it crosses the side seam, or place small pieces of Wundaweb at intervals all round between the facing and the garment; then press.

**Shaped facing**
A piece of fabric attached to a shaped edge, such as a neckline. The facing has one edge cut to the same shape as the garment edge. The outer edge is often parallel with it although this edge will be less likely to be visible through the main fabric if angled corners are trimmed to curves. If a particularly intricate shaped edge is required, such as scallops, then the edges of both garment and facing are cut straight until after the two have been stitched together. This eliminates any possibility of stretching or overhandling the area.

(See *Facings* and *Attached Facings.*)

## FAGOTTING

Joining two finished edges with an embroidery stitch.
(See *Insertion Stitches.*)

## FAILLE

This is also called facing ribbon. A decorative firm and serviceable ribbon in plain weave, finely ribbed. It is now usually made from triacetate ('Tricel') and most commonly found in cardigans as a backing for the buttons and buttonholes. It should be shrink resistant when purchased. It can be used for stabilising seams in knit fabrics.

## FALL

Fall has two meanings, the most usual being that part of the collar that folds down at the back and shoulders of a classic tailored coat collar. The depth of fall should always be sufficient to cover the neck join.

Secondly the word is used to describe the way in which the fabric of a full garment hangs, for example the 'fall' of a skirt.

## FAN PLEATS

A series of pleats starting at nothing at the top and widening to fan shape at the hem of a skirt. A separate piece of fabric is cut and pleated (there may be only one or two pleats of the Sunray type) and inserted into a seam. The insertion may run the whole length of the skirt or it may be smaller to create interest near the hemline.

## FASTENING STITCH

A stitch used at the end of a row to fasten off and prevent the stitches coming undone. In hand sewing the fastening stitch consists of two back stitches worked over each other, or, for more strength, three or four stitches. In machining reverse for two or three stitches. Alternatively, some machines have a lock-stitch device that can be employed to fasten off.

## FASTENINGS

The fastening on a garment may form a decorative feature in which case it should be chosen carefully to blend or contrast depending on the effect required. If a fastening is only functional choose the least obtrusive type that is efficient. Consider also comfort (avoid dome buttons down a back opening); stability (buttons and thread loops often come undone); strength (the waist takes a lot of strain); convenience (can back fastenings be easily reached); frequency of use (trouser openings must be strong but easily undone). The following list refers to the features of various fastenings. Often one main type can be used with a secondary back-up fastening for strength.

*Buttons*  Strong, visible, wide choice of types. Choice of functional or decorative, plain or contrast. Dome type tends to wobble. Strongest fastening is made with the buttonhole running in the direction of strain e.g. horizontally on cuffs, waistbands. Use vertical buttonholes only on looser clothes, e.g. shirt.
*Hooks*  Strong, choice of size to suit position, should not be visible. Hooks with bars or loops are stable; with eyes they move.
*Press studs*  Firm but will not take excessive strain Choice of size to suit position. Plastic studs flatter but fiddly to fasten.
*Velcro*  Strong; no movement; easy to use; excellent for disabled or handicapped. Adjustable. Three widths available, the medium width in a wide choice of colours. Easily cut to any size and shape, easy to sew on. Must use sufficient length for strain at the point it is used. May be too bulky for some fabrics.
*Ties*  Ties in fabric, cord etc., move in wear but are decorative, cheap, easy to apply.
*Fabric loops and buttons*  Decorative: suitable for a limited number of positions.

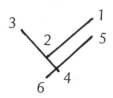

*Frogs* Very decorative; not strong, inclined to move in wear.

## FEATHER STITCH

A wide embroidery stitch worked in lines. The needle and thread are brought to the surface of the work, the needle inserted to the right of this first stitch, then a small angled stitch taken to the centre, while the thread is held down by the thumb. The next stitch is taken to the right and so on, with the thread always under the needle, and the stitches and the angle of the needle always identical.

## FELLING

Felling is rather like hemming stitch, but is stronger and deeper and less visible. It is used for attaching linings. Work from right to left inserting the needle fairly deeply into the cloth but not through to the right side. It should be virtually invisible. A good felling stitch is worked no more than 2 mm ($\frac{1}{8}$ in.) apart. Leave the thread slightly loose to avoid puckering then press with the toe of the iron to cover the stitches with the lining.

## FICHU

The term used to describe any softly draped or folded fabric added to a plain neckline. It may also extend down the centre front of a blouse or dress. It may be detachable, and is usually made from contrasting fabric except in the case of some sculptured evening dresses.

## FINDINGS

The additional items needed to make a coat such as canvas, linen, tape, wadding.

## FISHBONE STITCH

A flat embroidery stitch worked with diagonal stitches. The needle is drawn from the outside of the shape to be filled, into the centre. It is sometimes useful to draw a line down the centre of the shape as a guide. Open fishbone stitch is worked in the same way, but slightly wider apart.

## FITTING

This is probably the biggest single problem encountered by the largest number of people. Many people lament at having no-one around to fit them but the truth of it probably is that unless that person is extremely expert you may be better off on your own. At least you know your own problems and it is not difficult to look at problems in the back area by observing in the mirror from the side.

**Remember the following rules**
Fit only one problem at a time. Never try to fit the whole thing at one go because often an adjustment will affect another part.

If you know you have a problem alter the pattern, and then, at fitting, solve that problem first.

Good fit is more a matter of shaping than of violent taking-in or letting-out.

Do not fit a problem area too closely or it will tend to emphasise it.

It is often best to alter only one side of a seam, i.e. back or front of the garment, not both together by equal amounts.

Every garment should hang from the top, even if it is shaped to fit closely at some point lower down. Often an adjustment at the top will cure problems lower down.

Vertical folds are usually the result of excess width, though not necessarily to be removed at the sides.

Horizontal folds indicate excess length. Go to the top and lift the garment.

Horizontal creases indicate tightness so the nearest

seam should be let out.

A well-fitting garment is more comfortable than one that is ill-fitting. Check each area for comfort before altering it.

If you know you have a particular problem make sure the seams are marked; it makes the adjustment easier to judge.

Take account not only of your way of life in general, but also of the particular purpose the garment is intended for.

Try moving before finally deciding on the amount of an alteration.

Try on the garment as many times as necessary; on the whole, the more problems there are, the more frequently the garment will need to be tried on.

Look at darts, or other shaping, and adjust if necessary.

Next look at horizontal folds (excess length) and correct by lifting.

Then look at horizontal pairs of features such as armholes, hips, and make sure each piece of the garment is smooth and not being lifted out of line. If it is is it allowed to drop, from the top.

Next look at seams, starting with those running down or across the body and afterwards looking at side seams.

### Darts

At the point of a dart a bulge of fabric appears and, in order to make the garment fit, it has to fall over a bulge of the body. The bulge of fabric has to be the right size. It can be increased by widening the base of the dart. Conversely a reduction is achieved at the other end of a dart and this helps with fitting a waist etc., but do not increase the width of a dart only to achieve a tighter fit unless the increase is also needed at the point of the dart. Two smaller darts will provide a more general shape than one large one.

Use darts or the equivalent, such as gathers, to provide shaping for the bust, shoulder blades, stomach, elbows, bottom and make sure they run in the correct direction, over the bulge. Darts can be moved, shortened or lengthened without difficulty; if they are too long they restrict movement. In general, if there is a figure problem, it can be fitted provided there is a dart or a shaped seam at that point. This includes all the common figure problems such as large bust, prominent bust, large hips, plump arms, round back, sloping or square shoulders.

### Seams

Seams are essential for good fitting as they provide more gentle shaping over a longer distance than darts. Take in or let out seams as necessary even creating new ones where needed for fitting, for example, the centre back of a skirt on a hollow-backed figure. Make sure seams run straight on the part of the body, for example, vertically on a skirt, along the top of the shoulder on a bodice.

### Dress fitting

| | |
|---|---|
| *Problem* | Tight neck or armhole. |
| *Solution* | Snip raw edges to release tension, If that is not enough, mark a new lower seam line. |

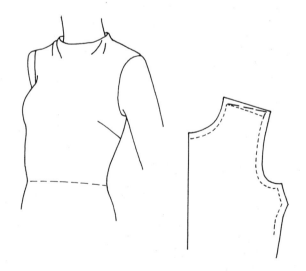

| | |
|---|---|
| *Problem* | Neckline stands away and folds below. |
| *Solution* | Release shoulder seam and let it out at the armhole end. |

*Problem* Neckline stands away and gapes — usually only occurs with low necks.

*Solution* Lift at front shoulder seam. Lower dart point if necessary.

*Problem* Folds across skirt below waist.

*Solution* Undo the side seam from below armhole and let out until dress hangs smoothly.

*Problem* Fold across back bodice.

*Solution* Undo shoulder seams and lift the whole back. Pin out a pleat on the pattern, place on the back and re-cut to give new shoulder, armhole and neck.

*Problem* Front opening does not meet, or folds appear running from side seam.

*Solution* Undo shoulder seam and let it down at armhole end. Lift dress at front neck and mark new lower neckline. If possible make base of bust dart smaller.

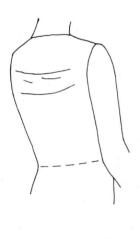

*Problem*    Folds below bust dart.
*Solution*    Undo dart and part of side seam. Lift shoulder a little, re-pin a bigger dart and pin the side seam to take out the surplus fabric.

*Problem*    Baggy below bottom.
*Solution*    Raise skirt at waist at back only and pin.

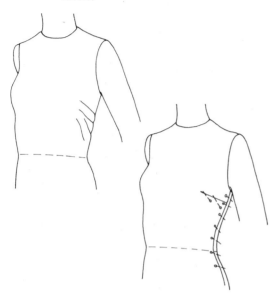

*Problem*    Low waist.
*Solution*    Put waist fitting aid round waist and re-mark waistline. Remove and tack skirt to new waistline. Try on again.

*Problem*    Gaping armhole.
*Solution*    Undo dart and pin out a bigger dart, making sure it runs towards the bust. Lift shoulder seam at armhole.

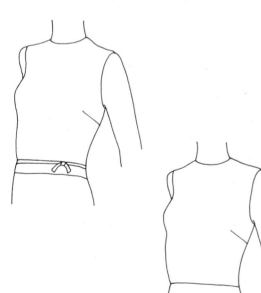

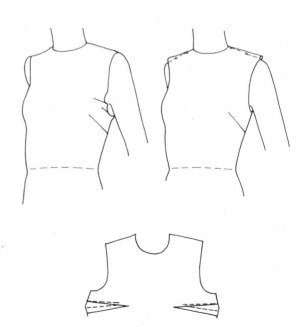

*Problem* Shoulder seam lies towards front of shoulder.
*Solution* Undo shoulder seam and release front seam allowance only.

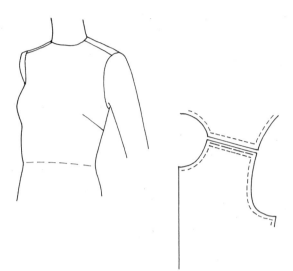

### Skirt fitting

*Problem* Folds across back below waist.
*Solution* Lift back skirt, using fitting aid to hold it up. Re-mark back waistline. Check length of darts if any, and lengthen after lifting skirt. It will also help to take in the centre back seam below the waist, if there is a seam.

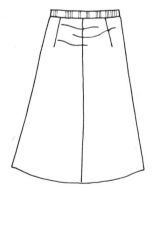

*Problem* Baggy folds under bottom.
*Solution* Drop skirt at front waist and raise it at the back. It may also help to let out the side seams above the hip.

*Problem* Side seams swing towards the front.
*Solution* As above, lift back and drop front at waist.

*Problem* Side seams swing towards back.
*Solution* Let down back waist and raise at front.

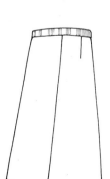
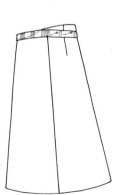

**Sleeve fitting**

*Problem*   Folds across sleeve below the top.
*Solution*   Mark a new fitting line below the existing one, over the sleeve head.

*Problem*   Sleeve hangs towards front or back producing folds at front or back of sleeve.
*Solution*   Remove sleeve and turning in the seam allowance, pin it to the armhole making sure there are no folds and ensuring that the vertical and horizontal grains are correct.

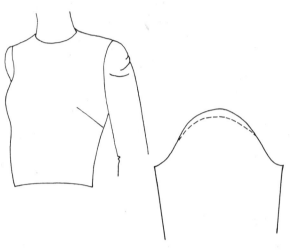

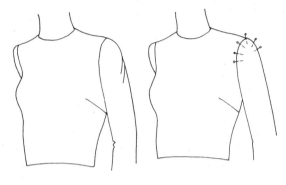

*Problem*   Lateral creases across the sleeve at upper arm or below elbow indicating tightness.
*Solution*   Release the sleeve seam and let it out.

*Problem*   Folds on each side of sleeve, running down to underarm.
*Solution*   Re-mark seam allowance at underarm of sleeve.

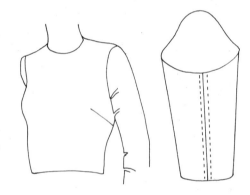

*Problem*   Sleeve pulls at back armhole.
*Solution*   Unpick seam and let out seam allowance on bodice and sleeve.

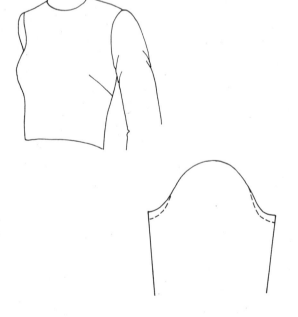

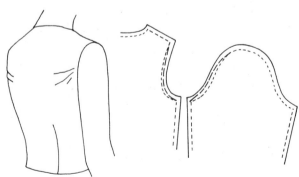

**Trouser fitting**

*Problem*   Trousers are tight at waist or hip, or leg. Creases appear where shown.

*Solution*   Unpick the area of seam and release. Re-pin at waist and over hip. If more ease is needed undo the inside leg seam and let it go from crutch half-way to knee. Taper adjustments into original seam.

*Problem*   Trousers tight below waist. Creases as shown on stomach.

*Solution*   Release darts and reduce width and length, or in some cases dispense with them totally. Also unpick the side seams and release. Re-pin.

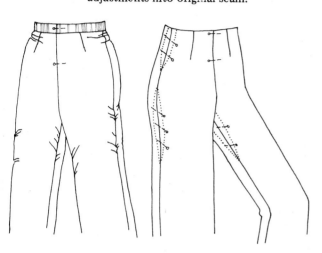

*Problem*   Trousers are loose at waist, hip or leg. Creases appear where shown on leg, and trousers stand away at waist.

*Solution*   Take up excess fabric at side and pin to run into original seam lower down. Alternatively, for a large bottom, make the dart a little bigger and longer. Pin out excess at hip and lower leg area on outside seam. If that is insufficient pin out at inside leg from crutch down to just above knee.

*Problem*   Trousers too high at waist. Horizontal folds may appear below waist level, or, trousers may stand above the waist, or if loose, crutch may be too low. Trousers too long.

*Solution*   Unpick the darts and side seams and smooth the trousers up. Replace the petersham fitting aid and pin new darts and new side seams to fit.

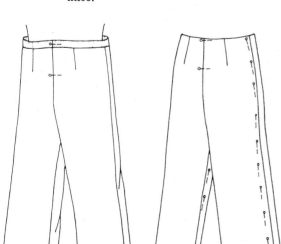

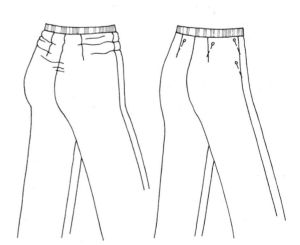

*Problem*  Trousers tight over stomach or crutch.
*Solution*  Unpin centre seam and let it out. Also shorten darts. Release inside leg seam from crutch to mid-thigh. It might also be necessary to lower the crutch curve slightly.

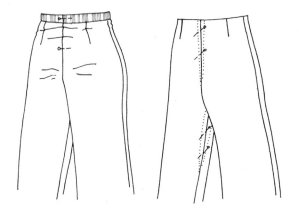

*Problem*  Tight across bottom. Creases appear as shown.
*Solution*  Release the inside leg seam from crutch to above knee. Undo back crutch seam and side seam over hip, re-pin.

*Problem*  Baggy folds below bottom and loose legs.
*Solution*  Take off and re-tack a new crutch seam scooped out below the bottom as shown. Put trousers on and lift more at the waist, take in back crutch seam to compensate. It may also be necessary to take some out of the inside leg seam.

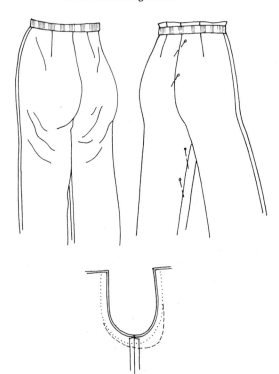

*Problem*  Vertical folds beside front seam, below waist level.
*Solution*  Undo the front seam and darts and smooth out fabric to pin out the front seam.

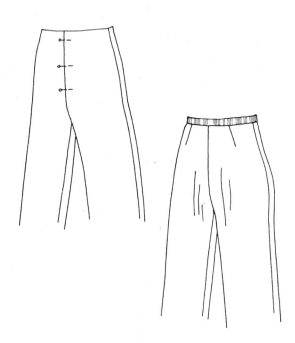

## Waist fitting

Establishing the correct position and fit of a waistline is not easy. Although, as with all fitting, comfort for the wearer is the prime consideration, good appearance and balance must be considered. Trousers or a skirt may be fitted carefully and quite often during early construction and yet still, once the waistband is attached, wrinkles and discomfort appear. Avoid this by always attaching the waist fitting aid or at least passing it round over the garment at each fitting even if other areas only are being adjusted. If a waistband is to be attached eventually, the width of it will affect the fit and comfort of the garment, particularly if it is fairly wide. In this case prepare the waistband and have it ready to put round at each fitting. If a petersham is to be attached, the top of the skirt or trousers is usually finally lower on the body so consider this too when fitting in the early stages. The waist of a dress is easier to fit as the garment should be hung from the shoulders and the fit does not rely solely on the waist.

*Skirt*   Complete all seams, pleats, etc., but not the hem or the zip. Put on the skirt and pin the opening. If possible this should be at the left side to leave the centre back seam as a fitting point if necessary. A back zip emphasises any problem such as a hollow back and adds a rigid line which prevents the back

Skirt: waist fitting

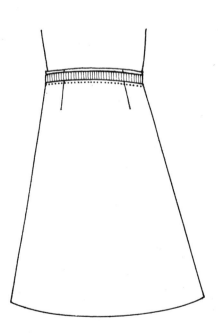

from responding to any pressing to shrink fullness away. It also draws unnecessary attention to the back. Sometimes style features prevent the zip from being placed in the side, in which case consider the centre front or even a panel seam before deciding to put a zip in the back.

Put the waist-fitting aid round the waist over the skirt and fasten it. Smooth out the skirt. Make sure there are no excessive amounts of skirt ease under the petersham aid. If there are it means the skirt is too big and it should be taken in before going further.

When satisfied with the appearance of the skirt from all round, mark the waistline. Mark with tailor's chalk along the top of the petersham if a petersham finish is to be applied or the bottom if a waist band is to be applied. Use pins only if the chalk does not show up on the fabric.

Remove the skirt and inset the zip with the slider at the waist mark. Tack the waistband or petersham to the skirt in the correct position and try on to check it before finishing.

*Dress without waist join*   If a waist level is marked on the pattern it is best to transfer this to the dress when cutting out as it acts as a guide. Also note any extra length allowed in the design for blousing above the waist. The shoulder seams should be tacked only at this stage.

Put the dress on, pin any opening, put the waist-fitting aid round. Distribute any fullness if the style is straight or full. Ensure centre front and centre back markings are central and side seams are in position.

On a fitted style the waist marking should fall under the fitting aid. If it does not, first see if the dress needs raising or lowering at the shoulders at either back, front or both to put the waistline in position. Lifting the back at the shoulder is nearly always the solution to a droopy back waistline as it has the effect of shortening the entire back of the dress. If the waistline rises above the fitting aid at the front, perhaps due to a large bust or very upright posture, this may be cured by letting the dress drop through letting it down at the front shoulder.

If the style is straight and full and bloused, arrange the dress so that the marked waist lies beneath the fitting aid. Look at the amount of blousing all round. If the fold produced is too deep, pull the skirt down evenly all round, or at front or back only to improve the appearance.

Finally, when satisfied, mark the waistline. Remember that a little ease for movement is needed between waist and underarm on fitted dresses, a lot is needed with low armholes or dropped shoulders. Provided the fitting aid is fastened firmly the true waist lies along the bottom edge. Mark with chalk. Use pins only if chalk does not show. Remove dress, run a row of tacking round the mark as a guide for attaching a stay or elastic inside.

*Dress with waist join*    The waist must be fitted so that the join follows the natural waist. If the back bodice is too long or if the figure is hollow backed, folds will be visible above or below the waist or both. Those above are removed by lifting the dress at the shoulder seams; those below by undoing the waist join and lifting more skirt into that seam.

At the front, if the bodice is too long, a fold will be visible below the bust. Lifting the shoulders may correct this on a small or high-busted figure. Otherwise undo the waist seam and take more bodice into it.

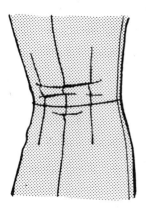

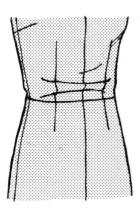

If the waist seam is too high either let down the shoulders or let out the bodice at the waist join.

Whilst attending to the waist level remember that the join must be in a position that is comfortable. The large-busted or short-waisted person is often happier with a slightly lower, looser waist. The small-busted slim figure usually prefers a higher tight waistline. Also remember that if an uneven waist, often the result of a hollow back, is fitted too well it will emphasise the figure imperfection. It may be best to make a more level waistline and then let out the dress a little for comfort. Remove the fitting aid and see how the dress looks. If a belt is to be worn with the dress, put it on to see the effect before finishing the waist join. If an elastic waist stay is inserted in the join do not make it too tight — the effect will be to raise the level of the waist join.

*Dress with gathered or pleated skirt*    Fit the waist of the bodice on its own by putting it on and adjusting the fitting line at the waist to the natural waist. Use the fitting aid as a guide for this. Mark a new waistline if necessary along the lower edge of the fitting aid. Take the bodice off, add the skirt and try on again to check before making the join.

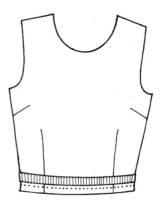

**Waist fitting aid**

It helps with fitting to keep a piece of curved petersham which, when fastened round the waist, fits. This can be put round the waist over a dress or skirt, the lower edge settling the waist line. Use tailor's chalk and mark the waist on the garment. The petersham is also used to hold up a skirt or trousers while fitting adjustments are made. It is also useful as a guide for cutting waistbands the correct length to fit, instead of using the paper pattern.

The waist marker in the illustration has Velcro attached as a fastener.

**Figure problems**

Any of the above fitting faults may crop up in the fitting of any garment even if the pattern was adjusted; even if it was correct in all aspects and required no adjustments. Even if there are no known figure problems, fitting is still essential because patterns and fabrics vary so much. So, in addition to these, the following figure problems will create the following fitting faults, which have to be corrected.

*Bust: fuller or smaller than average*    If the bulge of fabric is insufficient for the bust, the dart must be made a little wider at the base. If there is too much shaping and the bust is not filling it, the dart should be made smaller at the base.

The point of the dart may be raised or lowered so that it is on the same level as the bust point. To do this, undo the tacking almost to the base of the dart and re-pin, coming to a point at the correct position. If the dart point has to be moved more than about 1.3 cm ($\frac{1}{2}$ in.) then undo the whole dart and a section of the side seam and re-pin from a new base, higher or lower, whichever is required.

*Waist darts of bodice: thick waist, fleshy underarm*

Front darts should run up under the bust but not too close to it. On a short-waisted or low-busted figure they may look better fairly short. On a thick-waisted figure, reduce the width of the dart at the base. Waist darts should only be made wider at the base for the figure with a full bust and small waist.

Back waist darts should run up to the widest part of the back. On a thick-waisted figure or one that is full under the arm and across the back these darts should be quite short.

*Shoulder darts: round back, round back neck, widely spaced protruding shoulder blades*    A pattern will normally provide a dart in the back neck or in the shoulder seam. Sometimes, however, instead of a dart the back seam has to be eased onto the front. This produced a general shaping which may not provide the shaping or the comfort needed especially by those with the figure features mentioned. Place the dart where it is most needed.

Examine the back carefully, looking for pockets of material. With a severely round back or back neck it

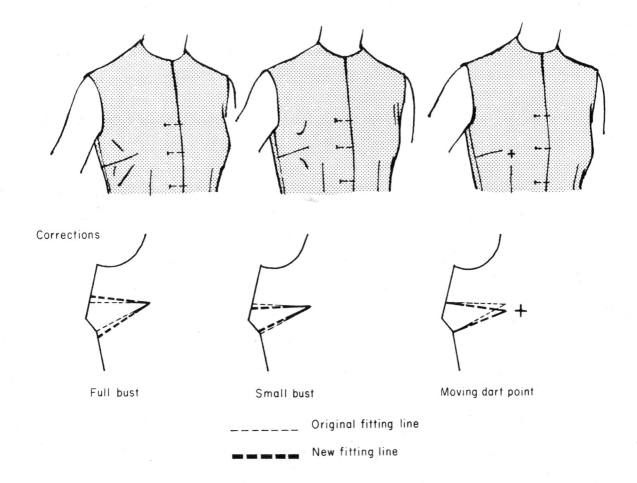

Corrections

Full bust      Small bust      Moving dart point

– – – – – – Original fitting line

━ ━ ━ ━ ━ New fitting line

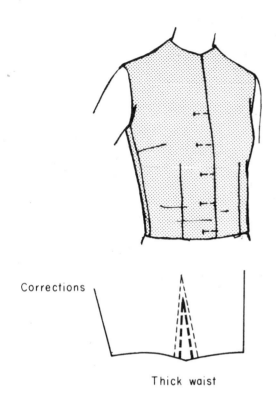

Corrections

Thick waist

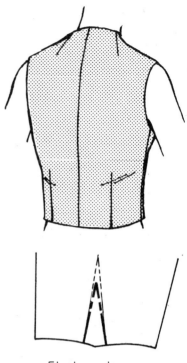

Fleshy underarm

may be better to move the dart into the neckline. For a figure that is flat at the centre of the back but has wide-apart bony shoulder blades (often goes with square shoulders) put the dart along and into the shoulder seam.

To move the dart, undo the tacking, smooth the fabric over that area and pick the surplus fold up in the position required, pinning to a point. It is important to move the arms when testing this particular area as these darts should also provide for ease of movement. Tightness can indicate that the darts are not in the best position for the figure.

Shoulder darts

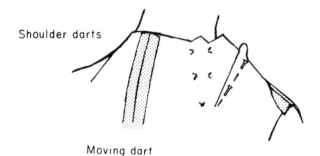

Moving dart

*Front skirt darts: high stomach, thick waist, small waist with large hips*   If the skirt seems tight over the stomach but there are pockets of fabric below, shorten darts at the same time making them smaller at the base.

*Elbow shaping: slim arms, long arms*   Elbow shaping in long or three-quarter length sleeves is provided either by ease or slight gathering or by a dart. If it is too wide at the base the sleeve will appear to be drawn up, if too high or too low, the back of the dress will feel tight and uncomfortable. Check the position by bending the arm to see where the dart settles with the arm in this position. Alter length, width and position if necessary.

*Centre back seam: round back, hollow back, small waist, narrow back*   The centre back seam on a bodice and skirt pattern is usually straight but it can be shaped to accommodate figure problems. If it is to be cut to a fold, but there is a known figure problem, add a seam. The seam can be shaped in at the neck and waist.

The seam can also be flared slightly at the hem. For a back that is narrow across the shoulder blades, take in the back seam all the way down to avoid altering the grain line, and then let out the side seams to compensate.

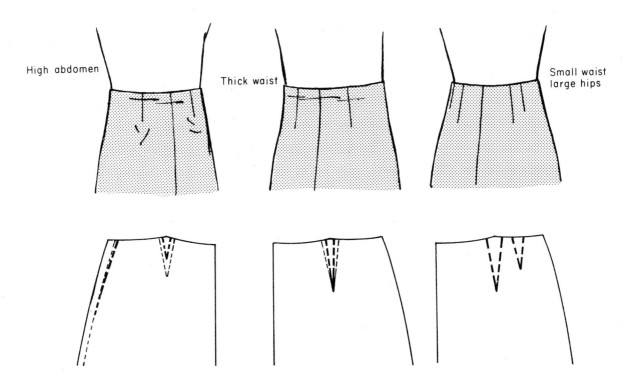

High abdomen

Thick waist

Small waist
large hips

*Side seams: thick waist, small waist, narrow back, large rib cage* These should be fitted as closely as the wearer can tolerate. The exact amount of ease needed will depend on the fabric being used and also on the size of the person, but a bodice that is too loose will present problems with setting in the sleeve and in wear it will be uncomfortable.

For a thick waist let out the seams; for a small waist, take them in, sloping from the armhole.

For a narrow back, release the seam and take in

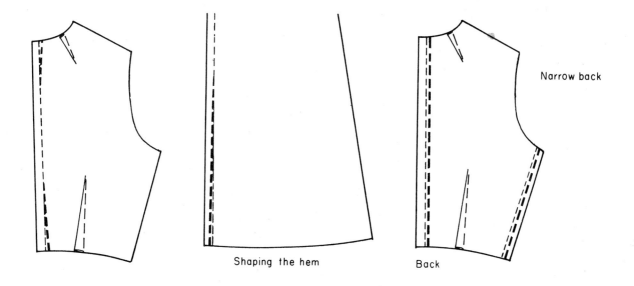

Narrow back

Shaping the hem

Back

the back only, remarking the armhole line. A few women have a large rib cage or diaphram which necessitates letting out the front only.

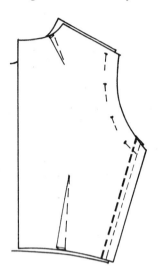

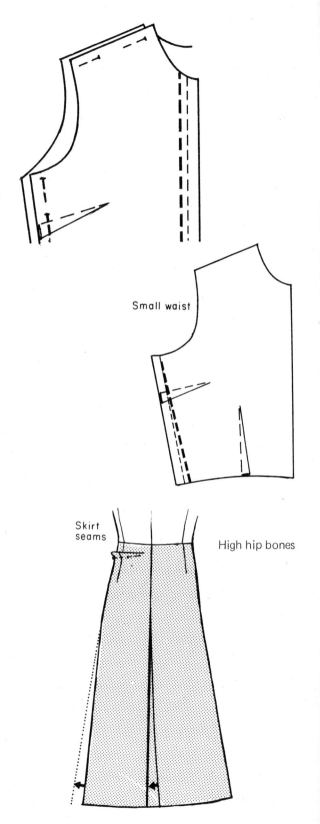

Small waist

*Centre front seam: broad chest, narrow chest, hollow chest, slim neck*　Many patterns are cut with the centre front to a fold and this makes it difficult to correct these problems. Any style with a seam or front fastening is easily adjusted.

Release the tacking and re-pin. If you are taking it in above the armhole, you will have to pin out an even amount right down the seam or the grain of the fabric will be distorted. It may also be necessary to undo the shoulders and move the whole bodice inwards towards the neck. Re-pin the shoulders. The surplus turnings at the neck and armhole should not be trimmed off until the new neckline and armhole lines have been marked.

On the small waisted figure the seam can be taken in below the bust.

Skirt seams

High hip bones

Front

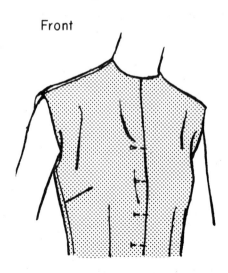

*Skirt waist: high hip bones*    If the skirt appears tight from the waist down to the hips, lift the whole skirt by pinning out a fold right round the waist. Then re-cut the waist line.

*Arm: plump, muscular, small wrist*    Fit the sleeve seam by slipping it onto the arm, anchor with a few pins over the top and bend the arm. It should feel comfortable but there should be no surplus width. Fit it more tightly in a jersey fabric than a woven one.

Even if the pattern has been altered to allow for a plump top arm it may be necessary to let the seam out still further above the elbow.

For a muscular lower arm, straighten the seam slightly from elbow to wrist.

For a small wrist, slope the seam in for the bottom part of the seam.

Finally, make sure the hand will slip through the wrist easily if there is no opening.

*Shoulders: sloping, square*    Folds of fabric will appear either sloping down towards the armhole and under it, or near the neckline.

For sloping shoulders, the shoulder seam should be lifted, usually on both back and front at the armhole edge, but not at the neck. Having done this you may find it necessary to take a little out of the centre back seam. The front is usually unaffected because the shoulder bone protrudes and supports the fabric.

For square shoulders, release the shoulder seam at outer edge, leaving joined at neck edge and re-pin, raising the seam at the armhole edge and also taking a little off at the neck.

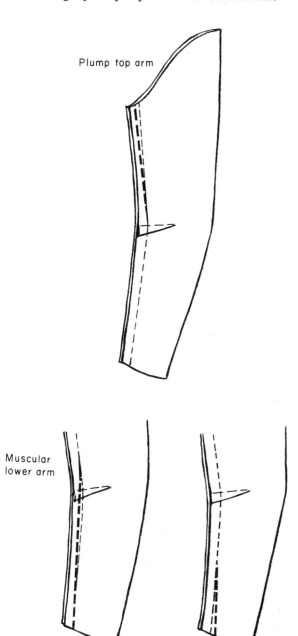

Plump top arm

Muscular lower arm

Small wrist

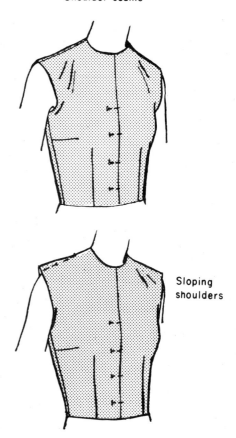

Shoulder seams

Sloping shoulders

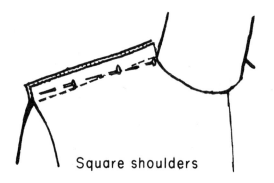

Square shoulders

*Neckline: sloping or upright neck, forward posture*
Someone with a slim upright neck will probably want the neckline higher and tighter than someone with a broad based short neck; some people with a protruding top vertebra like a low neck at the back that won't cut across it. Very often too, it is not the centre front or centre back that is too low but simply that the neckline needs to be higher at the sides.

Examine the figure from the side, some necks slope forward and therefore the front neckline only needs lowering a little but the back remains the same or even needs raising a little. A very upright figure with shoulders held back can produce a neckline that is too wide at the back but pulling at the sides. In this case release the shoulder seams a little and take in the centre back seam.

If the dress 'rides up and chokes you' it is not a matter of altering the neckline itself but either the front is too long or the back is too short. Let down the front shoulder seam. Also, if the bust darts are

too long or if the dress is tight across the chest this will make the riding up that much worse. The clearest way to see this problem is to put on a dress that does this, stand normally and ask someone to unpick a shoulder seam and lift the front up higher but let the back down, so creating a gap at the shoulder seam. Pin extra paper or fabric in here, take the dress off and it will be clear which section needs adding to, and which needs shortening in future, before cutting out.

## FITTING LINE

The line on the piece of fabric on which the seam is to be stitched. On single-size printed patterns the fitting line is usually marked. The fitting lines should be marked on the fabric after cutting out using tailor tacks, carbon paper, etc. When the garment has been tacked up, matching the fitting lines, it is tried on. At this stage the fitting lines may have to be adjusted and re-marked in order to make the garment fit.

## FLARE

The description for a type of shaped fullness that results from using a piece of fabric that is basically triangular. An example is a flared skirt. This is made from triangles that are trimmed at the top to a waist. curve and at the bottom to a hemline. The skirt is said to flare because the hemline is much wider than the waist size. There are degrees of flare: A-line is slight; full flare is what it says, it may even be almost circular.

## FLASH BASTING

Flash-basting is upright basting but with a back stitch worked horizontally at each stitch. It is stronger than

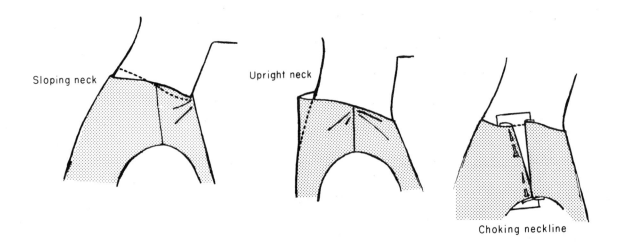

Sloping neck     Upright neck     Choking neckline

basting, and is used for joining linings to seam turnings, and in other places where two inside edges require joining.

## FLAT BINDING

(See *Bound Edges.*)

## FLAT STITCH

An embroidery stitch worked in the same way as fishbone stitch, but stitches overlap at the centre of of the shape being worked. In this case two lines may be drawn as guidelines for stitch length.

(See also *Fishbone Stitch.*)

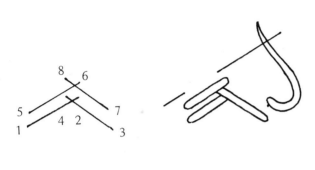

## FLEECE

(See *Lambswool.*)

## FLOUNCE

The term used to describe a piece added to the hem or sleeves of a garment. The flounce may be flared or gathered in order to add width at the hemline and create movement. Obviously soft fabrics add the most movement. Flounces are used in profusion on dance-dresses both modern and traditional.

## FLUTING

Also called lettuce edging, this is a way of finishing the edge of fine jersey fabric. The fabric is stretched while stitching so it flutes and results in a decorative edge. Suitable for full sleeves, frills, dress hems.

Use a normal sewing thread and set the machine to a small close zig-zag stitch — almost satin stitch. Trim the garment edge so that there is only 3 to 5 mm ($\frac{1}{8}$ to $\frac{1}{4}$ in.) surplus fabric. Place the edge under the machine right side up, folding under the surplus. Lower the foot and stitch so that the needle clears the fold when it moves to the right. Work a little way and then take hold of the hem as it emerges at the back of the foot.

Pull the fabric at the front as it goes under the foot and also hold it at the back. The amount you stretch it will depend on the type of fabric being used. After stitching use the points of small scissors to trim off the raw edge close to the stitching on the wrong side. Do not press.

This finish will also work on fine fabrics cut on the cross.

It is an excellent hem finish if short of fabric or when it may be very difficult to get a really level hemline on the garment.

RS

## FLY-RUNNING STITCH

A simple short stitch worked through a single layer of fabric. A very small amount of fabric is picked up on the needle so the threads on the surface are longer than the gaps between. Used where long rows of gathering are needed, for example in smocking. Begin at the right and hold the needle with the point on the surface of the fabric, weave the needle rapidly in and out while moving forward, holding the fabric taut with the left hand. Hold the right hand with palm slightly up and the thumb upper-most on the needle, this brings the needle closer to the fabric. When the needle is full of even wrinkles of fabric take the point and pull it through. Repeat until the end of the line.

It is important to use a thread of sufficient length for the area.

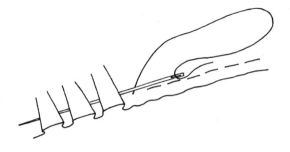

## FLY STITCH

A basic fly stitch for embroidery consists of one stitch taken from left to right with the thread looped at the centre by a small downwards stitch. The stitch can be worked singly in horizontal rows or joined vertically in a number of variations.

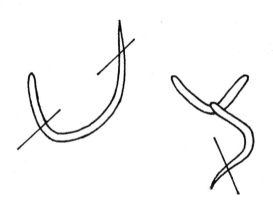

## FOLD-A-BAND

An iron-on strip of non-woven material. It is used as an interfacing in belts, cuffs, straps, waistbands and many other places. The strip is precisely 6 cm (2⅜ in.) wide but down the centre is a row of oblong perforations. This makes it excellent as a guide for marking the centre of the perforations, the fabric folds very easily on these perforations so eliminating some tacking and measuring. Fold-a-Band is made in two weights the heavier one for waistbands. Both are sold in pre-packs containing instructions for application.

## FOREARM SEAM

If a sleeve is cut in two pieces as on a man's coat, and sometimes on well-cut women's coats, there are two seams. The one that falls at the front of the coat is the forearm seam.

## FOREPART

The name given to the front section of a coat or jacket in men's tailoring.

## FORK

The point on trousers where the inside leg seams and the crutch seam meet.

## FRAY

The term used to describe threads of woven fabrics that drop off cut edges or are caused to come away by the handling they are receiving. When buying fabric look to see if it frays easily. It is not possible completely to avoid these fabrics but they should be avoided by beginners and it helps to be aware of the problem of fraying before cutting out.

Most woven fabrics containing shiny or slippery yarns will fray easily as will loosely woven fabrics. Either cut out allowing a wide seam allowance or prepare to have to apply Fray Check fluid especially on edges that are to be extensively handled.

## FRENCH KNOTS

A much used knotted embroidery stitch for making dots, seeds, etc. The needle is brought through at the point where the knot is required and the thread twisted round the needle before the needle is inserted again close to its original position. As the thread is pulled through the knot will appear close to the fabric.

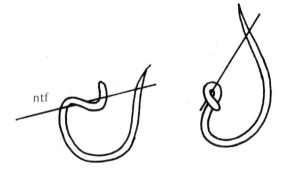

The thread is twisted around the needle

## FRENCH TACK

A bar of threads running between two pieces of fabric. It is used where pieces need joining but where they have to be able to move independently. These places include anchoring a skirt lining to a skirt, a coat lining to a coat and holding back a wide cuff.

Use double thread, lightly waxed, start with a knot in the heavier fabric. The two layers should be pinned together about 1 cm ($\frac{3}{8}$ in.) from the point of the tack; the best place for the tack is at a seam. Lift the top layer and take a stitch through it. Work four stitches across the two layers, putting them close together as a bar, and leaving them loose. The length of a tack is between 3 and 5 mm ($\frac{1}{8}$ to $\frac{1}{4}$ in.) depending on the probable movement at that point. Cover the threads with close loop stitch or buttonhole stitch.

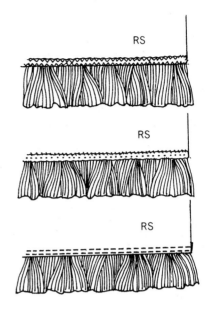

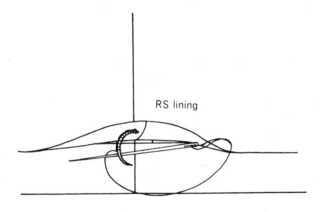

RS lining

## FRINGES

A fringe can be of any strands of any yarn of any length and either added to an edge or enclosed in a seam.

Fringeing bought by the metre can be expensive. It should complement the garment in texture and therefore hang as well as in colour. Plain white cotton fringeing can easily be dyed.

### Attaching to an edge
This is done by placing the finished beaded edge of the fringe over the garment edge (if the latter is single, zig-zag it first), then set the machine to a zig-zag stitch of a size suitable for the type of fringe and stitch. A variety of stitches are possible and they may be worked so that they fall partly over the beaded edge, or entirely within it. If two parallel rows are needed, work both in the same direction. Do not sew right to the end but turn under and hand sew the last 3 mm ($\frac{1}{8}$ in.) of fringe, hemming across the end as well. If the end of the fabric is a raw edge to be joined to another part then machine the entire length of fringe.

When attaching to a difficult fabric, e.g. velvet, or a very bulky one, sew the fringe by hand, felling over the edge then prick stitching through the centre a short distance away from it.

When using silky fringe apply two rows on top of each other for additional luxury.

An alternative method of attaching that can be used if the edge of the fringe is unattractive is to turn under the edge of the fabric and lay it over the fringe, treating it as an overlaid seam.

### Inserted in a seam
To do this, machine the fringe to the right side of one piece of fabric. Place the second piece on the top right side down, tack and machine the seam. Treat this as similar to a piped seam, making sure the first row of stitching is accurate and then using that as a guide for the second.

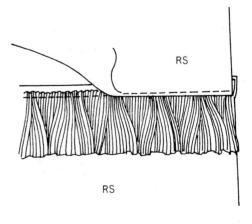

## Making a fringe

A fringe can be made from lengths of cut wool, or from strands taken from the fabric; fringeing can be bought ready made up. A long silky fringe looks more luxurious if a double row is applied.

## Fringe in a seam

Lay lengths of yarn on the right side of the fabric and place the other piece of fabric right side down. Tack and machine. Work two rows of stitching to prevent the fringe from falling out. Fold the fabric over and tack and press. Trim the fringe.

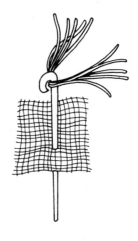

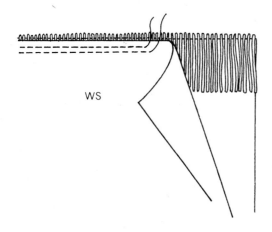

## Knotted fringe

Apply this to a finished edge; it is usually successful only on woven fabrics where a hole is easily made between the threads. Use a small crochet hook to pass bundles of yarns through the edge of the fabric. Pull the ends of the yarn through the loop and pull the knot tight.

## Fringed fabric

Woven fabrics can be unravelled to produce a fringe. Prevent further unravelling by working a small zig-zag stitch over the edge in a perfectly matching thread.

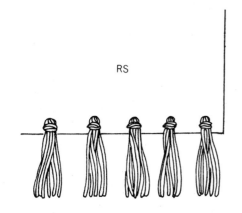

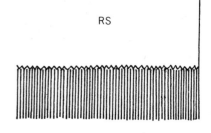

## FROG FASTENINGS

A frog is a loop made from cord or rouleau and fastened over a toggle, an oblong button or a ball button. The frog is usually of a looped design, one on each side of an edge-to-edge or an overlapping opening. It is necessary to try out a design to obtain the correct size for the garment and also for the thickness of cord being used. Draw the design on paper and make enough copies for the number of frogs to be made. Tack the cord to the paper over the design. Where the cord crosses, stitch together firmly then remove the tackings to detach the paper.

Place the frogs in position on the garment and stitch through the centre with a few stab stitches. If thin cord has been used the remainder of the frog may be slip-stitched from the right side. If this is difficult turn the garment over and use back stitch, feeling the cord beneath, and sewing through the fabric and into the cord.

The button is sewn on one side in the section of the frog nearest to the opening.

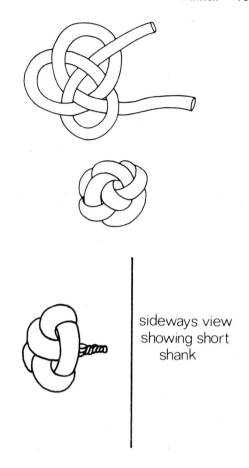

sideways view
showing short
shank

 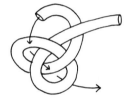

## FUNTEX

A non-woven craft felt made by Vilene and sold in pre-packs containing a number of pieces in different colours. It can be used for all the usual felt uses. It does not fray, it is washable and in addition it can be attached by using Bondaweb.

## GATHERING THREADS

To draw up excess fabric to make it fit a shorter edge, a thread is inserted. Gathering threads are used on frills, ruffles, yokes, but never where fabric is only being eased. Gathers are visible and decorative, whereas ease is only slight excess to be added for movement or comfort. Examples of both are: insert a gathering thread in a sleeve head that is deliberately full and high and gathered as a feature, but never insert a gathering thread in a plain set-in sleeve head.

When fabrics were more limited in range and lacked finish, two or even three rows of thread were inserted, squashing the area into place. Now, however, nearly all fabrics have finishes which make them springy and resilient so flat, even tubes of fabric are difficult to achieve. The answer is to use only one gathering thread, inserted on the fitting line or 1 mm ($\frac{1}{16}$ in.) above it. The fabric is then wrinkled at one point only, left to spring up on either side. It is much easier to achieve an even gathering like this.

### Gathering by machine

This is the quickest method and produces the most even results. Set the machine to a long straight stitch. Insert the fabric with the right side up. Lower the foot and reverse to fasten the thread. Stitch forwards to the end and take out the fabric. Leave the thread ends here but at the start of the row snip them off. It is the underneath or spool thread that must be pulled up, not the top thread.

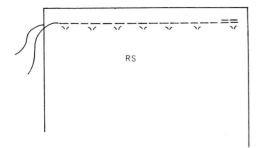

RS

### Gathering by hand

Insert threads by hand if only a very short area is to be gathered or if hand preparation is part of the process, e.g. smocking.

Thread a needle with sewing thread (or Machine Embroidery thread no. 3 on very fine fabrics and if little strain is to be exerted on it, e.g. several rows for smocking), measuring the length of thread against the length of the fabric. Put a knot in the end and work fly-running, leaving the thread free at the end. (See *Fly-Running Stitch*.)

After pulling up gathering threads wind the end round a pin to hold it, then even out the gathers along the row before pinning and tacking to another piece of fabric. Work with the gathered area uppermost the whole time.

## GAUCHO

Goucho pants are flared trousers coming to below the knee, or just covering the tops of boots. They are plain and masculine with patch pockets and leather or matching belt, and the style lends itself well to firm plain cloth such as flannel, camel-cloth, tweed, as well as to suede and suede fabric.

(See also *Culottes*.)

## GAUGING

Gauging is visible gathering, used as decoration, usually in short sections, often decorating an entire area, e.g. yoke.

Work several parallel rows of large machining, using synthetic thread (such as Coats' Drima) for strength. The distance between the rows will depend upon the thickness and design of the fabric and the size of the area of gauging. Work all rows of stitching, pin each end to a piece of tape or fabric the correct size and pull up the threads by grasping all the spool thread ends together. Fasten off all the ends by sewing them in on the wrong side. To prevent stretching or breaking, cut a piece of fabric or lining material the length of the gauged section plus turnings, hem the top and bottom edges, turn in the two ends and place wrong side down onto the back of the gauging. Hem in place across the two ends.

If an entire area is gauged the thread ends will be enclosed in seams later.

## GIMP

Gimp is a thick, silk-covered, wiry thread used for putting in hand-worked buttonholes in coats. (See *Tailored Buttonholes*, page 51, for instructions on use.)

## GIMP NEEDLE

A big needle with a round eye large enough to take gimp.

## GLOSS

Shiny or smooth areas that develop on woollens, worsteds and fabrics containing mostly wool fibre. The gloss is caused by the iron and it can be removed by pressing very lightly over a very damp pressing cloth folded double. Remove the cloth and brush the surface of the fabric gently. Allow to cool before moving.

## GODET

A flared insertion piece, usually triangular in shape, but possibly with a curved lower edge. They are used as style features singly or in series in skirts, sleeves, hip length jackets, etc. The feature is very popular in Twenties and Thirties styles.

The godet may be inserted in the base of a seam or the fabric is cut to the depth of the triangle. Insert as an angled seam or an overlaid seam.

## GOOSE

A heavy tailoring iron. It can be heated by gas or electricity, or it can be a flat iron. Before electricity was commonly used they were heated by gas or, like a flat iron, on a stove.

## GORGE

In a collar and rever or lapel the gorge line is the seam running between the lapel and collar. On a tailored garment this seam is stitched by hand from the outside, with the edges of lapel top and collar turned in to meet each other in a gentle curve that lies on top of the seam underneath.

## GRADING

(See *Layer*.)

## GRAIN

The grain is a straight yarn on woven fabric. All main pieces of a garment should have the warp threads, or grain, running the length of the piece. These threads are stronger and more stable than those running across the fabric. The exceptions to this occur when a design on the fabric has to take precedence. Small pieces of a garment, such as collars and cuffs, may safely be cut across the fabric.

Grain, or straight grain, on a pattern piece is marked with a long arrow. This arrow should be placed exactly on a lengthwise or warp thread of the fabric. The position of this straight grain is determined by the designer according to the effect wanted.

To cut something 'on the straight grain' means to cut it with the warp grain running down the centre. (See also *Bias*, page 26, which is a line on the fabric between warp and weft.)

Knit fabrics have no grain strictly speaking but the straight grain arrows should be placed parallel with the selvedge of the fabric.

## GUSSET

A gusset is a small section of fabric inserted in a seam to provide more room for movement than is provided by the overall shape. The gusset is usually triangular or diamond shaped. Examples of gusset use include under the arm of a fitted kimono sleeve to prevent splitting the seam when the arm is raised, and in French-style knickers and camiknickers to provide space between the flared legs.

There is usually strain on the gusset in wear and so they are often double. The inner fabric could be lining or lawn for instance, to reduce bulk.

There are two main methods of inserting a gusset. The first is to place the gusset and garment edges right sides together and join the edges, taking a very narrow seam. It can produce a poor result if the needle is left in at the corners to pivot round to the next edge, so treat it as an angled seam, working the three or four seams separately. Use a piece of Bondaweb at the corners of the garment if it is likely to fray. The second method is much easier. Turn in the edges of the gusset and press. Place it on to the outside of the garment, wrong side down. Tack in place. Attach either by working a row of machining on the edge of the gusset or, on outer garments, slip stitch invisibly. If a backing is applied, turn in and press the edges, place it on the wrong side of the attached gusset, tack and hem round the edge.

## HAIRCLOTH LAPTAIR

This mixture of cotton and horsehair is available in various weights according to the cloth being used. In tailoring it is used for supporting the chest and front edge of coats and jackets.

## HALF BACK STITCH

A smaller, neater, stronger stitch than back stitch, worked in a similar way to prick stitch but larger. Use half back stitch where machining would normally be used but where, in order to manipulate the process, it is better to stitch by hand, for example setting in sleeves. It is also useful for short lengths of stitching that are easier to reach by hand than by machine. If a strong seam is needed as on a trouser crutch seam, or sewing in sleeves, use the thread double and wax it first.

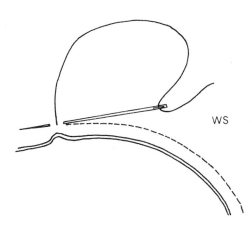

Work from right to left taking a small stitch forward. Pass the needle half way back to the previous point, take a stitch forward. Pass the needle halfway back and so on. Pull the thread fairly tight to embed it in the fabric. Fasten off very strongly at the end of the piece of thread. Always work from the side that will be most often seen as it is neater than the underside. Press well.

## HALTER

The neckline of a dress or top held up to the neck with a band or straps, passing round the back. The styles are many and varied but the feature common to them all is that the entire arm and shoulder is bare.

## HAM

A firm padded cushion, oval in shape, a ham is inserted under the bust or chest areas when pressing. They vary in size for different purposes. Tailors' hams are covered with linen or wool and filled with sawdust.

## HAND SEWING

Very little can be made successfully without some hand sewing, although with the development of versatile sewing machines it can be greatly reduced. Often the amount of hand sewing can be adapted to personal preference. Most people, after learning the correct techniques and equipment, find hand sewing extremely satisfying and enjoyable, even relaxing. These people will always hand sew a hem, the inside of a waist band, the step of a collar, etc., where it is good for the finished effect. A few people never feel at ease with hand sewing and they are the ones who will keep it to a minimum and substitute machine processes instead. However, it is as well to remember that time and again it is the odd tip that makes it all come right, and also if any skill remains unused for a long period not only are these tips forgotten but so are many of the basic movements.

The three kinds of hand sewing involve temporary stitches, permanent stitches and embroidery stitches.

**Temporary stitches**
These include tailor tacking and tacking or basting. A fairly large needle may be used as the stitches are large, although the needle must not leave holes in the fabric. Also, if the needle does not penetrate the fabric easily, a smaller size must be used. Usually a no. 5 or 6 will be suitable. Always use tacking or basting thread, for example Anchor, as it is soft and fluffy. Ordinary sewing thread is strong and shiny and may damage the fabric. Use a long piece, single for tacking but pulled through double for tailor tacks. Make a knot in the end of single threads and fasten off with a back stitch. These stitches are removed after the permanent stitching has been done.

If possible have the fabric on a wooden surface. Arrange the layers flat and stitch by inserting the needle, pushing the fabric onto the point and at the same time using the wooden surface to bounce off the needle point. Swivel the work to turn it rather than lift it. The reason for this is that it is at this early stage that edges can become stretched and once two layers are tacked together the work can safely be lifted in order to machine or fit. There are times when the fabric must be lifted, for example when easing a longer edge on to a shorter one, but only that part should be lifted, leaving the bulk of the weight of fabric on the table while the stitching is done.

Use a thimble for speed and comfort, keep the hand rather above the table than resting on it, and if you stand up and bend over you will be more comfortable and work faster.

### Permanent stitches

These stitches should remain in place for the life of the garment and so must be as small as the fabric allows. They should also be neat and even-sized for your own satisfaction. Results are often better if several areas of the garment are tacked simultaneously because a relaxed rhythm can be built up and also the thread becomes more even, so producing more uniform stitches.

Use normal sewing thread, the same as used for machining the garment, start with a knot except on very fine fabrics, and finish off each piece of thread really well.

There are a number of things to remember, all of which combine to make hand sewing not the daunting task that some people feel it to be.

Use the smallest Between needle that you can; it will slide into the fabric much more easily than a large one. A size 8 or 9 will suit most fabrics. If you find the stitching the least bit hard going change to a smaller needle.

Use short pieces of thread, even though you have to stop and re-thread the needle more often. Long pieces tangle easily and they also suffer wear as you constantly pull the entire piece through with each stitch. In addition once you have settled down to sew, the head and shoulders should not move too far out of position. A short thread ensures that only the hand and forearm moves with each stitch, a long thread means moving the whole arm out, which moves the shoulder, which in turn lifts the head. It takes time to bend over and re-settle and to focus on the stitching again. It is that sort of movement that destroys the rhythm and causes stitches to be uneven. It is also terribly slow.

Sit down comfortably. Either sit with the work in your lap and bend over or have it on a table, not too high, and bring the part to be sewn towards you. Never lean back and never hold work in mid-air. The work rests on lap or table, your elbows rest on your hips or thighs as you sit, and your hands rest on the work in a perfectly relaxed way. Your fingers manipulate the fabric and needle.

Always prepare by tacking and also pressing the part to be stitched. Afterwards, remove the tackings gently, using a bodkin and pulling on the knot. Then press again to embed the stitches in the fabric and smooth the wrinkles.

Sometimes thread will twist while sewing. If this happens stop and push the needle to the base of the thread and run beeswax along the thread once from the needle to the end. If double thread is being used it will have been waxed before starting, so stop and re-wax and re-twist if necessary.

The action of making a stitch involves one smooth continuous movement keeping control of the needle throughout. Hold the needle between thumb and forefinger, insert the point, with the side of the thimble resting against the end of the needle and the other fingers curled up underneath, so that the hand is close to the fabric. In one movement push the needle in and out again, release finger and thumb (but retain control by keeping the thimble on the needle) and quickly move them to take hold of the point to draw the thread through. Note the amount of pull required to form a flat neat stitch and apply it evenly to every stitch in that area. Working in this way is quick, produces even stitches and ensured that your fingers are correctly placed to start the next stitch.

It is essential to use a tailor's thimble — it has no top — and a Bewteen needle, it is short and therefore you really can take hold of the point and yet still have the side of the thimble on the needle.

### Embroidery stitches

Embroidery stitches are thicker and so require a larger needle with a bigger eye. Crewel needles have long eyes for this, tapestry needles have blunt points and are used where threads have to be counted and the needle inserted only between the threads of the fabric. The thicker the yarn, the larger should be the needle so that the hole it makes is the right size for the thread to slip through easily. For example, use a small crewel needle with two strands of Anchor Stranded Embroidery thread to work smocking on a baby's dress, but a large tapestry needle with Tapisserie wool or knitting wool to embroider a border round a tweed skirt.

As the needle is larger the hand is not clenched as in hand-sewing stitches, but more open, often almost flat as the point of the needle is stabbed back and forth. The threads are left looser to lie on the surface of the fabric but tension control is important for an even appearance. Begin and end with back stitches, not knots.

Unlike hand-stitching, the needle is often inserted in the fabric, the fingers let go entirely, the thimble pushes the needle through and then the hand moves to allow the fingers to take hold of the point. For this method of sewing the thimble with a top may be used if desired.

## HANGING LOOPS

These are necessary on coats, jackets, skirts, and at the waists of dresses if the dress will not remain on a hanger. It is also useful to attach loops to the waist of children's trousers. Stitch all types firmly to double fabric.

### Coat loops

Either make a tube of rouleau from lining 8 cm ($3\frac{1}{8}$ in.) long cut on the cross and insert the ends under the lining at the neckline, or make a stronger hanger by folding an 8 cm ($3\frac{1}{8}$ in.) length of straight grain lining. Fold in each edge, fold again to a finished width of 5 mm ($\frac{1}{4}$ in.). Tack and press. Slip stitch the folded edges together.

Turn in each end and hem in position, back stitching firmly across the end to form a square of stitching. This hanger should be stitched close up against the edge of the lining at the back of the neck.

Alternatively, narrow petersham ribbon may be used, or, a special ready-make loop which is part elastic. These are available in packs in normal tailoring colours. They are very strong.

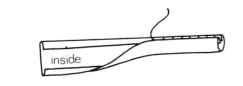

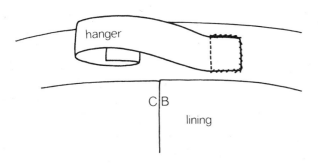

### Skirt loops

Cut two pieces of narrow petersham ribbon 20 cm (8 in.) long, or make lengths of rouleau from lining fabric. Fold each in half and press the fold. Arrange the ends side by side and insert at least 1 cm ($\frac{3}{8}$ in.) inside the skirt under the waistband before the final row of stitching is down. If sewing this by hand return and stitch underneath the loops as well.

Position the loops according to the style; it is not always best to place them at the side seams. If the skirt has pleats make sure they will not be pulled out of position when it hangs by the loops.

If the skirt has a petersham waist-finish slip the loop ends under the petersham and machine across them.

### Dress loops

A dress with narrow shoulders, a pinafore dress, anything with straps or a bib top, a dress with a particularly heavy skirt, a wedding dress, or a dress made from stretchy jersey or hand knitting is best hung from the waist. Also, a long dress too long for the wardrobe should have waist loops attached.

Make a length of rouleau or use narrow petersham ribbon and cut up into two pieces 4 cm ($1\frac{5}{8}$ in.) long and two pieces 15 cm (6 in.) long.

Fold the two longer pieces in half and press the fold. Hold the ends side by side and attach to the dress waist seam by machining to the seam allowances. The loop ends should be tucked under the seam allowance. Machine twice for strength. The position of these loops is important: place them both on the same half of the waist — either the front or the back, and make sure the distance between them is equal to the size of the coat hanger to be used. If they are too close together they will not reach the ends of the hanger; if they are too far apart they will slip off.

Attach the two short loops to the other side of the waist, exactly opposite the long ones. Turn under the ends and hem or machine in a square leaving some loop standing up. To hang the dress thread the long loops through the short ones and then on to the hanger.

This type of double loop is useful as it has more grip and can be made any length. If a skirt or dress tends to fall away at the middle when hanging, causing creasing, a double loop can be attached to the centre of the waist in addition to the usual side loops.

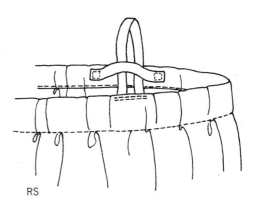

## HARD FINISH

Used to describe a smooth fabric, usually a worsted suiting that has no nap or surface. Also called a clear finish.

## HAREM

A skirt or trousers made in flimsy fabric, cut very wide and gathered at the hemline or ankles.

## HEEL STAY

(See *Kick Tape*.)

## HEM LENGTH

A hem is the amount of fabric turned up at the edge of a dress, coat, sleeve, skirt, etc., and held there by a variety of methods depending on a number of points. Among those to be considered are: the type of fabric; whether weight is needed to add to the hang; the shape of the garment edge and the number of seams; the effect required on the outside of the garment.

The depth of the fabric turned up is also governed by these points and as this one thing can completely spoil the appearance of a hem it is vitally important.

### Skirt hems

It is best to ignore the hem surplus at first, that is, the fabric to be turned up, and concentrate on the line of the fold because that will be visible in wear. On a skirt this lower edge should be parallel with the floor when wearing shoes and as the height of heel affects the length and level of the skirt it is a good idea to decide at least what type of shoes will always be worn with the outfit.

When deciding on the hem length of a coat make sure it is sufficiently long to cover anything likely to be worn underneath.

Although fashion influences hems to an extent, one's own figure, height, leg length, posture, etc., should not be ignored. Women with long legs may wish to wear a longer skirt to balance their proportion, but conversely they may wish to wear shorter skirts if they have exceptionally nice legs. Those with short legs should examine the length of thigh and compare it with the distance from knee to ankle before deciding whether to wear a short skirt or a longer one. The latter would help to lengthen the waist-to-thigh effect. Similarly apparent length can be added by wearing high waisted styles or at least avoiding those with low waists.

Anyone non-average with unusually long or short legs should adjust their hemlines only minimally when fashion decrees that they should be raised or lowered.

Style affects the length too. Consider a short person wearing a very full skirt; she should not make it too long or the remainder of her leg will be so short as to be lost. If she wants to wear that length she should wear a less full skirt. The taller person usually has fewer problems although anyone with very long legs may prefer to avoid high waisted styles when hemlines are low.

## HEM MARKER

There are various types of hem marker available. They consist of a base with a vertical measure marked off in centimetres. A container of chalk is attached to the measure and it can be adjusted to the height required. Attached to that is a tube and plastic bulb which is squeezed to spray a thin chalk line from the container onto the garment. An alternative type of marker has a jointed metal rule which is squeezed and clamped onto the fabric of the skirt in order that a pin may be inserted.

With a chalk marker if the chalk is not visible, pins may be inserted instead. The marks should be no closer than 10 cm (4 in.).

These markers are best used by a second person while the wearer of the skirt stands still or revolves slowly. However, it is possible to at least use it as a guide when alone simply by setting it to the correct height and then, wearing the skirt with the hem already marked or even tacked up, by standing in front of a mirror with the hem marker beside you, and turning slowly. It is then possible to see whether or not the hem is level all round.

## HEMMING INTO MACHINING

A small, neat, strong stitch. It is very easy to work because the machine stitches act as a guide to size of stitch and to keeping straight. Used where a folded edge meets a row of machining. Examples include finish of a bound edge on the inside, across the back neck of a collar in lightweight fabric, inside cuffs, and waistbands.

Tack and press the edge then work towards you sliding the point of the needle under the thread of a stitch and up into the fold. Take as little as possible of the fold, and work into every machine stitch, pulling the thread tight.

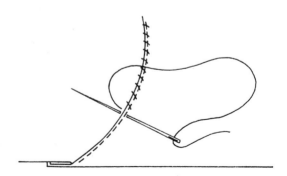

## HEMMING STITCH

A very small strong stitch worked over one edge lapped on to another. It should not be used on hems that show because the stitches are deep and are visible on the right side. Use inside garments. The upper edge may be folded under, or it may be flat. In the second case the stitches have to be larger, otherwise the fabric edge will be pulled away even though it will usually have been neatened with zig-zag stitch or something similar.

Work towards you, inserting the needle across the body, producing slanting stitches. Make the stitches as small and close as possible.

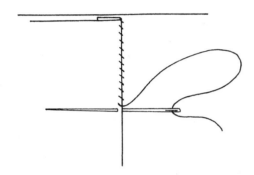

## HEMS

### Hem finishes

The word 'hemline' most often applies to the bottom of a skirt or a dress but a hem, the folding over of the raw edge, is used in other positions too, including sleeves, coats, jackets, trousers, blouses, tops, lingerie and nightwear. The choice of hem finish therefore depends on the position on the garment as well as on the garment itself and its future use and on the fabric. The other point to consider is the effect required. The hem finish may be deliberately visible either because of the type of fabric or because that finish may have been used elsewhere on the garment. If the hem finish is intended to be invisible, care should be taken to ensure that it is. If it proves impossible to do this, either through the nature of the fabric or due to lack of experience, then another, visible, hem finish should be substituted.

In addition to these considerations the hem finish chosen should be one that can be worked successfully on that particular shape. For example, most finishes are suitable for straight edges but many hemlines are shaped, some are even circular, and the finish must be selected accordingly.

### Hem depth

The depth at which a hem is trimmed and finished depends on the shape of the edge, on the type of fabric, and on the effect that is required. Decide first on the method of finishing it, whether by machine or hand and make the hem at the depth that is correct for that type of finish.

On a dress or skirt a certain amount of weight will keep it to hang well but too much depth will cause bulging. A sleeve hem can be narrow, but not so narrow as to allow the edge or the inside of the sleeve to show in wear.

A dress hem should be at least 2 cm ($\frac{3}{4}$ in.) in depth but preferably 3 to 4 cm ($1\frac{1}{4}$ to $1\frac{5}{8}$ in.). If there is insufficient fabric for a 2 cm ($\frac{3}{4}$ in.) hem then an alternative type of hem should be selected. In addition consider the amount of flare. If the 4 cm ($1\frac{5}{8}$ in.) hem produces a problem of excess fullness, it should be reduced in depth.

The hemline should be marked and turned up, tacked and pressed, before then marking the depth of the hem. The fact of having the hem partly tacked up in this way provides a guide as to the most suitable depth. Use an adjustable marker or cut a cardboard marker and use it to chalk a line on the hem.

On many garments such as blouses, lingerie, nightwear, children's clothes, the depth of hem is dictated by the type of finish employed on the rest of the garment.

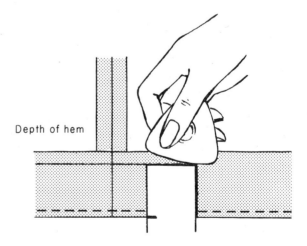

Depth of hem

### Blouse hem

This type of hem can be used on any edge that is unseen in wear and also on frills and on lingerie. Its advantage on a blouse is that there is no bulky edge to show through a skirt. It is suitable for all light-weight fabrics.

Turn under the hem to the correct length, tack and press. Set the machine to a very close zig-zag stitch, but not a satin stitch. Machine over the folded edge, working from the right side. Trim away the surplus edge on the underneath.

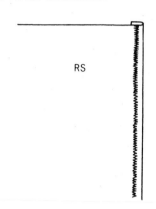

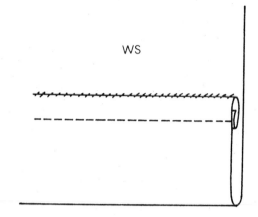

than on an adult garment. The machine stitch can be large to enable it to be removed easily for letting down.

## Bound hem

A hem edge may be bound in the same way as a coat hem, if the fabric is lightweight but frays. Use soft dress net cut into 2 cm ($\frac{3}{4}$ in.) strips, machine this to the right side of the hem and even from the fold. Use the iron to press the net flat then roll it under so that it encloses the raw edge and machine with a straight or zig-zag stitch. Tack the hem flat to the garment and work catch stitch between the net and the garment fabric. This method avoids adding any bulk.

Never use straight seam binding or skirt binding on a hem as it will make the hemline show badly.

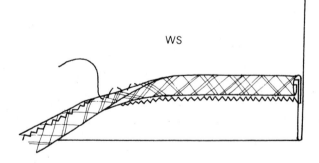

## Children's hems

Hems on children's clothes must be very secure to withstand wear and washing and to prevent accidents. In addition it may be wise to allow the facility for letting them down as the child grows.

Wherever possible turn up a double fold of fabric, tack and press and machine. The hem can be deeper

## Circular hem

*Fine fabrics*    Mark the hemline level and work a row of machining 2 mm ($\frac{1}{8}$ in.) below it. When working on fine synthetic fabric or on chiffon, eliminate any tendency to wrinkle by using a slight zig-zag stitch and by putting tissue or typing paper underneath the fabric. Tear the paper away before proceeding to the next stage. Trim the surplus fabric to within 1 mm ($\frac{1}{16}$ in.) of the machining. Turn up this edge by a small amount, as little as possible, depending on the fabric, and machine again. This time use a small zig-zag stitch or even satin stitch as an alternative to a straight stitch, but try it first in case it is unsuitable for the fabric.

Another way of completing the hem is to use the hemming foot or shell hemming foot on your machine.

If you wish to hand finish the hem work the row of machining as described above but then trim and roll the edge a little at a time. Hold the hem with either small hemming stitches or whip stitch which is taken right over the entire hem. Remember to moisten your fingers when rolling a narrow edge.

*Medium to heavy fabrics*    A deep hem in self fabric will show very badly so the part turned up must be kept as narrow as possible.

On jersey or soft fabric mark the hemline and turn up and tack on the fold. Press carefully on the fold. Press in short sections arranging each area in a curve on the pressing surface. Leave each part to cool before moving it, as it is very easy to stretch the fabric and finish up with a fluted hem. Never press this hem with the skirt over an ordinary ironing board. If you haven't a table or other surface for pressing put the ironing board close to a table of the same height, arrange the hem in sections on the board while keeping the remainder of the skirt supported on the table.

Trim the hem surplus to no more than 1 cm ($\frac{3}{8}$ in.) and tack down. Work herringbone stitch by hand over the raw edge, keeping the stitches fairly loose. Remove tackings. Press again lightly on the right side, using the same care as previously.

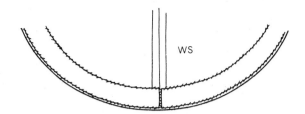

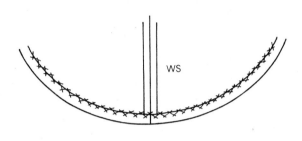

On heavier fabrics or those that are firmly woven a false piece must be added to ensure that the hemline does not show. Prepare bias strips, not on the full cross, about 6 cm ($2\frac{3}{8}$in.) wide, and join them until you have sufficient length for the entire hem. Turn in and press 5 mm ($\frac{1}{4}$ in.) all along one edge of the piece. Although this is now similar in appearance to purchased bias binding, it is best to cut your own strip from a lightweight soft fabric such as lining or nylon jersey. Using the iron, shape the strip into a curve.

Mark the hemline and trim away the surplus fabric to within 5 mm ($\frac{1}{4}$ in.) of the line. Turn up and tack near the fold. Press carefully as described above. Cut narrow strips of Wundaweb, no more than 3 mm ($\frac{1}{8}$ in.) in width, and slip them under the hem and press. The pieces should be very short as the hem is shaped, and need not connect; in fact a better result will often be achieved by leaving gaps of 1 to 2 cm ($\frac{3}{8}$ to $\frac{3}{4}$ in.) between pieces of Wundaweb 3 cm ($1\frac{1}{4}$ in.) long. Press with a damp cloth but fairly lightly at this stage.

Place the prepared lining strip with the wrong side down to the wrong side of the skirt with the pressed fold 2 mm ($\frac{1}{8}$ in.) from the hem fold. Tack. Join the strip at the centre back or a side seam by turning in the two edges to meet each other. Work hemming or felling along the lining edge with very shallow stitches.

Arrange the skirt on the table with the hem wrong side up, work in short sections with the hem flat on the table and turn under and tack down the raw edge of the lining. Press very lightly and work loose slip hemming or catch stitch. At the join, work slip stitch.

### Coat hem

A coat usually has a loose lining, i.e. the hem of a coat and lining hang separately. Coat fabric is usually substantial in weight and it may also fray so binding the hem with bias strips of lining provides a good hard wearing edge and it looks attractive. This method can be used on other lined garments such as skirts but avoid using it on lightweight fabrics as it will cause a ridge. It can also be used on unlined coats and jackets and if lining fabric is not available, purchased bias binding may be used although it does not look as good.

Mark the hemline, turn it up and tack near the fold. The thicker the fabric the further from the fold the tacking will be in order to hold the hem. Press well. Decide on the depth of the hem. This can be from about 5 to 8 cm (2 to $3\frac{1}{8}$ in.) and draw a chalk line on the hem surplus at this depth. Cut bias strips of lining fabric 2 cm ($\frac{3}{4}$ in.) wide and join to form sufficient length. Lift the hem away from the coat and place one edge of the bias strip against the chalk line.

Attach following instructions for *Binding*, page 28.

Tack the hem to the garment. Work catch stitch under the edge between the bound edge and the coat. Do not pull stitches tight but fasten off ends of thread firmly.

### Coat hem corners

At the front edges of the coat open out the facings, press open any seams and trim the turnings. The bottom row of tacking near the fold should continue across the facing but 2 cm ($\frac{3}{4}$ in.) above this the surplus hem material should be cut away.

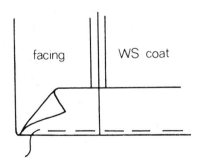

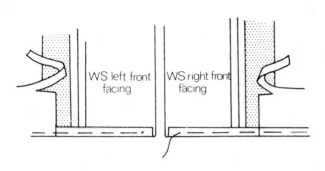

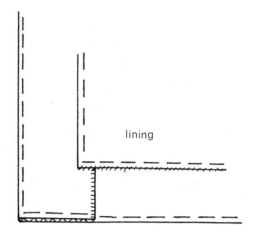

Tack the hem edge to the coat. Fold facings into position and tack. Press well. Compare the two corners and the front edges to make sure they are equal. Complete the hem with catch stitch under the finished edge. Complete the corner by slip-stitching the two folds together at the lower edge and working close loop stitch over the raw edge of the facing to hold it to the hem. Press.

Trim the lining so that it is about 2 cm ($\frac{3}{4}$ in.) longer than the coat. Turn up a hem on the lining 4 cm ($1\frac{5}{8}$ in.) deep. Finish it with slip hem or a machine embroidery stitch. Alternatively, turn up the lining so that it is 2 to 3 cm ($\frac{3}{4}$ to $1\frac{1}{4}$ in.) shorter than the coat and tack it to the coat hem. Finish by felling to the coat. With the first method the lining should be attached to the coat hem with three or four long bar tacks.

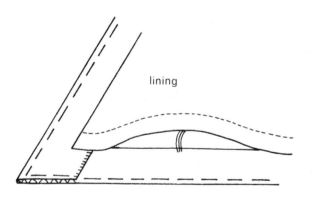

An alternative is to turn a narrow double fold and machine it and then turn a deeper hem and hand sew it, preferably using hemming stitch for strength.

On girls' dresses a couple of tucks can be made above the normal hem to be let down as necessary. Stitch the tucks with a large machine stitch.

### Dress hem

This is the hem that should not show. It is sometimes called a couture hem or blind hem. It can be used on all fabrics of any style, in any position on the garment, and of course it can be used not only on dresses but on anything. There are a number of techniques involved and several processes that apply to all hems.

The care needed to work this type of hem ensures that there is a good fold at the hem, that the area hangs properly, especially if it is a skirt, and that there is no sign of the hem depth inside. If this type of hemline shows, it is not usually because the stitches have been taken through the fabric, but it is more likely to be due to excess bulk of hem or to bad pressing, or to the wrong choice of method of finishing the raw edge.

Stitches disturb the weave of the fabric so the thicker the fabric the less danger there is, but still if the thread is pulled too tight it will produce a visible line. The softer and looser the weave or the more stretchy the fabric, the looser the stitches must be, to allow for movement during wear.

The raw edge of the hem that is turned up must be neatened. The choice of neatening depends on the type of fabric, often the method used on the remainder of the garment will be the most suitable. The exception to this would be if the hem was to be seen as in a coat. (See *Coat Hem*.) The raw edge may be neatened by machine with a zig-zag stitch adjusted to suit the fabric, or with a stitch combining straight with zig-zag such as is used on jersey fabrics, or even a straight stitch within the raw edge is suitable on non fraying fabrics. A more laborious method is to overcast the edge by hand but on short stretches of hem, such as sleeves, it may be more convenient than machining. If the fabric frays badly work a row of straight machining near the edge then trim it a little before overcasting over the stitching. The advantage of this hand sewing is that it keeps the hem soft and at the same time the thread is pulled tight. Sometimes machining will stretch the edge, and if that happens trim off the edge and start again using a different method. If a machined finish is wanted then run a thread under the stitch, which can be pulled up afterwards.

Turn up the hem, with the marked hemline on the fold, and tack. If it is a shaped skirt hem place it on the table right side out and with the hem towards you. Fold back the top layer of the skirt and begin by tacking a short section in front of you. Swivel the skirt and tack the opposite section. Turn it again and tack the sides so that the entire hem is now tacked along the lower edge. Keep the hem flat on the table as you tack. Tacking in sections in this way will prevent dragging and it keeps the flare evenly distributed. On fine fabrics tack close to the edge, on thicker ones tack further away.

Trim the turnings of any seams that fall within the hem to reduce bulk. If the hemline is very shaped it helps to snip the turnings in towards the seam line. This is especially helpful in keeping a hem turn-up flat on small circular hems where the hem depth cannot be reduced, for example a long shaped sleeve.

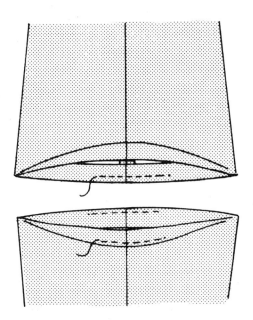

Press the tacked fold on the wrong side of the garment. Use the sleeve board to make sure the hem will not be stretched. Press a short section at a time. Press the fold only, not the entire depth of the hem fabric. Use the pressing method being used on the remainder of the garment but work slowly and take special care as it is at this stage that heavy pressing can cause marks, but light pressing will be inadequate. In any case press sharply to avoid the risk of the tacking stitches making imprints. Move the hem gently to press the next section as it may stretch while warm. To press small hems such as on sleeves and trousers turn the garment inside out in order to slide the hem on to the sleeve board.

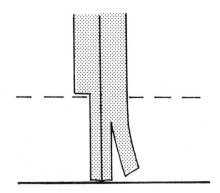

If the length has to be checked tack or pin up the surplus fabric and try on. Adjust if necessary.

To complete the hem, mark the depth suitable for the fabric with a chalk line. Neaten the edge, trimming off the surplus. It is not normally necessary to press this neatening but if it has to be done, remember to lift the edge off the skirt to press, otherwise it will cause a mark.

Arrange the skirt on the table in the same way as before and tack the hem itself to the skirt. The tacking should be placed just below the neatened edge. Tack in sections as before, easing in any extra fullness created by a shaped hemline. Do not press this fullness against the skirt, allow it to be raised in slight bubbles between the tacking stitches. If the surplus is impossible to manage in this way it means the hem is too deep, the neatening must be cut off to reduce the depth and it must be done again.

Stitch the hem by working catch stitch just under the neatened edge. Lift the edge, folding it towards you, and work loose stitches working from right to left. See *Catch Stitch*, page 57. Take up only one thread from the back of the garment, but a deeper stitch in the edge for strength. Start and finish the thread in the neatened edge. When stitching jersey fabrics leave even more thread in the stitching by leaving a small loop every 2 or 3 cm ($\frac{3}{4}$ to $1\frac{1}{4}$ in.).

Remove all tackings and press the hem lightly from the right side but do this when the entire garment is complete. Any separate pressing of the hem should be done on the wrong side and only with a towel or a piece of fabric placed with one edge against the hem edge, to prevent marks appearing.

### Faced hem

This can be made on a shaped or straight hem edge and it is especially useful where there is insufficient fabric to turn up a hem of the correct depth. The extra fabric used will also weight the hem well.

There are two methods of facing a hem, one using a light fabric or a mediumweight one. The other method involves the addition of a firm fabric which could even be a strip of the same fabric as the garment.

*Using a lightweight facing*   Turn up and tack and press a narrow edge at the hemline. Stitch the edge either by working catch stitch under the edge, or herringbone stitch over the edge, or even work a row of machining which will appear on the outside as a decorative top stitch.

Cut crossway strips of fabric such as lining or cotton lawn about 5 cm (2 in.) wide, or less if the hemline is curved. Join the strips if necessary. Turn in and press one edge of the strip and tack it to the wrong side of the hemline with the fold above the bottom edge of the garment. The stitched edge of the fabric must be well covered otherwise a ridge will be apparent on the outside of the garment. Turn under and tack the other edge of the facing. Do not turn under too little of the edge or this too will cause a ridge to show. Make a join by turning both edges to meet each other. Finish by slip hemming the upper edge and hemming or felling the lower edge. Keep the stitches loose. Remove all tackings and press lightly.

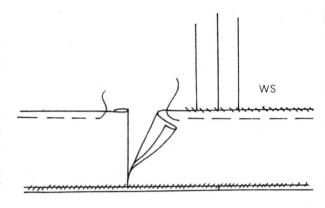

*Using a heavier fabric*   Cut a strip of self fabric or cotton, calico etc., 3 to 4 cm ($1\frac{1}{4}$ to $1\frac{5}{8}$ in.) wide, on the bias but not necessarily on the true cross. Also cut a piece of lightweight interfacing 2 cm ($\frac{3}{4}$ in.) wide. This may be sew-in or iron-on but if the latter is used test it on a piece of fabric to make sure it does not stiffen the hem too much.

Set the machine to a running zig-zag, elastic zig-zag stitch or something similar. Butt together the hem edge and the edge of the facing strip with the interfacing beneath. If iron-on interfacing is used it can be pressed lightly first. Work the machining across the two raw edges. Work a second row if it is not close enough to prevent fraying. Make joins in the facing strip by working herringbone stitch across the edges.

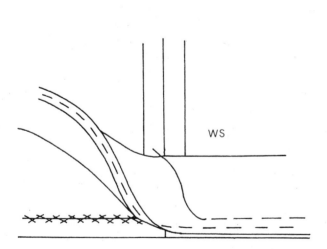

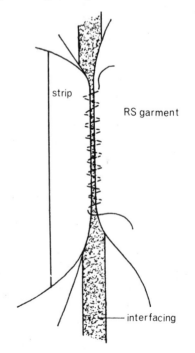

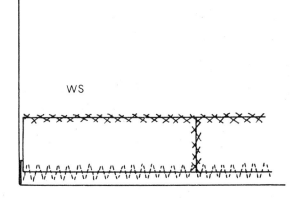

Finish by turning the hem to the wrong side, tack and press the lower edge. Neaten the other edge of the strip, tack it to the garment and then work catch stitch to hold. Remove tackings and press lightly.

### Fur hem
Attach 4 cm ($1\frac{5}{8}$ in.) wide strips of interfacing to the wrong side of the fur, with one edge on the hemline. Trim the fur edge to 1 cm ($\frac{3}{8}$ in.) and fold it over the interfacing and oversew it in place.

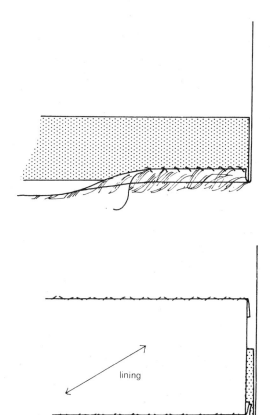

Cut bias strips of lining 8 cm ($3\frac{1}{8}$ in.) wide and turn in and press a fold of 5 mm ($\frac{1}{4}$ in.) along each edge. Tack this in position with the lower edge just covering the over-sewing on the fur. Tack both edges and slip hem.

### Hand-rolled hem
A very narrow hem suitable for straight or shaped edges on fine or soft fabrics. The edge must be freshly cut with no fraying fibres. Hold the fabric with wrong side towards you and, using the thumb and forefingers of both hands roll both thumbs and the edge will roll over. Allow the raw edge to turn right under out of sight. If the fingers slip, moisten them with your tongue to get a grip. Turn under the smallest possible amount, the finer the fabric the narrower the hem can be.

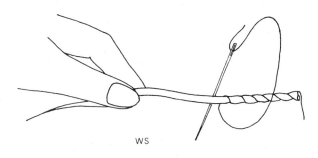

There is a choice of two stitches for holding the hem. Thread a small needle with a short piece of thread so that the hand does not have to move too far from the hem. Either work very small hemming stitches as the edge is rolled, or whip the edge by taking the needle right over the hem. The second stitch will not be as firm.

If the fabric proves difficult to roll and no other hem finish is suitable try working a row of small straight machine stitching first, trimming the edge close to it and then rolling it.

### Hem for transparent fabrics
A double edge of fabric will be clearly visible on voile or georgette for example, and even a narrow rolled hem will be visible. A good solution is to turn under the fabric edge once only, which will show only slightly and then machine with a small very close zig-zag stitch from the right side. This dense stitch will draw attention from the double edge and will be obviously decorative especially if a contrasting colour thread is used. Trim the edge to 5 mm ($\frac{1}{4}$ in.) longer than needed, turn the edge under and machine from the right side without tacking. Press well after stitching. Trim off any surplus raw edge on the wrong side.

## Jacket hem

Hems on heavy fabrics can be treated in the same way as a coat, see page 145. Lighter jackets will hang better if the hem is weighted.

Make sure the hemline of a jacket or short coat is parallel with the floor and that it appears level on the body. Some fitting adjustments distort hemlines. Also establish the length of the jacket at a suitable level for the skirt, dress or trousers that it will be worn with.

Mark the hemline. Open out the jacket and the front facings and trim away seam allowances. Reinforce the hemline with strips of soft interfacing or tailor's linen, attaching with catch stitch or herringbone stitch. The reinforcement should slightly overlap the jacket interfacing and it should be either slightly wider than the width of the hem or slightly narrower. Use the wider width on soft fabric. The width of the hem when finished should be between 2.5 and 3 cm (1 to $1\frac{1}{4}$ in.).

Turn up and tack the fold of the hem and press from both right and wrong side. Trim the raw edge of the hem to the correct depth, tack and catch stitch it in place.

Fold over the facing and tack the front edge. Holding the corner in place, open it up and trim off the surplus fabric. The easiest way to do this is to snip the edges of the fabric and then open it right out and cut it away. Turn up and tack the lower edge and fold the corner back into position. Tack well all round and press.

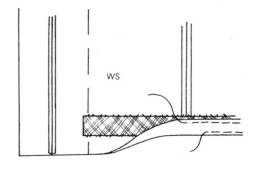

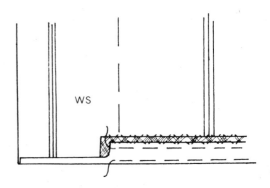

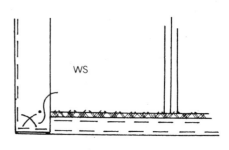

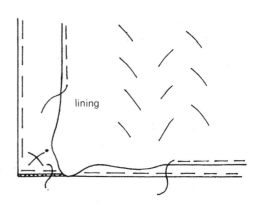

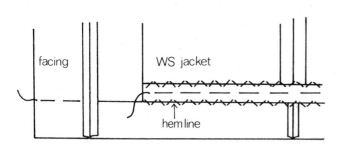

Slip stitch the lower edge and work buttonhole stitch over the raw edge. Work catch stitch over the edge of the facing, or, insert a few pieces of Wundaweb to hold it back.

Bring the lining down over the hem, trim it to 1 cm ($\frac{3}{8}$ in.) longer than the jacket. Turn up the lining so that it is 1 cm ($\frac{3}{8}$ in.) shorter than the jacket then pull it back a little to introduce ease and tack but not quite to the corner. Tack the lining to the facing in the same way. At the corners the lining should be made a little tighter to ensure that the jacket corners curl the right way, towards the body. Push the lining edges under and tack. Press lightly and fell the lining edges. Remove all tacking and press.

### Jersey hem
Many jersey fabrics including the shiny synthetic knits and also fabrics such as velour are improved by machining the hem rather than trying to hand sew invisibly.

Mark the hemline and turn it up and tack and press. Tack down the surplus hem fabric 3 cm ($1\frac{1}{4}$ in.) from the fold. On the right side draw a chalk line 2.5 cm (1 in.) from the edge. If chalk does not mark the fabric well make a dotted line with tailor's chalk or a chalk pencil. Alternatively work the previous tacking accurately and stitch 1 cm ($\frac{3}{8}$ in.) inside it. Set the machine to a decorative zig-zag stitch, even a blind stitch will suffice, and work it on the line from the right side. Do not use a stretch stitch or a satin stitch as it may stretch the hem.

If fabric is limited the hem may be as narrow as 1 to 1.5 cm ($\frac{3}{8}$ to $\frac{5}{8}$ in.) but in this case work two rows of machining, one of them on the lower fold of the hem.

### Lace edge
Finish the hem of nightwear and lingerie by adding narrow lace edging. Mark the hemline, place the lace on the right side with one edge on the mark. Use a small zig-zag stitch and sew inside the edge. Press the fabric edge back on the wrong side, away from the lace, and machine again, this time over the edge of the lace. On the wrong side trim away the surplus fabric.

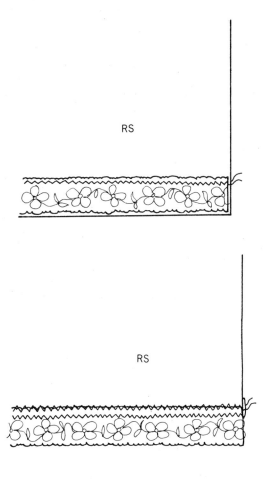

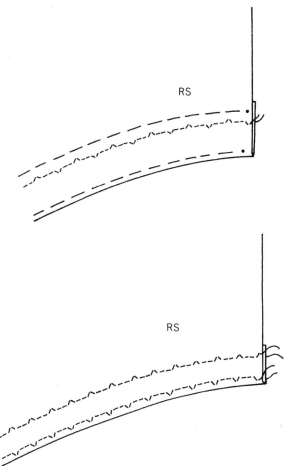

### Lace hem
Cut a strip of dress net 6 cm ($2\frac{3}{8}$ in.) wide and machine it to the hemline mark, with right sides together. Fold the net to the wrong side, roll and tack the lower edge, then turn in the other edge of the net. Tack and slip hem to the lace.

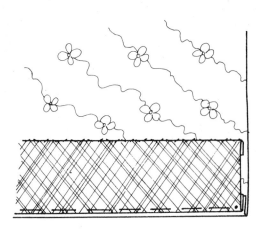

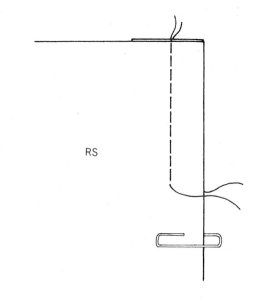

RS

### Leather hems

The choice of finish lies between machine stitching
and adhesive and although the latter sounds easiest
very few machines, old or new, will refuse to stitch
leather and this produces a more pleasing appearance.

Mark the hemline on the right side with tailor's
chalk. Trim away seam allowances within the hem
area or they will cause the hem to bulge. Leather cannot be tacked so trim the hem depth below the chalk
line before turning it up. Keep the hem depth to
3 cm ($1\frac{1}{4}$ in.). Turn up the hem and hold the folded
edge with paper clips or clothes pegs, inserting a few
at a time along a short stretch of hem. Machine from
the right side with a large stitch and using a spear
point leather needle. The stitching should be at least
1 cm ($\frac{3}{8}$ in.) from the fold. Remove the paper clips
as they approach and replace them further along the
hem. A second row of machining can be worked above
if desired. Alternatively if the hem does not lie flat
after pressing with a warm iron and brown paper or a
dry cloth, work another row of stitching slightly
nearer the hem fold.

When using adhesive, mark the hemline on the right
side with tailor's chalk and trim the surplus to 3 to
4 cm ($1\frac{1}{4}$ to $1\frac{5}{8}$ in.). Also trim seam allowances. On
the inside mark the total hem area with a chalk line
and spread adhesive thinly within this area. Follow
the instructions with the adhesive. Fold up the hem
carefully and press firmly, making sure the chalk line
is exactly on the fold. If the leather is heavy the hem
can be flattened by hammering evenly.

If the edge to be turned up is curved, mark, turn
up and hold with paper clips then snip out V-shaped
sections from the hem edge so that edges meet without overlapping. Remove paper clips and proceed to
turn up and fix the hem with adhesive or machine
stitching.

Similarly if the hem curves the other way, as on a
sleeve, the hem depth must be snipped to allow it to
lie flat.

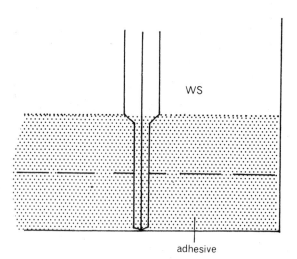

WS

adhesive

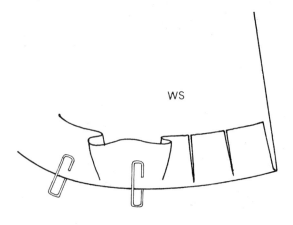

WS

### Machine rolled hem

A hemming foot is a standard additional sewing machine attachment. The edge of the fabric must be freshly cut and fed into the metal curl of the foot. Use a straight machine stitch set to a length that is suitable for the fabric. Always try out the hemming foot as it does not work satisfactorily on all fabrics. It is most successful on crisp lightweight material such as cotton but with care it can also be used on softer sheer fabric like voile.

### Machined blind-hemming

The blind hem stitch on a machine should be tried out carefully on a spare piece of fabric because it is not suitable for lightweight fabrics. Attach the correct foot and adjust the stitch according to the instructions in the machine manual. Mark the hemline, turn up tack and press and also press under a narrow fold on the hem surplus. This may be tacked although the stitches should be kept away from the edge.

Fold the hem back and insert the fabric under the machine with the wrong side of the garment uppermost and to the left. The machine stitch should run beside the fold but with the zig-zag part of it just catching the fold.

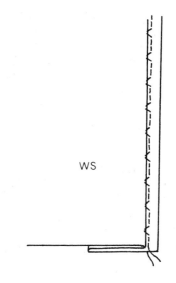

### Narrow hems

A narrow hem, for example less than 2 cm ($\frac{3}{4}$ in.), will not add any weight or improve the hang of a garment so it should be confined to garments where this is not important. Examples include very full or long skirts, children's clothes, nightwear etc. A narrow hem is also suitable for use on other edges than skirt hems.

Mark the hemline, turn it up and tack and press, or press only. Trim the raw edge level and fold it under on lightweight fabrics, or neaten it on heavier fabrics. Tack again near the edge and machine, with a straight or a zig-zag stitch, or stitch by hand. The hand stitch may be hemming or slip-hemming. Thicker fabrics should be held by catch stitch or by herringbone stitch provided the latter does not make the hem show on the right side. Herringbone stitch is a useful way of holding down curling edges of jersey, velvet etc.

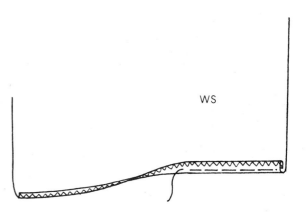

### Shell hems

A decorative edge suitable for fine fabrics. To work it very simply by machine, turn under a narrow edge of the fabric and work the blind hem stitch or similar stitch over the folded edge. There is no need to tack the edge although it may help if it is pressed first. Experiment with the length and width of the stitch until a pleasing effect results. It should not be necessary to trim away the raw edge afterwards on the wrong side unless too much has been turned under.

To make a shell edge by hand, start by turning and tacking a narrow hem then work the stitch, holding the wrong side of the fabric towards you. The thread is taken right over the hem vertically, and pulled

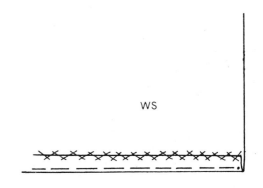

slightly, then take a second stitch over it to hold it firmly. Pull only sufficiently to wrinkle, not pleat, the edge. Next work two hemming or running stitches along the fold. Running stitches will be insufficient if the fabric is springy. Work the vertical stitches again over the hem and so on. Work out the distance between the shells according to the depth of the hem to form a pleasing proportion. Carefully remove tackings and if pressing is necessary place the hem on a thick towel and press only lightly.

This narrow shell hem can also be reproduced on the machine. A shell hemming foot is a standard attachment with most machines. The cut edge of the fabric is fed into the foot which curls it into a hem. The stitch used will be one that combines two or three straight stitches with one zig-zag stitch and this makes the actual shell. Experiment with spare fabric until you have the knack of feeding in the fabric as it easily slips out of the foot.

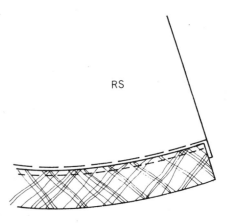

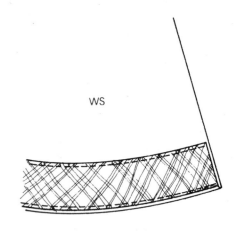

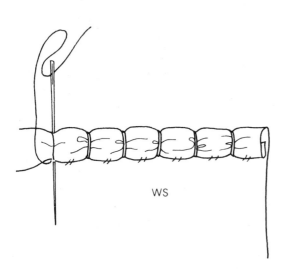

### Stiffened hem

A long skirt in a heavy or crisp fabric will be improved by stiffening the hem. This method of finishing is employed on wedding dresses and it is also useful on some areas of stage costume. There are two ways of doing this.

The first method uses horsehair braid. Mark the hemline and place one edge of the braid on the mark. Machine in place or hem by hand. If the skirt hem is curved the braid will easily follow the edge. Trim off a little of the surplus hem edge under the braid but leave at least 1 cm ($\frac{3}{8}$ in.). Fold the braid to the wrong side of the garment, tack near the lower edge and machine. Turn the skirt over in order to machine from the right side, keeping an even distance from the edge. The edge of the braid should be 1 to 2 mm ($\frac{1}{16}$ to $\frac{1}{8}$ in.) in from the hem edge.

Tack the other edge of the braid to the garment and herringbone or catch stitch over the edge. If the hemline is curved, pull up the thread that runs along one edge of the braid. If there is no thread use the thread securing the hem, pulling up the braid every few stitches. Alternatively the second edge of the braid may be secured by another row of machining worked from the right side and then one or two additional rows added for decoration.

Another way of stiffening a hem is to use Vilene. Select a weight that is suitable for the fabric. It may be iron-on or sew-in but try several types before making a decision.

Mark the hemline with tacking then cut Vilene 4 to 6 cm ($1\frac{5}{8}$ to $2\frac{3}{8}$ in.) wide with the lower edge exactly the shape of the hemline. Press in position of tack and then herringbone over both edges. Trim the hem edge and neaten it. Fold it over the Vilene and tack. The hem should not cover the Vilene otherwise the strain of stitching will make the hem show. Catch stitch the hem edge to the Vilene.

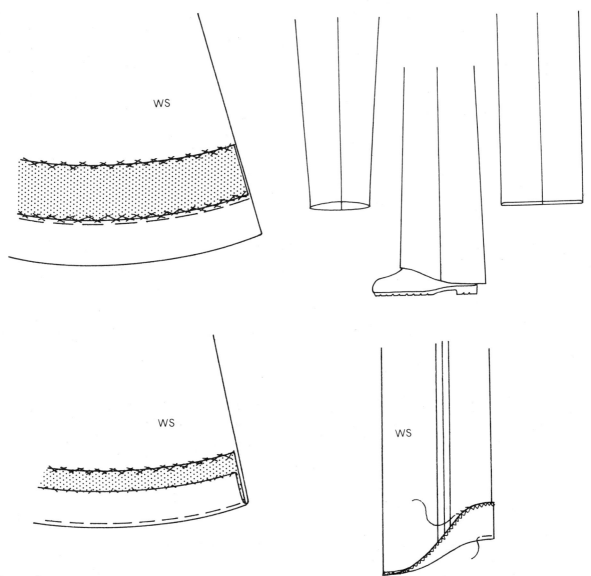

### Trouser hems

When trousers are very short and tapered the hemline should be curved. When they are long and wide or flared the hem should curve down over the heel but up over the toe of the shoe. At the outside of the foot the trouser should be longer than at the inside leg. Between these two extremes the hem is straight.

Turn up and tack the bottom fold of one trouser leg and try on. Adjust if necessary. Turn up and press both hems. Trim the surplus to 4 cm ($1\frac{5}{8}$ in.) and neaten. The best way to finish a trouser hem is to insert Wundaweb because it provides a good crisp line. The alternative is to machine, in which case the hem may be made narrower. If the trouser hem is to be hand stitched this must be firmly done with a hemming stitch worked just under the neatened edge.

### Wundaweb hem

This is suitable for most medium and heavyweight fabrics. It is not satisfactory on sheer fabrics because the adhesive web will come in contact with the iron. It should also be avoided on most pile fabrics because the pressure required by the iron will harm the surface. However, on all fabrics test a small piece first because the Wundaweb slightly stiffens the fabric.

Mark the hemline, turn it up and tack very close to the fold. Press well. Trim the hem surplus to 3 mm ($\frac{1}{8}$ in.) wider than the Wundaweb, i.e. 3 cm ($1\frac{1}{4}$ in.) and neaten the raw edge. Arrange the hem wrong side up on the sleeve board and slip the Wundaweb under the hem with the edge close to the tacking at the fold. It should be completely covered by the hem fabric to prevent it sticking to the iron. Press in short sections only and before pressing pull the fabric of the hem, excluding the Wundaweb, to make sure there is sufficient of the strip in the hem. It can happen that the strip is inserted tightly, the 'give' in the fabric not allowed for, and the result can be a tight looking hem.

Use a damp cloth and a hot iron and press the hem sharply, not heavily pressing twice in each place on the hem before moving on and arranging the next part of the hem. The Wundaweb can be cut or broken at curves and edges can be overlapped without any adverse effect. On completing the first press and when the entire hem is in place, remove the tackings and press again lightly but still using a damp cloth. Finally, turn the garment right side up and press again. This final pressing can be done when the garment is entirely finished.

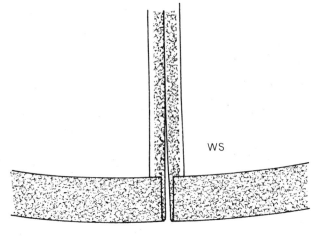

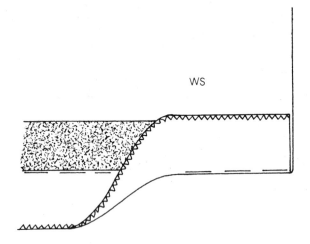

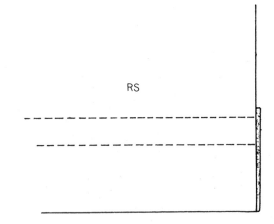

Wundaweb should be used at its full width or possibly with a little trimmed off if there is insufficient fabric to make a 3 cm (1 $\frac{1}{4}$ in.) hem. If it is too narrow it may not stick some fabric satisfactorily and also it may be inclined to produce a wavy hem if it is too narrow. However, this rule may be broken if a short section of a firm fabric is to be held in place, rather than an entire skirt hem. Such short stretches of hem include holding back seam allowances to form side slits in a skirt.

When using firm cotton fabrics that press into a good crease, such as some curtain fabric, the hem can be pressed as described and then the tacking stitches removed before inserting the Wundaweb. The Wundaweb can then be pushed down as far as the fold to produce a very sharp hem when pressed. This is entirely suitable for household articles but will generally be found to be rather sharp on clothes.

It is generally unsatisfactory to try to use Wundaweb in the top part only of a wider hem but Wundaweb can be very usefully employed in this way to reinforce a hem before top stitching it by machine.

## HERRINGBONE STITCH

In hand sewing, this is a wide stitch with crossed threads. It is not very strong but is neat and decorative. Normally used in short stretches only where a raw edge lies on top of another layer of fabric. Examples include the end of a neckline facing on top of the seam allowances of a shoulder seam or the bottom corner of a coat where the facing edge lies across the hem.

It is not successful when used on hems because after a while the weight of the garment pulls at the thread and the hemline shows on the right side.

Work from left to right taking very small horizontal stitches in two parallel lines. The distance between the rows depends on the thickness of the fabric but they should be as close as possible. Start and end threads in the upper layer of fabric. Do not pull the thread tight. Press lightly afterwards.

A herringbone stitch is also an open embroidery stitch. Work from left to right, with needle pointing from right to left. Bring the needle through at the bottom left of the row to be worked, take a diagonal stitch to the top right, a small stitch under the fabric to the left, then a diagonal stitch to the bottom right. By working another small stitch to the left the needle is back in position to begin the next stitch.

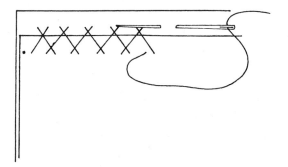

## HIPS

The wide area of the body below the waist. The hips are formed by the pelvic bones. The hipline varies in position between individuals but will be found between 15 and 25 cm (6 to 10 in.) below the waist. Those with a high pelvis should take the measurement high up, over the bones. On some people it is lower but it is seldom lower than 18 to 20 cm (7 to 8 in.) below the waist.

The hips must not be confused with the thighs. If the thighs, which are found level with and below the crutch, are bigger than the hips then they should be measured and checking of pattern width, etc., should be done at both levels.

Buttocks may be included when the hip measurement is taken but this depends on the position of the buttocks. If they are low they will more likely be almost at thigh level.

## HIPSTER

Trousers, jeans or skirt with less depth than normal between the hipline and the waist, so that the top of the garment rests on the top of the pelvic bone. Whatever finish is applied, for example petersham, facing, band, it must be shaped and fitted to the body. Depending on the figure, hipsters can be uncomfortable or difficult to keep up. Often worn with a belt to overcome this.

## HOBBLE

A style of skirt not often in fashion. As the name implies, it is not easy to walk when wearing one because the hem is gathered into a band round the calves or above the ankles.

## HOLE-AND-BUTTON CUFF

This term is used to describe a tailored cuff opening fastened with one to four buttons. The buttonholes are often worked without cutting the cloth and the buttons are sewn on top. The exception is with a blazer-type button where there is a shank to conceal. In this case proper buttonholes have to be made.

## HOLLAND

Holland is linen cloth of fine texture, used in tailoring for reinforcing and for stays. Shrink before use.

## HOOKS, EYES AND BARS

Hooks provide a very strong fastening provided they are sewn on correctly. They are fastened into bars or into eyes. Use bars where possible as there is always a tendency for a hook to move in an eye. However, the latter must be used at an edge-to-edge fastening. If sewing on several hooks it is essential to space and position them perfectly accurately otherwise not all of them will be taking equal strain. Hooks can be used in almost any position and they are reliable on tight-fitting garments.

Cards of hooks with eyes or hooks with bars can be bought in black or silver in sizes 0000 (difficult to obtain) up through 00 which is a good medium size for most things, to size 3 which is large and the most suitable for heavy wear or points of excessive strain such as waistbands. (See also *Trouser Hooks*.)

Always attach hooks to a double layer of fabric, and preferably interfacing as well. Take time to use buttonhole stitch as it is strong and neat. Use short pieces of thread, run through wax for medium and heavy fabrics. Use normal sewing thread either to match the fabric or, in the case of black hooks, black thread can be used.

Use the smallest hook possible if it is likely to be obvious, but use large ones for strength. Attach the hook by holding it in position a little way back from the edge of the garment. Work about eight strong, deep stitches (but not through to the right side) under the head of the hook, then pass the needle to the loops and hold each loop in position with one

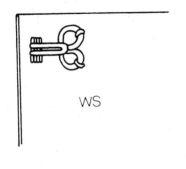

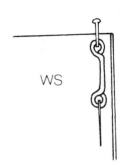

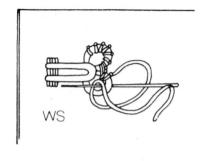

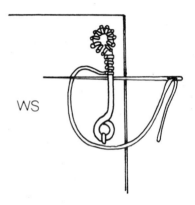

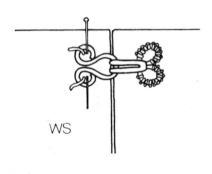

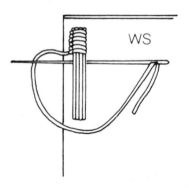

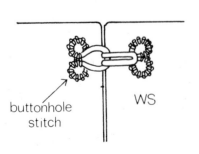

buttonhole
stitch

oversewing stitch. Finally fill the loops with close
buttonhole stitch.

To use an eye with the hook, loop it onto the
hook and pass a pin through the loops of the eye to
hold it in position. Work a single oversewing stitch in
each loop, remove the pin and work close buttonhole
stitch round each loop.

When using bars hold with an oversewing stitch
and attach with buttonhole stitch. If the bar is likely
to show, cover it completely with loop stitches

between the metal loops. These can be difficult to fasten, so do not use in places that are awkward to reach. Only cover large bars, as small ones would be almost impossible to fasten.

A bar made entirely of thread is the least visible of all, but it is not very strong. It is inclined to pull away from the fabric as the stitches all fall in one place. Use only where there is little strain (e.g. tops of zips).

Make a bar of about four stitches (more for a larger bar) taking the stitches as deep as possible, work close loop stitches over the entire bar.

If you have to attach a number of hooks to a special garment, you may prefer to partly cover them after sewing them: cut a strip of lining on the cross (or use bought bias binding), press in the edges, and slip it under the heads of the hooks. Hem in place with small stitches.

## HORSEHAIR BRAID

A wide braid made of plaited strands of nylon or polyester filament, though no doubt it once was made from horses' hair. The main use of this braid is for stiffening the hemline of long dresses and to emphasise some style features of period stage costume.

## HORSEHAIR CANVAS

(See *Haircloth.*)

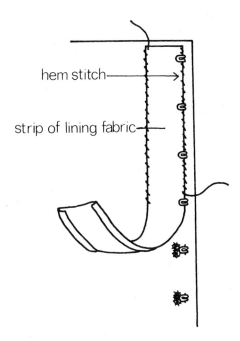

hem stitch

strip of lining fabric

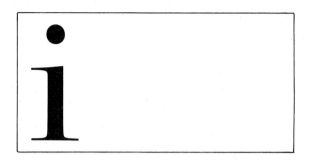

## INSERTION STITCHES

These stitches are worked to join two pieces of fabric in a decorative fashion. It is important always to turn under and press both raw edges if hems are not to be finished. Tack both edges to tissue paper leaving an even distance between.

A type of herringbone stitch may be used to join the two edges, inserting the needle vertically through the edge instead of horizontally. Alternatively a twist can be added by twisting the needle point round the central thread before re-inserting it on the opposite side.

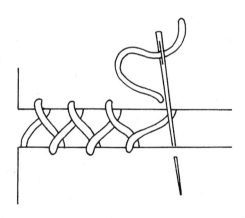

## INSIDE LEG

This is a length measurement used to establish the length of trouser legs. The inside leg seam runs from crutch to ankle. The precise position of the hem depends a little on fashion and also on the style of the trousers. Flared trousers are usually worn much longer than straight ones: sometimes tight trousers finishing above the ankle bone are fashionable. With women's trousers the height of heel to be worn should be included when deciding on the correct inside leg measurement.

It is difficult to measure the inside leg accurately: the best way to do it is to measure the seam of a pair of trousers, adjusting, if necessary, to allow for shoes and fashion.

When cutting out trousers use the inside leg measurement to establish the length but also check that the outside leg length is sufficient.

## INTERSECTING SEAMS

Where completed seams have to match, insert a pin across the fitting line, precisely in the two seams. Do not push the pin in too far. Stitch the joining seam, sewing over the pin. This will ensure that the two seams remain in place.

If the seams are bulky it helps in addition to machine across this section first, then return to the start of the seam and sew it without fear of a bulge of excess fabric working up as you near the seams.

If the actual seam is free, as with a narrow seam or french seam, it helps to have the two being joined facing in opposite directions to reduce the bulk.

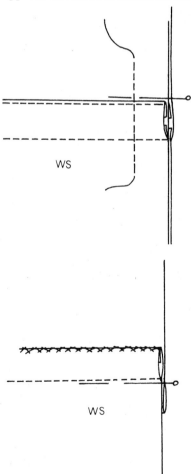

WS

WS

# INTERFACING

An interfacing is an extra layer of fabric put on the inside of the garment. It is put in selected positions depending on the style of the garment and the use to which it will be put. For example a heavy winter coat has the prospect of years of wear and being constantly put on and fastened and it would almost immediately look amateurish, creased and limp if interfacing were not used. In an item such as that the collar, lapels and buttoned area would need interfacing, so would the pockets; it would improve it to also interface the hemline and sleeve hems and because of the weight of the fabric the shoulder area too should be interfaced. At the other end of the scale interfacing is not required in nightwear, except perhaps for the buttonholes of pyjamas and it would be a definite disadvantage to use it in underwear or in such things as T shirts and track suits which need to remain soft and pliable.

With all the items between, including dresses, blouses, skirts, holiday wear, children's clothes, trousers, shirts, pinafore dresses, the decision as to which areas to interface will vary. Paper patterns will indicate where interfacing should go and the areas suggested will include collars, cuffs and places where buttons and buttonholes will be placed. However, the decision also depends on the fabric being used so it is necessary to consider other positions on the specific item you are making. The following may be a guide:

**Positions to use interfacing**
— Collars to keep them shaped in wear.
— Exception: soft cowl or roll collars.

— Cuffs to keep them flat and crisp.
— Exception: double ribbed cuffs that have no opening.

— Button and buttonhole areas.
— Collarless necklines including round, square, V or decorative.

— Patch pockets.
— Exception: not if it would make the pockets too obtrusive.

— Cut pockets. Always back the area with interfacing before making the cut.

— Flaps, welts etc.

— Yokes: sometimes it may not be necessary but always consider it.

— Belts.
— Exception: very soft or single layer tie belts.

— Bands and strappings.

— Decorative features including scallops, facings finished on the outside of the garment, embroidery and any area that will be handled a lot while the decoration is being worked.

The next consideration is what material to use for interfacing. Occasionally an extra layer of the garment fabric is sufficient, or a piece of lining fabric or nylon jersey. At one time interfacing was not used at all in women's clothing — hence the rather limp look of most outfits of the Thirties. Some reinforcement then began to be used but it was generally organdie or lawn or some other non-specific fabric. Probably the only field in which special materials were produced was in the tailoring industry. Canvasses and linens of all types and weights have always been available for use in men's clothes and in women's coats and suits. These are still used, and in traditional hand tailoring on the best cloth, they still produce results second to none in the hands of skilled craftsmen. Even amongst the non-professionals, when a woman has achieved success through experience of making a very wide variety of clothes, it is no bad thing for her to at least try out the old traditional techniques of hand tailoring. It will not only give her an infinite respect for the craft and for all the dedicated people who devote their lives to it, but she may well derive pleasure and satisfaction from working in that way for a change.

The revolution in special interfacing materials took place largely during the 1950s with the emergence of methods of making materials like fabric but which were neither woven nor knitted, together with the possibility of being able to fuse or stick these new materials in place with specially developed adhesives. The initial development of adhesive that is attached to the interfacing material but yet is dry and non-sticky until heat is applied, after which it dries again, has led to an ever widening use of things that stick on, including badges and embroidery as well as such things as Wundaweb. The latter consisting purely of the web of adhesive with nothing attached to it.

All adhesive type interfacings have been developed initially for use in the ready-to-wear industry and subsequently selected ones become available for home dressmaking. It is not too surprising that they are used successfully in factories because special presses etc., can be used to apply the correct temperature for the correct length of time. What is remarkable is that these fusible interfacings have been developed to such a high degree that they are successful in the hands of the home dressmaker — iron settings are notoriously unreliable and she certainly does not time herself nor measure the amount of pressure she is exerting.

A few of these interfacings are of woven material and may be with or without adhesive, but by far the widest range is in the non-woven type, also with or without adhesive. The choice as to whether to iron-on or sew-in is mainly personal but partly dependent on the type of fabric being used and on what types of interfacing are stocked by the shop. The early non-woven interfacings tended to be stiff, collars had angles in them instead of curving smoothly round the neck. As fabrics have become softer and more fluid so interfacings too have become softer and lighter. The secret of making the correct choice between various grades is that whilst the area should look smooth, it should not stand out as being totally different from the rest of the garment. It should certainly not be possible to mentally 'shade-in' the interfaced areas because the edges of the pieces show through.

Vilene is the best known and widest distributed of the non-woven interfacings, both sew-in and iron-on. They produce an extensive range for the making-up trade and a selection of these are available for home dressmaking. Vilene's entire range, known as Highline, include sew-in and iron-on varieties in several weights and also a group called Supershape. These are manufactured in a slightly different way.

Previously all Vilene was produced from short fibres lying in more or less random direction and bonded together. Supershape can be observed to have a distinctly warp direction emphasis. The three Vilene in this range, light, medium and heavy, are very soft and pliable and have a degree of elasticity which makes them easy to handle against all types of fabric.

The choice of weight of Vilene depends on the fabric being used. As a general rule the lighter the fabric the lighter and softer should be the interfacing. However, the interfacing must do its jobs for the life of the garment. For example if a child's playsuit or dungarees are made in a light cotton fabric the lightest interfacing would not be sufficient to stablise the buttons and buttonholes on the straps, so a heavier one would be used. Similarly if a dress or jacket is being made in a medium weight fabric but with gathers or soft pleats and a roll collar, a heavy interfacing might spoil those features even though that weight could be used for strength at button and buttonhole positions.

The following chart may act as a guide to choice but remember that different weights of Vilene can be used in different areas of the same garment. It is often impossible to be absolutely sure which will be the best one until you begin handling it. So try to keep a stock of all weights.

### Vilene Highline interfacings

*Sew-In range*
Light Sew-In: For lightweight and sheer fabrics, e.g. voiles, silks and taffetas. Washable and dry cleanable. Width 81 cm (32 in.).

Light Sew-In — Charcoal: For lightweight and sheer fabrics, e.g. voiles, silks and taffetas. Washable and dry cleanable. Width 81 cm (32 in.).

Medium Sew-In — White: Suitable for all medium-weight fabrics where a firmer handle is required. Washable and dry cleanable. Width 81 cm (32 in.).

Heavy Sew-In: For use with heavy fabrics such as satin, brocades, heavy cottons and tweeds. Ideal for craft work. Washable and dry cleanable. Width 81 cm (32 in.).

*Supershape Iron-On range*
Light Iron-On: For light and sheer fabrics, e.g. voiles, silks, taffetas, chiffons, crêpe de chine. Washable and dry cleanable. Width 90 cm ($35\frac{1}{2}$ in.).

Light Iron-On — Charcoal: For light and sheer fabrics, e.g. voiles, silks, taffetas, chiffons, crêpe de chine. Washable and dry cleanable. Width 90 cm ($35\frac{1}{2}$ in.).

Medium Iron-On: For use with jersey, double knits, woollens, wool mixtures and tweeds. For large areas. Washable and dry cleanable. Width 90 cm ($35\frac{1}{2}$ in.).

Heavy Iron-On: Suitable for double knits, gaberdine, flannel, suit and coat weight wools. For large areas. Washable and dry cleanable. Width 90 cm ($35\frac{1}{2}$ in.).

*Soft Iron-On Vilene*
Suitable for lightweight cotton and cotton mixtures. Use in small areas. Washable only. Width 81 cm (32 in.)

*Firm Iron-On Vilene*
Suitable for medium to heavyweight cotton and cotton mixtures. Use in small areas. Washable only. Width 81 cm (32 in.).

### How to interface

It is not easy to make rules about this because so much depends on the type of fabric being used and the style of the garment. The finished effect also plays a part. For instance, iron-on interfacings, although washable, should be included in a garment seam because at some stage during washing they will become detached. (Easily re-fixed of course, if necessary putting in a piece of Wundaweb.) However if, as on a shirt, some types of cuff, some top-stitched garments, there will finally be a row of machining penetrating the fabric and the iron-on interfacing, there is no need to do anything in the early stages except press the Vilene in place.

The following list may be of help, but use it only as a guide; the final decision is made while actually sewing.

The great advantage of iron-on interfacing is that it is quicker to use but if in doubt try it out because the pressure of attaching it may cause a line on the garment. As a general rule, if the interfacing is evident it is probably too heavy for the fabric. The lighter the better — you can always add to it as for example a shirt collar.

### Cutting and marking interfacing

*Iron-on varieties*    Cut to shape and size, using the section of garment as a template, especially if alterations have been made to the pattern. Trim about 2mm ($\frac{1}{8}$ in.) from any outside edges to prevent them sticking to the ironing surface. When interfacing a

Neck facing for basic dressing

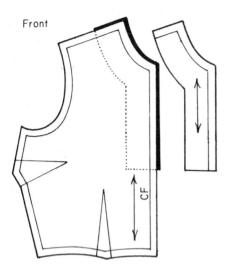

Front

CF

buttoned edge that will have a facing cut the interfacing to shape but trim at least 5 mm ($\frac{1}{4}$ in.) from the long curved edge to ensure that it will be entirely covered by the facing later.

Place fabric pieces wrong side up on the ironing surface making sure large pieces are supported and not being stretched. Place interfacing adhesive side down on top. To avoid error work in pairs, placing both halves of each garment, both cuffs for example, side by side to ensure one right and one left side. Make sure the adhesive is downwards facing. If you do make a mistake and it sticks to the iron, quickly rub your Iron-Clean stick on the hot base plate and wipe with a cloth to remove it. Press the iron onto the interfacing, do not run it along the surface. Use a damp muslin if necessary. Leave the fabric to cool before moving it.

Place pairs of pieces of fabric wrong sides together, pin the pattern back in position and mark any necessary seam allowances, etc. These may have to be tailor tacked but if only one side requires marking, slip carbon paper, folded, between the layers and mark with a tracing wheel. The marks will appear only on the interfacing.

| Item | Weight and type | How to attach |
|---|---|---|
| Collar: Stand | Medium iron on or sew-in. | Included in seam. |
| Shirt | Several layers of light iron-on plus medium at points. | Included in seam. |
| Roll | Light iron-on or sew-in narrow strip at neck edge. If sew-in catch loose edge down. | Included in seam. |
| Buttoned opening | Light or medium iron-on. | Include in seam or cut to extend beyond fold line. Buttons will hold in place. May be taken into armhole in some garments. If sew-in is used it will have to be caught to the fold line if there is no seam. |
| Yoke | Light iron-on or sew-in in entire yoke. | Include in seams. |
| Cuffs | Light iron-on over entire cuff. Alternatively use mediumweight and take it only to the fold line of the cuff. | Include in seams. |
| Pockets | Iron-on or sew-in. | Include in seams. |

*Sew-in varieties* Cut to shape and size using the pattern pieces. Mark any seam allowances with carbon paper and a tracing wheel. Arrange fabric pieces wrong side up and place interfacing on top. Insert a couple of pins to hold. Turn the whole piece over and work rows of basting all over each piece. Do this from the fabric side because once the garment is constructed it can be difficult to remove all the stitches.

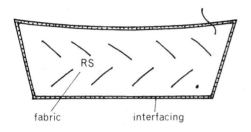

fabric interfacing

When using heavy Vilene that is too thick to include in the seams, trim it away on the dotted carbon line and attach with catch stitch over the edge. In the case of a waistband it may be machined if preferred, and also possibly in pockets, decorative bands etc., provided the later seams are stitched accurately.

If the Vilene is included in the seams, trim it down after machining and before pressing the seams. If sharp corners are to be machined, cut off the corner of the Vilene before stitching, it makes it easier to turn through and produces a flatter corner.

Note that if you decide to interface a section of garment but it is not indicated on the pattern, draw the shape of it on the pattern piece, place the pattern on Vilene and outline with carbon paper and tracing wheel. Remove pattern and cut out the Vilene.

If woven interfacing is used, whether iron-on or sew-in the grain should be the same on the interfacing as on the garment. Also with Vilene Supershape that has a certain amount of 'give', take care to cut it with the 'give' running in the most advantageous position for the area.

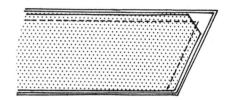

### Joining interfacings

In order to economise, use up odd pieces or cut from a small length of interfacing, to make joins. With medium or heavy interfacings they should be joined edge to edge to avoid a ridge showing through the garment. The pieces can be cut, placing the join in a fairly unobtrusive place if possible, then the edges

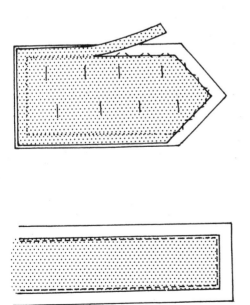

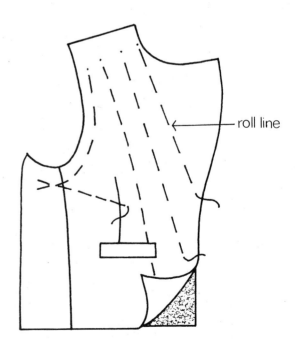

roll line

butted together and joined with a wide zig-zag or running zig-zag stitch. If the interfacing is likely to fray, e.g. canvas, place a narrow piece of fabric behind the join. The selvedge cut from the edge of lining is suitable for this.

Light and soft interfacing may wrinkle if joined with a large zig-zag stitch so allow an extra 5 mm ($\frac{1}{4}$ in.) on one edge when cutting then overlap and work a zig-zag or a combination of straight and zig-zag stitch, over each raw edge.

If darts are to be made in interfacing, cut out the shape of the dart, bring the edges together and work a wide zig-zag stitch to join the edges together. With light interfacing stitch the dart in the usual way but then trim off the surplus to 3 mm ($\frac{1}{8}$ in.) and press open.

*Interfacing a coat or jacket with canvas*    Most men's suit and coat weight fabrics will need canvas in the main part of the coat front, with a layer of tailor's felt or domette, plus haircloth in the chest area. In a woman's coat the padding (domette or felt) is usually omitted although often the entire front of a coat is backed with canvas if the cloth is very soft. With all coats add a piece of linen to the front where the buttons and buttonholes will come.

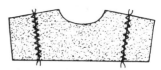

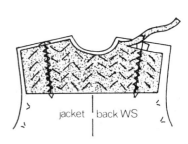

place cut edges together — zigzag edge to edge

jacket ¦ back WS

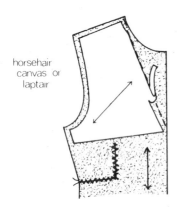

horsehair canvas or laptair

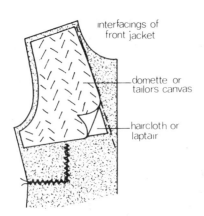

interfacings of front jacket

domette or tailors canvas

haircloth or laptair

Cut canvas on the same grain as the jacket or coat front. Cut a piece of haircloth for a man's coat, on the cross, to cover the chest to below the armhole. Trim it away on the lapel roll line. The domette or felt is cut the same size.

Stitch darts into the canvas, joining edge to edge.

Place the haircloth, or the canvas, and the domette on top of that. Baste all three together. Use tacking thread but remember that the stitches will not be removed. Press well on both sides with a damp cloth. Place canvas assembly on the table with the domette uppermost. Place the coat front on top wrong side down. Line up the edges and baste from shoulder to hem, another row nearer to the front edge, one row on the lapel line, with a final one round the armhole.

As women's coats are made from softer fabric it helps to support it by inserting interfacing across the back neck and shoulder area. Make any darts, place interfacing to the wrong side of the jacket back, and baste in position. The interfacing may be included in the seams later or it may be cut away at this point to the fitting line and caught down to the fabric.

## INTERLINING

The same as interfacing. The term 'interlining' is used in the ready-to-wear manufacturing industry but it is one that can be slightly confusing to the home dressmaker who may think it concerns lining. Interfacing is the additional material placed on the wrong side of fabric to reinforce it either to keep that area in shape or to take the strain of wear.

(See *Interfacing* and *Underlining*.)

## IRON

The iron is used at various temperatures and preferably in combination with moisture. As the range of light-weight fabrics is so wide the most useful iron is a steam iron. It can be used dry, directly on fabric, or with a damp cloth on heavy fabric, as well as being set on steam for a wide variety of light and medium fabrics. Care must be taken, however, to ensure that the holes in the base of the iron do not leave imprints on soft fabrics.

If it is possible to have two irons then a dry iron in addition is very useful indeed. In fact if tailoring is to be done or heavy fabrics handled often, then it is almost invaluable for its weight and smooth base plate.

Some steam irons have additional features which can be used to good effect. These include several different 'steam' settings, a button for releasing additional steam and another for spraying water.

When using an iron on a damp pressing cloth, set the iron slightly hotter than the correct setting for the particular fabric or insufficient heat will reach it.

## IRON CLEANER

A small stick that removes marks from the base of an iron. Heat the iron and rub on the stick. Wipe off the resulting liquid. It also removes interfacing adhesive that may be on the iron, and helps to unblock the holes in a steam iron.

Iron cleaner is in a transparent tube attached to a card and sold as a haberdashery item and also in electrical and hardware departments.

## IRON COVER

An iron-shaped metal frame covered with a perforated paper substance. When fixed on to the base of an iron it protects the fabric from direct heat, but, with a steam iron still allows steam through the holes. A useful tool for difficult fabrics that may mark easily, such as velvet, satin etc.

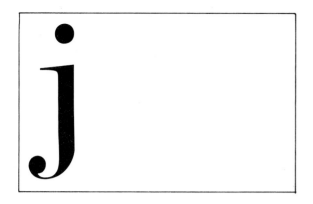

## JABOT

A decorative feature on the front of a blouse or dress. The jabot may be narrow pieces of fabric, in several layers, gathered onto a straight band, or it may be rings of fabric with the inner edge attached to the band. The jabot, sewn on or made detachable with Velcro or press studs, usually hangs from the neck down the centre front. It is a decoration much used for blouses under edge-to-edge Chanel-type jackets.

## JACQUARD

Named after the inventor of a loom, jacquard fabrics are those with patterns woven in. The weft threads pass over the required number of warp threads; this varies with each row of the pattern, and so the same pattern in reverse is formed on the wrong side of the fabric.

## JACQUARD RIBBONS

Luxury ribbons that have an intricate woven pattern, too intricate for the type of loom used to weave plain or simple-figured qualities. The term comes from the inventor of the part of the loom that allows for this infinite control of the warp, namely Joseph-Marie Jacquard (1752-1834). Jacquard ribbons, often floral, are much more pleasing in appearance than similar designs achieved by printing. Woven labels, as found in good clothes, are examples of jacquard weaving. Rich effects are created in jacquard ribbons by combining exotic colours and threads, including gold and silver.

## JERSEY

(See *Knitted Fabrics*.)

## JERSEY STITCH

(See *Stretch Stitches*.)

## JIGGER

The inside button on a double-breasted coat used to hold the underneath in position.

## JOINS IN FABRIC

When short of fabric for cutting small pieces such as facings and belts, the joins will be less obvious if they are made on the cross. The fabric will 'give' at the join and there will be no likelihood of it bubbling.

However, if a small piece is to be joined to a larger section of fabric the join must be on the straight. For example, when cutting a flared skirt and the fabric is not wide enough a small triangle may be needed. The join must be on the straight because the weight of the whole would cause a bias join to stretch.

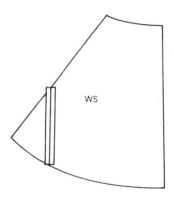

## JUMP SUIT

Similar to a boiler suit or cat-suit in that it is an all-in-one garment, but the jump suit can be made in less workmanlike materials, such as velour, plush and velvet. The jump suit can be fairly close fitting with a variety of style features and it is much more comfortable and easy to fit if made in knit fabrics.

## KICK TAPE

Also known as heel tape. A narrow fabric woven specifically for providing scuff resistance to the inside of the bottoms of trouser legs. It is worth adding even to ready made trousers where the manufacturers have failed to take this precaution. On the Continent trousers without kick tape are practically unknown. These tapes are tough, being woven from either polyester or nylon. Avoid iron-on qualities as these almost invariably come off after a succession of dry cleanings.

## KIMONO

A straight, loose Japanese garment with wide sleeves cut in one with the main part. This traditional garment has been adapted for western wear and features such as the wrap-front, wide belt and sleeve line, are often incorporated into other sytles.

A kimono sleeve is frequently used; it is an extension of the bodice and the shoulder seam may be either horizontal or following the slope of the arm. If it slopes, arm movement may be restricted but this is corrected by inserting an underarm gusset. A true kimono sleeve is loose at the wrist often with turn-back cuff, but we frequently vary this by adding fitted cuffs, still referring to this loose full armhole as kimono.

## KNICKERBOCKERS

Trousers that finish below the knee, gathered into a band and buttoned or fastened with Velcro. Made in firm, hard-wearing fabrics such as cord and tweed, they are a sporting garment but they sometimes appear in other fabrics, even satin, and are called 'pedal-pushers'.

## KNITTED FABRICS

Knits or jersey fabrics are all those which are constructed on a knitting machine from one continuous thread. The fabric may be knitted flat in which case it has a selvedge, often very rough, or it may be made on a circular knitting machine. The latter will have a cut edge when sold.

Welt knits are those made by running one thread back and forth. These fabrics are firm, often closely constructed and may have similar right and wrong sides. Warp knits are made from a large number of vertical yarns being knitted at once. These fabrics have an easily visible right and wrong side and are often quite thin with a lot of 'give' in them.

Knits should be handled according to their weight and construction and according to the result wanted.

## KNOT

Most hand stitching begins with a knot. This is easily made with the fingers. The thread is broken from the reel, moistened, threaded through the needle with the right hand and the end taken with the left. Take this end with the left thumb and forefinger and pull it until there is sufficient pulled through. At the maximum point, while still taut, wind the thread once round the forefinger under the thumb. Immediately slide the thumb to the end of the forefinger, pushing the thread. As it reaches the fingertip bring in the second finger and use its tip against the tip of the thumb to slide the knot out to the end of the thread.

This should all be done in one quick, smooth movement.

## KNOTTED CABLE CHAIN STITCH

A thick embroidery stitch worked as for chain stitch but at the beginning of each stitch work a small knot by laying the thread along the line of the design, taking a small stitch over the thread, then passing the needle and thread under this first stitch. Then work the chain stitch, work the knot and so on.

(See *Chain Stitch*.)

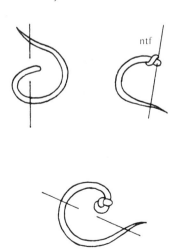

## KNOTTED LOOP STITCH

A looped embroidery stitch worked exactly as for loop stitch, but the thread is twisted round the needle before the downward stitch is made. Loops are tightened round the head of the needle by pulling the thread gently before the stitch is completed.

(See also *Loop Stitch*.)

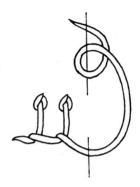

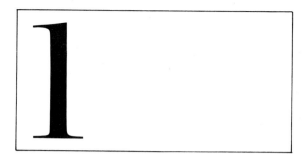

## LACE APPLIQUE

Decorative motifs may be bought, cut from piece lace — possibly old lace — or made from tatting or crochet.

Make sure the weight of the motif and the fibre from which it is made are suitable for the fabric. Place the motif in position. For a solid effect slip a small piece of fabric adhesive (such as Wundaweb) underneath, and press both sides using a damp muslin. Attach round the edge with oversewing or loop stitch in a thread exactly matching the lace, or use zig-zag stitch. If you wish to trim fabric away on the wrong side for an open effect you cannot use adhesive, so insert a few tacking stitches instead.

Carefully snip off all ends of thread. Remove tacks if used. Cut away the fabric behind the motif, snipping close beside the stitching. Press on a towel.

loop stitching edge of motif to garment

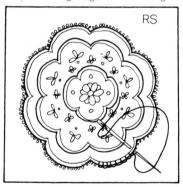

## LACE EDGING

Select a lace of suitable fibre and texture for the fabric; it could even be hand-made lace. Choose a suitable method of attaching from the following methods.

Lay the edge of the lace over the fabric and hem, trimming and neatening the fabric raw edge underneath. Turn a narrow hem on the fabric and hem or machine it before putting the edge of the lace to it, then oversew or whip the two together. Work a small zig-zag or satin stitch by machine over the lace edge and trim off the surplus fabric.

To introduce gathers of fullness into the lace choose a hand method and every 3 to 5 mm ($\frac{1}{8}$ to $\frac{1}{4}$ in.) take a stitch through the lace only then insert the needle in its correct position close to the previous stitch. This will cause a tiny pleat to form in the lace.

Some types of lace edging have a thread running through the edge that can be pulled up to gather the lace.

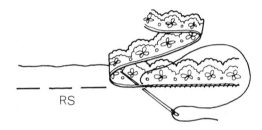

RS

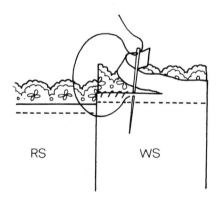

RS          WS

trimming and neatening on WS

## LACE INSERTION

The lace used is usually one with both edges finished in the same way. This may be straight, picot, scalloped; but lace with differing edges may be used. Choose a lace suitable in style and fibre, remembering that the feature of insertion is to cut away the fabric behind the lace.

Either a hand or machine stitch can be used. For example hemming, felling, loop stitch, feather stitch, zig-zag, satin stitch; whatever the stitch it must be very small and extend only over the first bar at the edge of the lace. If working round small scallops it is easier to choose a hand stitch.

Place the lace in position on the right side and tack. Stitch both edges. Press. Trim away the fabric on the wrong side with sharp scissors and neaten with hand-overcasting.

trim away at back

trim ends close to oversewing

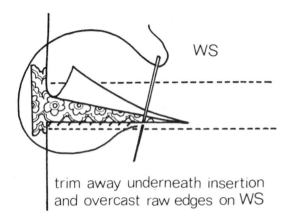

trim away underneath insertion and overcast raw edges on WS

## LACE SEAMS & JOINS

### Piece lace

A French seam or narrow finish seam is acceptable on most garments if the lace is lightweight but on heavy lace such as Guipure the seam will not only be unsightly but it will be almost impossible to press it to a good finish. With this type of heavy lace cut and fit the lining and use it as a pattern to avoid waste and alterations to the lace and mark the seam lines with tacking. On each seam lap the front garment edge over the back, match up the seam lines and tack. Set the machine to a very small zig-zag and stitch from the right side through both layers. Follow any obvious outlines in the design without moving too far in either direction. Remove the tacks carefully then with small pointed scissors trim off the surplus lace edge on both right and wrong side.

Net can be joined in the same way but with a straight row of stitching.

### Edging or insertion

To join lace edging or insertion overlap the two ends, and work close oversewing stitches across the width of the lace, following the outline of part of the design. Trim away the excess lace close to the stitching on both the right side and the wrong side.

To mitre a corner mark the angle of the mitre on each end of lace, and overlap the two ends, matching the tack marks. Oversew closely round a main part of the design. Trim away the surplus lace on the right side and the wrong side.

To press the lace place the right side down onto a folded towel; press lightly with a steam iron.

## LAMBSWOOL

Also called fleece, lambswool is similar in texture to wadding but more wiry and resilient. Used to make sleeve head rolls, the sausage shapes that support the top of a sleeve in a tailored coat. May also be used to make shoulder pads in place of wadding.

## LAPEL

The lapel is the part of the jacket front that rolls back between the collar end and the top button.

(See *Tailored Collar* page 71, for sewing instructions.)

## LAYER

Layering is trimming a number of raw edges to different widths to reduce bulk and lessen the chance of a ridge. Always trim the narrowest edge as narrow as possible, depending on how much the fabric frays and leave other edges a little wider. To avoid any chance of a ridge appearing with medium or heavy fabrics, the widest edge should be the one that will lie against the garment.

## LAYERED LOOK

Layers have always been worn during winter but it is only comparatively recently that the term 'layered look' has been used by designers to describe co-ordinating outfits comprising several pieces, often of varying lengths as well as colour and texture, to be worn one over the other. The emergence of this type of outfit co-incided with the increase in the variety of lightweight fabrics.

## LEAF STITCH

A flat embroidery stitch worked in a similar way to fishbone stitch, but the two lines of diagonal stitches overlap in a cross stitch effect at the central line.

(See also *Fishbone Stitch*.)

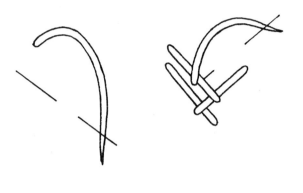

## LINEN

Embroidery linen is made in various weights and colours. Tailoring linen is made in limited dark colours and white and it is used for such things as backing pocket areas and reinforcing hems.

## LINING

A lining is a separate layer of fabric inside a garment. The lining is partly made, the stage reached depending on the garment, and inserted against the wrong side of the garment, wrong side down. In all linings there are points to be matched with the garment, for example, seams, centre back, centre front, darts; and these must be matched first, pinning if necessary, then tacking or basting. Never pull the lining taut or it will cause wrinkles in the outer fabric when worn. When inserting the partly made lining begin by matching and tacking the important points, then work towards the outer edges. Finally the raw edges are dealt with, the size of the lining being accurately adjusted and finished at those outer edges.

A loose lining hangs separately inside the garment. In a dress or skirt it is added for comfort, and it prolongs the life of the garment. It will rarely prevent creasing or seating because it is loose, unlike mounting. The lining is inserted near the end of the garment construction; it can even go in after the hem has been turned up if it is carefully made to fit.

Cut out the lining using the pattern pieces, but omitting areas where facings occur. Remember to add turnings to the lining where leaving off a facing. Cut out slightly outside the pattern edge all round to allow ease, because most lining fabrics have no 'give' in them. Alternatively if extensive pattern alterations were made, place the cut-out fabric pieces on the lining and cut out.

Tack up the lining and try it on, making any adjustment made on the garment when it was fitted. Stitch the lining seams and press open, or use narrow seams. Remember that the side towards the body will be the right side as the lining is made up.

### Lining a skirt

Place the lining in a skirt before attaching the waistband but after inserting the zip. Put the edges of the skirt and the lining together at the waist, and baste. Also baste at the seams through lining and fabric.

Attach the waistband. Turn under the edge of the lining by the zip and hem. Turn up the lining hem so that it is about 3 cm (1¼ in.) shorter than the skirt. At the hem, work bar tacks at the side seams and at the centre front and centre back. Make the tacks 5 cm (2 in.) so that movement is not restricted.

When lining a pleated skirt, make a seam in the lining where the pleat comes, and stitch the seam down to just below the level of the pleat. Leave the seam open below this. At the hem work bar tacks at the seams only, not where the pleats fall. Alternatively to hold the pleats in position, leave the slit at the side of the skirt.

### Lining a dress

Make up the lining. Match up the shoulder seams of the lining and dress, and baste wrong sides together. Use a dress dummy for this. Baste around the neck and armholes and down the seams taking the stitches through both lining and fabric. Stitch loosely. Finish the neck edge according to the style of the dress. Turn in the edge of the lining, tack and hem to dress collar, facing etc. Prick stitch down the side seams as far as the waist working from the right side through fabric and lining.

On a sleeveless dress, turn in the lining edges, and fell a little way back from the armhole edge. Turn up the hem so that it is 3 cm (1¼ in.) shorter than the dress. Work bar tacks at intervals. The lining hem may be finished by hand or machine.

### Lining sleeves

For short sleeves, stitch the dress and lining seams, and press. There is no need to neaten the edges. Put the sleeve and the lining right sides together, tack round the lower edge, and machine. Trim the seam, turn the lining through, roll the lower edge, tack and press. When rolling make sure the lining is a little back from the sleeve edge. Smooth the lining over the sleeve, pulling it up well so that it will not drop in wear and show at the hem. Baste the two layers round the sleeve head but not too near the edge.

To set the sleeve to the armhole, leave the lining free. Back stitch the lining turnings to the armhole turnings then turn the sleeve edge of the lining over, and bring it onto the armhole turnings. Tack and fell. Never pull the lining taut.

For long sleeves, tack and machine the under sleeve seam. Stitch a little way outside the fitting line to allow some ease. Press seam towards the back. Do not neaten. Tack and machine the other seam, matching balance marks to ease in any fullness. Stitch just outside the fitting line. Press to one side. Note — sleeve may have only one seam. Hold sleeves and linings wrong sides out and place the turning of the under sleeve seam against the same seam on the sleeve. Be sure to put the right lining to the appropriate sleeve. Using a long back stitch, attach the lining turnings to the sleeve turnings on both under and upper sleeves. End the back stitching 5 cm (2 in.) below the sleeve head and 12 cm ($4\frac{3}{4}$ in.) above the cuff to enable the edges to be handled easily.

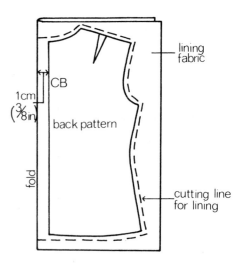

Draw the lining through by putting one hand through the wrist and up to the sleeve head; take hold of the lining and sleeve, and pull through. With the lining now right side out, work a couple of rows of basting through the lining and sleeve to hold the lining in place. Work another row of basting round the top of the sleeve about 4 cm ($1\frac{5}{8}$ in.) in from the raw edge, leaving plenty of room to cope with setting in the sleeve.

*Hems*    Trim the raw edge of the lining if necessary, turn up the lining so that 2.5 cm (1 in.) of sleeve is visible, and crease the lining. Turn under the lining edges beside the cuff opening if there is one. On the button side the lining runs level with the edge, on the buttonhole side it slopes in to a point 3 cm ($1\frac{1}{4}$ in.) from the edge to allow room for the buttonholes. Tack down, but when working round the hem of the sleeve draw the lining back about 3 mm ($\frac{1}{8}$ in.) to allow ease. Finish by felling with small invisible stitches. On a plain long sleeve, simply turn up the sleeve hem then trim and fell the lining.

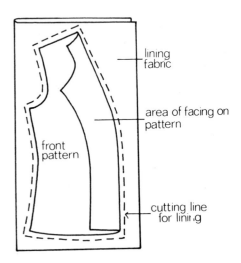

Set the sleeve into the armhole, omitting the linings. Back stitch the armhole lining turnings to the dress armhole, then bring the sleeve lining edge over and fell.

### Lining a coat or jacket
Use the pattern pieces or the cut out pieces of coat, but place the back against the fold of the lining 1.5 cm ($\frac{5}{8}$ in.) from it to allow a pleat. If a back neck facing is given in the pattern do not use it if a collar is to be added, but cut the back lining up to the neck. Cut the front linings minus the width of the front facing. For all pieces, cut a little outside the edge, as the lining must be bigger than the garment to prevent tight ridges on the fabric in wear.

Stitch and press any darts or tucks. If there is a separate pattern for the lining it may well suggest tucks in some places instead of darts which is correct. Tack the pleat in the centre back of the lining. On a jacket, stitch the pleat on the wrong side from the hem to just above the waist. On a full length coat it helps in providing ease to leave the pleat tacked right to the hem. Press the pleat to one side.

In a man's jacket, front linings are first joined to the facings to enable the inside pocket to be made. The facings are then joined to the coat at the front edge and the lining joined by hand at the side seams. Tack the turnings together at the side seams.

In a woman's coat or jacket there is no need to join the front lining to the facing, so the facing can be attached and finished on its own, and the lining side seams joined. Stitch outside the fitting line to allow ease. Press the turnings towards the front.

Line up the centre back pleat against the centre back of the coat and baste from below neck to above hem. Smooth out the lining as far as the side seams and work another row of basting on each side of the centre and down through the dart if there is one. Baste across the back neck and round the armhole keeping at least 3 cm ($1\frac{1}{4}$ in.) inside the edge, and baste down beside the side seam. Avoid basting where the shoulder pads will be placed.

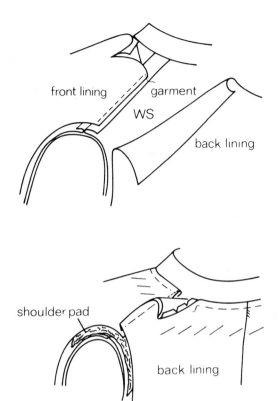

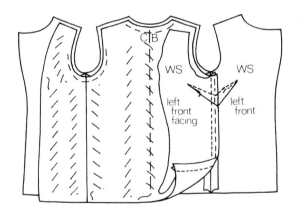

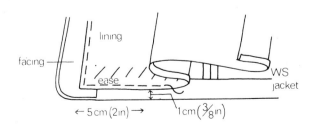

On a woman's coat, back stitch or flash baste the lining turnings to the coat turnings. Start at least 3 cm ($1\frac{1}{4}$ in.) below the armhole. Smooth out the front linings on the lower half of the coat and work a couple of rows of basting from the hem up to the bust shaping. Then lift the top of the coat onto your hand, smooth the lining over the bust, and baste in the centre of the shoulder. Baste round the armhole and down the front edge. Holding it like this will ensure that the shape is retained.

Hold the lining in place by working a row of basting along the hem 5 cm (2 in.) from the edge. Do this from the right side of the jacket.

Turn in all raw edges round the hem and front edges or side seams, folding under the raw edge before pulling it back slightly, about 3 mm ($\frac{1}{8}$ in.) to tack it down. At the hem, 1 cm ($\frac{3}{8}$ in.) of hem should show on a jacket but 2.5 cm (1 in.) on a full length coat.

On a full length coat you may prefer to finish the lining hem separately, leaving it hanging loose from the coat and attach only at the seams with 2 cm ($\frac{3}{4}$ in.) bar tacks. It is more usual on a man's overcoat to stitch the lining to the hem. Stitch the coat shoulders and smooth the front lining up to the shoulder and back stitch the lining edge to the shoulder seams, or to the shoulder pads.

Smooth the back lining up so that it falls over the front shoulder. Turn under the raw edge of the lining across the back of the neck, including the pleat, and tack down.

Turn under and tack the lining edges across the shoulder. Fell across the shoulders and the back neck, hemming down the edge of the pleat for 2 cm ($\frac{3}{4}$ in.) down the centre back to keep it flat.

## LINK BUTTONS

These may be used in place of cuff links or as a decorative fastening. Two buttonholes are required. Another place where the principle of joining two buttons is useful is on heavy leather or suede coats where the strain of stitching through the leather may make a tear. To use a link button punch a small hole in the coat and work buttonhole stitch round it. Join the coat button to a small flat backing button, working through the hole.

Two buttons are joined by forming several strands of double waxed thread then loop stitching over the connecting threads.

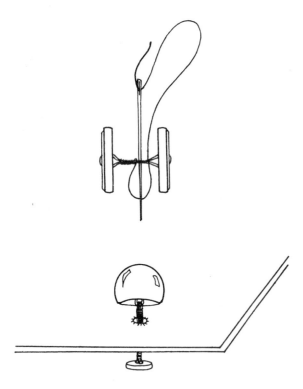

## LONG & SHORT STITCH

A variation of satin stitch, but used as a filling stitch where satin stitches would be too long. The first row is formed using alternative short and long stitches round the outline of the area to be covered. The following rows are worked to fill in the area. A shaded effect can be achieved by working rows in different shades.

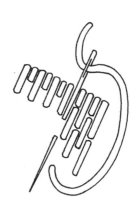

## LOOP STITCH

This has two meanings. First, it is a loose, rather weak hand stitch used when a raw edge overlaps another and needs lightly attaching. Work from left to right inserting the needle back from the raw edge and, catching both fabrics, bring it straight towards you. The thread from the last stitch must lie under the point of the needle. Do not pull the thread tight. The size of the stitch depends on the weight of the fabric but make it as small as possible. The stitches should be square in shape.

Loop stitch may also be used over a single edge. If it is decorative in purpose use a thick thread. If it is to prevent fraying, work on only small areas. It is laborious to do long lengths and it is not as effective as overcasting for containing fraying.

(See also *Buttonhole Stitch*, page 41, with which loop stitch is often confused.)

Another stitch, strictly loop stitch in construction, but not like it in finished appearance, can be worked out of sight between two layers. It is a loose attachment so is not suitable for hems but only for short areas such as holding a front facing to a coat. Lift the facing, work from left to right taking a tiny stitch in the garment and fold. The thread must run under the needle point. Stitches should not be smaller than 2 cm ($\frac{3}{4}$ in.) and can be much longer. Do not pull the thread tight.

Its second meaning is a looped raised embroidery stitch sometimes called buttonhole stitch or blanket stitch, but this is incorrect in sewing terms. The thread begins on the lower line of the stitch. Take a straight stitch up, with the thread under the needle point. As the stitch is pulled up the loop is formed. The stitch is worked close together, and may be used in cut-work embroidery, working round a shape, the fabric then being cut away from the centre.

(See also *Buttonhole Stitch*, in hand sewing, page 41 and the first meaning of loop stitch, above for other uses.)

## LOOP STITCH WITH PICOT

An embroidery stitch for edging worked in the same way as loop stitch, but when a picot (or knot) is required the thread is twisted round the needle and pulled towards the worked loop stitch. The next stitch is made into the last loop.

(See also *Loop Stitch*.)

The thread is twisted around the needle

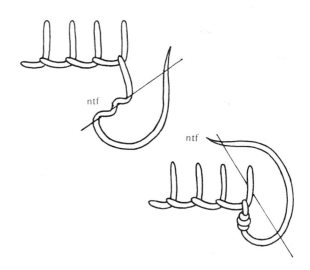

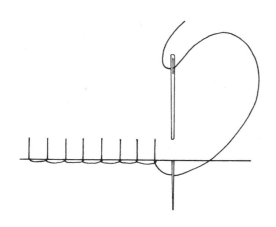

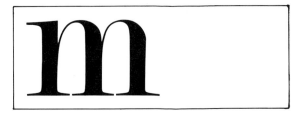

## MACHINE BASTING

Basting, or tacking, by machine is quicker than by hand, but it should not be used where there is a curve or where fullness has to be distributed. Use where a number of straight seams can be sewn, or where hand tacking would not withstand the strain of fitting.

The simplest stitch to use is the largest straight stitch. This is quickly removed after stitching permanently by taking hold of the spool thread and easing it out.

Details of how to set up your machine for basting will be described in the machine manual. On some models a special foot is attached, on others the feed teeth have to be dropped and the stitch length controlled by you.

Basting thread cannot usually be used on the machine so there is a risk of damage to the fabric when the stitches are removed. Reduce this risk by working the permanent machine stitching beside the basting so that the latter is not caught under the needle. Alternatively, machine embroidery thread can be used safely and easily removed because it is soft and will break when gently pulled.

## MACHINE STITCHING

If you look after your machine and keep it clean (many do not need general oiling now) it should sew on any fabric without any trouble.

Obviously the length of the stitch must be adjusted so that it looks right on the fabric; remember that it will vary on different thicknesses — double layer, single layer, etc. Also the length must be adjusted in conjunction with the width when working zig-zag or embroidery stitches. Both the adjustments are easy to make on good modern machines.

Sometimes the tension may need altering *slightly*. The top thread is held in check by various hooks and discs before it passes through the needle. The bottom thread is wound onto the spool, which is inserted in a case. The thread is pulled round until it is caught under a spring, so it is then under control. These two threads loop together to form what is known as the lock stitch. The interlocking takes place between the two layers of fabric. However if, because of the type of fabric, thread, or number of layers, the stitch does not look similar on both the upper and under sides, then the tension may have to be adjusted. If the top

thread is visible like little knots or loops on the under side of the fabric it indicates that the tension on the top thread is too loose and needs tightening. If the bottom thread can be seen on the top of the fabric then loosen the top tension a little. Consult your sewing machine manual if you don't know how to do it.

Occasionally the spring on the spool container needs adjusting, but only if a thick thread or elastic has been used. A tiny screw can be moved a little to produce the correct tension. When the spool is in its case and you hold the end of the thread and gently bob it up and down, the spool case should move slowly down the thread. If it moves too fast or not at all it is likely that it needs adjusting.

If the stitch is not satisfactory, try changing the size of the needle. Change the type of thread if possible, although good modern machines are designed to accept all the threads available. Another remedy with fine fabrics is to place a piece of paper under the fabric. Use tissue or light typing paper. It can be easily torn out after stitching.

Beginners often worry about faults in stitching, probably because they are not sufficiently experienced to know how to adjust the machine for the fabric and because they are not familiar with the machine. Most faults in stitching are simply remedied, most are the fault of the user, not the machine.

If the machine does not stitch properly, unthread it and start again. It is most likely that the thread has missed one of its control points.

If the stitch is still unsatisfactory, check and correct as follows.

*Thread breakage*
1 Improper threading of either top or bobbin thread.
2 Starting machine with needle incorrectly positioned.
3 Rough spots on needle eye, throat plate or bobbin case.
4 Lint or thread ends around bobbin case.
5 Needle too fine for fabric or thread.
6 Needle improperly inserted.
7 Bent needle.
8 Tension too tight.
9 Top thread caught around spool holder or another point on the machine.

*Irregular or skipped stitches*
1 Sewing in spurts.
2 Needle wrong size for thread or fabric, or wrong type of needle.
3 Pressure too light.
4 Pulling fabric as you sew.

*Machine stuck*
Bits of thread caught in bobbin case holder. Clear out regularly, especially when using synthetic thread.

*Needle breakage*
1   Wrong needle for machine.
2   Presser foot improperly set.
3   Stitching over pins, zip, etc.
4   Bobbin inserted incorrectly.
5   Needle improperly inserted.
6   Wrong size needle for fabric.
7   Pulling fabric as you sew.

## MAGYAR

A type of sleeve cut in one piece with the bodice. It is similar in effect to the kimono sleeve but the latter is usually wider and has a lower, looser armhole. The magyar style is taken from a sleeve in a typical Hungarian costume.

## MANDARIN

A stand collar with the ends meeting at the centre front of the neck even if the opening is elsewhere, either shoulder or centre back. This type of collar is a copy of the Chinese style, it is narrow and the two front corners are usually curved.

(For details of methods of making and attaching see *Stand Collar*, page 70.)

## MAN-MADE FIBRES

These are the fibres derived, mainly, from mineral sources and having different properties of warmth, absorbency and reaction to heat from the natural ones. The man-made, or synthetic fibres include acetate, acrylic fibres, modacrylic fibres, cupro, modal, polyamide, polyester, triacetate, viscose and others used in smaller amounts including polyvinyl chloride.

Most man-made fibres can be used alone in fabric manufacture or mixed with natural fibres, so making possible an unbelievably wide range of fabrics for clothing.

## MARIBOU

This is feathered trimming. The feathers, or fluffy synthetic substitutes, are attached with thread to a central cord and they tend to lie in one direction. The trimming is bought by the metre or in cut lengths; it varies in thickness.

It can be attached by working oversewing stitches over the centre cord. Keep the thread loose or the fabric will wrinkle, and make sure the attachment line is marked on the fabric because it is difficult to position the maribou accurately due to its fluffiness.

The trimming may or may not be washable. If the garment is dry cleaned the trimming may have to be removed, or, at the very least, the cleaners will point out that they will not be responsible for the results of

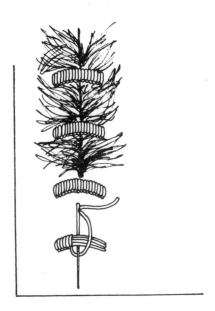

the cleaning.

In any case, maribou is expensive so for ease of removal it can be attached with bar tacks. These are worked at intervals in a thread to match the trimming, not the fabric, and the maribou threaded through them. This also produces a better appearance as the fabric is not likely to wrinkle.

When attaching maribou to a very fine fabric such as silk, back the area with a strip of net to take the strain of stitching.

## MARKING FABRIC

After cutting out a garment and before removing the pattern there will be some information to be transferred to the fabric to make sure the pieces are assembled correctly. With simple styles there may be few essential marking points, with others, especially close-fitting styles, it may be wise to mark all seam lines as well as matching points.

The folds of the fabric should always be marked and this is best done with tacking. Also mark darts and any points where the fabric is to be cut later. Any special features requiring accuracy must be marked, including angles, decorative curves, collars and pockets. If there is a fastening, such as buttons, then the lines on which these are to go should be marked. There is usually no need to mark balance marks on straight seams but always mark them on curved seams, gathered seams and where two edges of different shapes are to be joined, including the armhole and the sleeve head. In addition if there is a point that invariably produces a fitting problem, mark the balance marks and the seam lines in that area as it makes accurate fitting much easier if there are some guide lines. The decision as to how much marking is done also depends on whether there will be help available at fitting. If there is likely to be little or no help it will make this stage easier if all seam lines are marked that will be visible at the first fitting. These include neckline, armholes, waistline and hem-line. Mark with tailor tacks so that with the garment tacked up and being worn you can look in the mirror and see clearly where the tack lines run on the figure.

The method of marking fabric should be chosen according to the type of fabric, the time available and how long the garment is going to take to complete (some marks wear off quickly). The following list gives an indication of the benefits and shortcomings of each method.

*Tailor tacking*    Best; suitable for all fabrics. Mark two layers at once; lasting; easy to remove; will not harm fabric; very accurate. Modern machines will tailor tack; useful where lots of long seams need marking but not for single marks.

*Trace tacking*    Takes a long time; marks one layer at a time; confine to very important delicate clothes that will be in the making for a long time.

*Carbon paper and tracing wheel*    Always test first as marks may be permanent; dark colours often penetrate the fabric; use white and yellow paper only and mark wrong side of fabric only. (The best tracing wheel is smooth edged; it does not make holes in the table.) Difficult to draw straight lines well as much pressure is needed. Quick, marks two layers at once if small strips of paper folded colour outwards are slipped between the two layers of fabric. May be durable though it seems that carbon dots either come out as soon as the iron is put near them, or they are im-movable even by washing. Dots may not show at all on pile or bouclé fabrics. Never use on white fabric.

*Chalk pencil*    May be white or blue. Use for marking dots or points, not for continuous lines. Marks one side only. Comes off easily so not long lasting, but safe on right side of fabric. Good for marking button-hole sizes.

*Tailor's chalk*    Easy to use, excellent for marking straight lines with a ruler, on long seams. Marks one side only, brushes off so use as temporary marker. Good for fitting adjustments. Must be kept sharp. A wax square is also useful, lines are melted by the iron. Does not show up well on all fabrics.

*Chalk wheel*    There are various types, some with a 1.5 cm ($\frac{5}{8}$ in.) measure attached. As for tailor's chalk, marks on one side only but easy to remove. Excellent tool, very quick to use.

## MARK STITCHES

The term that tailors often use to describe thread markings on cloth. Dressmakers call the stitches 'tailors' tacks'.

## MAXI

When the term was first introduced it referred to any unusually long skirt (coat, dress or skirt) in contrast to the mini it was superseding. Gradually maxi-length has come to mean only full length, i.e. ankle or floor length.

(See also *Mini* and *Mid-Calf*.)

## MEASUREMENTS, METRIC and IMPERIAL

Whether measurements are used in centimetres or in inches, it is essential to have some knowledge of both scales, even if it is necessary to consult a chart for the equivalent in the other scale.

### IMPERIAL TO METRIC (SLIGHTLY ROUNDED)

| in. | cm | in. | cm |
|-----|-----|-----|-----|
| $\frac{1}{8}$ | 0.3 | 19 | 48.5 |
| $\frac{1}{4}$ | 0.6 | 20 | 51 |
| $\frac{3}{8}$ | 1 | 21 | 53.5 |
| $\frac{1}{2}$ | 1.3 | 22 | 56 |
| $\frac{5}{8}$ | 1.5 | 23 | 58.5 |
| $\frac{3}{4}$ | 2 | 24 | 61 |
| $\frac{7}{8}$ | 2.2 | 25 | 63.5 |
| 1 | 2.5 | 26 | 66 |
| $1\frac{1}{4}$ | 3.2 | 27 | 68.5 |
| $1\frac{1}{2}$ | 3.8 | 28 | 71 |
| $1\frac{3}{4}$ | 4.5 | 29 | 73.5 |
| 2 | 5 | 30 | 76 |
| $2\frac{1}{2}$ | 6.3 | 31 | 78.5 |
| 3 | 7.5 | 32 | 81.5 |
| $3\frac{1}{2}$ | 9 | 33 | 84 |
| 4 | 10 | 34 | 86.5 |
| $4\frac{1}{2}$ | 11.5 | 35 | 89 |
| 5 | 12.5 | 36 | 91.5 |
| $5\frac{1}{2}$ | 14 | 37 | 94 |
| 6 | 15 | 38 | 96.5 |
| 7 | 18 | 39 | 99 |
| 8 | 20.5 | 40 | 102 |
| 9 | 23 | 41 | 104 |
| 10 | 25.5 | 42 | 107 |
| 11 | 28 | 43 | 109 |
| 12 | 30.5 | 44 | 112 |
| 13 | 33 | 45 | 115 |
| 14 | 35.5 | 46 | 117 |
| 15 | 38 | 47 | 120 |
| 16 | 40.5 | 48 | 122 |
| 17 | 43 | 49 | 125 |
| 18 | 46 | 50 | 127 |

## ZIP LENGTHS

| in. | cm. | in. | cm. |
|---|---|---|---|
| 4 | 10 | 16 | 40 |
| 5 | 12 | 18 | 45 |
| 6 | 15 | 20 | 50 |
| 7 | 18 | 22 | 55 |
| 8 | 20 | 24 | 60 |
| 9 | 23 | 26 | 65 |
| 10 | 25 | 28 | 70 |
| 11 | 28 | 30 | 75 |
| 12 | 30 | 36 | 90 |
| 14 | 35 | | |

## FABRIC WIDTHS

| in. | cm. | in. | cm. |
|---|---|---|---|
| 25 | 64 | 50 | 127 |
| 27 | 70 | 54/56 | 140 |
| 35/36 | 90 | 58/60 | 150 |
| 39 | 100 | 68/70 | 175 |
| 44/45 | 115 | 72 | 180 |
| 48 | 122 | 108 | 275 |

## FABRIC LENGTHS

| yards | metres | yards | metres |
|---|---|---|---|
| $\frac{1}{8}$ | 0.15 | $5\frac{1}{8}$ | 4.70 |
| $\frac{1}{4}$ | 0.25 | $5\frac{1}{4}$ | 4.80 |
| $\frac{3}{8}$ | 0.35 | $5\frac{3}{8}$ | 4.95 |
| $\frac{1}{2}$ | 0.50 | $5\frac{1}{2}$ | 5.05 |
| $\frac{5}{8}$ | 0.60 | $5\frac{5}{8}$ | 5.15 |
| $\frac{3}{4}$ | 0.70 | $5\frac{3}{4}$ | 5.30 |
| $\frac{7}{8}$ | 0.80 | $5\frac{7}{8}$ | 5.40 |
| 1 | 0.95 | 6 | 5.50 |
| $1\frac{1}{8}$ | 1.05 | $6\frac{1}{8}$ | 5.60 |
| $1\frac{1}{4}$ | 1.15 | $6\frac{1}{4}$ | 5.75 |
| $1\frac{3}{8}$ | 1.30 | $6\frac{3}{8}$ | 5.85 |
| $1\frac{1}{2}$ | 1.40 | $6\frac{1}{2}$ | 5.95 |
| $1\frac{5}{8}$ | 1.50 | $6\frac{5}{8}$ | 6.10 |
| $1\frac{3}{4}$ | 1.60 | $6\frac{3}{4}$ | 6.20 |
| $1\frac{7}{8}$ | 1.75 | $6\frac{7}{8}$ | 6.30 |
| 2 | 1.85 | 7 | 6.40 |
| $2\frac{1}{8}$ | 1.95 | $7\frac{1}{8}$ | 6.55 |
| $2\frac{1}{4}$ | 2.10 | $7\frac{1}{4}$ | 6.65 |
| $2\frac{3}{8}$ | 2.20 | $7\frac{3}{8}$ | 6.75 |
| $2\frac{1}{2}$ | 2.30 | $7\frac{1}{2}$ | 6.90 |
| $2\frac{5}{8}$ | 2.40 | $7\frac{5}{8}$ | 7.00 |
| $2\frac{3}{4}$ | 2.55 | $7\frac{3}{4}$ | 7.10 |
| $2\frac{7}{8}$ | 2.65 | $7\frac{7}{8}$ | 7.20 |
| 3 | 2.75 | 8 | 7.35 |
| $3\frac{1}{8}$ | 2.90 | $8\frac{1}{8}$ | 7.45 |
| $3\frac{1}{4}$ | 3.00 | $8\frac{1}{4}$ | 7.55 |
| $3\frac{3}{8}$ | 3.10 | $8\frac{3}{8}$ | 7.70 |
| $3\frac{1}{2}$ | 3.20 | $8\frac{1}{2}$ | 7.80 |
| $3\frac{5}{8}$ | 3.35 | $8\frac{5}{8}$ | 7.90 |
| $3\frac{3}{4}$ | 3.45 | $8\frac{3}{4}$ | 8.00 |
| $3\frac{7}{8}$ | 3.55 | $8\frac{7}{8}$ | 8.15 |
| 4 | 3.70 | 9 | 8.25 |
| $4\frac{1}{8}$ | 3.80 | $9\frac{1}{8}$ | 8.35 |
| $4\frac{1}{4}$ | 3.90 | $9\frac{1}{4}$ | 8.50 |
| $4\frac{3}{8}$ | 4.00 | $9\frac{3}{8}$ | 8.60 |
| $4\frac{1}{2}$ | 4.15 | $9\frac{1}{2}$ | 8.70 |
| $4\frac{5}{8}$ | 4.25 | $9\frac{5}{8}$ | 8.80 |
| $4\frac{3}{4}$ | 4.35 | $9\frac{3}{4}$ | 8.95 |
| $4\frac{7}{8}$ | 4.50 | $9\frac{7}{8}$ | 9.05 |
| 5 | 4.60 | 10 | 9.15 |

When taking body measurements in preparation for choosing a pattern, whether buying fabric or selecting a zip, you may find you have measured in one scale (usually your own tape measure or information from a pre-metric paper pattern) but the goods are sold otherwise.

The above charts show the accepted equivalents in both scales.

## MEASUREMENTS

### Taking measurements and adjusting patterns

If possible wear something thin with a round neck and set-in sleeves. It is almost impossible to find some of the vital body lines if clothes are not worn. If a tight measurement, such as the waist, is required, this can be taken with clothes on too.

Apart from a tape measure, have a narrow belt or piece of fabric, tape or petersham to put round the waist, and a ruler is useful for one of the measurements. If there is someone reliable to help, so much the better, but most measurements can be taken alone accurately enough to locate problems.

*1 Bust/chest*

Take this measurement by running the tape round under the arms and over the bust points. Make sure the tape is horizontal all the way round. This is of course the total measurement and when it comes to deciding whether to adjust a pattern, for women, you will need to have some idea of how average in size the bust prominence is.

For example, two people may measure the same but one may have a narrow back and large bust, the other a small bust but large back. The same size pattern may well be used but both people may need to make an adjustment, one to alter the back, the other the front. When taking the bust measurement take note of the shape of the figure. (You are probably already aware if you have a problem by the bra cup size you wear as well as by the actual bust measurement of the bra.)

This measurement on men and children is the chest, taken firmly round the body in the same position.

Do not add any ease as this will already be included in any pattern bought to that bust or chest size.

## 2 Hips

Men and children are usually fairly straight so the measurement can be taken round the hip bone, keeping the tape level all round.

Women have more of a problem because their more rounded shape makes it difficult to locate the hip level. Find the most prominent part of the pelvic bones and measure at that level. It may not be the widest part of the figure, in which case see *Thighs*, page 192. Make a note of the depth down from the waist at which this measurement is taken; you may need to refer to it later.

Do not add ease, the pattern you buy to that measurement will include the correct amount of ease for movement in skirts, trousers etc. Note that skirt patterns and also men's and children's patterns may well be bought by waist measurement which is fine for the average figure but otherwise check the hip size on the pattern and go by that rather than the waist if the figure is not average.

## 3 Waist

Easy to locate on women. Run the tape tightly round the waist. Do not allow ease and take the measurement firmly even if a loose fit is preferred. The precise size is determined in fitting, this measurement is for deciding on a pattern size. On men and children it may be necessary to discuss where the waistline is before measuring. Take note of personal preference as well as actual shape, e.g. tummies on young children (or men) when measuring, as it will affect the choice of style when selecting the pattern.

The following are used to check the actual pattern piece. Have ready pieces of paper and pins. The surplus edges of patterns are useful for inserting strips to lengthen patterns.

## 4 Back length

Measure straight from the top spinal bone down to the level of the natural waist (leave a tie round the waist as a guide). Measure in the normal posture for

accuracy. This measurement will appear on the list of measurements on the pattern envelope. It is for information, indicating whether you have to lengthen or shorten the pattern. A pattern would not be purchased purely according to this measurement. Measure men, women and children in the same way and check and alter the pattern. The figure on the envelope will tell you how much to add or take off. If you are measuring the actual pattern piece from neck to waist add 1 cm ($\frac{3}{8}$ in.) for ease (2 cm ($\frac{3}{4}$ in.) for large sizes and growing children). Also, make quite sure the pattern neckline is the natural neckline (this information is usually given).

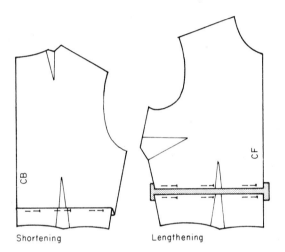

Shortening          Lengthening

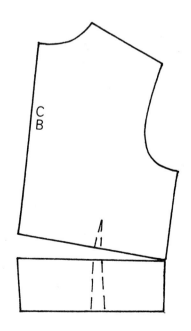

Lengthen or shorten the pattern as shown. There is usually a line on the pattern on which to make the alteration.

Women with hollow backs and average busts must make a wedge-shaped alteration on the back pattern.

*5 Neck to waist*

a) Measure men and children from the hollow at the front of the neck down to the waist. Check the pattern pieces, adding 1 cm ($\frac{3}{8}$ in.) for ease. Since you will have altered if necessary when adjusting for back length, this is just a check because on some very upright or very stooping postures the front pattern may now have to be made longer or shorter.

b) Women should take two measurements, the first from mid-shoulder down to the tip of the bust. If the figure is rounded and the points difficult to locate, measure slightly lower than higher to ensure comfort. On a close-fitting garment a fine adjustment can be done at fitting. If there is specific bust level shaping, such as a dart or a shaped seam, on the pattern, check the distance from shoulder seam to bust point and adjust. A slight adjustment, up to about 1.5 cm, ($\frac{5}{8}$ in.) can be made simply by moving the dart point, otherwise pleat the pattern, or add to the length, above the dart but below the armhole, as shown.

If a curved or angled seam runs over the bust the alteration is made in the same way. Note that the total length is unaltered, so the side seam will still match the back pattern.

If the bust is large, regardless of depth (although in fact it will nearly always be low) the shaping must be increased, even if this is in addition to the alteration described above. The illustration shows how to cut the pattern through the dart and from its point to the centre front. Part the pieces and insert extra paper. The dart is re-drawn to a new point but from the original, wider base points. Make a similar lengthening alteration for any style of pattern as the prominent bust requires the extra length. On a curved seam it will help to curve the seam edge a little more as well. If it is not needed it can be removed at fitting.

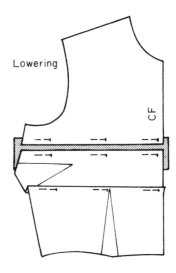

Lowering

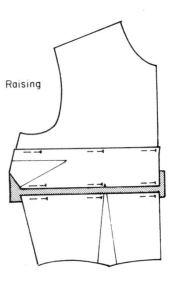

Raising

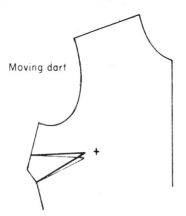

Moving dart

If a pattern has a yoke with gathers the bust will be accommodated at any level. If there is a shoulder dart or tucks running down towards the bust, these too will usually provide satisfactory space for the bust, whether high or low. However, for the figure with a *prominent* bust for its size, as described above, always cut and lengthen the pattern, otherwise the garment hemline will rise at the front.

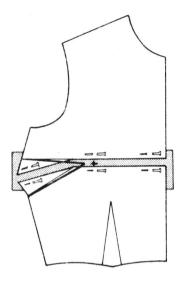

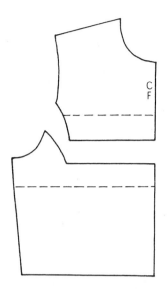

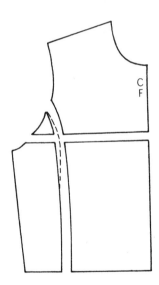

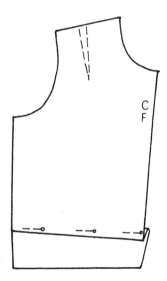

On women with a particularly stooping or upright posture, a very low bust and/or short waist it helps to measure from the bust point down to the waist. Check the pattern, allowing 2 cm ($\frac{3}{4}$ in.) for ease and lengthen or shorten the front only with a wedge-shaped alteration. This will often be required if back neck to waist was altered earlier.

*6 Armhole depth*

On men, women and children, the correct depth of armhole contributes to comfort. This should be checked and altered in conjunction with the adjustment below for wide or narrow shoulders as they affect each other. It does not matter which alteration is made just as long as the resulting armhole is correct.

Occasionally an armhole may be too high, but is more usual for it to be too low. You will know it because other garments will lift when you raise your arms. This is more of a problem in women's clothes because the bust needs room for movement, but children should be comfortable too, and men's coats should not ride up when they move about.

Begin by holding a ruler close up under the arm as illustrated, the top edge provides the level of the armhole. Measure from neck bone to ruler. Draw a line across the back pattern and check the armhole depth. Place the front pattern beside it, matching the seam. If the armhole is too deep, move the back pattern down a little. This reduces the distance

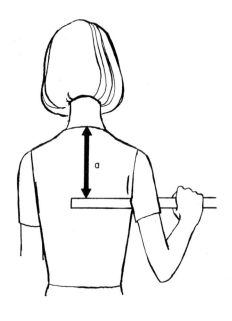

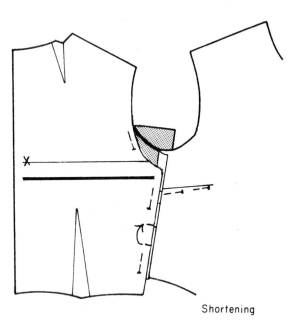

Shortening

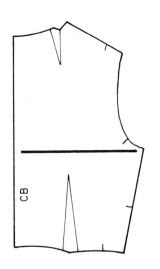

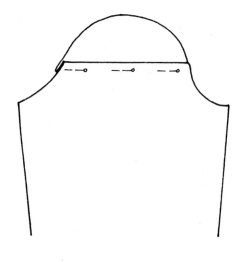

between the neck and the new underarm. Put in a new piece of paper and fill in the back armhole curve to join up with the front.

Check the back and front neck to waist length again and find out whether the small amount of surplus at the waist on the back needs trimming off (unevenly for a low-waisted figure) or whether you will have to add a piece of paper to the front (probably a wedge-shape) to level the front waist.

Adjust the sleeve pattern by folding out a small wedge-shaped pleat as shown.

### 7 Top arm

If a sleeve pattern is a fitted shape, measure women and plump children round the plump part of the arm. Add extra to the measurement for ease: 2 cm ($\frac{3}{4}$ in.)

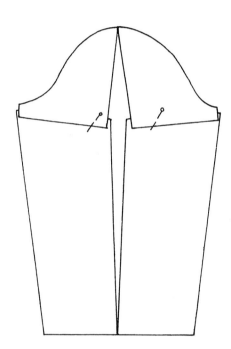

long enough. Even if you have short arms, it will save fabric if the pattern is altered before cutting out. The length varies according to style, so measure the underarm seam of an existing sleeve of similar style and check the pattern length, excluding the hem. Also exclude the cuff if there is one. On a two-piece sleeve such as found on men's coats, measure at the underarm, between the seams. Lengthen or shorten the pattern on the line indicated on the pattern. On a sleeve fitted with an elbow dart make sure the dart level remains approximately at elbow level.

### 9 Skirt length

On women and children measure from the waist to the hem and check the pattern. If a small alteration is needed it can be made at the bottom of the pattern piece, otherwise lengthen or shorten on the line provided. This measurement is often easiest to take from an existing skirt.

### 10 Hip depth

On women check the measurement previously taken and make sure the hip line (often marked) is up at the

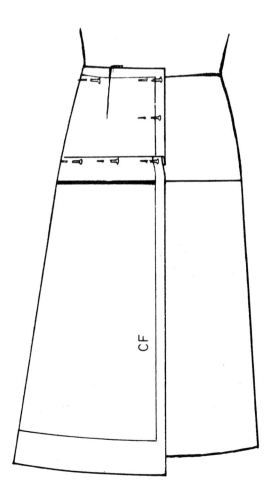

for women, 1 cm ($\frac{3}{8}$ in.) for children, and check the pattern width. If it is too small cut the pattern across and down the middle but try not to cut right through the edges of the paper. Place on to a strip of extra paper and open out the centre a little as shown. Keep all four sections flat and allow the two edges to overlap. This is the new pattern. It will still fit the original armhole.

### 8 Sleeve length

The final adjustment must always be made at fitting when the sleeve is in the armhole, but if you have long arms you must at least make sure the pattern is

level of the hip bone. This is often easier to see if the
pattern is pinned on the figure. This should be done
in conjunction with measuring the skirt length,
checking the length as the pattern may then need
lengthening. Also check the thigh measurement if the
thighs are plump. Measure round the thighs adding
4 cm ($1\frac{5}{8}$ in.) for ease and check the pattern at that
depth. Usually only straight or slightly shaped patterns
will need a little added to at the sides. If the thigh
size is very large, then a larger pattern should be
chosen, and the waist and hips reduced at fitting.

*11 Inside leg*
On men, women and children the trouser length must
be checked. This is easiest to do on the inside leg
seam of an existing pair of trousers, excluding the
hem. Make sure the trousers are plenty long enough
to allow for any lifting that might have to be done
at fitting.

This completes the alterations that may be needed
as a result of measuring the body. Other problems
may be known too, or they may appear at fitting,
indicating that in future the pattern should be altered.
Although the illustrations show a female figure the
problem occur in men too, although they may not be
so severe since the clothes generally are looser.

The exact amount of adjustment cannot be given
as it depends on the severity of the problem.
Remember that too close a fit will emphasise a
problems occur in men too, although they may not
be so severe since the clothes generally are looser.

(See also *Paper Patterns*.)

**Other pattern alterations**
It often helps to pin the pattern on the body to alter it.

*Rounded back or back neck*
Cut the back pattern across half-way down the armhole and open it up a little at the centre back edge
only. Insert extra paper. The pattern should be laid
flat to cut out in fabric. If cut to a fold, place the
neck section a little way from the fold to make a
straight edge.

If cutting to a seam allow the extra, but it may
make for a better fit if the seam is actually shaped in
at the neck. Also at fitting it may be necessary on
women to insert a neck dart. If there is also a
shoulder dart in the pattern, omit it.

*Hollow or narrow chest*
This may accompany the previous problem. The front
pattern may be too long and/or too wide in the area
between the neck and the underarm, or in the case of
women, the start of the rise of the bust. Surplus should
be pinned out horizontally and also if necessary, the
front edge taken off the pattern. Note that it is
usually a wedge-shaped alteration in both directions.

Rounded back or back neck

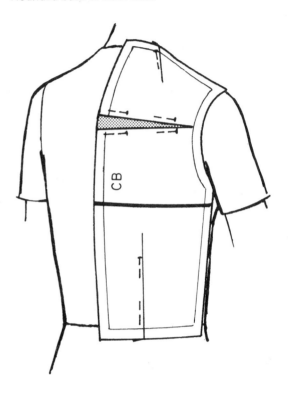

Chest width

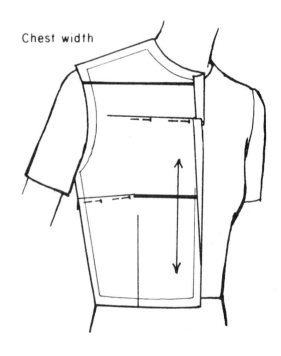

*Back width*

A small addition can be made to the back width by filling in the armhole. Also, a little could be added at the centre back. If the pattern is a little too wide take some off at the centre back. If the problem is very severe either cut or fold the pattern lengthwise from shoulder to waist and make a wedge-shaped alteration. Avoid any dart.

*Width of shoulders*

This may be a figure problem or it may be the result of a previous pattern alteration that the length of the shoulder seam is wrong. For narrow shoulders, cut the pattern from mid-shoulder down to mid-armhole. Overlap the pieces a little at shoulder only. For broad shoulders open out the pieces. Take a ruler and draw a new shoulder seam from the neck point to the shoulder point.

*Neck width*

This is usually a back problem but in women sometimes occurs at the front too. You will know from experience if necklines are usually too wide or too narrow. To widen the neck at back or front pin the pattern on to paper and raise the neck point, where the shoulder seam starts. Re-curve the neck and re-draw the shoulder. To reduce the width lower that point and re-draw the shoulder seam. Note that these alterations affect the slope of the seam. This may or may not need adjusting at fitting.

Back width

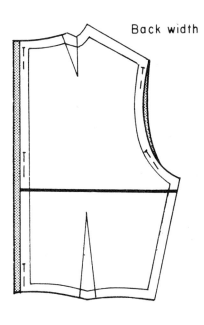

Back neck width

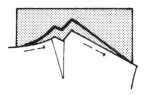

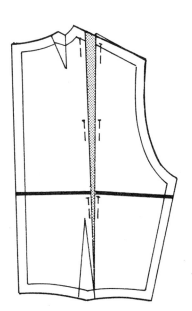

*Slope of shoulders*

As with the other problems, if you know it exists alter the pattern anyway. If you want to check it pin the pattern to the body. The shoulder seam should run along the top of the shoulder, if it does not, or if there are signs of pulling or of excess fullness in the armhole, the seam edge must be altered. To adjust for sloping shoulders make a new line from neck down to armhole. If the figure slopes a great deal it may be necessary to add extra paper at the neck point, but remember that shoulder pads help to disguise sloping shoulders.

For square shoulders add extra paper and make a new, less sloping, seam. In severe cases cut the pattern across from the base of the neck and open it up there instead.

Make this alteration after any other to neck, back and shoulders. Alter back and/or front depending on the figure.

*Crutch depth for trousers*
If you normally have a problem fitting this area then check the pattern and adjust it. You will still have to fit carefully but the problem may be easier to solve. Run the tape measure from back waist through to front waist between your legs, which gives you the total crutch seam length. Place the two pieces of pattern together at the inside leg and measure the seam length. This will only tell you if the total is correct or not but it will not tell you whether it is the back or front or both that is wrong. For this you will have to cut out and try on the trousers, or you may already know if you are extra short or long from

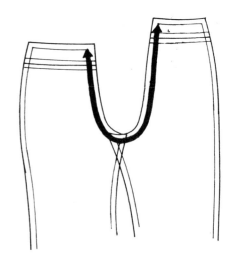

### Checking the trouser pattern

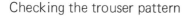

crutch to waist at front or back. However, the following will certainly make fitting easier. If the total crutch length is too short, separate the pattern pieces and add a triangular shaped piece to the inside seam of the back. Continue the curve of the crutch. This is seldom needed at the front. If the total crutch length is too great, take a horizontal fold out across each pattern piece about 8 to 10 cm (3 to 4 in.) below the waist. If by chance you remove too much, the crutch can be lowered at fitting provided you have allowed a long enough leg length.

*Thigh width for trousers*
If tight trousers are in fashion or if you have big thighs, measure one, add 2 cm ($\frac{3}{4}$ in.) for ease and check the pattern. Add to the pattern at the side. If the thighs and bottom are very slim and trousers always seem too wide, take out a small fold down the centre of the pattern from waist to hem at back, front or both.

*Length*
If you habitually have a problem with achieving a good hang on trousers, it will help to measure the outside leg length as well as the inside, subtract one from the other and measure the pattern straight down from waist to crutch level. You will know at fitting whether in future the front, or back, or both need lengthening or shortening below the waist. Finally posture affects the hang a great deal. Legs that are open as in the illustration require a shorter side seam compared with the inside leg. Figures whose legs or thighs are angled the other way need a shorter inside leg seam. Any of the horizontal adjustments can be wedge-shaped to achieve this.

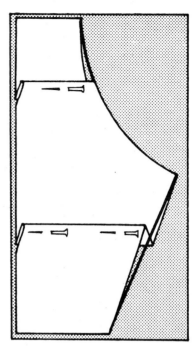

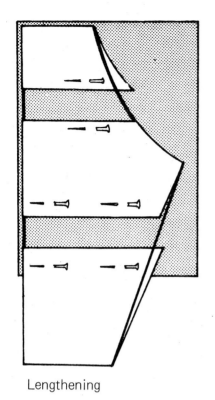

Trousers

Shortening

Lengthening

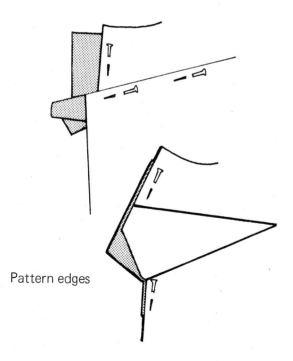

Pattern edges

### Pattern edges

Pattern alterations throw out the smooth edge of a pattern piece. After adjusting always re-draw. Use a ruler for straight seams. Also make sure the seam allowance is correct and even. On curved edges, quite new curves may have to be drawn especially if quite a large lengthening or shortening operation has been done. If darts are affected re-draw them correctly to a point. If darts, tucks, for instance, are altered or are affected by an alteration make sure pattern edges are correct by pinning up the dart and drawing a new seam edge across the fold. Cut on the line with the paper folded. When opened out the correct shape will be revealed.

### Measurement tables

The table of body measurements shown overleaf refers to Burda patterns; you will see that measurements vary slightly from the chart on page 183. A Burda size 40, the equivalent of McCall's size 14, shows bust, waist and hips as 92, 73 and 98 cm against McCall's 92, 71, 97 cm. The differences are very small but it is as well to consult these charts when buying a pattern to make sure that you select the size closest to your measurements, at least until you are familiar with the differences between the various makes of pattern.

## BURDA MEASUREMENT TABLE FOR WOMEN'S STANDARD SIZES (66-in. HEIGHT)

These measurements are net measurements. The necessary allowances for comfort in wear suited to the individual style and intended use of the garment are included in Burda paper patterns.

| Burda size | | 34 | 36 | 38 | 40 | 42 | 44 | 46 | 48 | 50 | 52 | 54 |
|---|---|---|---|---|---|---|---|---|---|---|---|---|
| corresponding sizes | | 8 | 10 | 12 | 14 | 16 | 18 | 20 | 40 | 42 | 44 | 46 |
| 1  Bust | cm | 80 | 84 | 88 | 92 | 96 | 100 | 104 | 110 | 116 | 122 | 128 |
| | in. | $31\frac{1}{2}$ | 33 | $34\frac{3}{4}$ | $36\frac{1}{4}$ | $37\frac{3}{4}$ | $39\frac{1}{4}$ | 41 | $43\frac{1}{4}$ | $45\frac{3}{4}$ | 48 | $50\frac{1}{4}$ |
| 2  Waist | cm | 63 | 65 | 69 | 73 | 77 | 81 | 85 | 91 | 97 | 103 | 109 |
| | in. | $24\frac{3}{4}$ | $25\frac{1}{2}$ | 27 | $28\frac{1}{2}$ | $30\frac{1}{4}$ | 32 | $33\frac{1}{2}$ | 36 | 38 | $40\frac{1}{2}$ | 43 |
| 3  Hips | cm | 86 | 90 | 94 | 98 | 102 | 106 | 110 | 116 | 122 | 128 | 134 |
| | in. | $34\frac{3}{4}$ | $35\frac{1}{2}$ | 37 | $38\frac{1}{2}$ | 40 | $41\frac{3}{4}$ | $43\frac{1}{2}$ | $45\frac{1}{2}$ | 48 | $50\frac{1}{2}$ | $52\frac{1}{2}$ |
| 4  Front waist length | cm | 42.5 | 43.5 | 44.5 | 45.5 | 46.5 | 47.5 | 48.5 | 49.5 | 50.5 | 51.5 | 52.5 |
| | in | $16\frac{3}{4}$ | 17 | $17\frac{1}{2}$ | 18 | $18\frac{1}{2}$ | $18\frac{3}{4}$ | 19 | $19\frac{1}{2}$ | 20 | $20\frac{1}{4}$ | $20\frac{1}{2}$ |
| 5  Back width | cm | 33 | 34 | 35 | 36 | 37 | 38 | 39 | 40.5 | 42 | 43.5 | 45 |
| | in. | 13 | $13\frac{1}{2}$ | $13\frac{3}{4}$ | $14\frac{1}{4}$ | $14\frac{1}{2}$ | 15 | $15\frac{1}{4}$ | 16 | $16\frac{1}{2}$ | 17 | $17\frac{3}{4}$ |
| 6  Back waist length | cm | 40 | 40.5 | 41 | 41.5 | 42 | 42.5 | 43 | 43.5 | 44 | 44.5 | 45 |
| | in. | $15\frac{3}{4}$ | 16 | $16\frac{1}{4}$ | $16\frac{1}{4}$ | $16\frac{1}{2}$ | $16\frac{3}{4}$ | 17 | $17\frac{1}{4}$ | $17\frac{1}{2}$ | $17\frac{3}{4}$ | 18 |
| 7  Neck | cm | 33 | 34 | 35 | 36 | 37 | 38 | 39 | 40 | 41 | 42 | 43 |
| | in. | 13 | $13\frac{1}{2}$ | $13\frac{3}{4}$ | $14\frac{1}{4}$ | $14\frac{1}{2}$ | 15 | $15\frac{1}{4}$ | $15\frac{3}{4}$ | $16\frac{1}{4}$ | $16\frac{1}{2}$ | 17 |
| 8  Shoulder width | cm | 12 | 12.5 | 12.5 | 13 | 13 | 13.5 | 14 | 14 | 14 | 14.5 | 14.5 |
| | in. | $4\frac{3}{4}$ | 5 | 5 | 5 | 5 | $5\frac{1}{4}$ | $5\frac{1}{2}$ | $5\frac{1}{2}$ | $5\frac{1}{2}$ | $5\frac{3}{4}$ | $5\frac{3}{4}$ |
| 9  Sleeve length | cm | 58 | 58 | 58 | 58 | 58 | 59 | 59 | 59 | 59 | 59 | 59 |
| | in. | $22\frac{3}{4}$ | $22\frac{3}{4}$ | 23 | 23 | 23 | $23\frac{1}{4}$ | $23\frac{1}{4}$ | $23\frac{1}{4}$ | $23\frac{1}{4}$ | $23\frac{1}{4}$ | $23\frac{1}{4}$ |
| 10  Upper arm width | cm | 25 | 26 | 27 | 29 | 31 | 33 | 35 | 37 | 39 | 40 | 41 |
| | in. | $9\frac{3}{4}$ | $10\frac{1}{4}$ | $10\frac{1}{2}$ | $11\frac{1}{2}$ | $12\frac{1}{4}$ | 13 | $13\frac{3}{4}$ | $14\frac{1}{2}$ | $15\frac{1}{4}$ | $15\frac{3}{4}$ | $16\frac{1}{4}$ |

## McCALL'S BODY MEASUREMENTS

### MISSES

Misses patterns are designed for a well proportioned, and developed figure; about 1.65 to 1.68 m (5′ 5″ to 5′ 6″) without shoes.

| Size | | 6 | 8 | 10 | 12 | 14 | 16 | 18 | 20 | 22 | 24 |
|---|---|---|---|---|---|---|---|---|---|---|---|---|
| Bust | cm | 78 | 80 | 83 | 87 | 92 | 97 | 102 | 107 | 112 | 117 |
| | in. | $30\frac{1}{2}$ | $31\frac{1}{2}$ | $32\frac{1}{2}$ | 34 | 36 | 38 | 40 | 42 | 44 | 46 |
| Waist | cm | 58 | 61 | 64 | 67 | 71 | 76 | 81 | 87 | 94 | 99 |
| | in. | 23 | 24 | 25 | $26\frac{1}{2}$ | 28 | 30 | 32 | 34 | 37 | 39 |
| Hip | cm | 83 | 85 | 88 | 92 | 97 | 102 | 107 | 112 | 117 | 122 |
| | in. | $32\frac{1}{2}$ | $33\frac{1}{2}$ | $34\frac{1}{2}$ | 36 | 38 | 40 | 42 | 44 | 46 | 48 |
| Back waist length | cm | 39.5 | 40 | 40.5 | 41.5 | 42 | 42.5 | 43 | 44 | 44 | 44.5 |
| | in. | $15\frac{1}{2}$ | $15\frac{3}{4}$ | 16 | $16\frac{1}{4}$ | $16\frac{1}{2}$ | $16\frac{3}{4}$ | 17 | $17\frac{1}{4}$ | $17\frac{3}{8}$ | $17\frac{1}{2}$ |

## MISS PETITE

This size range is designed for the shorter Miss figure; about 1.57 to 1.60 m (5' 2'' to 5' 3'') without shoes.

| Size | | 6mp | 8mp | 10mp | 12mp | 14mp | 16mp |
|---|---|---|---|---|---|---|---|
| Bust | cm | 78 | 80 | 83 | 87 | 92 | 97 |
| | in. | $30\frac{1}{2}$ | $31\frac{1}{2}$ | $32\frac{1}{2}$ | 34 | 36 | 38 |
| Waist | cm | 60 | 62 | 65 | 69 | 73 | 78 |
| | in. | $23\frac{1}{2}$ | $24\frac{1}{2}$ | $25\frac{1}{2}$ | 27 | $28\frac{1}{2}$ | $30\frac{1}{2}$ |
| Hip | cm | 83 | 85 | 88 | 92 | 97 | 102 |
| | in. | $32\frac{1}{2}$ | $33\frac{1}{2}$ | $34\frac{1}{2}$ | 36 | 38 | 40 |
| Back waist length | cm | 37 | 37.5 | 38 | 39 | 39.5 | 40 |
| | in. | $14\frac{1}{2}$ | $14\frac{3}{4}$ | 15 | $15\frac{1}{4}$ | $15\frac{1}{2}$ | $15\frac{3}{4}$ |

## JUNIOR

Junior patterns are designed for a well-proportioned shorter waisted figure; about 1.63 to 1.65 m (5' 4'' to 5' 5'') without shoes.

| Size | | 5 | 7 | 9 | 11 | 13 | 15 |
|---|---|---|---|---|---|---|---|
| Bust | cm | 76 | 79 | 81 | 85 | 89 | 94 |
| | in. | 30 | 31 | 32 | $33\frac{1}{2}$ | 35 | 37 |
| Waist | cm | 57 | 60 | 62 | 65 | 69 | 74 |
| | in. | $22\frac{1}{2}$ | $23\frac{1}{2}$ | $24\frac{1}{2}$ | $25\frac{1}{2}$ | 27 | 29 |
| Hip | cm | 81 | 84 | 87 | 90 | 94 | 99 |
| | in. | 32 | 33 | 34 | $35\frac{1}{2}$ | 37 | 39 |
| Back waist length | cm | 38 | 39 | 39.5 | 40 | 40.5 | 41.5 |
| | in. | 15 | $15\frac{1}{4}$ | $15\frac{1}{2}$ | $15\frac{3}{4}$ | 16 | $16\frac{1}{4}$ |

## JUNIOR PETITE

Junior Petite patterns are designed for a well-proportioned petite figure; about 1.52 to 1.55 m (5' to 5' 1'') without shoes.

| Size | | 3jp | 5jp | 7jp | 9jp | 11jp | 13jp |
|---|---|---|---|---|---|---|---|
| Bust | cm | 76 | 79 | 81 | 84 | 87 | 89 |
| | in. | 30 | 31 | 32 | 33 | 34 | 35 |
| Waist | cm | 56 | 58 | 61 | 64 | 66 | 69 |
| | in. | 22 | 23 | 24 | 25 | 26 | 27 |
| Hip | cm | 79 | 81 | 84 | 87 | 89 | 92 |
| | in. | 31 | 32 | 33 | 34 | 35 | 36 |
| Back waist length | cm | 35.5 | 36 | 37 | 37.5 | 38 | 39 |
| | in. | 14 | $14\frac{1}{4}$ | $14\frac{1}{2}$ | $14\frac{3}{4}$ | 15 | $15\frac{1}{4}$ |

## HALF-SIZE

Half-size patterns are for a fully developed figure with a short backwaist length. Waist and hip are larger in proportion to bust than other figure types; about 1.57 to 1.60 m (5′ 2″ to 5′ 3″) without shoes.

| Size | | | 10½ | 12½ | 14½ | 16½ | 18½ | 20½ | 22½ | 24½ |
|---|---|---|---|---|---|---|---|---|---|---|
| Bust | cm | | 84 | 89 | 94 | 99 | 104 | 109 | 114 | 119 |
| | in. | | 33 | 35 | 37 | 39 | 41 | 43 | 45 | 47 |
| Waist | cm | | 69 | 74 | 79 | 84 | 89 | 96 | 102 | 108 |
| | in. | | 27 | 29 | 31 | 33 | 35 | $37\frac{1}{2}$ | 40 | $42\frac{1}{2}$ |
| Hip | cm | | 89 | 94 | 99 | 104 | 109 | 116 | 122 | 128 |
| | in. | | 35 | 37 | 39 | 41 | 43 | $45\frac{1}{2}$ | 48 | $50\frac{1}{2}$ |
| Back waist length | cm | | 38 | 39 | 39.5 | 40 | 40.5 | 40.5 | 41 | 41.5 |
| | in. | | 15 | $15\frac{1}{4}$ | $15\frac{1}{2}$ | $15\frac{3}{4}$ | $15\frac{7}{8}$ | 16 | $16\frac{1}{8}$ | $16\frac{1}{4}$ |

## WOMEN

Women's patterns are designed for the larger, more fully mature figure; about 1.65 to 1.68 m (5′ 5″ to 5′ 6″) without shoes.

| Size | | | 38 | 40 | 42 | 44 | 46 | 48 | 50 |
|---|---|---|---|---|---|---|---|---|---|
| Bust | cm | | 107 | 112 | 117 | 122 | 127 | 132 | 137 |
| | in. | | 42 | 44 | 46 | 48 | 50 | 52 | 54 |
| Waist | cm | | 89 | 94 | 99 | 105 | 112 | 118 | 124 |
| | in. | | 35 | 37 | 39 | $41\frac{1}{2}$ | 44 | $46\frac{1}{2}$ | 49 |
| Hip | cm | | 112 | 117 | 122 | 127 | 132 | 137 | 142 |
| | in. | | 44 | 46 | 48 | 50 | 52 | 54 | 56 |
| Back waist length | cm | | 44 | 44 | 44.5 | 45 | 45 | 45.5 | 46 |
| | in. | | $17\frac{1}{4}$ | $17\frac{3}{8}$ | $17\frac{1}{2}$ | $17\frac{5}{8}$ | $17\frac{3}{4}$ | $17\frac{7}{8}$ | 18 |

## GIRLS

Girls' patterns are designed for the girl who has not yet begun to mature. See chart below for approximate heights without shoes.

| Size | | | 7 | 8 | 10 | 12 | 14 |
|---|---|---|---|---|---|---|---|
| Breast | cm | | 66 | 69 | 73 | 76 | 81 |
| | in. | | 26 | 27 | $28\frac{1}{2}$ | 30 | 32 |
| Waist | cm | | 58 | 60 | 62 | 65 | 67 |
| | in. | | 23 | $23\frac{1}{2}$ | $24\frac{1}{2}$ | $25\frac{1}{2}$ | $26\frac{1}{2}$ |
| Hip | cm | | 69 | 71 | 76 | 81 | 87 |
| | in. | | 27 | 28 | 30 | 32 | 34 |
| Back waist length | cm | | 29.5 | 31 | 32.5 | 34.5 | 36 |
| | in. | | $11\frac{1}{2}$ | 12 | $12\frac{3}{4}$ | $13\frac{1}{2}$ | $14\frac{1}{4}$ |
| Approx. height | cm | | 127 | 132 | 142 | 149 | 155 |
| | in. | | 50 | 52 | 56 | $58\frac{1}{2}$ | 61 |

## YOUNG JUNIOR/TEEN

This size range is designed for the developing pre-teen and teen figures; about 1.55 to 1.60 m (5' 1'' to 5' 3'') without shoes.

| Size | | 5/6 | 7/8 | 9/10 | 11/12 | 13/14 | 15/16 |
|---|---|---|---|---|---|---|---|
| Bust | cm | 71 | 74 | 78 | 81 | 85 | 89 |
| | in. | 28 | 29 | $30\frac{1}{2}$ | 32 | $33\frac{1}{2}$ | 35 |
| Waist | cm | 56 | 58 | 61 | 64 | 66 | 69 |
| | in. | 22 | 23 | 24 | 25 | 26 | 27 |
| Hip | cm | 79 | 81 | 85 | 89 | 93 | 97 |
| | in. | 31 | 32 | $33\frac{1}{2}$ | 35 | $36\frac{1}{2}$ | 38 |
| Back waist length | cm | 34.5 | 35.5 | 37 | 38 | 39 | 40 |
| | in. | $13\frac{1}{2}$ | 14 | $14\frac{1}{2}$ | 15 | $15\frac{3}{8}$ | $15\frac{3}{4}$ |

## CHUBBIE

Chubbie patterns are designed for the growing girl who is over the average weight for her age and height. See below for approximate heights without shoes.

| Size | | 8½c | 10½c | 12½c | 14½c |
|---|---|---|---|---|---|
| Breast | cm | 76 | 80 | 84 | 88 |
| | in. | 30 | $31\frac{1}{2}$ | 33 | $34\frac{1}{2}$ |
| Waist | cm | 71 | 74 | 76 | 79 |
| | in. | 28 | 29 | 30 | 31 |
| Hip | cm | 84 | 88 | 92 | 96 |
| | in. | 33 | $34\frac{1}{2}$ | 36 | $37\frac{1}{2}$ |
| Back waist length | cm | 32 | 34 | 35.5 | 37.5 |
| | in. | $12\frac{1}{2}$ | $13\frac{1}{4}$ | 14 | $14\frac{3}{4}$ |
| Approx. height | cm | 132 | 142 | 149 | 155 |
| | in. | 52 | 56 | $58\frac{1}{2}$ | 61 |

## MEN (height approximately 178 cm (5' 10''))

| Size | | 34 | 36 | 38 | 40 | 42 | 44 | 46 | 48 |
|---|---|---|---|---|---|---|---|---|---|
| Chest | cm | 87 | 92 | 97 | 102 | 107 | 112 | 117 | 122 |
| | in. | 34 | 36 | 38 | 40 | 42 | 44 | 46 | 48 |
| Waist | cm | 71 | 76 | 81 | 87 | 92 | 99 | 107 | 112 |
| | in. | 28 | 30 | 32 | 34 | 36 | 39 | 42 | 44 |
| Hip (seat) | cm | 89 | 94 | 99 | 104 | 109 | 114 | 119 | 124 |
| | in. | 35 | 37 | 39 | 41 | 43 | 45 | 47 | 49 |
| Neckband | cm | 35.5 | 37 | 38 | 39.5 | 40.5 | 42 | 43 | 44.5 |
| | in. | 14 | $14\frac{1}{2}$ | 15 | $15\frac{1}{2}$ | 16 | $16\frac{1}{2}$ | 17 | $17\frac{1}{2}$ |
| Shirt sleeve | cm | 81 | 81 | 84 | 84 | 87 | 87 | 89 | 89 |
| | in. | 32 | 32 | 33 | 33 | 34 | 34 | 35 | 35 |

| Size | | BOYS | | | | TEEN-BOYS | | | |
|---|---|---|---|---|---|---|---|---|---|
| | | **7** | **8** | **10** | **12** | **14** | **16** | **18** | **20** |
| Chest | cm | 66 | 69 | 71 | 76 | 81 | 85 | 89 | 93 |
| | in. | 26 | 27 | 28 | 30 | 32 | $33\frac{1}{2}$ | 35 | $36\frac{1}{2}$ |
| Waist | cm | 58 | 61 | 64 | 66 | 69 | 71 | 74 | 76 |
| | in. | 23 | 24 | 25 | 26 | 27 | 28 | 29 | 30 |
| Hip (seat) | cm | 69 | 71 | 75 | 79 | 83 | 87 | 90 | 94 |
| | in. | 27 | 28 | $29\frac{1}{2}$ | 31 | $32\frac{1}{2}$ | 34 | $35\frac{1}{2}$ | 37 |
| Neckband | cm | 30 | 31 | 32 | 33 | 34.5 | 35.5 | 37 | 38 |
| | in. | $11\frac{3}{4}$ | 12 | $12\frac{1}{2}$ | 13 | $13\frac{1}{2}$ | 14 | $14\frac{1}{2}$ | 15 |
| Height | cm | 122 | 127 | 137 | 147 | 155 | 163 | 168 | 173 |
| | in. | 48 | 50 | 54 | 58 | 61 | 64 | 66 | 68 |
| Shirt sleeve | cm | 57 | 59 | 64 | 68 | 74 | 76 | 79 | 81 |
| | in. | $22\frac{3}{8}$ | $23\frac{1}{4}$ | 25 | $26\frac{3}{4}$ | 29 | 30 | 31 | 32 |

## CHILDREN'S MEASUREMENTS

Measure around breast. Toddler patterns are designed for a figure between a baby and a child. Dresses are shorter than the child's dress and pants have a diaper allowance.

## TODDLERS

| Size | | ½ | 1 | 2 | 3 | 4 |
|---|---|---|---|---|---|---|
| Breast or chest | cm | 48 | 51 | 53 | 56 | 58 |
| | in. | 19 | 20 | 21 | 22 | 23 |
| Waist | cm | 48 | 50 | 51 | 52 | 53 |
| | in. | 19 | $19\frac{1}{2}$ | 20 | $20\frac{1}{2}$ | 21 |
| Finished dress length | cm | 35.5 | 38 | 40.5 | 43 | 46 |
| | in. | 14 | 15 | 16 | 17 | 18 |
| Approx. height | cm | 71 | 79 | 87 | 94 | 102 |
| | in. | 28 | 31 | 34 | 37 | 40 |

## CHILDREN

| Size | | 2 | 3 | 4 | 5 | 6 | 6x |
|---|---|---|---|---|---|---|---|
| Breast or chest | cm | 53 | 56 | 58 | 61 | 64 | 65 |
| | in. | 21 | 22 | 23 | 24 | 25 | $25\frac{1}{2}$ |
| Waist | cm | 51 | 52 | 53 | 55 | 56 | 57 |
| | in. | 20 | $20\frac{1}{2}$ | 21 | $21\frac{1}{2}$ | 22 | $22\frac{1}{2}$ |
| Hip | cm | | | 61 | 64 | 66 | 67 |
| | in. | | | 24 | 25 | 26 | $26\frac{1}{2}$ |
| Back waist length | cm | 22 | 23 | 24 | 25.5 | 27 | 27.5 |
| | in. | $8\frac{1}{2}$ | 9 | $9\frac{1}{2}$ | 10 | $10\frac{1}{2}$ | $10\frac{3}{4}$ |
| Approx. height | cm | 89 | 97 | 104 | 112 | 119 | 122 |
| | in. | 35 | 38 | 41 | 44 | 47 | 48 |
| Finished dress length | cm | 46 | 48 | 51 | 56 | 61 | 64 |
| | in. | 18 | 19 | 20 | 22 | 24 | 25 |

## MELTON

Melton is a close, durable wool, thin and firm almost like felt. It is used for tailored under-collars as it does not fray, and is available in basic dark colours and in white.

(See *Tailored Collar* page 71, for instructions on how to use.)

## METRE RULE

A substantial boxwood rule with brass ends. The sides are vertical which make it easy to use with tailor's chalk, for marking fabric grain, straight seam lines, etc. Also used for pattern drafting and pattern alterations. In addition the rule can be used on end for checking hem levels in place of a hem marker. When felt pen has to be used take care not to use the rule on fabric until dry. The most useful rule has inches on one side and centimetres on the other.

## MID-CALF

The term used to describe a hemline that is well below the knee. Since its introduction as a new fashion, after the mini and the maxi, it has been in constant vogue and has been adopted permanently by a number of women as the correct length for their style and body proportion.

## MILITARY

Any coat or jacket with some of the features of a military uniform. They include convertible or high stand collars, double breasted fastening, decorative brass buttons, epaulettes, buttoned half belt at the back, usually with a vent. The coat will usually be made in a firm plain cloth.

## MINI

A sudden and initially shocking change in hemlines to above the knee introduced in the 1960s. Skirts became shorter and reached mid-thigh length for a few years. The introduction of fine denier tights as hosiery was a direct result to replace suspenders. Skirts are unlikely to be so short universally again except in a prosperous economic situation because so little fabric is needed.

## MITRES

If a facing or binding passes round an angle or into a corner some surplus fabric will result and this has to be made into a neat mitre. Also if a hem is being turned round a corner and it is likely to be visible in wear, it should be mitred. The advantage of the mitring process is that it distributes the bulk evenly but the disadvantage is that it is very fiddly to do and in the case of a bias edge, the manipulation necessary is likely to stretch it out of shape.

The precise method of making the mitre will vary according to the fabric and the angle but it helps to remember two things. Firstly, cut away as much surplus as possible but only after stitching the mitre. Secondly, stitch from the angle outwards on both sides of the mitre position. This will lessen the chance of a bulge of surplus fabric at the corner.

To mitre a hem, turn in and tack and press the hem to within 3 to 4 cm ($1\frac{1}{4}$ to $1\frac{5}{8}$ in.) of the angle. Mark the exact corner with a pin. Fold over the corner and press the diagonal crease with the toe of the iron. If you find it difficult to locate this point by observing the grain of the fabric, continue to turn in both hems

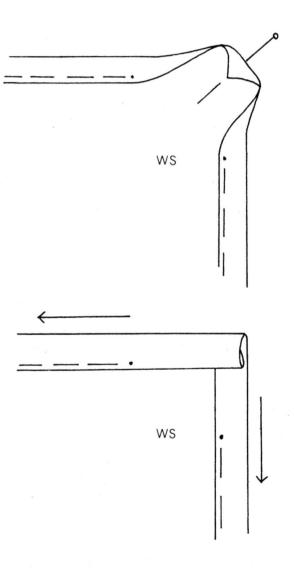

right to the corner, lapping one over the other. Press well and then open out again. The corner is where the creases cross. Next cut off the corner leaving only 3 mm ($\frac{1}{8}$ in.) of fabric. Remove the pin and fold over the hem, tacking from the corner outwards.

To mitre a facing, attach the fabric which may be a straight or bias strip, stitching from the corner outwards. Fasten off the stitching. Move the remainder of the facing so that it lies in position along the other edge. Snip from the edge to the end of the stitching just inserted. Press the corner, lift it up and stitch on the crease. This is usually easier done by hand. Trim off the surplus at the mitre leaving 2 to 3 mm ($\frac{1}{16}$ to $\frac{1}{8}$ in.). Tack and stitch the remainder of the facing from the corner outwards. After trimming and folding the facing to the wrong side it will lie flat.

When facing an inward corner, stitch from the corner outwards on one side, snip the facing so that it will go round the corner then stitch the second side. Trim and press the facing to the wrong side, pressing the mitre flat at the angle. Slip stitch the fold by hand then lift the facing and trim off the surplus fold of fabric. Complete the facing.

When mitring a binding, that is a piece of fabric enclosing an edge, work the mitre in two parts. First attach the binding, stitching from the corner outwards. Trim the raw edges and press the binding outwards. Press the binding into a fold at the mitre and slip stitch by hand. On the wrong side snip off the surplus fabric. Continue to bind the edge in the usual way, tacking and hemming to within 3 cm of usual way, tacking and hemming to within 3 cm

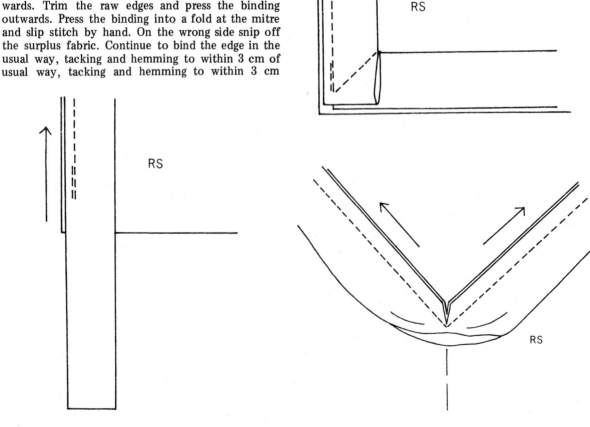

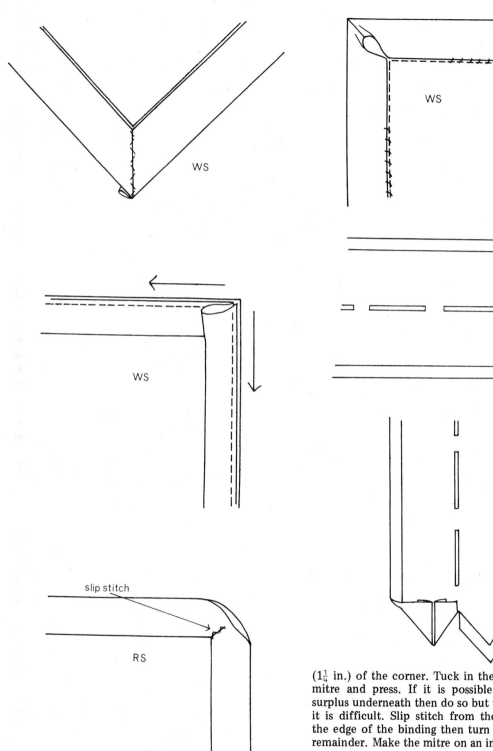

(1¼ in.) of the corner. Tuck in the surplus to form a mitre and press. If it is possible to snip away the surplus underneath then do so but with a narrow bind it is difficult. Slip stitch from the corner almost to the edge of the binding then turn under and hem the remainder. Make the mitre on an inward corner in the same way.

If a mitre is to form a feature of a band, belt etc., the most accurate way to make it is to cut the interfacing (possibly Fold-a-Band) to the shape required, press the fabric over it and then trim the surplus before tacking the fabric to the interfacing. Stitch the folds of the mitre together by hand. If this is a belt treat the other side in the same way and lay it on top of the first one. Hand sew or machine to finish. If it is a short band applied to a garment place the first point on to the garment and machine or slip stitch in place then turn in and hem the second piece on the back.

## MOUNTING

Mounting, sometimes called underlining, means backing the fabric with another material of lighter weight. The effect of this, if it is done correctly, is to support the garment and reduce creasing, produce a better outline, and lengthen the life of the garment. It increases the cost, but it is worthwhile when used on an important item that will be worn for a long time.

At one time it was quite a good idea to mount everything but since fabrics have become much less prone to creasing, and while fashion fabrics tend to be light in weight, mounting an entire garment may not only be inappropriate but may actually spoil the outer fabric.

However, there are always occasions for mounting. The first is when using a traditional fabric that may lose its shape especially when straight skirt styles are in fashion. These fabrics include open-weave materials such as mohair, hand-woven and locally produced tweeds. The second is when a fabric is transparent and requires backing: in this case it may be best to mount fitted areas such as bodice and sleeves but loose-line a skirt.

Another time when mounting is still worthwhile is in a classic coat being made of expensive fabric when it will have a long life. This has the added benefit of additional warmth.

Finally, certain areas of a garment will often benefit from mounting especially if they are to support a larger part of the garment. These areas include yokes, inset bands, shaped waist areas and other parts that are to be fairly closely fitted and therefore rather more subject to strain and creasing. It may be that interfacing these parts is sufficient but often a layer of mounting added to the back of the fabric first will improve it even more. In addition, if a special treatment has been worked on a small area, mounting will help it keep its shape and wear better. This includes embroidery, appliqué, pin-tucking, beading, quilting.

It is essential to choose a mounting fabric that is lighter in weight than the top fabric, otherwise the top fabric will lose its essential nature. The only exception to this might be in a fitted dress in something like chiffon which would obviously need to be mounted onto an opaque fabric.

Choose cotton lawn or any other soft weave fabric, or use the garment fabric if the area is small. Ordinary lining fabrics can be used as a last resort but they tend to part from the top fabric, may not be very comfortable next to the skin, and some of them split at seams and points of strain. The exception is Cupro (Bemberg) which is soft and comfortable. For lighter weight fabrics use polyester voile, cotton voile, triacetate crêpe. For knits and jersey always use nylon jersey and always use it to back any fabrics with 'give'.

Cut out the garment in fabric, then lift the pieces to be mounted without removing the pattern and place them on the mounting fabric. There is no need to pin down as the weight holds them in place. Cut out. Turnings have to be marked, preferably on the mounting as this will be on the wrong side. This could be done with carbon paper and a tracing wheel. A better but more laborious method is to go ahead and do the mounting and then place all pieces in pairs again, replace the pattern, and tailor in the usual way. In places where accuracy is essential this will have to be done.

Remove the pattern pieces and lay each piece of top fabric onto its mounting. Smooth it out flat on the table and baste together with rows of stitching worked up and down over the piece. The stitches should be about 4 cm ($1\frac{5}{8}$ in.) long and the rows 4 or 5 cm ($1\frac{5}{8}$ or 2 in.) apart. Use tacking thread, e.g. Anchor or, on fine fabrics, use machine embroidery thread, and not too big a needle or you may leave holes in the fabric

Now make up the garment as usual, treating it as one layer of material. Hems, darts, etc., should be sewn as usual. Trim well at bulky points.

If the garment is to be loose-lined as well (e.g. a coat) the lining is inserted in the usual way.

## MULTI-SIZE

A pattern containing more than one size. This usually takes the form of one tissue with the pattern lines printed on it but there are several lines, the inner one indicating the smallest size. The sizes are carefully graded so the distance between the lines varies and it is important to follow the line marked with your size when trimming the pattern pieces.

The advantages of multi-size patterns are that figure variations can be catered for by gradually proceeding from one size to the next at the appropriate point, and also one pattern can be shared by people of different sizes.

Some pattern companies produce a selection or a particular type of design as multi-size. Others, for example Burda, produce all patterns in two or three sizes. The maximum number of sizes is usually four because the grading becomes difficult and the lines look confusing.

## NAP

Surface fuzz or finish which causes shading on fabric. Any fabric with surface interest should be cut with all pattern pieces lying in one direction to ensure the nap lies one way and no shading occurs. Fabrics that should be cut in this way include velvet, plush, velour, bouclé, faced cloth, suede.

Paper patterns will indicate fabric quantities required as 'with nap' or 'without nap' because extra fabric is nearly always needed to cut with the nap running in one direction only. Many printed fabrics have a one-way pattern and should be treated as 'with nap'.

## NATURAL FIBRES

These are fibres obtained completely from natural sources and some have been in use since man first wore clothing. The natural fibres include cotton, flax, wool and silk and, in smaller amounts, fur, leather and several types of hair such as Angora and Cashmere. The main properties of each natural fibre are well known and fabrics are chosen according to the way they will be required to behave in wear. The four main natural fibres can of course be used satisfactorily on their own but in addition many fabrics are made from mixtures of more than one fibre in varying proportions. Natural fibres can be mixed together or with man-made fibres in order to produce differing results.

## NEATENING RAW EDGES

Some fabrics either cannot be neatened, e.g. fur, or clearly do not need it, e.g. suede, plastic. Others do not fray so neatening is not required to prevent fraying but a row of machining will often improve the appearance of the cut edges and also prevent them curling up inside the garment. These include jersey fabrics.

Of the remaining fabrics there are open knits that do not fray but may shed chunks of knitting; woven fabrics that hardly fray at all; and woven fabrics that fray badly. All these fabrics must be neatened to prevent fraying or curling, under the friction of wear and washing.

Experiment with various methods and decide which is the most suitable for your fabric. Remember that nearly all raw edges will be single fabric. Whatever method you select can be used throughout the garment, including hem edges.

Trim the raw edge neatly just before neatening it.

### Machine neatening

Zig-zag stitches must be worked over the edge otherwise the fabric may curl up, and the length and width carefully adjusted so that it looks right. On the whole the smaller the stitch the better.

A plain zig-zag stitch or overlock stitch is suitable for most fabrics but vary it by trying out some of the other stitches your machine offers. Many combination stitches and stretch stitches work well over a single edge.

Zig-zag stitches have largely superseded the method of turning under a raw edge and straight stitching it. This can be used on very fine fabrics but any others are too bulky. The other disadvantage of it is that the normal 1.5 cm ($\frac{5}{8}$ in.) seam allowance is not sufficient to turn under the stitch satisfactorily. If this method is used, trim off the surplus raw edge underneath afterwards.

### Hand neatening

Use on very short lengths where it is difficult to reach with a machine. This includes ends of facings and seams that have been snipped.

The best stitch to use is overcasting as it is quick and leaves the edge flat. On longer stretches it helps to work a row of straight machine stitching close to the edge then trim even closer and overcast. Alternative stitches are loop stitch, and, for a very small stretch, buttonhole stitch.

There is no necessity to neaten the seam allowances of a lined garment where the lining is to be fixed all round. Similarly the lining fabric need not be neatened unless perhaps the seam allowances were very narrow and might later pull out of the seam altogether.

## NECK STAND

The part of a stand or fold-over collar that stands close up against the neck in wear. A shirt collar open at the front has a neck stand only round the back, a high stand collar or a roll collar has neck stand of equal depth all round the neck.

## NEEDLE THREADER

A flat piece of thin metal with a fine wire loop attached. Pass it through the eye of the needle, pass the end of the thread through it and pull it back, so bringing the thread through. This gadget can be used on machine needles and on larger hand-sewing needles. There is also a larger device which will stand, or can be stuck, on the sewing table.

Many sewing machines have a threading device attached to the needle bar, which is very quick and effective. There are also several types of threader for machine needles which will rest on the machine bed for use.

## NEEDLEBOARD
(See *Velvet Board*.)

## NEEDLES FOR HAND SEWING

The needle is the oldest sewing tool and the basic tool. We have available for use a wide range of needles in a type and size for every sewing job there is and yet too few people select sensibly. Some people don't select at all but use any needle. Small wonder that they find hand-sewing laborious and uncomfortable.

It is worth buying a selection of all the needles likely to be used, so that they are always to hand. Select the correct type of needle for the job and then choose the size that is right for the fabric and for the thread.

### Dressmaking needles

*Betweens*
The basic needle for dressmaking is the Between, at one time always called Egg-Eyed Betweens and labelled as such on some packets. They are perfect for all hand sewing because they are short and if held correctly are easily inserted in and out of the fabric in one continuous movement. Neat, even stitches result with little effort because the needle is controlled — you never let go of it, leaving it stuck in the fabric. Tailors, professional dressmakers, and experienced amateurs have always used them. Beginners are sometimes more difficult to convince because they see other needles that are larger and think that they might be easier to use, but this is utterly untrue. The most difficult needle to use is the thick, long one because it is hard to force through the fabric, it may leave holes, and certainly the stitches will be uneven.

Betweens are made in sizes 1 to 12 but size 12 is almost impossible to obtain. Packets of assorted sizes contain sizes 3 to 9 or 5 to 10. The possession of packets of assorted sizes encourages sewers to use various sizes for different jobs, but for those who sew regularly a packet or two in each size should be kept.

Size to use
On lightweight fabric and closely woven ones, use
Size 6 for tacking
Size 7 or 8 for hand finishing
Size 6 for sewing on buttons.

On medium and heavy fabrics use
Size 5 for tacking
Size 7 for hand finishing
Size 4 for sewing on buttons.

The finer needle is always used for finishing because the stitches must be small, neat and even; a larger one is used for tacking because the thread is thicker and in the case of tailor tacking it is double so a larger hole must be made in the fabric to take it. A large, strong needle is used for sewing on buttons because the thread is double and also twisted and waxed which makes it even thicker. In addition the needle has to penetrate a least three layers of fabric.

Do not use a hand sewing needle for too long. Although made from fine nickel steel they become blunt. Needles are individually inspected and carefully packed in rust-preventative black cloth. If the needles are blunt, rusty or bent, or the point snags, it is because you have not taken care of them.

*Sharps*
These have the same eyes as Betweens and are made in the same range of sizes but they are longer. They are more difficult to sew properly with because while holding them near the point for inserting into fabric, the thimble finger has to let go, thereby lessening control. If the thimble remains on the end, the thumb and forefinger are further from the point and so control over inserting it is lessened. Sharps needles are widely distributed in general shops and often purchased by people wanting a few needles for repair jobs. Between are obtained in specialist shops and those catering for the needs of the dressmaker, as they are aware of the subtle advantage of the Between.

*Ball points*
Since close-knit fabric in synthetic yarn has been made a needle with a rounded point has been available. The principle of this is the same as for the ball point machine needle — easier penetration. They are a good idea but not a vital piece of equipment. If a fine knit is difficult to hand sew use a smaller size Between needle and there should be no more problems.

*Self-threading needles*
These are needles with a double eye and the thread is simply pulled down to thread the needle. They are excellent for those with poor sight but they are long like Sharps and are not made in small sizes.

### Embroidery needles
There are various types for different kinds of embroidery.

*Tapestry needles*
These have long eyes and rounded points so that yarns such as tapestry wool can be threaded easily and so that the needle penetrates easily in all types of canvas work. They are made in a limited number of sizes. Choice of size is very important as it should not be so large that it distorts the weave of the canvas but it must be large enough to take the yarn, otherwise

the latter will wear thin when pulled through. Tapestry needles are excellent for stitching up hand knitting.

### Crewel needles

These are for most types of embroidery. They have very long eyes so that embroidery threads, flattened at the end, can pass through easily. Made in sizes 1 to 12 but usually most easily available in assorted packets containing 3 to 9 or 5 to 10. The packet may be labelled 'Crewel Needles', 'Embroidery Needles' or both. Very large versions can be obtained, usually two on a card. They are short like tapestry needles with very large eyes. Often one will have a sharp point, the other a rounded point.

### Glovers' needles

These are for sewing leather, suede and plastic. They have a sharp spear point which cuts the leather easily. Instead of a round hole the needle leaves only a small cut which closes up round the thread. Made in a wide range of sizes. Available in assorted sizes in one packet. Very large glovers, or leather needles may be found with only three sizes on a card. These are used for repairing heavier leather items.

### Beading needles

These are very long so that many beads can be threaded at once, and they are very thin and fine so that the fabric is not marked, and so that they pass easily through beads, sequins, pearls baguettes, etc., of all sizes.

### Specialist needles

Other types are usually found separately or in sets on cards and are for the odd special purpose. It is worth keeping one of each, most are made in only a few sizes. They include: mattress needles (curved) for upholstery, etc.; sack needles, long with a curved spear point; carpet needles; sail needles. Use whenever the thickness or type of fabric requires it.

## NEEDLES FOR MACHINING

Machine needles are made in a variety of sizes and types. The type should be selected according to the construction of the fabric and the size should be selected according to the weight of that fabric. The type of thread also comes into it, but to a lesser degree, because there are fewer varieties of thread to choose from. Having tried the chosen needle, if you are not satisfied with the trial stitching, first change the needle as that will nearly always solve the problem.

Keep a good supply of general purpose needles and a few specialist needles, in all sizes. Only make a couple of outfits before you throw away the needle and insert another one. They blunt easily especially on synthetic fibres.

As there are so many sizes and types, you may forget which one is in the machine if you stop sewing for a while, or if you are making several different things. If this is likely to be so, keep a small square of fabric from each garment near the machine and as you finish remove the needle and put it in its fabric. This serves several purposes. You know you will be using the same needle when you come back to that garment; it avoids the risk of putting the needle back in the wrong packet; you will know from the fabric which type you used and it may help when trying to select for a similar fabric; you will know how much it has been used, according to what you made; and you will know when it is time to throw it away.

### Machine needle size

Needles are made in two measurements; standard, also called US or American, and European. The needles are the same, only the numbers are different. Needle packets have both numbers on them. The chart overleaf shows the range of sizes in both the numbering systems and also gives some of the fabric types. Use this table as a guide only. Often the type of fabric will be of such a structure that it requires a different needle, despite the fabric weight. If in doubt go down a size to a smaller needle.

The chart shows the three needles required for normal sewing on conventional fabrics, the basic needle, ball point needle and special purpose needle. This last one has a longer groove in it and is called a scarfed needle and one type with a deep groove is named 'perfect stitch' others 'stretch', although they are useful on many fine woven fabrics, not just knits.

The basic needle is pointed, has a short groove above the eye, for the thread to fit, and a long groove to take the thread right down the other side of the needle.

The ball point needle has a shorter, rounded tip for pushing into knit fabrics. The scarfed needle has a much longer, more defined groove above the eye of the needle. The advantage of this is that the thread remains close to the needle as the stitch is formed. Often stitches are missed, especially on knit fabrics, because the thread tends to move out in a loop away from the needle and therefore it does not catch the underneath thread to form the stitch. These needles are for knits and stretch fabrics but also often produce a better stitch on many fine fabrics than the basic needle.

### Special purpose needles

*Basting needle* This has two eyes, the top one being threaded when long stitches are required.
*Leather needle* This, like the hand sewing leather needle, has a spear point which cuts the fabric rather than making a hole in it.
*Twin needle* This is a double needle on a single shaft. Two reels of thread are used, one thread through each eye. Two parallel rows of stitching result. There are many variations in stitching using this needle, including using different coloured threads, and using decorative stitches.

*Basic*

Standard/metric

| Size | 9/70 | Voile, crêpe de chine, chiffon, |
| Size | 11/80 | batiste, taffeta, georgette, lace, gingham, silk, cotton, crêpe, velvet. |
| Size | 14/90 | Cotton, flannel, mediumweight material, wool, cord, brocade, heavy cotton, curtain fabric. |
| Size | 16/100 | Denim, gabardine, heavyweight material, fur, tweed, overcoating. |
| Size | 18/110 | Canvas, upholstery, heavy material, or top stitching. |

*Spear*

| Size | 11/80 | Lightweight, jersey backed plastic, soft pliable leathers, light plastic, suede. |
| Size | 14/90 | Mediumweight leathers, heavy suede, medium plastic. |
| Size | 16/110 | Heavyweight leathers, calfskin. |

*Ball*

| Size | 9/70 | Delicate and sheer fabric, fine lace, fine silk, fine jersey, crêpe de chine. |
| Size | 11/80 | Lightweight knit fabrics, synthetic or natural, single, double-knit. |
| Size | 14/90 | Mediumweight knit. |
| Size | 16/110 | Heavyweight knit, heavy elastic, bonded knits. |

*Special purpose* (Called: stretch, jerseys, knit needles, perfect stitch.)

| Size | 11/80 | Lightweight knit with stretch, jersey and any others that cannot be sewn with a ball point. |
| Size | 14/90 | Mediumweight stretch fabrics, jersey, tracksuit fabric, towelling. |
| Size | 16/160 | Heavyweight stretch fabric, some simulated suedes. |

*Wing needle*   This has a wide spear section above the needle which makes large holes in the fabric. Used for decorative sewing on fine fabrics. May also be a twin needle, the other part being a basic needle. Used for hemstitching.

**Threading the machine needle**

Cut the thread cleanly and hold it near the end to push it through. If you have difficulty use a needle threader; the type with the long wire is best. Some machines include an attachment that can be used. Some, such as some Pfaff machines, have a built-in needle threading device which is very quick and easy to use.

## NET SEAMS & JOINS

(See *Lace Seams & Joins*.)

## NON-WOVEN

The term used to describe fabrics that have, in the main, the properties of woven (or knitted) fabrics, that is they are suitable for items of clothing. Non-woven fabrics are made by laying down short fibres, in all directions, and then bonding them together to form a sheet. The main use of this type of non-woven fabric in clothing is as interfacing such as Vilene, although there is also a small amount made into items such as disposable underwear and household items like tablecloths and dish cloths.

## NOTCHES

The edges of a pattern have printed marks, usually triangles, to show where one edge is to be matched to another. The positions of these marks must be transferred to the fabric. When large quantities of ready-made clothes are being cut out they are usually marked by a snip in the edge of the fabric, hence the term 'notch'. However, in hand work it is preferable to use the term 'balance mark' to avoid the implications that the fabric is to be snipped. Snipping weakens the edge and means that fitting adjustments are limited, seam neatening and pressing are not easy.

(See also *Balance Marks*.)

## NOTIONS

The collective American term to describe the items of haberdashery required to make a garment. It includes such things as buttons, hooks, zips, elastic and braid.

## OFF-GRAIN

The term used to describe a length of fabric with weft threads lying out of position and not at right angles to the selvedge or warp threads. Knitted fabrics are frequently off-grain. The fault usually lies in poor finishing in manufacture; no care has been taken in ensuring the yarns are lying correctly. A printed fabric will be off-grain if care is not taken to apply the print correctly.

Examine fabric before buying and avoid off-grain fabric if possible. However, it may not be possible, in which case take care with cutting out. Cut with the lengthwise grain correctly placed. Cutting each piece on single fabric will help because folding can worsen the problem or obscure it. When cutting singly place and cut only one piece or pattern at a time.

Regular patterns such as stripes, checks, lines of spots, must be exactly on the grain because the pattern is so pronounced. Either keep to woven patterns for these or ensure that the printing is accurate before buying. For small items and trimmings on small areas, the fault in off-grain fabric will not be noticed.

The term 'off-grain' is also used to describe a part of a garment that has been cut wrongly. For example a cuff must have the warp along one edge and the weft on another or it will be off-grain. This is avoided by placing all pieces of pattern with the grain line exactly on the straight grain of the fabric and when cutting any piece with a right angled corner make sure the edges of the pattern lie on the correct grain line.

(See also *Straightening Fabric*.)

## ONE-PIECE DRESS

A term that sometimes confuses the beginner; it does not necessarily mean a dress made from one piece of fabric, although occasionally this is so. The one-piece dress is a design which eliminates a waist join and is cut in one piece from the shoulder to the hem.

## ONE-WAY

This term usually refers to a fabric that has a design or finish that should be seen from one direction only. Nearly all prints are composed of patterns that differ if turned the other way. Even checks and stripes are often not regular. All these are one-way and therefore all pattern pieces should be placed with the top towards the same end of the length of fabric, ensuring all pieces of garment are up the same way. Pile fabrics too are one-way, because usually if pieces are cut in both directions shading occurs.

When cutting out one-piece fabrics follow the correct cutting out plan, i.e. the one called 'with nap'.

## OPEN CHAIN STITCH

An embroidery stitch worked as for chain stitch, but the ovals are open at the top; the stitch inside the loop is wider apart, producing a square effect. Stitches may vary in width to produce a 'spider's web' effect.
(See *Chain Stitch*.)

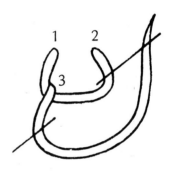

## OPENINGS

The choice of type of opening depends on the fabric being used and on the finished effect required. There are no longer any rules related to which opening must be used where, for instance, a shirt sleeve opening can be used successfully in other positions. It looks good when made in such fabrics as denim so this should be the guide as to choice.

Openings divide into obtrusive and unobtrusive, overlapping and edge-to-edge. They may be fastened with any type of fastening that is suitable for the position on the garment; they may just be drawn together at the top by a cuff or a tie. Edge-to-edge openings can be fastened invisibly if necessary, at one point. Use a very small piece of Velcro and sew one piece completely under one side of the opening, the other opposite but sewn only across the end so that it extends. Alternatively, a tiny press stud can be attached. Sew the knob part under one side of the opening and attach the well opposite but sew only through one hole so that the press stud extends.

All openings should be long enough to allow the body through easily and remember to allow for such activities as rolling up the sleeves. If there is no seam and the fabric has to be cut, remember that a small piece of Bondaweb will reinforce weak points and help to prevent fraying.

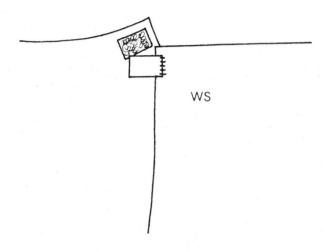

WS

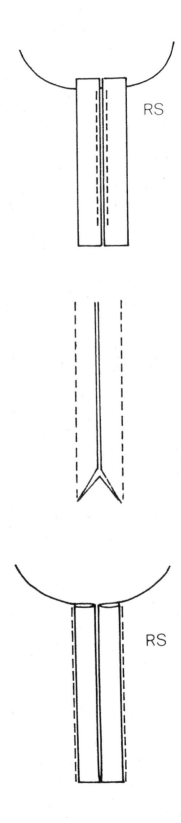

### Bound opening

An opening formed by cutting a slit in a neckline or sleeve where there is no seam so the raw edges are finished with binding or fabric cut on the cross. This fabric may be matching or contrast and it may extend beyond the end of the opening so that there is sufficient length to tie. Otherwise there may be a collar, cuff, etc., added to finish the top of the opening.

*Straight bound opening*

Chalk a line on the right side of the garment to indicate the position of the opening.

Cut two crossway strips of fabric the length of this line plus 1 cm ($\frac{3}{8}$ in.), and 2 cm ($\frac{3}{4}$ in.) wide. Place the strips on the right side of the garment, right side down with the raw edges meeting on the chalk line. Pin.

Machine 3 mm from each raw edge, fastening off each row of stitching at the base. The two rows must be parallel and the same length.

Turn the work over and cut the garment fabric between the rows of stitching. Snip to within 1 cm ($\frac{3}{8}$ in.) of the bottom before cutting out at an angle to the ends of the two rows of stitching.

Use the toe of the iron to press over the strips. Fold the raw edge of each strip over twice bringing the fold to cover the machine stitches. Tack. Press.

Turn the work over and machine from the right side stitching exactly in the dent formed by the strip. Fasten off at the lower end.

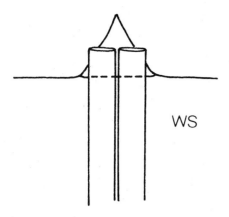

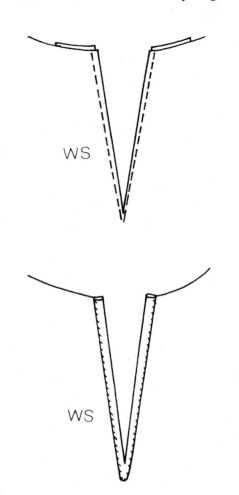

Fold the bindings down on to the lower part of the garment so that the triangle cut earlier stands upright. Insert a pin across the bindings to hold them together and machine across the base of the triangle, attaching the strips. Fold the opening back and press.

If the fabric frays easily press a small square of Bondaweb to the wrong side of the garment at the end of the chalk line, before you start.

*V bound opening*

Mark the length of the opening on the right side of the garment. Cut a crossway strip of fabric 2 cm ($\frac{3}{4}$ in.) wide and twice the length of the opening.

Cut the opening, cutting a V 2 cm ($\frac{3}{4}$ in.) wide at the top. Place the strip right side down to the right side of the garment and pin. Have the raw edges level at the top of the V but gradually reduce the turning taken on the garment until, at the base of the V, you take only a couple of threads. Tack. Turn the work over so that the garment is uppermost and machine. It helps to open out the V as straight as possible. Take a 3 mm ($\frac{1}{8}$ in.) turning all the way along the crossway strip.

Use the toe of the iron to press the strip outwards. Fold its raw edge over twice so that it covers the machine stitches. Pin across the strip and tack. Remove the pins. Turn the work right side up and machine in the well formed by the strip.

If the fabric frays easily press a small square of Bondaweb to the wrong side of the fabric at the base of the marked opening, before cutting it.

Use a small machine stitch to attach the crossway strip, especially at the base of the V.

*Continuous bound slit*

This may be bulky on some fabrics, although it looks attractive on some casual garments. Cut a strip of fabric on the cross, turn in 5 mm ($\frac{1}{4}$ in.) along each edge and press on to wrong side.

Cut an opening in the neckline, sleeve, etc., place right side of strip to right side of opening and with raw edges level start tacking in the crease of the strip. After a couple of stitches take the needle through to the garment side and continue tacking, taking 5 mm ($\frac{1}{4}$ in.) on the strip — use the crease as a guide — but

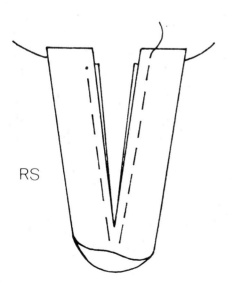

gradually take less and less turning on the garment until at the end of the opening only two threads are caught in. It helps to open out the slit horizontally to get the tacking even.

With the bias strip uppermost stitch in the crease from end to end. Turn garment over and work a second row of stitching about 2 cm ($\frac{3}{4}$ in.) long at the centre, for added strength. Remove tacking.

Cut a small strip of Bondaweb and place this over the double machining but with one edge on the stitching, not extending beyond it. Press with a hot iron and damp muslin. Allow to cool. Peel off the paper. This adhesive together with the double stitching should prevent fraying at the point.

Trim down the raw edges to within 3 to 6 mm ($\frac{1}{8}$ to $\frac{1}{4}$ in.) of the stitching. With the wrong side of the bias strip towards you, bring folded edge over on the machine stitches. Start at the centre and insert pins vertically to prevent strip from stretching. Tack near fold to hold down.

Finish by hemming into every machine stitch, taking the needle up into the fold of the bias strip. Remove tacking stitches and press. On a sleeve opening the part of the strip that will be at the buttonhole end of the cuff is pressed under, the other side will extend.

The opening may be made by attaching the strip to the wrong side of the sleeve first, bringing over the second edge to cover the machining. The edge can then be machined down with a straight stitch or a small zig-zag stitch worked over the fold. On shirts in suitable fabrics where this opening is used on cuffs, fasteners such as metal capped studs can be used to fasten the opening, matching up to the cuff by using capped studs there too.

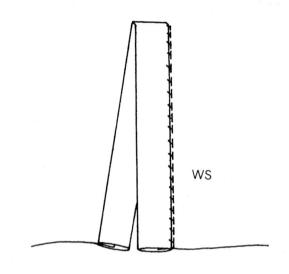

### Dart opening

A dart-shape is stitched for a short distance and a slit opening made below it. It is not a particularly attractive opening, can only be used where the fullness of a dart is required and is therefore normally confined to long tight sleeves where the dart can extend from the wrist towards the elbow.

Measure the length of opening required and stitch the dart down to this point. If this type of opening is not indicated on the paper pattern it can easily be positioned by putting on the sleeve and pinning out a long dart in a line from the little finger towards the elbow. Stitch the dart and fasten off the stitching.

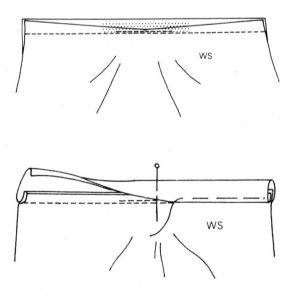

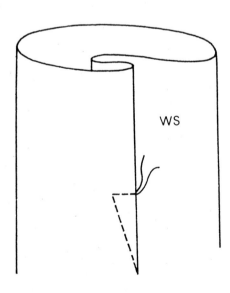

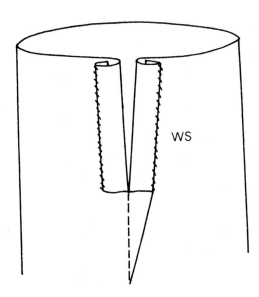

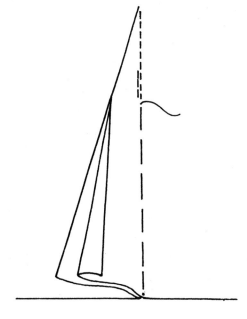

WS

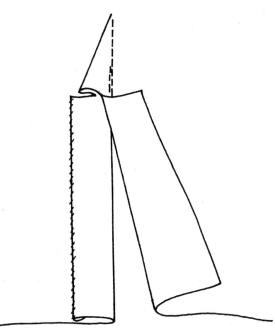

Press to one side. Cut down the fold of the fabric as far as the stitching and snip the top fabric above the horizontal machine stitches. Turn back the edge into a narrow rolled hem and do the same on the other side. Hem both sides. Press.

Fasten at the wrist with a button and thread loop or attach a cuff that fastens.

### Dart opening with fastening

This is mainly used in long tight sleeves with no cuffs, on elegant outfits. The fastening used is often covered buttons and rouleau loops.

Mark the opening 15 cm (6 in.) in length. Fold fabric right sides together and tack a dart from that point down to the wrist making the dart at least 4 cm ($1\frac{5}{8}$ in.) wide, or whatever is required to make the wrist fit. Machine only the top 5 cm (2 in.) of the dart from the point. Cut the fabric along the fold of the dart from the edge up to a point level with the end of the machining. Open up the dart, and with wrong side uppermost press the dart towards the front of the sleeve and turn under and hem the raw edge below that. For a neat result trim a little off the edge to make an even hem. Trim and neaten the other raw edge and fold it back so that it lies neatly and vertically below the dart. Slip a narrow strip of Wundaweb underneath and press. Note that it will be necessary to make two snips into the fabric, level with the base of the stitching in order to get these hems to lie flat.

If buttons and loops are used, the buttons will fall beyond the opening edge, on single fabric. Either place a piece of tape or seam binding alongside the opening to provide a double layer or, instead of neatening the second raw edge, join a narrow strip of fabric to it and then neaten and press it back with Vilene underneath.

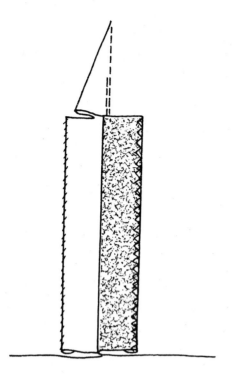

### Faced slit opening

This is frequently used on sleeves with cuffs and occasionally in other positions such as a neckline where it would be bound and tied or fastened with a button and loop.

It is a suitable opening for any fabric although with heavy or bulky fabrics the facing piece should be cut from lining fabric to reduce bulk.

Cut pieces of fabric 6 by 3 cm ($2\frac{3}{8}$ by $1\frac{1}{4}$ in.) and neaten the two long edges and one short one.

Press a narrow strip of paper-backed adhesive (such as Bondaweb) to the wrong side. Tear off the paper. Place the piece right side down to the right side of the sleeve where the opening is to be. Mark the centre of the piece as a guide to stitching.

Machine two parallel rows of stitching 5 cm (2 in.) long, tapering to a point at the top. The distance between the rows varies according to the type of fabric. Cut up between the stitching, right to the point. Turn the patch to the wrong side of the roll, and tack the edge and press well. The adhesive holds the patch in position and prevents fraying.

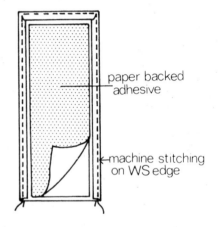

paper backed adhesive

machine stitching on WS edge

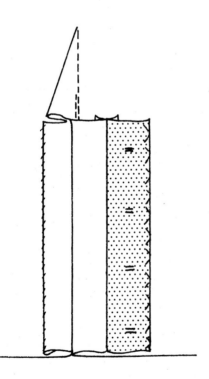

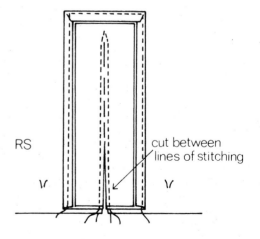

RS

cut between lines of stitching

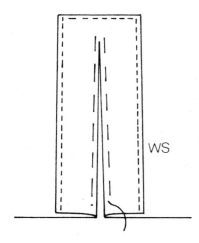

## Horizontal opening

This is a quick, neat way of making an opening but its use is almost entirely confined to full gathered sleeves with cuffs, and possibly in some places on children's clothes. Due to the fact that it creates a gap it cannot be too wide. The horizontal section folds in half when the cuff is fastened and is concealed amongst the gathers.

Make two snips 1.5 cm ($\frac{5}{8}$ in.) deep and 2 cm ($\frac{3}{4}$ in.) apart in line with the little finger position on the sleeve. This is the usual place for the sleeve opening.

If the fabric is woven, overcast this little piece of raw edge between the slits. Press. Hold it back with a small piece of fabric adhesive (such as Wundaweb). Proceed to attach the cuff.

## Hemmed opening

Although without bulk, this opening is not suitable for any position where it can be seen in wear. This limits its use to sleeves with a cuff or bound finish and other similarly unobtrusive places.

The opening is rather weak at the top and should only be used on lightweight fabrics. Cut a 7 cm ($2\frac{3}{4}$ in.) slit in the sleeve. Turn in a narrow hem, opening the slit out straight, and hem. The hem becomes very narrow at the top of the opening. Proceed to attach the cuff in the normal way.

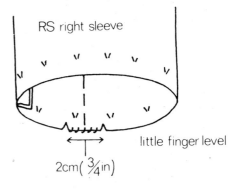

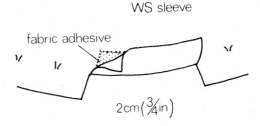

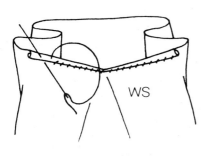

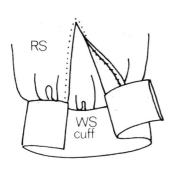

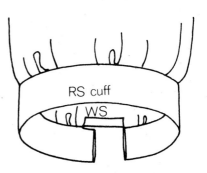

**Placket opening**
This is an old fashioned term that was used to describe
a conventional side opening in a dress or skirt before
zips were in general use. It is useful to know how to
construct it for its possible occasional use now.

Stitch the seam and neaten the edges as far as the
base of the opening. Press open, or if a French seam
or welt seam has been made, snip it so that the seam
allowances are released. On the upper side, if the
turning is wide enough it will provide the double
layer necessary for attaching fastenings. Neaten the
edge and hold it down with a piece of Wundaweb.
The alternative is to attach an extra strip of fabric to
press back. Cut this on the bias to avoid wrinkling
the garment.

On the underside snip the seam allowance as far as
the seam stitching. Trim the seam allowance to 5 mm
($\frac{1}{4}$ in.). Cut a strip of fabric on the bias, or use lining
or purchased binding, 3 cm ($1\frac{1}{4}$ in.) wide. Place it to
the edge just trimmed right sides together and
machine, taking a 5 mm ($\frac{1}{4}$ in.) turning. The machining should meet the machine stitching of the seam
below. Trim the edges, press the strip so that it
extends, fold under the edge 5 mm ($\frac{1}{4}$ in.) and bring it
on to the machining. Hem into the machining. Trim
and neaten the lower edge of the strip. Back stitch
the strip to the other seam allowance underneath. On
the right side work a bar tack for strength. This opening may be fastened with press studs or hooks or
both, or with small buttons.

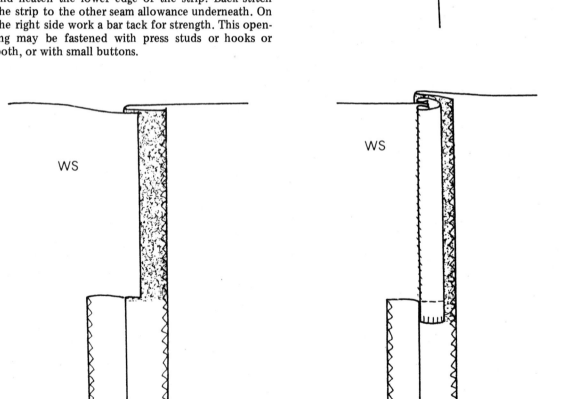

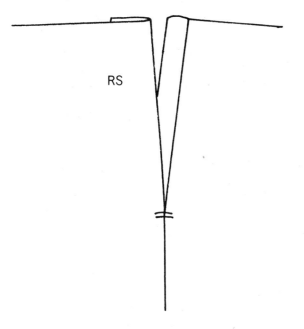

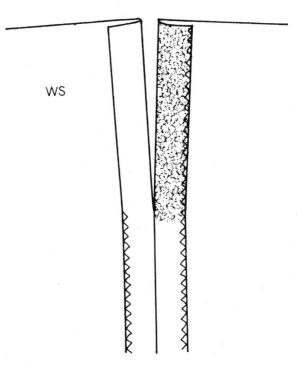

### Seam opening

This is the least bulky of any opening because no additional fabric is used. The main positions for use include undergarments, nightwear, children's clothes, a full sleeve with cuff or binding, and a full skirt where the opening is concealed by gathers or a pleat.

Stitch the seam, fastening off where the opening is to come. A sleeve opening for an adult should be about 7 cm (2¾ in.) in length, on a skirt it must equal the length of the zip it is replacing. In other positions calculate the length, making sure no strain will be put on the seam in use as it is not a strong opening.

Press the seam open and neaten the raw edges, including the edges of the opening. If an open seam is not used the fabric should be clipped at the top of the stitched part of the seam, so that the seam allowances may be pressed back. Neaten the raw end of the seam with buttonhole stitch.

Cut strips of Wundaweb to slip under the seam allowances. The Wundaweb must be completely covered by the turnings and the strip should be 1 cm (⅜ in.) longer than the opening. With the Wundaweb in place arrange the opening on the pressing board with the edges together and press using a damp cloth. Attach waistband, cuff, etc., in the usual way. When used on a sleeve as illustrated the opening causes the cuff to fasten at the underarm so the fastening chosen must be flat and unobtrusive.

This opening can be made to overlap if desired. This would not be necessary on a sleeve but may be desirable on a skirt. Allow a wider seam allowance when cutting out, then after stitching the seam press back one side with Wundaweb but leave the other seam allowance extending.

### Seam opening with wrap

This opening can be inserted in any seam with fullness which will conceal it. It is normally a short opening without fastenings, often used in a skirt below a yoke on a child's dress, at the neckline of nightwear etc.

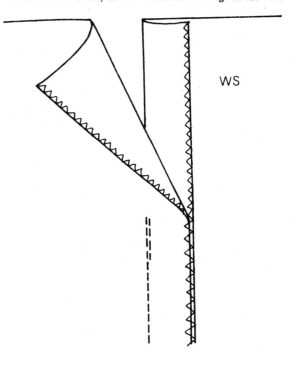

Cut out leaving at least 2 cm ($\frac{3}{4}$ in.) seam allowance on the seam. Stitch the seam, leaving the opening. Press the seam open and then to one side including the edges of the opening. Neaten the raw edges separately down to the base of the opening, then together to the hem of the garment.

### Self-bound seam

This is often used as a method of neatening a gathered seam, e.g. yokes, frills. It is not suitable for bulky fabrics. Stitch the seam with the gathers in the usual way and remove the gathering thread. Trim down the gathered edge to 2 to 3 mm ($\frac{1}{16}$ to $\frac{1}{8}$ in.). Make sure the other seam allowance is even in width. Turn this one down twice so that the fold lies on the machine stitching. Tack and hem into the machining.

This seam is particularly useful on children's clothes and on others that have to withstand constant wear and washing. Often the hemming can be replaced by machining. If this is to be done do not bring the folded edge quite so far down.

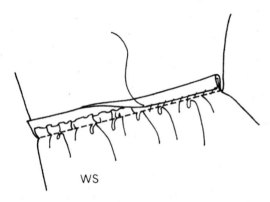

### Shirt sleeve opening

Several types of opening are suitable for shirt sleeves but this is the one conventionally used on men's shirts, casual jackets, etc. In the method described below both edges are finished with a strip of fabric but in fact the under side could simply have a narrow hem turned which is the way most ready-made shirts are finished now.

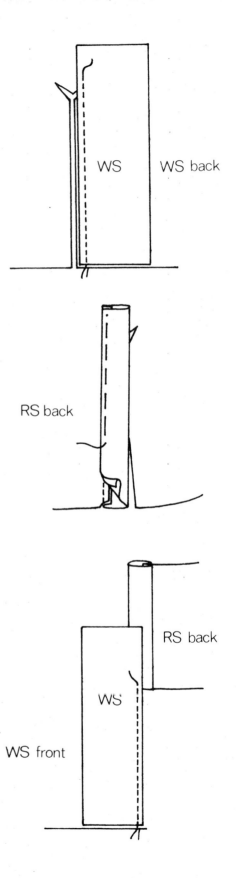

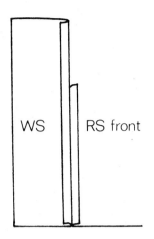

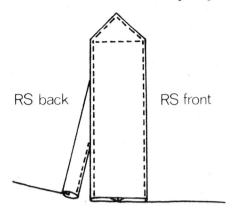

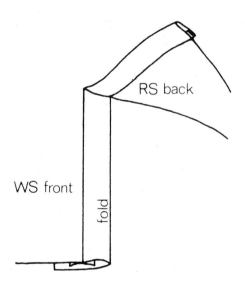

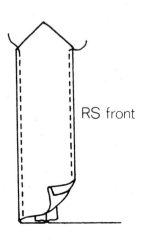

Make sure the opening in a man's shirt sleeve is quite long, to enable the sleeves to be rolled up.

Cut the opening and make a small 3 mm ($\frac{1}{8}$ in.) snip at the top at right angles. Cut a strip of fabric on the straight grain, longer than the slit and 5 cm (2 in.) wide. Place this to the wrong side of the sleeve, against the raw edge at the back of the sleeve. Machine from the end of the slit to the wrist, taking 3 mm ($\frac{1}{8}$ in.) turnings.

Press the strip outwards, roll it to the right side, turn under the edge, baste and machine. Cut a longer strip of fabric 4 cm ($1\frac{5}{8}$ in.) wide, place one edge to the raw edge of the slit, with the right side to the wrong side of the slit. Machine, taking the stitching to the top of the slit.

Press the join open. Press the strip over to the right side but allow it to extend 1 cm ($\frac{3}{8}$ in.). Turn in the outer edge of the strip and press. Turn in the top edge of the strip and press. This can be made into a point. Press.

Baste the side of the strip to the sleeve, and machine on the edge. Also machine the fold if required.

Baste the top of the strip to the shirt, making sure that it covers the slit underneath. Machine round the top. Machine across the strip just below the original snip to catch in the underneath strip. Press right and wrong side.

### Slit and pleat opening

This is particularly useful on full clothes such as nightwear, children's skirt, lingerie, gathered skirt. It is not usually fastened down its length. Most patterns can be adapted if necessary so that this opening can be made. When adding this type of opening allow at least 4 cm ($1\frac{5}{8}$ in.) extra on the width of the garment.

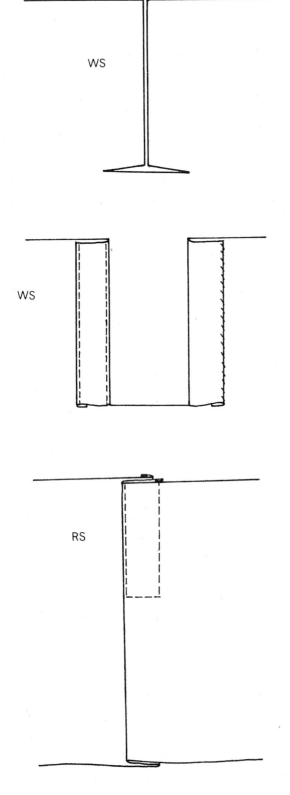

Mark and cut the opening. At the base snip horizontally for 2 cm ($\frac{3}{4}$ in.) on each side (or half what has been allowed). Fold back and press the 2 cm ($\frac{3}{4}$ in.) and either neaten and hold down with Wundaweb, turn under and hem, or turn under and machine. Decide on whatever is most suitable for the garment and the fabric. A combination of two methods may be best.

With the right side uppermost, bring one edge over the other and press in the knife pleat that forms. Stitch across the base of the opening about 5 mm ($\frac{1}{4}$ in.) above the bottom.

### Strap opening

This is the type of opening, usually found at a neckline, where the edges are finished with a strap of fabric. The straps lie on top of each other and may have buttons and buttonholes or other fastening. It may be a short neckline opening or it may extend to the waist or below the waist to eliminate the necessity for a zip, often a feature of a shirtwaster dress. Instructions for working the opening will be included in the pattern but the whole operation is made easier by using a Fold-a-Band. Fold-a-Band is produced in a standard width which means the strapping will be that width when finished. It is worth accepting this limitation in order to simplify the process, even if this method is used to learn how to do it and then later perhaps, future openings could be of different widths. However, even then, remember that Fold-a-Band has a useful line of perforations that can be used as a guide for a folded edge.

Fold-a-Band can also act as the interfacing in the strap. If the neckline is to have a rever opening the piece of fabric used will not be rectangular but it will be shaped to extend round into the shoulder seam and front neckline. In this case apply interfacing but then use Fold-a-Band on top so that it can still be used at the difficult point, the base of the opening.

Work the opening as early as possible on the garment. A short opening should be checked for depth carefully, others should be adjusted if the length of the garment is altered. There may or may not be a centre front seam.

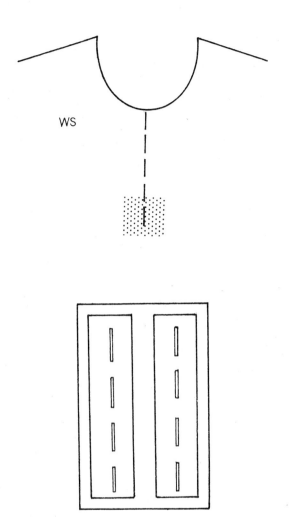

Place the strip right side down on to the right side of the opening, exactly over the marked line. Tack just off the edge of the Fold-a-Band on both inner edges. Machine close by the tacking, starting at the base of the opening and reversing to fasten the thread. This produces two exactly parallel rows of stitching. Remove tacking and press the stitching.

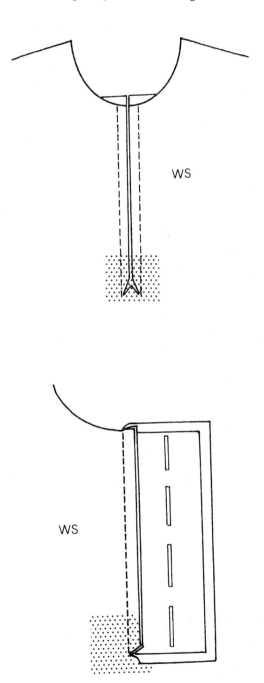

Mark the depth of opening on the garment. Cut a piece of Bondaweb 2 cm ($\frac{3}{4}$ in.) square and press over the base of the line on the wrong side. Peel off the paper.

Cut two strips of Fold-a-Band the length of the opening plus 1 cm ($\frac{3}{8}$ in.) to allow for the shape of the neckline. Place one strip on fabric, matching the perforations to the straight (or bias for a crossway effect) and press.

Place the second strip next to it but exactly 3 cm ($1\frac{1}{4}$ in.) away, i.e. the width of two seam allowances. Press. Cut out round the outside allowing an even 1.5 cm ($\frac{5}{8}$ in.) seam allowance.

If the opening has a rever, place the paper pattern provided on fabric and cut out, and place it to a fold in the fabric — open out the piece and interface, then place the Fold-a-Band on top, 3 cm ($1\frac{1}{4}$ in.) apart. Trim the top edges of Fold-a-Band to follow the neckline curve 1.5 cm ($\frac{5}{8}$ in.) from the edge.

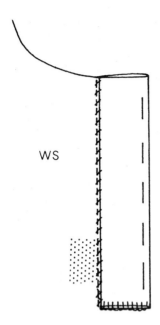

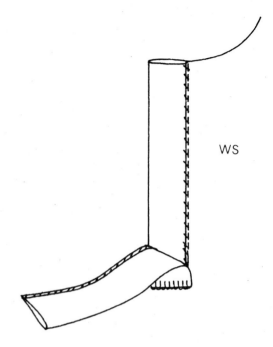

Turn the fabric over and cut the two layers between the rows, stopping 1.5 cm ($\frac{5}{8}$ in.) above the bottom and from there out to the stitching. Trim the raw edges, but not the triangle at the base, to 3 mm ($\frac{1}{8}$ in.) and 5 mm ($\frac{1}{4}$ in.) respectively.

Fold each strip over so that it extends and run the toe of the iron along the join on the right side. The turnings should extend outwards too. Do not press at the extreme base of the opening as there is Bonda-web beneath.

Complete the left or underneath strip first. Fold it along the Fold-a-Band perforations and tack. Fold in the raw edge and tack down, leaving the machining showing. Hem into the machining. Keep the triangle at the base free of the strip. At the bottom, trim the folded strip off to 1 cm ($\frac{3}{8}$ in.), loop stitch across the bottom and slip stitch as far as the start of the hemming.

Complete the outer, right, side. Trim the seam allowance along the bottom of the strip to 4 mm ($\frac{1}{4}$ in.), fold this over the Fold-a-Band and tack. Fold the strip along the perforations, turn in the seam allowance on the long edge and tack down, leaving the machining showing. Hem into the machining and slip stitch along the bottom of the strip. Press both strips. Mark buttonhole positions and work the buttonholes. The bottom one can be omitted and the button sewn on later through both strips. This is not only easier, saving making a buttonhole in that position, but it makes a strong base to the opening.

Arrange the outer strip in position on the garment and pin. Slip stitch it to the garment along the base and up the edge for 2 cm ($\frac{3}{4}$ in.). Hide the stitches under the edge.

Push the triangle of fabric over so that it hangs down between the outer and inner strips. Pin the two strips on top of each other and back stitch across the base of the inner one, taking the stitches through to one layer of the outer strip. Sew on the buttons, sewing the bottom one through both strips.

If a shaped strip is wanted, cut the Fold-a-Band accurately to the required shape to start with and use it as a guide when constructing the opening.

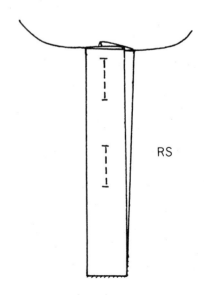

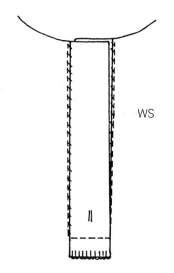

WS

## OUTSIDE LEG

This is a length measurement from the waist, taken at the side of the body, down to the hemline position of trousers. It is a useful measurement because if the inside leg measurement is subtracted from it the resulting figure represents the crutch depth of the trousers.

When cutting out trousers use the inside leg measurement to establish the length, but also check that the outside leg length is sufficient.

(See also *Crutch Depth for Trousers*, page 192.)

## OVERCAST STITCH

An outline embroidery stitch worked from left to right. Work a line of small running stitches, then work close overcasting over it to resemble satin stitch. A similar effect is obtained by working satin stitch over a thread laid on top of the fabric. This is called trailing stitch.

## OVERCASTING

A stitch made by throwing the thread completely over the fabric edge. It could sometimes be found useful as a joining stitch but is mainly used for preventing fraying of a cut edge. The size of the stitch depends on the weight of fabric but it has to be sufficiently deep to contain the fraying otherwise the edge will come away altogether. The stitch is now mainly used only if a zig-zag or overlock machine stitch is not available and for neatening very short fraying edges where it is hardly worth using the machine.

Use short lengths of thread, start with a knot and end each thread by working a horizontal back stitch in the fabric. There will be no strain of wear on the stitch so do not fasten off heavily. Work from left to right holding the raw edge out flat with the fingers of the left hand (if you are right-handed). Trim the raw edge, a little at a time before you overcast. Determine a suitable depth of stitch and then work very quickly to hold down the fraying yarns. Insert the needle at a slant and do not pull the thread tight or the edge will roll. Press the stitching, keeping the edge away from the rest of the garment.

If the fabric frays very badly work a row of straight machine stitching about 1.3 cm ($\frac{1}{2}$ in.) from the seam line; it helps to chalk a straight line, otherwise use the machine foot as a guide. Trim the fabric, using medium scissors, a few centimetres at a time, and overcast. Work from left to right taking the needle under the machine stitches and pulling the thread quite tight to compress the narrow raw edge, and hold the fraying fibre firmly down. If possible, work in the direction the fibres lie so that you flatten them as you work.

Press the stitching to finish, pulling the edge slightly to remove any tightness that has been caused by the stitching.

This is an excellent finish, though time consuming, and can be used on any weight of material.

The tailoring term for this neatening stitch is serging and it is usually worked from right to left inserting the needle straight, not at an angle.

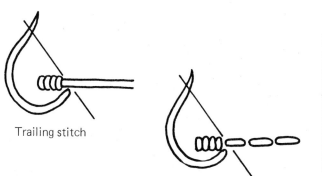

Trailing stitch

Overcast stitch

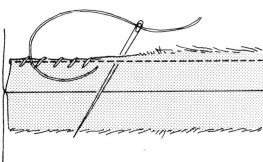

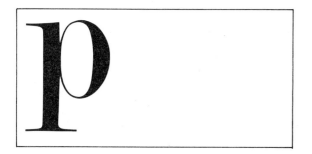

## PAD STITCH

Pad stitch or padding is the small diagonal stitch used to attach canvas to collars and lapels in hand-tailored clothes. Use a small needle and a short length of sewing thread, work up and down in vertical rows with the canvas uppermost. Hold the work up in the hand so that the fabric beneath curls and the canvas follows it as you stitch. This natural shape is utilised in the shaping of the collar and lapel later. Insert the needle across the body and take the smallest possible stitch. The point of the needle will penetrate the canvas completely and just pick the fabric beneath. Take deep stitches but do not attempt to deliberately penetrate the fabric. If you are holding the work as described the way it curls will ensure you pick up the fabric.

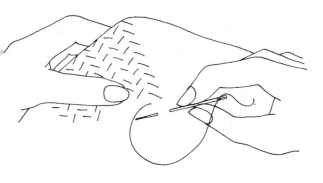

The threads should be 4 to 5 mm ($\frac{1}{4}$ in.) in length, the horizontal gaps about 2 mm ($\frac{1}{8}$ in.). Start with a knot, end with one back stitch. Work only to just short of the fitting line round all edges, so that the pattern can be replaced and the canvas trimmed accurately after padding. The padding must be well-pressed on both sides to smooth it out, using a hot iron and a damp cloth. On the underside marks are visible where tiny stitches have been made.

(See *Tailored Collar*, page 71.)

## PAPER PATTERNS

Normally use the pattern nearest to your bust size because with the checking that comes later, and the fitting, the other areas can be corrected. Also, it is easier to adjust the hips, by taking in or letting out the seams, than it is to alter the bust size. If, however, your bust and hips are excessively out of proportion, it would be easier to choose the smaller pattern and make it larger where needed. The size of your frame may help you to decide, and also whether you have a particular figure problem, or one area that is out of proportion. Length is relatively unimportant at this stage because it is easy to adjust, and also we have to consider the proportional length of each part of the body before finally establishing such things as skirt and sleeve length. (For details of how to take measurements and adjust patterns, see *Measurements*.

However, here are some examples of figure types and things that you should consider when deciding which pattern to use. These points also apply if you fall between sizes.

1   A tall, well-built woman with a small bust, but otherwise relatively in proportion, would be best to choose a large pattern which fits her everywhere except at the bust, and reduce the bust dart before she begins.

2   A petite woman with small bones but with one area out of proportion, for example, a prominent D cup bust, should start with the small pattern and enlarge the bust dart and front length.

3   The pear-shaped person, as a general rule, will get on best with the pattern that fits her bust, especially if her waist and rib cage are small and her arms are short, as is often the case, because she can alter the pattern for her hips or thighs without too much trouble.

4   The person with a narrow back, narrow shoulders and chest, thin arms and small armholes, but large, low bust and thick waist (and possibly very slim hips and flat bottom) should use a small size pattern because the subtle curves at neck and armhole are more difficult to adjust than the bust and waist.

Paper patterns that you buy are prepared to a set of standard, average measurements which have been discovered to be as close as possible to most figure types. You may find that one make fits you with less adjustment than the same size in others, but this is because the amount of ease for movement that is allowed on top of the body measurement varies.

Pattern companies produce patterns in some or all of the following categories, although there is a much greater choice of style amongst one group, Misses, than the others because more women fall into this category. The categories are Misses; Women; Half-size; Men; Young Junior; Teen; Boys; Children; Toddlers.

Every woman is made aware of where her own

measurements deviate from average when she tries on ready-made clothes. Fortunately different manufactures have different ideas of the proportion of the average woman, and so it is usually possible to find something that fits or nearly fits by trying different makes. However, ready-made clothes, and also paper patterns, are still made to standard sets of measurements and so they cannot take account of slight deviations let alone definite peculiarities of shape. After all, something as basic as short legs will mean that neither ready-made trousers nor paper patterns will fit without adjustment.

Most women become aware of their own peculiarities through experience, although girls and young women often find it difficult to accept that they are not the perfect shape. Quite a lot of points can be corrected when the garment is tried on at the fitting stage, but the amount of fitting can be reduced greatly by knowing exactly where the problem is and by altering the pattern before cutting out. A few women have several figure problems, and therefore make a lot of their clothes, most women have between one and three places where neither a paper pattern nor a ready-made garment will fit correctly. Knowing a few body measurements obviously helps to identify the problem areas and therefore makes pattern alterations possible, but the information is also of help when buying ready-made clothes as it enables you to avoid things that are obviously closely fitted at one of your problem areas.

Since a paper pattern is selected by bust size or by hip size within the pattern category that is nearest to your body type, it is essential to know what these currently are, making sure they are revised if weight changes. In addition to these 'around-the-body' measurements, you must know where the length of various parts of your body differs from a pattern measurement. It is quite unnecessary, and very uninteresting, for mature women repeatedly to take all their measurements. You will know where the problem is, so measure only that part of you. There is no need to measure yourself each time you adjust a pattern, but do it occasionally because the problem will get worse as you get older. There is no escaping that long backs get longer and low busts get even lower with time.

The following illustrations show the correct place for taking measurements, all shown together on one body, but apart from bust and hips, only keep a note of others that are necessary. Several of the length measurements are easier to take from an existing garment that fits, especially if you have no help where it is impossible to measure the length of a seam. When measuring garments remember that the result will include ease for movement.

Note that although ready-made men's shirts are sold by neck size, paper pattern details give the chest size as well, which is often a more useful guide. If

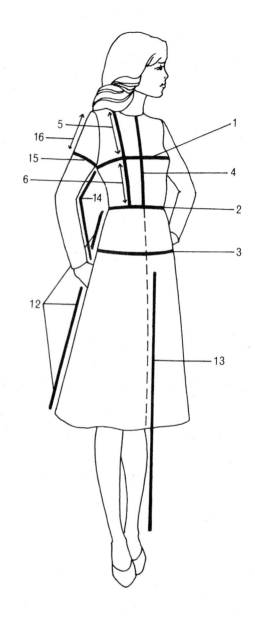

you do not know the neck size required, measure round the base of the neck, not tightly. When choosing the pattern size remember that the chest will be easy to adjust, the neck would be difficult to alter to fit. Other men's clothes such as casual tops and anoraks are sized by chest measurement.

Pattern pieces are printed on large sheets of paper. Identify those you need and cut them out on the correct cutting line, using old scissors or paper scissors. Make any alterations necessary (see *Taking*

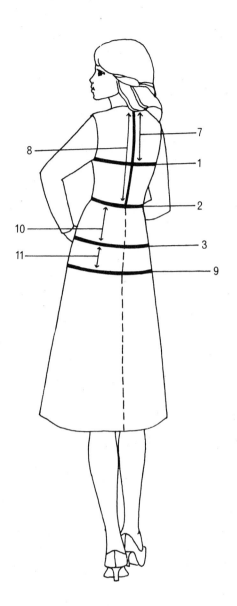

7

8

1

2

10

3

11

9

*Measurements and Adjusting Patterns*, page 184).
Smooth out each piece with a warm iron and place on
the prepared fabric.

## PASSEMENTERIE

A collective term used to describe ornate decoration
made up of a variety of things such as braid, lace,
gimps applied with couching and the addition even of
beads and sequins. More recently the term has come
to be used in describing ornate motifs worked on net

base fabric, using a variety of techniques, the motif
then being applied to the garment.

## PATCHWORK

A traditional craft used for household items as well as
clothes. Although it is a useful way of using up fabric
scraps, for clothes it is worth designing the patchwork
carefully and buying specific fabrics. Entire garments
can be composed of patches, or small areas such as
collars, cuffs and yokes. Where possible make a piece
of patchwork and cut out the shape afterwards. The
exception to this being large, rectangular shapes such
as quilts and pillows. Patchwork effect can be achieved
quickly by purchasing printed patchwork design
fabric by the metre.

If a large area is to be in patchwork it may be a
selection of large, almost random, shapes, joined by
machine on the wrong side, taking a narrow seam.
Where small repeating regular shapes are required,
templates are used. A selection, in metal and plastic,
can be bought. They are in pairs, the larger one the
size of each fabric piece and the small one the template for the temporary backing of each patch. The
advantage of buying templates is that they are
precision produced and the cut shapes will match
when joined. If you want individual shapes you will
have to cut your own master template.

The easiest way to make patchwork is to cut out
sufficient templates — traditionally paper, but soft
sew-in Vilene is easier to sew. Cut out an equal
number of fabric pieces with the straight grain in the
same position on each. When using various fabrics, a
plan should first be made to ensure that the correct
colours are being cut. Note that if a firm result is
required as on a yoke, collar, cuffs, belt, hemline
band, use light iron-on Vilene for templates, press
them to the wrong side of the fabrics and cut out
round each, allowing a small seam allowance.

With right side towards you, fold over the raw
edge of each piece and tack, near the edge but not
too close. Press carefully. Following your design, hold
the prepared patches together, right sides together,
and oversew with small stitches that pick up only a
little of each fold. It is vital that matching edges are
joined accurately. Continue in this way until all
pieces are joined. Press on the right side. If the backing
has to be removed, pull out tackings and take out the
backings. Keep them to use again. On the right side
additional decoration can be added with stitches such
as feather stitch, or on rich fabrics such as velvet, use
beads, etc. Whole areas of patchwork such as cuffs,
and collars, can be lined. Another method of finishing
edges is binding.

## PEASANT STYLE

A dress or skirt and blouse whose features include

hemline frills and gathers, possibly gathered tiers and even elastic in the waist instead of a waist band. Tops have long or short full gathered sleeves with elastic in the hems, the sleeves are usually raglan, the bodice straight and the neckline gathered with binding with ties or elastic inserted. The sewing processes are easy and quick to do and effective use can be made of lightweight fabrics of mixed colours and designs.

## PEDAL-PUSHERS

(See *Knickerbockers*.)

## PEG TOP

A style of skirt or trousers. Such skirts are often worn when straight skirts are in fashion. The hemline is quite narrow, the hips are fitted but the surplus fabric is reduced at the waist by wide fold tucks rather than standard darts. The trousers have the same waist construction and are straight-legged.

## PENCIL

A term applied to a tight-fitting straight skirt, i.e. pencil slim; it may be short or long.

## PEPLUM

A shaped piece added to the waist of a fitted bodice. It may be used on a jacket or a dress and is usually worn with a fairly straight skirt. This decorative feature suits only those with slim waistlines.

## PETAL

A feature comprising several shaped pieces of fabric, usually with curved outer edge, that are overlapped and then incorporated into a neckline as a collar, into an armhole as a sleeve, or into a waist as a skirt or over-skirt. Also used as a style for hats.

## PETER PAN COLLAR

A small, flat collar with little or no stand at the back and shaped to round corners at the front.

## PETERSHAM

Named after Lord Petersham, this term is used for crisp ribbons with a pronounced weft rib, and also for elastic. Petersham ribbons are made in two quite different types.

**Millinery petersham**
Used to trim ladies' hats, but also used widely in ready-made clothes, particularly nylon qualities which have better wash/shrink characteristics.

**Skirt petersham**
Heavier and stiffer to enable it to maintain the shape of the waistband and prevent roll. Recently there has been a strong swing to polyester fibre for straight petersham, and nylon for those that are shaped or curved making them particularly good for skirts that are worn low on the waist, and to aid the fitting of hollow backs. The curve in the best qualities is permanent, as is the firmness.

**Curved petersham**
Petersham made from polyester fibre and woven in a permanent curve that is not affected by washing. Available in black and white 2.5 cm (1 in.) wide. In pre-packs containing 1 metre (1 yd) and including a flat hook and bar the same width as the petersham so that it can be slotted on to the end, or the petersham can be bought by the metre.

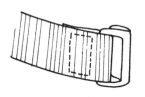 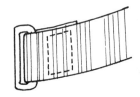

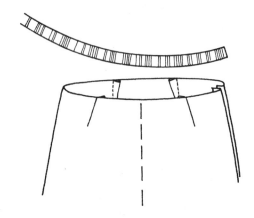

The concave or shorter edge of the length of petersham fits the waist, the convex or longer edge is below the waist. The main benefits of curved petersham are comfort and the fact that as it is waist-shaped it does not crease, roll or ride up.

Curved petersham can be used inside waistbands to make them curved and comfortable; attached to the top of skirts and trousers as a finish; inside curved belts; and it is also useful on other parts of the body where a curve is needed, for instance, upside down in the band of a bikini top.

### Elastic petersham

A stretch petersham with a soft edge each side. The main part is perforated and so is possibly more comfortable than solid elastic. Very useful in knitted skirts and comfortable in the tops of fabric skirts for those whose waist size varies. Can be inserted through a casing. If attached by one edge like ordinary petersham use a zig-zag or stretch machine stitch.

## PILE

Pile fabrics are those which have some yarns standing up on the surface. The pile is the result of extra yarns being introduced and they may be cut, as in velvet or plush, or they may be looped, as in towelling or chenille. On the whole the longer and silkier the pile the more difficult the fabric is to sew without wrinkling and without iron marks. If the pile has been flattened, as in panné velvet, it presents no problems provided sewing is done in the direction of the pile and not against it.

## PIN BASTE

This is a term used in some instruction books which simply means that pins are used to hold together a

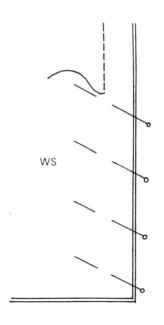

seam ready for stitching, rather than tacking or basting. It is best to insert the pins at right angles to the raw edges, picking up a very small amount of fabric on the pin, exactly on the fitting line. Do not push the pins in too far, leave the heads extending to the right so that they can be removed easily just as you approach them on the machine. In fact, if the pins are slightly angled they are quicker to remove.

## PIN CUSHION

A pin cushion is a useful place to place pins and needles temporarily as they are quicker to pick up again than taking from a box or container. However, many pin cushions, both purchased and home-made, contain fillings that may dull the ends of the pins and needles. Always replace all pins and needles in their packets when not in use.

A wrist pin cushion is useful for fitting sessions, this is one that is on a band that slips on to the wrist. One type of pin container, not cushion, can be attached to the rigid wrist band with Velcro (it is already in place) or the container can be put beside the machine, also attached with Velcro. This second piece can be stuck to the surface with a strong adhesive.

Another useful pin cushion is one that is on a plastic 'sucker'. This can be moved but remains in one place when moistened and pressed to the machine, table etc.

## PIN MARK

Where extreme accuracy is required and where the fabric is suitable the point of a pin will provide an indication of a point. An example of pin marking occurs when a buttonhole position is marked by inserting a pin. The buttonhole is snipped with scissors, the pin removed at the last moment and it is then possible to snip with the points of the scissors precisely into the hole left by the pin. Such a mark will not be visible on some fabrics, but on fairly fine or closely woven ones the pin-point will move the threads out of position and this mark is very useful. The threads will soon close up again so it is a very short-term method.

## PINKING SHEARS

Scissors that produce a serrated edge. At one time they were used instead of neatening raw edges but now that we can neaten by machine it is almost as quick and much more effective. In addition synthetic woven fabrics fray so easily that pinking raw edges has little effect, and the knits and jersey do not fray anyway.

Pinking shears are useful for cutting fabrics for

appliqué and possibly for trimming hidden raw edges such as on the bags of pockets in a lined garment. However, the use of these scissors is very limited. Never cut out fabric pieces with them, it reduces the seam allowance and it is irritating to handle fabric that does not have smooth edges.

## PINS

Good steel pins purchased in a box will not leave holes in fabric. They should be kept in the box because it will include a small piece of paper which keeps the pins dry and prevents rust. When sewing it is easier to put a few pins in a small shallow dish; the pins lie flat so you don't prick your fingers and they are quicker to pick up.

It is possible to buy long pins which are thinner than most. These are very suitable for fine fabrics including jersey.

Coloured headed pins are long and fine with plastic heads of different colours. They are attractive to use and very good where perhaps not many are needed and where it helps to be able to see the pin head, e.g. fitting. However, they are slow to use as it is not easy to grip the smooth round head, especially with thick or resilient fabrics.

At the first sign of bluntness or a bent pin, throw it away. And never keep needles mixed with pins.

Plastic pins are transparent, thick and not sharp. Their use is limited to open-knit fabrics.

## PIPING

Sometimes also called insertion braid. The function of piping is to emphasise a line, usually a seam, and to facilitate insertion it is woven with a sewing edge which disappears into the seam. Piping is available in three different forms: made from bias cut fabric; braided; and more recently, woven piping.

Woven piping is best made from polyester fibre and slightly elastic so that it will take the curve of a seam almost as well as the bias binding types. Fully elastic woven pipings are ideal for sports clothes made of stretch fabrics.

All purchased piping has a filled edge and a flat 'skirt' beside it. The latter being held in the seam allowing the filled part to show.

## PIPING CORD

Made of soft cotton yarns, usually white, this is a loosely twisted cord made in various thicknesses. It is used for inserting in bias strips to make piping and it can also be put into a length of rouleau tie to fill it. Other uses are mainly decorative including threading it between parallel rows of stitching to form Italian quilting, and twisting several lengths to make belts, bag straps etc.

Wash the piping cord before use since it may shrink.

## PIVOT

A technique in machining for turning corners accurately. The corner should be accurately marked. Machine up to that point and stop just short of it. Go forward with single stitches until the needle is in the down position exactly in the marked point. Raise the presser foot, swivel the fabric and lower the foot so that you can now proceed along the seam.

The angle is often a weak point but it can be strengthened by altering the stitch to a shorter one for a short distance on each side of the angle. This also helps to prevent fraying in woven fabrics.

## PLAIN SLEEVE

A fairly straight, basic sleeve with a standard sleeve head shaped to fit a basic armhole without any decorative features such as gathers. The sleeve may have slight elbow shaping in the form of ease or a dart on the back. The wrist is just wide enough to allow the hand to slip through without an opening.

## PLASTIC CURVE

A multi-purpose tool used in pattern drafting and also for accuracy in altering patterns. The outer edges are graded to assist with accuracy. The curved edges are different in shape so that they can be used for various parts of the pattern. The curves are usually marked with parts of the body. The transparent plastic tool also has a conventional ruler and a right angle, built-in.

## PLEAT STAY

If a fitted garment has several pleats in it, add a stay to the wrong side after completion. Cut a piece of lining fabric large enough to cover the area where the pleats are stitched flat, adding a seam allowance all round. Place lining to wrong side of garment and baste in position. Turn in the raw edges, tack, press and fell in place. When adding this stay to a skirt, leave a raw edge at the waist to be included when the waistband is attached. If the skirt fabric is bulky the backs of the pleats can be cut away before attaching the stay. Knife pleats that are not stitched can be held in place for a short distance below the waist by applying a piece of iron-on Vilene instead of lining.

Sometimes the backing of a pleat may not extend right up to the waist of a skirt, perhaps the result of economy of fabric. In this case attach a length of tape or straight seam binding to act as a stay and prevent the pleat from dropping in wear. Hem one end of the tape to the top of the pleat itself, tack the length of tape to the wrong side of the skirt up to the waist. Include this end of the tape in the waist finish, then remove the tacking.

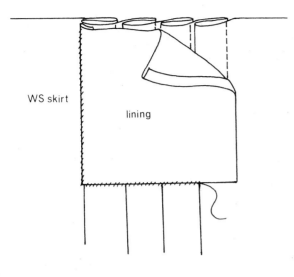

WS skirt

lining

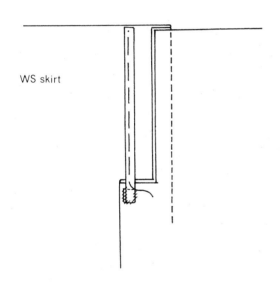

WS skirt

# PLEATS

Pleats are an attractive style feature and they can also provide room for movement. A pleat may be held in position at one end only, as at the centre back of a man's shirt; it may be held at both ends, e.g. pleat inserted down the centre of a patch pocket; or it may be held at one end and also stitched in place for part of its length, as in a skirt. Pleats that are held on one end but not stitched or pressed are unpressed pleats.

There are three main types of pleats: knife pleats, inverted pleats and box pleats, and they are all simply folds of fabric. A pleat can be added to any garment simply by allowing enough additional fabric where it is needed and folding it into place.

Wherever possible put the pleats in position in the fabric before doing any other process. When fitting a garment the entire pleat should be tacked down to ensure that none of its width is borrowed to make the garment big enough.

All pleats (except unpressed) must be very well and firmly pressed at an early stage and subsequent pressing of the garment will press them in even more.

Mark all pleat lines and hemlines before removing the pattern. Some skirt pleats may have the back part of the pleat as a separate piece to be attached. This often improves the hang, enabling the pleat to be slightly on the bias of the fabric; it may be done to economise on fabric or to enable it to be cut from a narrow width; it also makes it possible to use contrasting fabrics.

## Accordion pleats

Very narrow knife pleats. The effect is used on skirts, flounces on skirt hems and sleeves so that the fabric splays out like an accordion when moved. Pieces of fabric can be taken to a pleater to be treated. It is not easy to calculate exactly how much fabric you need for whatever depth of pleat you have in mind so it is best to have plenty done. You will usually be required to turn up the hem first but probably not join the seams.

Pleats inserted in fabrics made from synthetic fibres are permanent, those in natural fibres are not.

There is a wide range of accordion pleated fabric available by the metre and some very attractive effects can be achieved especially where matching unpleated fabric is offered as well.

If the garment is washable, place a series of rubber bands loosely round the pleated section, wash by hand without squeezing and drip dry.

## Box pleats

A box pleat is composed of two knife pleats facing in opposite directions. They are often used in skirts, stitched down for part of their length, and small box pleats may be used in the back of a shirt or in a decorative patch pocket. The two knife pleats may or may not meet at the back. If they do not the knife pleats should be stitched separately on the wrong side and then pressed.

If the pleats meet at the back, fold the fabric right side out, matching the marked pleat lines. Stitch for part of the way if desired, with a normal machine stitch and then for the remainder with a large stitch as for other pleats. If the pleat is not to be stitched down, tack for its entire length. Arrange the fabric on the sleeve board right side up. Open the fabric of the pleat and flatten it with the fingers, carefully pressing

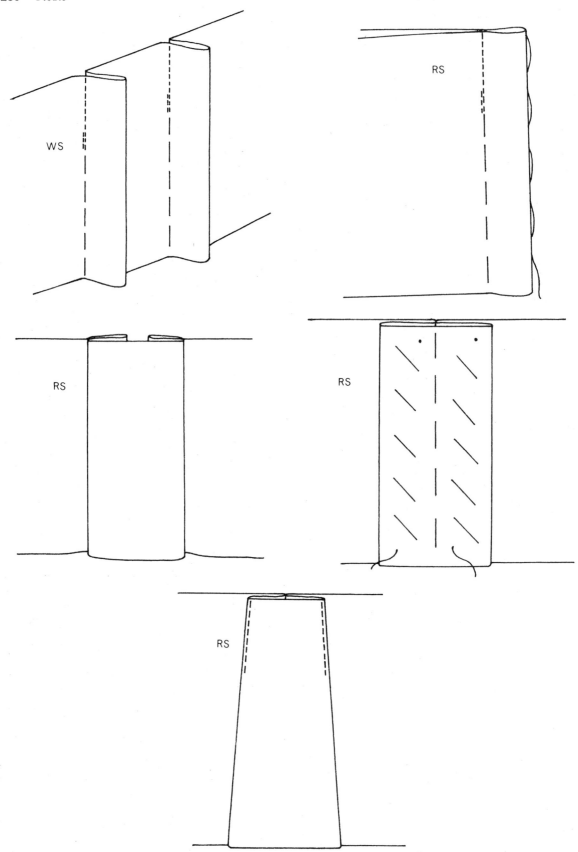

the centre marking of the pleat on to the stitched join beneath. Start at the bottom and press, following your finger with the iron. After initially pressing in place, press again to ensure good pleat edges. Baste the pleat through all layers for its length.

Pleats in pockets and shirts are held in place by later processes, after which the central stitching is removed. Skirt pleats must be stitched down on the right side to the required depth. Remove the lower section of stitching before turning up the hem.

### Inverted pleats

An inverted pleat is two knife pleats facing each other, meeting at the centre. The pleat is usually stitched down for a short distance from the waist, or for quite a long way if a small kick pleat at the hem is preferred. Make sure the pleat release point is either above or below the widest part of the figure otherwise too much attention will be drawn to that area.

The backing of an inverted pleat is nearly always cut as a separate piece. Tailor tack the centre front line. Place the two front skirt sections together, right sides facing, and match the centre front lines carefully. Tack. Put a chalk mark to indicate the top of the pleat. This depth can be varied from 10 cm (4 in.) to about 20 cm (8 in.). With normal straight machine stitch, machine from the chalk line up to the waist, fastening off the threads. Adjust the stitch to maximum length, lower the needle into the fabric exactly at the base of the first row of stitching and machine from there to the hem. Do not fasten off ends.

Press stitching flat, then use the toe of the iron to open the pleat on the stitching line. Press pleat open firmly, using a damp muslin. The pleat is not finished at this stage but the skirt is ready for a fitting. Make a chalk mark or put a pin on the right side level with the depth of pleat to show at fitting where the pleat ends.

After fitting, undo tacking in side seams and finish the pleat. Lay the skirt, wrong side up, on the table. Place pleat backing on top, right side down. Match the centre, with the pleat line beneath and tack up the middle. Slide a hand under the two layers of pleat and lift slightly so that you can baste together from hem to waist. Finally tack the two edges together on the seam line. Machine the pleat edges together. Trim and neaten to within about 7.5 cm (3 in.) of the hemline. Complete the skirt.

Put the skirt on and have the hem level marked with pleats stitched in. Remove skirt, run tacking thread round hemline but where pleat occurs work tailor tacks, penetrating all layers of fabric. As the tacks have to be snipped into three, leave long loops between the stitches. Part the three layers of fabric carefully, starting with the underneath one, and snip the tacks.

Undo the row of big machine stitches holding the pleats in. This can often be done by grasping one end of the thread and gently easing the fabric along. Press

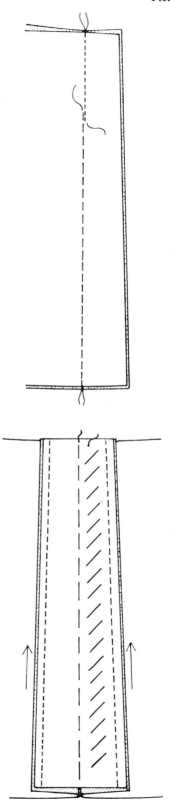

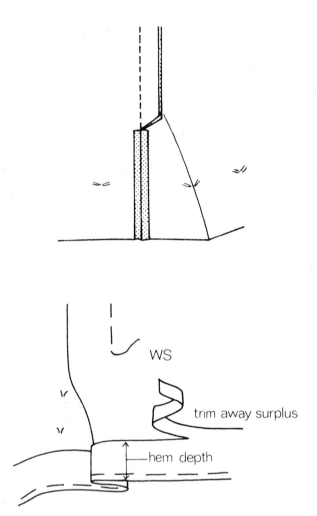

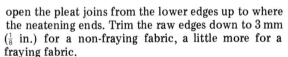

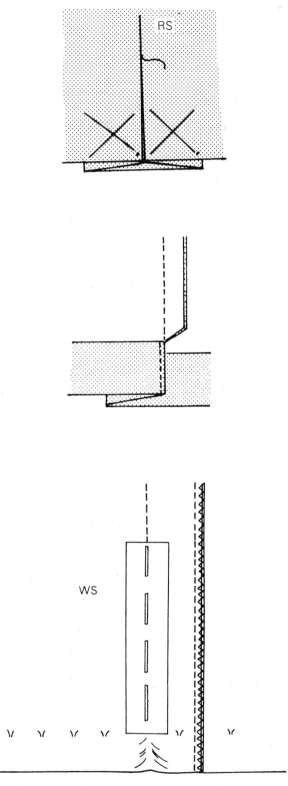

open the pleat joins from the lower edges up to where the neatening ends. Trim the raw edges down to 3 mm ($\frac{1}{8}$ in.) for a non-fraying fabric, a little more for a fraying fabric.

Turn up the hem in the usual way all round the skirt, pressing and trimming down and neatening the raw edge. Catch the hem down as usual but at the pleat joins, snip the raw edges in towards the seam and then stitch the hem down. Lift up the raw edges and complete the neatening, working round the corner at the bottom to finish off.

*Stitching pleats to prevent them opening*    Fold the pleat into position and tack with a double diagonal stitch. Turn to the wrong side and stitch from just inside the bottom up to the hem edge, sewing near the edge through all layers.   This can be done by machine if you can keep your stitching straight through this thickness, but it is often easier to back stitch by hand.

Press the hem in the usual way and re-press the pleat edges but as you have uneven layers of fabric, pad the board with a towel first as it is easy to finish up with pleat backing imprints showing in the hem.

The folds can be given a crisp edge and longer life by adding a strip of Fold-a-Band to the wrong side before turning up the hem. After removing the large machine stitches, centre a piece of Fold-a-Band over the pleat crease and press. The Fold-a-Band should run from the hemline mark to about 3 to 4 cm ($1\frac{1}{4}$ to $1\frac{5}{8}$ in.) above the release point. Re-press the pleat folds carefully. Turn up the hem.

### Kick pleat

A short pleat in the hem of a straight skirt providing room for movement. It is usually an inverted pleat with a separate backing piece. As the pleat is short the backing does not extend right up to the skirt waist. Construct as for an inverted pleat. If the pleat is shorter than about 20 cm (8 in.) it is easier to turn up the hem of the skirt and the pleat backing and finish both hems, before attaching the backing to the pleat. Ensure the hems are level by inserting firm tacks, then machine from the hem, through all layers up to the top of the backing. Stitch both sides in this direction. Attach the top edge of the pleat backing by working herringbone stitch over the edge and picking up small stitches in the fabric of the pleat.

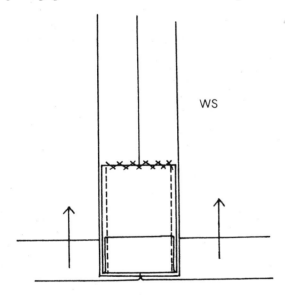

WS

### Knife pleats

A knife pleat is a single fold in the fabric, pressed to one side. They can be used singly, in pairs or groups, or continuously as in a kilt. With single pleats the fabric may simply be folded or, if it is a deep pleat, the skirt may be cut in two sections. In this case place the pieces right sides together, tack on the pleat line; stitch to the release point if desired. Join the two raw edges by stitching on the fitting line and then neatening. Press well. The hemline has to be handled carefully with this type of pleat so stop the neatening well above the hemline. It can be completed after the hem has been turned up.

If a skirt has knife pleats all round, it is easier to establish the skirt length and turn up and finish the hem completely before inserting the pleats.

Working from the right side fold the pleats, matching tailor's tack lines, then tack from hem to waist. Press well with a hot iron over a damp cloth. If the pleats are to be stitched down for part of the way, do this now. It helps to hold the pleats in position in wear if the back folds are machined at this stage. Begin at the hem and stitch up to the waist.

If the skirt has only a few knife pleats it is best to set them in position from the wrong side. With the fabric wrong side up, fold over each pleat, matching up the tailor's tacks. Tack from hem to waist. If the pleats are to be stitched down for part of their length,

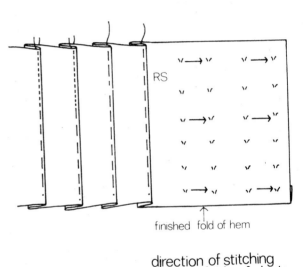

RS

finished fold of hem

direction of stitching on back folds of pleats on ws garment

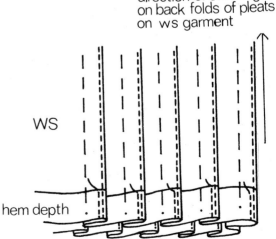

WS

hem depth

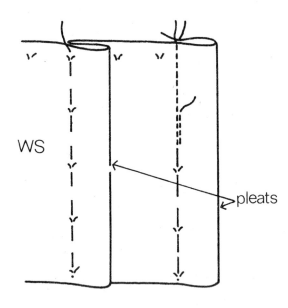

WS

pleats

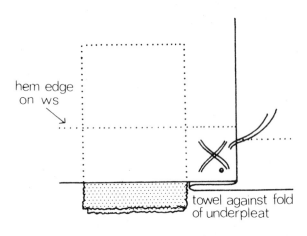

hem edge
on ws

towel against fold
of underpleat

If the pleat is in two pieces (if there is an actual seam at the back of the pleat instead of a fold), tack the pleat in the usual way, press, and stitch the seam. Turn up the hem with the seam trimmed and pressed open within the hem. Snip the seam turnings at the top of the hem, then neaten the turnings above the hem. Stitch the fold of the pleat through the hem.

## PLUNGING NECKLINE

A neckline, usually V or slit, that reaches the waistline of the garment. The plunge may be at the back or the front. If both back and front are designed to plunge then some anchorage has to be provided. This may take the form of a high stand collar.

## POCKETING

(See *Trouser Pocketing*.)

## POCKETS

### Breast pocket
The term used to describe an outside or inside top pocket on a man's coat. On the inside it is usually a jetted pocket made in the lining before the coat is constructed. It may have a zip or piece of Velcro attached for safety. It is usually inserted in the left side if the man is right handed or he may prefer it on the right side so that his wallet is then in his left hand ready for use. Always measure the depth and thickness of wallet, pocket book and other items and make the pocket to fit.

An outside breast pocket may be any of the cut pockets or a patch pocket and it is always on the left except on Safari-style jackets where one is made on both sides.

(For construction of *Jetted Pocket*, see page 238.)

### Cut pockets
Making these pockets involves making a slit in the fabric and they are therefore more difficult to do than other types of pocket. They have to be sewn accurately and strongly and as they cannot be moved once the fabric is cut it is essential to decide on the correct position and size before starting. They can be horizontal on the garment, or sloping, or even vertical as a style feature. All cut pockets may be made on men's or women's clothes and on any type of fabric.

Always reinforce the wrong side of the fabric first, using a piece of iron-on Vilene or a piece of soft canvas or linen. The strip should be 3 cm ($1\frac{1}{4}$ in.) wide and at least 5 cm (2 in.) longer than the length of the mouth of the pocket. Mark the position of the pocket on the reinforcement with tailor tacks worked through both parts of the garment if there is to be a pair of matching pockets. On the right side draw an accurate

do this now on the wrong side. Press well from the right side, making sure all pleats are facing in the correct direction. Finish the skirt, then turn up the hem. To do this remove the tacks in the pleats, open out the fabric, then turn up and finish the hem. Refold the pleats, and hold them in position with a double basting stitch through the hem. Press, placing a towel against the inner edge to prevent a ridge showing.

To keep the pleats in position, stitch down the folds on the backs of the pleats and through the hem.

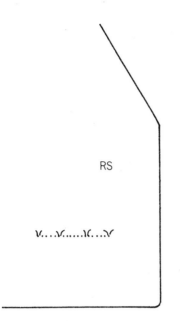

chalk line on the tailor tacks with further chalk lines marking the ends of the pocket.

The size of the pocket is related to the width across the hand plus ease, or, if the pocket is for a specific purpose or purely as a decorative style feature, calculate the length accordingly. The following is a guide.

Coat or jacket pockets: men's, 17 cm ($6\frac{3}{4}$ in.); women's, 12 cm ($4\frac{3}{4}$ in.).

Breast pocket: men's, 11 cm ($4\frac{3}{8}$ in.); women's, 8 cm ($3\frac{1}{8}$ in.).

Ticket pocket (a small pocket made inside a conventional pocket): men's, 5 cm (2 in.)

The size of the pocket bag varies accordng to the position and intended use of the pocket. The following is a guide, bag pieces should be cut approximately to these sizes but trimmed and shaped only in the final stages of construction. If the mouth of the pocket opens to reveal the inside, as with a jetted pocket, a narrow strip of the fabric of the garment must be joined to the bag to fall behind this gap. The bag is best made from strong fabric such as calico, strong cotton or pocketing for men's clothes and for women's coats. If the pockets are decorative or are likely to be little used the bag may be made from lining fabric. Avoid making the bag from garment fabric unless it is very lightweight.

After constructing cut pockets, work bar tacks at the ends of the pocket for strength then close the pocket by working a row of basting over the edges. Press but leave the basting in until the garment is complete. For additional strength on coat pockets

that are to be well used and therefore will pull the garment out of shape, attach a length of tape or a strip of linen to the end of the pocket on the inside of the coat. Baste the tape flat across the coat to the armhole and back stitch. The end will be stitched into the armhole seam later.

Begin by cutting all pieces of fabric, such as reinforcement or pocket bag material, then work the first stage on all pockets, then the second stage and so on. The straight grain on the fabric pieces should correspond with that on the garment unless it is deliberately cut on the cross for effect, as it might be with check fabric. Striped fabric is difficult to use; the stripes should either match the garment exactly or they should be on the cross.

As with most fiddly processes on small areas the small pieces for the pockets are easier to handle if narrow seam allowances of 5 to 10 mm ($\frac{1}{4}$ to $\frac{3}{8}$ in.) are used. This applies to jettings, pipings, flaps and welts.

### Flap pocket

The upper edge of the cut in the fabric has a flap attached to it to neaten it. The flap may be any size that is suitable and it usually has rounded corners as they are not so inclined to curl up as square corners. If a flap pocket is made on an angle the lower corner is often left with straight edges. The flaps may have interfacing inserted; this is wise in some soft suitings and coat fabrics and it is essential in flaps made from lightweight fabrics.

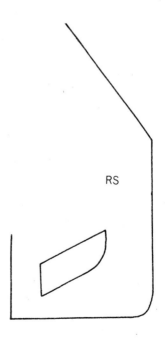

The lower edge of the pocket is neatened with a narrow strip of fabric attached like a jetting or piping on a jetted pocket.

Reinforce the wrong side of the garment. Mark the pocket positions. Prepare two pieces of pocket bag and one strip of fabric 6 cm (2⅜ in.) wide and 3 cm (1¼ in.) longer than the size of the pocket. Cut two pieces of fabric for the flap, cutting rectangles first then marking the exact shape on them with chalk. On heavy or bulky fabrics cut one piece in fabric and the other in lining material. Join the jetting to one piece of pocket bag and press the join to one side.

*Flaps without interfacing*   Place the lining and fabric right sides together, fabric uppermost, and tack, easing the fabric in slightly. This will prevent the flap from curling up in wear. Machine. Trim, snip and turn the flap right side out. Roll the edges so that the lining is slightly to the underside, tack the edge and press. If a swelled edge finish is wanted, work it now.

*Flaps with interfacing*   When using light iron-on such as Vilene Supershape, cut it to the same size as the flap, and make as described earlier. If a heavier interfacing is required cut it without turnings to the finished size of the flap. If using a sew in interfacing attach it with herringbone stitch round the outer edge.

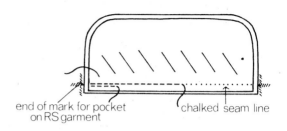

end of mark for pocket on RS garment    chalked seam line

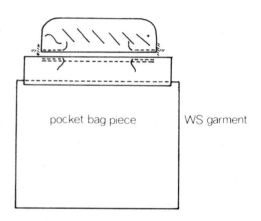

pocket bag piece          WS garment

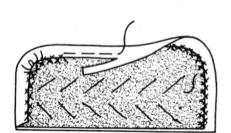

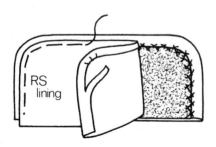

RS lining

Fold the edge of the fabric over the interfacing and tack and press. Snip the surplus at the corners. Trim the edge down to 5 mm (¼ in.) and work herringbone stitch over the edge. Do this only round the outer edge.

Place the lining wrong side down to the wrong side of the flap and tack. Turn in the raw edges, trimming a little off first, so that the lining is 2 mm (⅛ in.) in from the edge of the flap. Fell the lining to the flap.

With all flaps draw the lining piece tight on the fabric and tack along the raw edges. Press.

To make the pocket, place the flap with right side down to the right side of the coat, with the flap seam line exactly over the chalk line marking the pocket position. Baste. Make a chalk line on the flap on which to machine, as it is difficult to be accurate once the work is under the machine. Machine exactly from end to end of the flap.

Place the piece of bag with fabric piece right side down below the pocket line. Baste. Machine 3 mm (⅛ in.) from the previous row of stitching, making this line slightly shorter than the top row at each end.

Cut the pocket by snipping between the rows of stitching. Work from the wrong side and cut through the fabric and reinforcement only. Cut right to the ends of the machining, angling the snips for the final 2 cm ($\frac{3}{4}$ in.).

Push the lower piece through to the wrong side, trim the turnings, and carefully press open the join. Form a jetting by rolling the edge until it is very narrow, then prick stitch along the join. Bring the flap down over it and press the join from the right side, then baste the flap down flat.

Take the other piece of bag and place it against the flap turnings on the wrong side. Machine as close as possible to the row of stitching holding the flap in position. Work a row of prick stitches from the right side through the turnings just above the flap join.

Push under the triangles at each end. Mark the size and shape of the pocket bag and machine, stitching as close as possible to the end of the pocket, catching in the triangles if possible. Machine again 5 mm ($\frac{1}{4}$ in.) away. Neaten if garment is unlined.

Work a bar tack across the ends of the pocket beside the flap to the lower edge of the jetting, then press.

### Flap pockets with jettings

A flap pocket may have a jetting or piping along the top edge of the flap, especially on men's suits where it adds some stability for wear.

Attach jettings as described for a jetted pocket, turn them to the wrong side and prick stitch the joins. Push the end triangles through to the wrong side; press. Make up a flap 2 mm ($\frac{1}{8}$ in.) longer than the jetted pocket, to make it curve outwards, and push the raw edges into the pocket slit. Baste in position, making sure the flap is accurately in position. On the wrong side machine the flap to the upper jetting stitching as far in from the raw edges as possible. Finish by attaching the pocket bag as for a flap pocket.

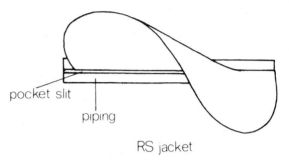

pocket slit

piping

RS jacket

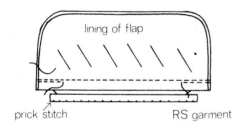

lining of flap

prick stitch          RS garment

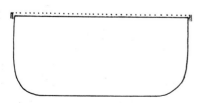

### Inset pockets

These are set below the waist, sometimes on skirts and often on trousers and jeans. The cut-away edge is curved or slanting and therefore liable to stretch and it is also subjected to strain. Mark the edge when cutting out but do not cut close to it until interfacing has been attached to the wrong side. On men's trousers also insert tape in the edge. One piece of

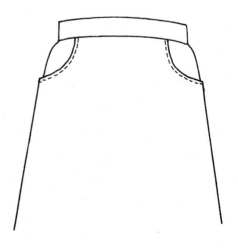

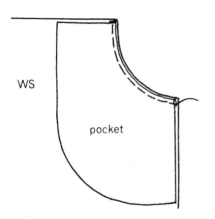

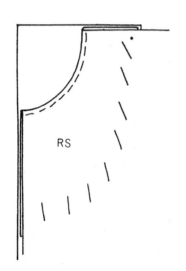

### Jetted pocket

The cut edges of fabric are neatend with a narrow piece of fabric producing the effect of binding. This type of pocket is sometimes called a piped pocket. The method described uses two pieces of fabric although this type of pocket can be constructed in the same way as a piped buttonhole with the same result. In this case it is possible to use bought piping, with a filled edge, instead of fabric, to produce a really raised piped edge.

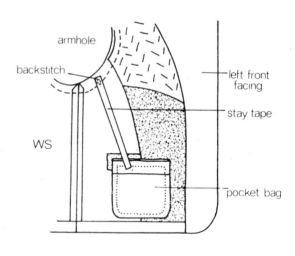

pocket has one edge cut to correspond with the cut-away edge and it is attached and turned to the wrong side in the same way as a facing. The second piece of pocket also forms part of the garment. Place it right side up underneath the edge and tack the pocket to it. Mark the pocket bag, machine and neaten it. Baste the pocket to the garment. Complete the garment.

On men's trousers the fabric extends only inside the pocket for a depth of 6 to 8 cm ($2\frac{3}{8}$ to $3\frac{1}{2}$ in.) and then pieces of pocketing are joined on for strength.

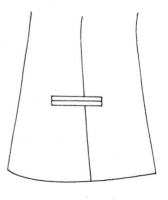

Reinforce the wrong side of the garment. Mark the pocket positions. Prepare two pieces of pocket bag and three pieces of fabric. One piece of fabric will be used to back the mouth of the pocket and all three should be 6 cm ($2\frac{3}{8}$ in.) wide and about 3 cm ($1\frac{1}{4}$ in.) longer than the proposed size of the pocket. Join one piece of the fabric to one piece of pocket bag and press the turnings to one side. The other two pieces are the jettings and one can be joined to the other piece of pocket bag at this stage. Press the join to one side.

Place this piece right side down against the pocket line on the right side of the garment, below the line, and the other piece right side down above. The raw edges must be close together. Machine 3 mm ($\frac{1}{8}$ in.) from each raw edge. The rows of stitching must be parallel and the same length.

Cut the pocket by snipping on the wrong side through the reinforcement and the garment only. Cut between the rows and then out to the corners, snipping right up to the end of the machining. Press open all seams, then pass the strips through the slit to the wrong side.

If the pocket is to be used frequently, the lower edge may stretch in wear, so reinforce it by slipping a length of stay tape under the lower jetting. Back stitch it to the reinforcing fabric close to the machining.

Pass both pieces to the wrong side. Roll and tack the jettings to form a narrow piping of even width along both edges. Prick stitch through the join from the right side, then press.

On the wrong side attach one piece of pocket bag by turning under one edge and hemming to the lower jetting.

On a man's coat there may have to be an inside ticket pocket. Make it now from two pieces of pocketing. This pocket should be about 9 cm ($3\frac{1}{2}$ in.)

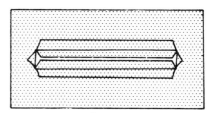

WS garment

reinforcement piece

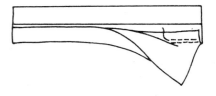

RS garment

RS garment

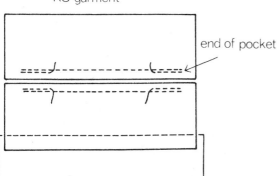

RS garment

end of pocket

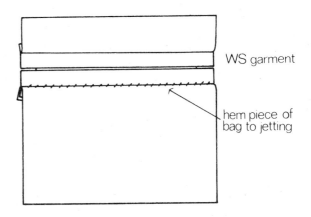

WS garment

hem piece of bag to jetting

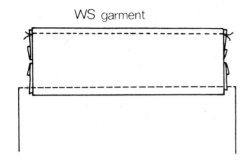

WS garment

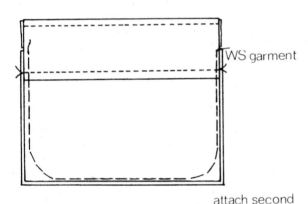

WS garment

attach second
bag piece

wide and inserted 5 cm (2 in.) below the top edge of
the pocket bag piece.

On the wrong side of the coat, place this pocket
bag piece right side down onto the back of the jettings
with the raw edge level with the raw edge of the top
jetting. Hold the bag edge and jetting edge together
and baste. Machine as close as possible to the top of
the pocket or it will hang down. It is worth using the
piping or zip foot for this in order to get close.

On the right side push the triangles of cloth that
have appeared at the ends, underneath the end of the
pocket. Do this with the point of a needle.

Place both bag pieces together, chalk the shape of
the pocket bag on the top one and machine round.
Begin and end very close to the pocket mouth and
catch in the little triangles if you can. Work two rows
about 5 mm ($\frac{1}{4}$ in.) apart. Trim the surplus. On an
unlined garment, neaten these raw edges.

On the right side baste the pocket edges together.
Work a bar tack through all the layers across the
width of the jettings, then press.

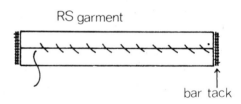

RS garment

bar tack

### Men's trouser pocket in seam

The edges of the pockets are made from fabric but the
remainder must be made from pocketing for strength.

Baste a strip of linen 6 cm ($2\frac{3}{8}$ in.) wide and 26 cm
($10\frac{1}{4}$ in.) long against the edge of the front trouser leg.

Cut two pieces of cloth 5 cm (2 in.) wide and 23 cm
(9 in.) long. Place one on the front leg and one on the
back, right sides together. The top of the pocket
opening comes 5 cm (2 in.) down from the waist, so
that is the position for the pieces. Stitch in position.

Sew the back and front trouser legs together at the
side seam, sewing down from the waist for a distance
of 5 cm (2 in.). Press open.

On the front trouser, roll the facing strip back to
the wrong side. Baste, press and prick stitch 5 mm
($\frac{1}{4}$ in.) in from the edge.

On the outer edge of the back piece turn a narrow
hem and machine or prick stitch to hold flat.

Make a pocket bag from a piece of trouser
pocketing 40 cm ($15\frac{3}{4}$ in.) wide and deep enough to
include not only the pocket opening and the depth of
the hand but also sufficient height for it to extend up

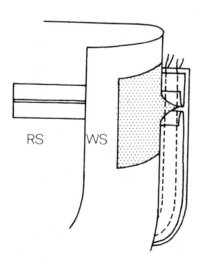

RS    WS

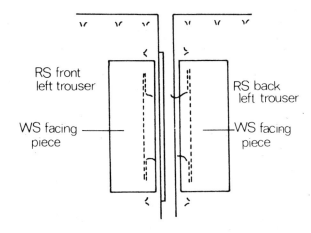

RS front
left trouser

WS facing
piece

RS back
left trouser

WS facing
piece

into the waistband later. Fold the fabric, cut the lower edge curved and make a seam round the curve. Trim the bag slightly so that it measures about 18 cm (7 in.) across the top (doubled).

Place in position on the facings and attach the front side first. Fold the top layer of the bag back, turn in the raw edge of the under piece and baste so that the edge is 2 cm ($\frac{3}{4}$ in.) back from the trouser edge. Fell this edge very firmly. On the right side baste up the pocket opening to hold closed. On the wrong side machine or back stitch the second edge of bag to the facing beneath.

At the base of the pocket strongly hem the pocket where it crosses the side seam of the trouser. On the right side work a strong bar tack at the top and bottom of the pocket, across the seam.

### Patch pockets

These may be of practically any size or shape if they form a style feature. If they are to be used they should be of the correct size and shape for the purpose. If a simple pocket is required just in case it is needed, make the size of it equal to the depth of the hand by the width of the hand plus ease.

Patch pockets intended for use will withstand wear better if they are interfaced, or at least have a strip of Fold-a-Band along the top edge. Patch pockets on a lined garment or in soft or fraying fabric should be lined. If the fabric is lightweight the pocket can be made double instead of using lining. If the garment fabric is soft, reinforce the back of the fabric by stitching a piece of cotton tape or seam tape at the place where the top of the pocket will come. In a lined garment press a strip of iron-on interfacing on instead.

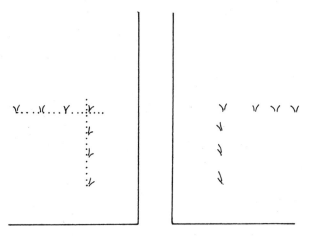

Pockets intended for hardwear, those on jeans or on children's clothes for example, should be machined in place for strength. For convenience put them on as early as possible in the construction of the garment. Other patch pockets can be hand-stitched in place and it may be best to put the garment together first in order to decide on the best position for them.

Avoid placing patch pockets on protruding parts of the body that are out of proportion, for example top pockets on a large bust or poacher's pockets on the side of trousers on a figure with large thighs.

Establish the best position and size by pinning the pattern to the garment and adjusting it. If no pattern is provided cut a piece of Vilene and try it, trimming it and moving it until satisfied.

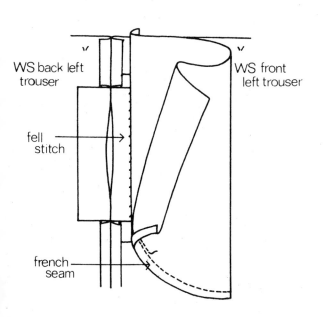

WS back left
trouser

WS front
left trouser

fell
stitch

french
seam

Mark pocket positions with one horizontal line of chalk and one short vertical line across it to mark one corner. For two matching pockets chalk and then tailor tack through both layers.

### Unlined patch pockets

Turn in the top edge of the pocket and press. Fold-a-Band may be inserted. Tack along the fold; press. Hold down the raw edge with a fabric adhesive (such as Wundaweb), with herringbone stitch or with a row of machining. Turn in the other three edges on the fitting line and tack. If the corners are rounded they should be snipped. Press. Place in position and tack round all four sides to hold.

Work a small slip stitch, just under the edge, around three sides. Work bar tacks at the top corners just inside the corners.

### Lined pocket

Turn in all outside edges of pocket and hold down with fabric adhesive or herringbone stitch.

Cut pieces of lining fabric the same size plus turnings. Place to the pocket wrong sides together, and baste. Trim the raw edges and turn under all round. Along the top edge the lining should just cover the raw edges; the lining is therefore about 1 to 2 cm ($\frac{3}{8}$ in.) below the top edge of the pocket. Around the other three sides, the edge of the lining should be about 2 mm ($\frac{1}{8}$ in.) back from the edge. Tack. Fell all round. Remove tacks, and press.

If top stitching is required do it at this stage either by machine or by hand.

If a box or inverted pleat is put in a patch pocket, insert the pleat and stitch it, then line the pocket as described.

Place the pockets in position, and attach by hand. If the edge has been stitched it looks better to work the slip stitch further in (i.e. under the edge stitching).

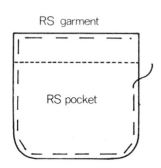

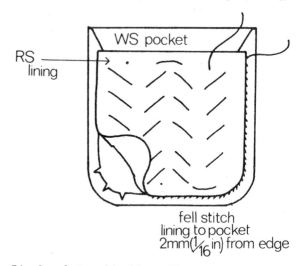

fell stitch
lining to pocket
2mm($\frac{1}{16}$ in) from edge

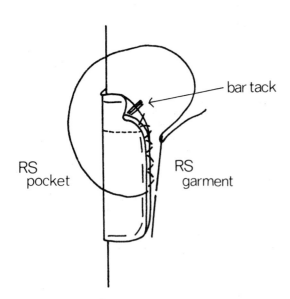

### Lined pocket machined in position

Cut the pocket with 4 cm ($1\frac{5}{8}$ in.) to turn in and cut a piece of lining 8 cm ($3\frac{1}{8}$ in.) shorter. Place the lining piece to pocket piece right sides together with top edges level and machine, taking 5 mm ($\frac{1}{4}$ in.) seam allowance. Press the turnings open if both layers are fabric, press towards lining if the smaller piece is made of lighter fabric.

Bring the three raw edges of pocket and lining together, insert pins round the outside, well within the outer edges. The lining is smaller than the pocket so you will have to force the edges to meet.

Using tailor's chalk and a ruler, chalk a line on which to stitch. Mark a gap 4 cm ($1\frac{5}{8}$ in.) long in one side through which to turn the pocket. If the pocket has curved corners use the paper pattern, or original Vilene pocket, as a guide to marking accurate pairs of curves.

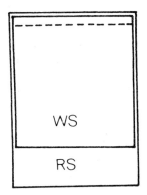

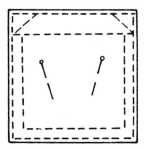

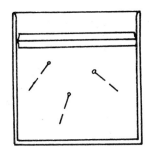

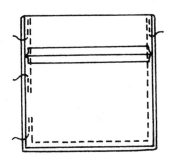

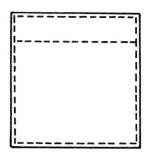

Machine all three sides, reversing at the top and at each side of the gap.

Remove pins. Trim raw edges to 3 mm ($\frac{1}{8}$ in.) and cut off the corners. Press the stitching flat. Push the pocket through the gap and turn it right side out. Roll the corners and edges and press the edge from the lining side. Press the raw edges inwards at the gap.

Edge stitch all round the outer edge of the pocket. Machine again across the top 2 cm ($\frac{3}{4}$ in.) down from the top edge. Press.

Place pocket in position on the right side of the garment, anchor with two pins. Baste the pocket across the top and then around the other three sides. Do not remove the pins.

Machine, starting at the edge level with the lower row of machining, stitch at an angle up to the top of the pocket, swivel the work, stitch along the top for three stitches, swivel and stitch round the pocket parallel with the edge. At the second corner repeat the triangle.

Remove pins and basting. Fasten off machine ends. Press well on both right and wrong sides of pocket.

### Seam pockets

Functional seam pockets are simply two bag-shaped pieces of fabric stitched to the seam allowance, a gap left in the seam and the bag pieces stitched together. It is probably the simplest pocket to construct but it may be bulky. This can be overcome by cutting one piece of the bag in lining fabric and by pressing light iron-on Vilene to it. Alternatively, if the fabric is lightweight, add Vilene to one piece to help the pocket to lie flat. Prepare both pieces and neaten the raw edge.

For accuracy stitch the seam of the garment leaving a gap for the hand. Tack or machine that gap then press the entire seam open.

Place the back pocket bag to seam allowance of back of garment, with right sides together, and machine taking a narrow seam allowance. Attach the front pocket (it may be lining) to the front in the same way. Press open the seams.

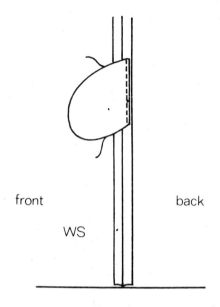

front                    back

WS

and finishing at the garment seam. Machine on this line starting and finishing on the garment seam whatever the shape of pocket. Remove pins. Trim the edges to 5 mm ($\frac{1}{4}$ in.) and zig-zag over the two edges to neaten.

Cut a piece of Wundaweb 12 cm ($4\frac{3}{4}$ in.) long and slip it under the pocket at the front. Push it into the fold at the seam between the garment and the pocket to hold the pocket in position. Press well to melt the adhesive. Remove the large machine stitches in the seam.

*Combined seam and patch pocket*
This is a very simple partly decorative pocket. Cut one pocket bag piece of fabric. This can be larger and perhaps a more interesting shape than the functional bag. Stitch the seam and leave the gap. Press open the seam. Neaten the outer edges of the pocket bag. Place this right side down to the wrong side of the garment matching the straight edge to the pressed seam of the garment. Machine the pocket edge to the back seam allowance. Tack the pocket flat to the garment. Turn to the right side, mark the pocket edge with chalk and machine.

The pocket piece may be circular and placed behind a panel seam, as an alternative.

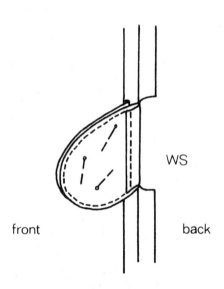

WS

front                    back

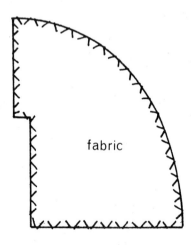

fabric

Re-press the back pocket so that it extends towards the front of the garment and lies on top of the front pocket piece. Snip the seam allowance on the back of the garment level with the end of the pocket, at the top and bottom. Neaten the edges of the garment seams.

Pin the pocket pieces together, inserting the pins well within the outer edge. Using tailor's chalk, mark the shape of the bag, drawing a line from the seam at the top of the pocket opening, round the outer edge

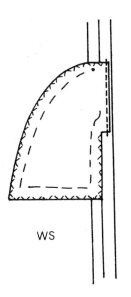

WS

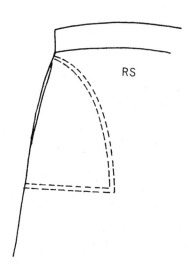

RS

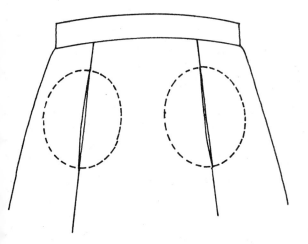

### Pocket in horizontal seam

This may be a yoke seam and the pocket can be placed underneath. The pocket will probably have to be quite small. Cut one piece of fabric and a piece of lining to reduce bulk. Stitch the seam, leaving a gap for the pocket. Stitch up the gap with machining or tacking. Press open the seam and add top stitching if appropriate to the design.

On the wrong side put the piece of pocket lining to the lower yoke seam allowance with right sides together. Machine 3 mm ($\frac{1}{8}$ in.) from the edge. Press so that the pocket lining hangs down.

Put the piece of fabric right side down on top of the first piece with the edge level with the edge of the

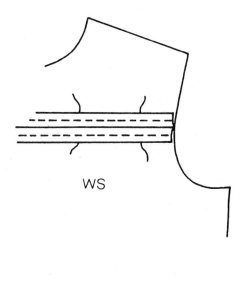

WS

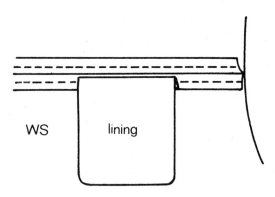

WS    lining

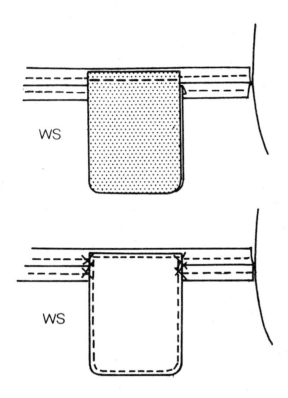

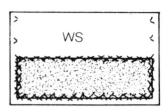

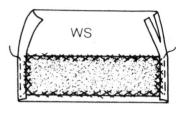

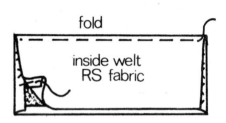

upper seam allowance on the yoke. Machine the two together 3 mm ($\frac{1}{8}$ in.) from the edge. Neaten the pocket edge by working zig-zag stitch over both edges.

Pin the pieces of pocket bag together. Mark the size and shape of the pocket with tailor's chalk. Machine round the bag, trim the turnings to 5 mm ($\frac{1}{4}$ in.) and neaten both edges together. Where the bag crosses the yoke seam, herringbone the edges of the bag to the seam allowances. Remove pins, press well and remove the large machine stitches in the seam.

### Welt pockets

A welt is a double fold of fabric attached to the lower cut edge of the pocket and extending upwards to cover the mouth of the pocket. Welts can be quite wide, between 2 and 5 cm ($\frac{3}{4}$ to 2 in.), and the ends are stitched down so there is no need to use a piece of the garment fabric to neaten the upper edge of the cut. The piece of pocket bag material can be used for this. The welt should be interfaced to keep it flat and to prevent stretching.

Prepare two pieces of pocket bag, and one piece of interfacing which is exactly the size you want the finished welt. Cut one piece of fabric twice this width and the same length but add a seam allowance all round. Mark the centre of the welt piece and place one edge of the interfacing on this line on the wrong side. Press in place if it is iron-on, otherwise work herringbone stitch all round.

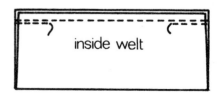

fold

inside welt
RS fabric

position of top of pocket

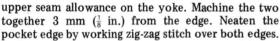

inside welt

RS garment

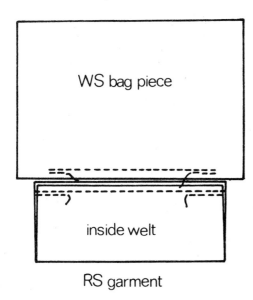

RS garment

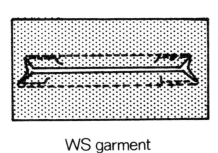

WS garment

On the wrong side of the garment cut between the rows of stitching and out to the ends of the stitching.

Push the pocket bag through the slit and allow it to hang down behind the opening inside the garment. Press the join open. Push the fabric triangles to the wrong side. Fold the welt up so that it covers the opening. Press the join with the toe of the iron. Baste the welt down firmly. Slip stitch the ends strongly, and work a row of prick stitch parallel with the ends, and also stab stitching through all the layers of fabric 2 to 3 mm ($\frac{1}{8}$ in.) inside the end.

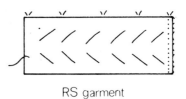

RS garment

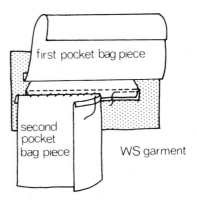

WS garment

Trim the edges of the other half of the welt at a slight angle, so that, when turned in and folded down, the edges are slightly to the underside of the welt. Baste the top and ends. Press and slip stitch the ends.

Place the welt on the right side of the garment, wrong side up. The position of the welt is below the marked pocket line, so that when the welt is folded up into position the pocket opening is correctly placed. Baste and machine along the raw edge of the welt, taking a small seam. Stitch exactly from end to end but do not allow the stitching to extend over the ends of the welt or it will show later. Trim down the raw edge of the welt quite narrow.

Place one piece of pocket bag right side down above the welt with its raw edge against the raw edges of the welt. Baste and machine, taking small turnings. This row of stitching must be shorter at each end than the row below to ensure that the welt completely covers it when the pocket is finished.

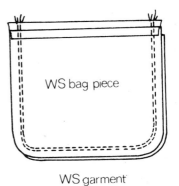

WS garment

Press over a narrow turning on the other piece of pocket bag; place this fold on the machine stitches attaching the welt on the wrong side then baste and hem to attach the fold to the welt turnings.

Bring the first piece of pocket bag down so that it lies on the underneath one. Baste the two pieces together round the outer edge. Chalk the correct size and shape of bag for the garment, with rounded corners. Machine round the bag starting very close to the ends of the pocket. Work two parallel rows of machining and overcast the edge if the garment is unlined.

## POINT PRESSER

This is a slim wooden device over which you can slip such processes as the corners of collars, lined pockets, etc. If you cover the top edge with a piece of blanket, cut exactly to size and stick it down, it can also be used in place of a seam roll.

## POLO COLLAR

A high collar cut on the cross and rolled over to its full depth. (For instructions for making and attaching see *Roll Collar*, page 66.)

## PONCHO

A simple poncho is a square of fabric of any type, or knitting or crochet, even a blanket, with a slit in the centre for the head to pass through. There are many fashion variations on the traditional South American shape. They can be oval or round, be fringed, bound, reversible, have pockets, where the wrists come they can be fastened or have cuff ribbing attached, and they can be any length. An elaborate poncho may be made of chiffon, beaded and fluted or pleated and made ankle length to complete a matching dress beneath.

## PRESS STUDS

A form of fastening that will not hold under the strain of body expansion. Once fastened there is no movement as there can be with buttons and hooks, so they are useful where accuracy is important. Use at such places as wrists and necklines but not at the waist or in place of buttonholes on a front fastening. However, they are flat and neat and their main use is to supplement other stronger fastenings.

Made in black and silver or nickel colour they range in size from 0000 (small and difficult to obtain) up through 1 and 2, to the very large press stud used on loose covers which can also be useful on waistbands as a back-up to hooks. Size 00 and 0 are the most useful sizes. There are also small ones in transparent plastic, not very strong but almost invisible, and others in pink and blue plastic. Tape with studs attached at intervals can be bought which is useful on furnishings, fancy costume and children's clothes but it is rather bulky and utilitarian for adult clothing.

Always sew press studs to at least two layers of fabric. Use the central hole in each part to locate the position accurately — insert a pin. Take the time to sew them on with buttonhole stitch; because it is neat and strong. Use normal sewing thread in short lengths. Start a new piece of thread for each section of press stud as the constant pulling through the metal holes tends to fray the thread. Use thread to match the garment, or in the case of black or coloured plastic press studs match the thread to the press stud so that they show less, provided your stitches are very neat.

### Attaching press studs

The 'knob' section is flatter and therefore goes on the outer part of the garment and the 'well' goes underneath. They are easier to fasten this way too. Thread the needle, put in a knot and run the thread through wax if working on medium or heavy fabrics.

Mark the position of the press stud, slip a pin through the central hole, insert the point exactly in position and make a back stitch under the pinpoint. Allow the press stud to slip on to the fabric and anchor by working one oversewing stitch in each hole. Remove the pin.

The press stud is now anchored in position, and you can attach it permanently by working buttonhole stitch close together to fill each hole. Fasten off beside the press stud or on the wrong side with a back stitch.

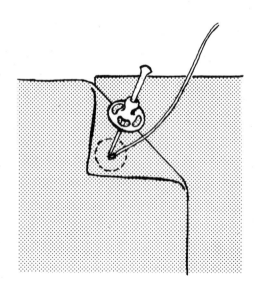

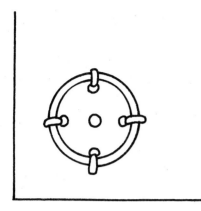

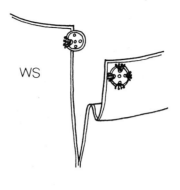

WS

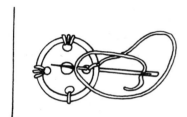

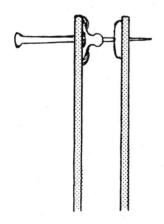

Slip a pin through the fabric and through the hole in the centre of the press stud; close up the section of garment and let the point of the pin enter the under part of the garment. Work a back stitch where the pin is, remove the pin, place the press stud over the stitch, and attach it as for the first half.

At slit necklines and edge-to-edge collars, use a transparent plastic press stud and sew the knob section in place close up against the edge of the fabric. Attach the well section to the other part of the garment by stitching through only one hole and allowing the remainder of the press stud to extend beyond the garment. When fastened, it brings the opening edge-to-edge.

### Covering press studs

This is worth doing on special fabrics and lined garments. Use a piece of lining fabric cut into circles large enough to wrap over the press stud, about twice the diameter. Run a gathering thread round the outer edge of each circle. Make a hole in the centre with a stiletto or large needle and force the knob through it. Pull up the thread and fasten off. Trim off the raw edges of fabric and press down. Cover the well sections in the same way, but without making a hole; this will occur automatically when the press stud is first fastened. Attach the press studs with button-hole stitch, using a thread which exactly matches the lining material.

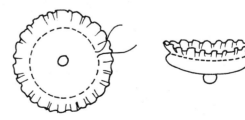

# PRESSING

There are probably three stages at which a garment has to be pressed during making, and all require a different technique apart from method.

First, creases must be removed from the bought length of fabric so that it lies flat for cutting out. If a pattern is placed on creased material it will be inaccurate. Select the method of pressing suitable for the type of fabric and the fibre content. Great care should be taken because pressure will be needed and the surface must not be impaired. Moisture might also be required, but there are no spare pieces of fabric yet to test the method of pressing.

During construction this flat piece of fabric must be subjected to heat, pressure and moisture in varying amounts in order to smooth all joins and edges so that the garment is permanently in position at all these points. There are numerous combinations of methods and techniques to be employed at different places even on the same garment in one fabric and experience can only be built up by making a variety of articles.

All sewing books have always stated that pressing must be done as you go along but too few explain why or how to do it. No sewing looks complete or professional until pressed so the iron and all the other equipment should be set up and ready. It is very important to make some sort of arrangement to enable you to press near the sewing area. If you have to rush downstairs to the iron, the pressing will be skimped or not done at all, but it is the most important aspect of sewing. No amount of superb machining, fitting and hand sewing will be worthy of the time spent on it if it is not pressed correctly. At one time it was only tailors who knew the value of pressing, spending almost as long on that as on sewing. It is only with the widespread availability of a variety of products from which to choose, enabling the construction of clothes in the home by amateurs, as against the professional dressmakers, that the attention given by tailors to the art of pressing has been adopted. The trouble is that too many women still confuse pressing with the ironing done after washing. The moment a dressmaker realises the difference, and the moment she employs her iron not only as a means of completing a process but also as a aid to accuracy (pressing folded edges etc.), she not only acquires an additional skill but she enjoys sewing more because it is easier and the results are better.

Another problem is that when this very pressure is applied, lack of care or experience may result in a spoiled fabric and the fear of this may deter the dressmaker until she gains confidence, Usually, in the hands of someone experienced these errors can be put right but the poor beginner does not know what to do. It cannot be stressed too much that pressing must be done, always, all the time; that it always improves the sewing; that the fabric is not likely to be spoiled if a few basic rules are learned; and that quite soon it dawns on everyone what valuable sewing aids the iron and water are.

### Remember

Press the process initially on the wrong side of the fabric — but in very few cases will it look right until the outside of the garment has been pressed as well.

Use only that part of the iron that is needed depending on the process, i.e. the toe for little things and for pushing into corners etc., the side of the iron on a long narrow edge.

If there is a ridge of any kind or a varying number of thicknesses of fabric, pressure on it for too long may cause a mark, usually only shine.

Use the pressing cloth. Mostly it needs to be damp otherwise very little will be achieved by using the iron alone, but if moisture is not needed, the dry cloth on the fabric will protect it from the base of the iron, prevent shine etc.

When using the cloth damp, keep it damp, never be tempted to continue when most of it has been used. Have two pressing cloths to save going so often to the water. Have a washing up bowl of water under the table if there isn't a tap handy. (Keep it away from the iron, the flex and the socket outlet.) Don't use a little bowl, you cannot wring out the cloth properly.

Use short, sharp bangs with the iron on the damp cloth for most fabrics, rather than prolonged pressure.

Pressing with an iron that is not hot enough to penetrate the damp cloth is not only ineffective but can actually cause marks on the fabric.

Get to know your iron and set it according to the amount of heat you know you will need rather than to specific fabric names on the dial.

Before pressing the process to shape it helps to run the iron over the actual stitches, hand or machine, to flatten them.

If an area is uneven, such as a hemline, either press only the edge or use fabric pieces or a towel to build up the remainder to the same level, and even then press comparatively lightly.

Stage three in pressing comes when the garment is complete. Even though it has been pressed properly all along, a final light press on the right side is essential. This is the only time that the process resembles 'ironing'. Remember though that on many fabrics the surface will have to be protected by the pressing cloth, even if it is dry.

### How to press

Try to get into the habit of adopting the same sequence for the following.

Collect several pieces of hand or machine sewing to be pressed. Switch on the iron. Damp the cloth. Arrange the sleeve board and anything else that may be needed. Have a piece of spare fabric to test if you have not pressed the fabric previously. See if there are any stray tacking stitches that could be removed from the fabric and which might cause marks.

Press: arrange the stitching wrong side of garment up and press it flat. Open out the process and run the toe of the iron along it. Look at the result and press again to exert more pressure and to have more effect. Turn the fabric over and press the right side — lightly. When it is cold move the fabric and arrange the next section to be pressed. Hang each piece to dry and cool before handling again.

### The technique of pressing

The aim is to combine the correct amount of heat, pressure and moisture, applied for the right length of time, without harming the fabric, yet pressing successfully. There are several combinations of the main agents to choose from.

*Hot iron:*

Single damp cloth, e.g. soft wovens, knits.

Double damp cloth, e.g. closely woven worsted, polyester.

*Medium-hot iron:*

Single damp cloth, e.g. thin synthetics, knit synthetics.

Dry cloth with damp cloth on top, e.g. medium fabrics with surface interest.

Damp cloth, then quickly remove it and dry off the fabric either with the iron on the fabric or with it on the dry cloth if necessary.

*Dry iron:*

Cool or warm, e.g. silk.

Hot, e.g. cotton.

## PRESSING BLOCK

This is used for banging in steam in order to set pleats and creases, hem folds, and on springy fabrics, seams. Remove the iron and pressing muslin and quickly bang down the block. Bang once or twice then leave the block in position until the fabric is cold and hard. Move the fabric along and press and bang the next section. Do not use the block on soft or spongy fabrics or those with surface interest.

Use a block of wood about 25 x 6 x 6 cm (10 x $2\frac{1}{2}$ x $2\frac{1}{2}$ in.) ensuring that the surfaces are very smooth — the bottom surface particularly. A handle may be made by shaping a ridge along the top.

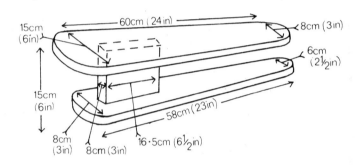

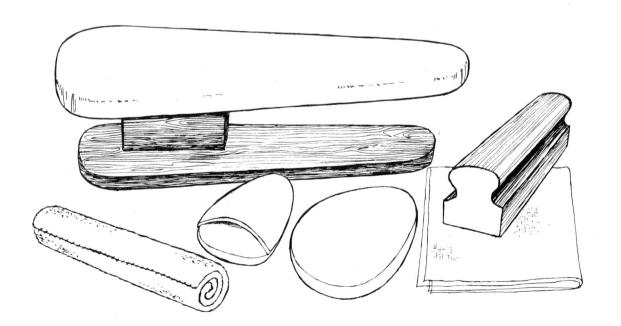

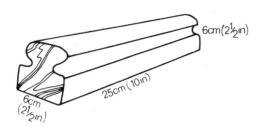

## PRESSING CLOTH

You really need two pieces of muslin because some fabrics need both a damp and a dry cloth. Buy 1 metre (1 yd) and cut it in half to make two manageable pieces. Muslin can be wrung out until nearly dry for light fabrics, made damper for medium ones, and folded over if more moisture is required. With such a variety of fibres, blends and textures available now, muslin is much more useful, and safer, than calico, which holds a lot of water and should be limited to coatings and suitings.

## PRESSING PADS

You can buy a variety of pressing pads of different shapes, the larger ones often called hams are heavy and are used in tailoring for pressing bust and chest areas and other shaping.

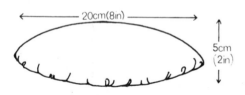

A pressing mitt is useful. You can slip your hand into one side to conceal your fingers while pressing shoulder areas in tailoring and anywhere else where the garment has to be lifted onto the hand to be pressed.

A small oval pad can easily be made and will suffice for most dressmaking pressing. Cut an oval of firm card about 15 to 20 cm (6 to 8 in.) long. Pile a filling (e.g. cut-up tights) on the top and make a fitted cover in strong cotton, such as calico, leaving a small opening to stuff in extra filling to make it firm. Sew up the opening. Make a detachable cotton cover by cutting an oval larger than the top of the pad and putting two or three rows of shirring round the edge.

## PRESSING SURFACE

If you can use a table or work top with a blanket on it and a piece of sheeting, this is best for pressing since it gives you a bigger surface for supporting the work. However, an ironing board may have to suffice and if this is so remember to support big pieces of soft fabric by placing a chair beneath or by placing the board close to the kitchen work top.

## PRICK STITCH

The least visible hand stitch; totally unseen when worked in a perfectly matching thread on a fabric with surface interest or texture such as tweed. The stitch is used in a variety of places including stitching zips by hand, forming a ridge or indentation on fabric and almost anywhere where stitching has to be done from the right side but is not to show.

Use a small Between needle and short pieces of normal sewing thread. Start with a knot on the wrong side or hidden between layers, and end each thread with at least two stitches on top of each other on the wrong side. Do not snip the thread at that point but run the needle forward or back a little way first. When starting a new thread, begin about 1 cm ($\frac{3}{8}$ in.) back. Prick stitch is not strong and this overlapping of thread avoids weaker points.

Work from right to left taking a stitch forward that is as short as the fabric will allow. On fine fabrics the stitches can be very close but remember that the resulting dents will be closer together and therefore more visible as a line.

Pull the thread through but not too tightly. Re-insert the needle at the place where the thread emerges but with the point to the back of the thread.

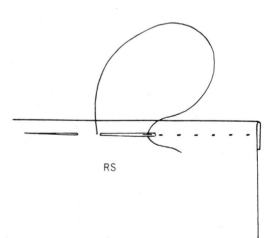

RS

This, in effect, makes the smallest back stitch possible but no thread should be visible on the surface after the stitch is made. Once again take a small stitch forward and so on. On the under side there will be a line of stitches and this is necessary for techniques such as sewing in a zip. If the stitch is being used decoratively, on a finished edge (see *Swelled Edge*, page 302) then the needle point must be brought up again as soon as it is felt by the forefinger of the other hand. In fact, with experience, it is possible to turn the needle point just as it picks at the bottom layer of the fabric but before it quite penetrates; this is not difficult with heavy fabrics. The stitch is occasionally called pick stitch, possibly for this reason.

On completion press the stitching only with the toe of the iron (over a damp cloth if necessary).

Remember to run the thread through beeswax if it twists while sewing. Also, it is best to stitch beside any tacking, not on it, as removing tacks will disturb the stitches.

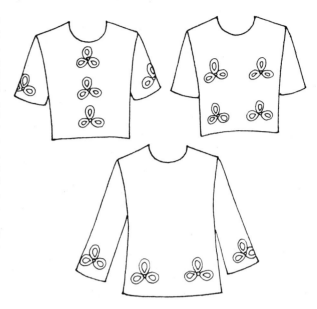

## PRINCESS

A princess-line dress is one which has seams running from mid-shoulder down the body to the hem. The seams are very useful for fitting as they pass over several of the body's bumps and hollows. They can be inconspicuous or be made decorative by adding piping, top-stitching or by making the central panel in a contrasting fabric.

## PRINTED FABRIC

Very little printed fabric has the design applied so carefully that it falls exactly on the grain for its entire length and width.

Always examine printed fabric and reject poor printing where possible, but when it has to be used, look carefully at the extent of the deviation. Often the print will be off grain only near one selvedge, in which case careful folding can ensure that those areas are reserved for small pieces such as collar, yoke, facings. If possible cut the main pieces at least on the correct grain, but this may not work on striped or geometric prints. In these instances the pattern must be placed so that the print is correct, ignoring the grain.

If the print contains a large motif, hold up the entire length of fabric and decide where these should occur on the body. Consider the effect on the sleeves and the back as well as on the front in conjunction with the individual figure. The illustrations show various effects. On the whole the best position is on the front and back, centrally at chest level and slightly lower on the sleeves. Avoid emphasising any figure problems by placing a large motif on them.

After making a decision draw an outline of the print on the pattern pieces to show the position of one motif. Cut out on single fabric matching the sketch on the pattern to the fabric beneath.

## PUCKERING

If a row of machining has puckered the fabric, snip a stitch near the end of the line then starting at the opposite end force the stitching along the fabric a little at a time to induce more thread into the seam. Work to the end where you will find the cut end of thread will have been pulled up a little. Press the stitching on both sides. If it is a seam, re-fasten the end with a couple of stitches.

To prevent puckering from occurring try out the machine stitch on a piece of fabric and adjust it before sewing the garment. It helps to place a layer of paper under very fine fabrics.

## PUFF SLEEVE

A very full short sleeve gathered at the sleeve head to fit the armhole and finished at the hem with elastic or a fitted band. It may be very short or elbow length. Always in fashion on little girls' and baby clothes.

## PUNCH

A punch is a tool used for punching holes to make tailored buttonholes and belt eyelets.

## QUILTING

A very old craft that has been used traditionally on household items such as quilts and also on clothes. It can be employed to add warmth to anoraks, jackets, coats, detachable linings, or as a fashion point in plain or printed fabric and also to great effect in small areas on any outfit including evening wear.

Quilting is done by making a sandwich of wadding between two layers of fabric. The wadding may be cotton or it may be kapok to give a bulky, uneven effect, or polyester wadding may be used which is an even thickness and retains its spring. The choice of type and of thickness (it is sold by weight per metre, e.g. 2 oz, 4 oz etc.) depends on the effect required, the type of fabric used, the warmth required and on whether the article has to be washable. The backing fabric may be anything suitable from lining, nylon jersey, lawn, muslin, or self or contrasting fabric.

Always prepare the quilting before cutting the pieces exactly to size as it gets drawn up by the stitching.

Place the three layers of fabric together and baste together all over. Do not pull the stitches tight. The stitching may be worked by hand, using prick stitch or running stitch, or it can be machined. Mark the design on the right side using sharp tailor's chalk and stitch. When quilting by machine, attach the quilting foot which has short toes which make it easier to see the design. The easiest design is one using straight parallel lines, possibly a deep border on sleeves

or hem or collar, or a diamond design. With both these draw only one chalk line with a ruler and start with that. Attach the quilting bar to the foot, set it to the required distance and continue the stitching, running the bar on the previous row. Work the same direction for all rows.

Note that if you have a dual feed foot it can be used on quilting. In fact the dual feed on the Pfaff machine is a builit-in device and the feed is so perfect top and bottom that quilting can be done without even any previous tacking, so saving a lot of time.

Single motifs can also be quilted, either geometric or circular. After stitching, parts of the design can be thrown into greater relief by snipping the backing fabric and tucking in a little more wadding.

Any quilting design can be added to, if so wished, with beads, sequins etc.

### Italian quilting

Often referred as 'Trapunto' work, this method of quilting also involves two layers of fabric, but the raised effect is a defined line. The method lends itself to many scroll and curved designs, as well as parallel lines. The lines of the design should be as long and unbroken as possible for ease of quilting.

Baste the layers of fabric together; the backing can be another fabric or it could be lawn, muslin, depending on the article. Mark the design and work parallel rows of running stitch or machining. When complete, thread the eye of an elastic threader or a bodkin with an eye, with soft thick yarn and thread it through between the rows of stitching. Do this from the underneath, piercing holes in the backing. The yarn may be wool, Anchor Soft Embroidery or Coton à Broder, even piping cord. Make sure the yarn will wash if it is used on a washable item. It is obvious that some practice must be done to determine the distance between the rows of stitching to take the chosen yarn comfortably. The design can be marked on the backing if preferred, possibly using a tracing wheel and carbon paper, and the stitching done from this side.

Always work the quilting before cutting pieces exactly to size. The exception would be on long borders and continuous cuffs for example. In these instances join all seams except one in fabric and backing, work the quilting and join the remaining seam.

## RAGLAN

A sleeve which incorporates a section of the shoulder of the garment. The seam runs from underarm to the neckline when attached. The seam may be curved or straight from the neck over the chest area depending on the style. The sleeve itself may be in two pieces, with a seam running down the outside of the arm from neck to wrist: this is often used on well-cut coat and jacket patterns. Alternatively, in more casual clothes, it is in one piece and looser. At the wrist or hem the sleeve may be loose or gathered into a cuff.

## RAISED CHAIN BAND

A composite, thick embroidery stitch which may be worked in contrasting colours for effect. Work horizontal straight bar stitches for the length required. Bring the thread through to the right side and pass it over and under the first straight stitch, without passing through the fabric. Keeping the thread under the needle, pass the needle over and under the bar stitch again, thus forming a chain loop. Proceed to the next bar and so on.

## RAVEL

A word sometimes used instead of 'fray' to describe those woven fabrics whose threads easily come off a cut edge. The description should really be 'unravel'.

## RAW EDGE

The cut edge of fabric, not the selvedge.

## REINFORCING

Some form of reinforcement is needed at points of strain in wear; in places where the sewing process involves a lot of handling, particularly if the fabric is soft or loosely constructed; or if the process involves cutting into the fabric and it is likely to produce a weak point. There are various methods of reinforcing and some quite simple techniques for providing sufficient strength.

Seams can have tape stitched into them to prevent stretching. A particularly weak point, where there is little surplus fabric, can be machined twice. Often changing the machine stitch will act as a reinforcement,

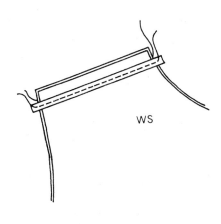

ws

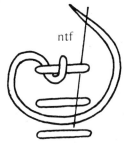

ntf

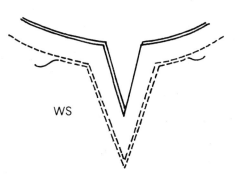

ws

for example, on a trouser crutch seam, use a slight zig-zag stitch, or better still a triple stretch stitch, which will allow the seam to give with movement and therefore it will not split. The application of interfacing at the right place, or just a small piece of iron-on interfacing or Bondaweb will hold a process in shape as well as preventing fraying.

Sometimes an area needs reinforcing before any work is done. For example, the wrong side of a coat or jacket should have the proposed pocket positions reinforced with interfacing or possibly a piece of tape stitched where the mouth of the pocket will be.

Similarly button positions must consist of two layers of fabric plus the interfacing at least and on heavy fabric it is wise to add a strip of linen or cotton fabric as well.

Decide from all these methods according to the fabric and the amount of wear the garment will have.

## REVER

The triangular area of fabric formed by folding back a front edge below a neckline. The rever may have a collar above it; it may be above a buttoned opening or above a slit or just a seam.

## REVERSIBLE

Anything that can be worn with either side outermost. A reversible garment may be made by putting two fabrics wrong sides together, perhaps quilting them, then binding the edges. Any fastenings must be made so that they work on both sides. Velcro is the most successful and unobtrusive fastening to use.

## REVERSIBLE FABRIC

Reversible fabric, other than quilting, is made of two fabrics of different colour and design. They are joined either by adhesive or by a thread running back and forth between them. Those joined by adhesive should be bound to make them reversible in wear, seams should be of the welt type.

The other fabric, usually expensive, can be parted into two layers by snipping the thread that joins them so eliminating the necessity for using binding. A rather more sophisticated garment can be produced with this type of fabric.

Part a sufficient area round the edges of the fabric pieces to enable the processes to be worked. The two fabrics will feel very soft so it will help to press pieces of Bondaweb to the wrong side of one piece before working the process. Afterwards, when the pieces are pressed together, they will feel firmer and be more durable.

Darts should be stitched separately in each fabric and cut open to reduce bulk.

Seams should be made in two stages. First join two

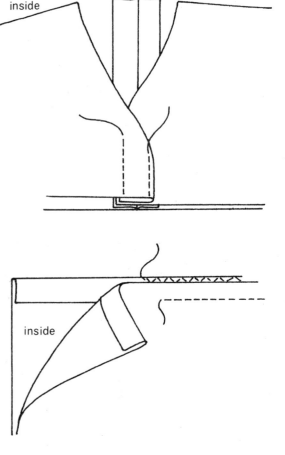

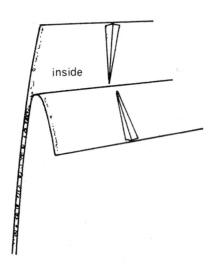

layers and press as an open seam, then lay one of the other edges flat on the seam, turning under the other on top of it. This edge is machined so that it simulates a welt seam on both sides.

Piped buttonholes should be made in one fabric and the other fabric used as a facing to finish the backs of the buttonholes.

To finish edges and hems turn in one side and tack, then turn in the other so that the two folds meet. Slip stitch them together. A row of machining can be worked within the edge if desired.

## RIBBED WAISTBANDS

Soft jersey skirts and sports or track suit trousers, and other items such as pyjama trousers and shorts, may have ribbing attached at the waist. This may be purchased or cut from firm ribbed fabrics. When purchased it is usually in a pre-cut length and quite wide, folded ready for use. The edges are usually overlocked to prevent unravelling, either together or separately. If using ribbed fabric make sure it will spring back to size easily and cut twice the desired finished width, plus 2 cm ($\frac{3}{4}$ in.) for seams.

With both types pass the ribbing round the waist and when it fits firmly, cut, leaving 1 cm ($\frac{3}{8}$ in.) for joining. Open it out and join the ends together with a stretch stitch. Fold the ribbing and baste if it does not lie flat. Divide into four and mark. Slip this inside the top of the trousers, match the join to the left or back seam and pin. Pin the opposite seam to the halfway mark on the ribbing. Pin the two quarter marks on the ribbing to the other seams. Using a stretch stitch, anchor the stitching firmly then stitch the ribbing to the trousers, stretching the ribbing out so that it fits the waist. Remove the pins as you approach them.

(See also *Cuffs*, page 30.)

## RIBBING

Ribbing is available in several colours. It is usually about 10 cm (4 in.) wide and folded in half. It is pre-packed in small circles for wrists and ankles and in longer lengths for waists. The raw edges are overlocked. Ribbed fabric can be cut up and used for the same purpose. Sections of knitting by hand or machine can also be made.

To attach to wrists or ankles, complete the seams and neaten them; insert a gathering thread in garment fabric. Slip the fabric over the ribbing and draw up the gathering threads until the fabric fits the circle of ribbing when it is stretched to its maximum. Insert a few pins, then machine. Use the free arm on the machine if possible, and slip the assembly over it with the fabric uppermost. Use a stretch stitch and machine, stretching the ribbing while sewing.

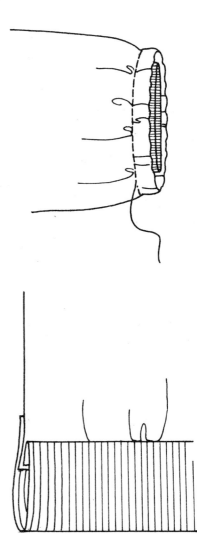

Lengths of waistline ribbing are folded but not joined so the garment can be machined to one edge only to begin with if it seems desirable to reduce bulk, or if it helps with inserting a zip. The second edge of ribbing can be laid flat on the wrong side and stitched down. Always use a stretch stitch or at least a slight zig-zag, to retain the character of the ribbing.

## RIBBON

Ribbons are generally defined as decorative woven fabrics, usually under 100 mm (4 in.) and often as narrow as 6 mm ($\frac{1}{4}$ in.). All ribbons are made from a warp and a weft (two systems of threads). Other narrow fabrics are tapes which are largely functional; webbing, heavier than tape; and braids. Braids are in a different group because they are made using only one system of threads and are constructed like a plait. Examples of braids are shoe laces, pyjama cords and some ropes, particularly as used in yachting. Elastics are either woven or braided.

Modern ribbons are usually made of nylon, polyester or triacetate, although viscose and viscose with cotton ribbons are still available. By selecting an appropriate yarn and weave, plain weave — taffeta, single-sided or double-sided satin, twill, etc., the ribbon weaver can offer a very wide variety of qualities suitable for many different purpose. To give some examples: nylon taffeta, ideal for hair ties and indeed other uses; polyester satin for lingerie and nightwear. Most ribbons are dyed after weaving, the technical term being 'piece-dyed', but checks and figured designs, whether dobby or jacquard woven, are produced from yarns already dyed. Ribbons can also be printed. Ribbons of all kinds are often the means of converting a plain or old garment into something updated or even unique. They also have a wide use in fastenings and craft work.

(See also *Jacquard Ribbon*, and *Velvet Ribbon*.)

## RIBBON WORK

Narrow, thin ribbons can be threaded into a large-eyed needle and used in place of embroidery thread. Ribbons are specially manufactured for the purpose, without a beaded edge, but the best ones in pure silk are difficult to obtain. An old form of decoration — thick, chunky designs — can be worked using, in the main, simple running or stem stitches.

## RIC-RAC

A wavy decorative braid made in a variety of colours and several widths. It may be used flat, or inserted in a join to form a picot edge.

(For attaching see *Braid*.)

## RIGHT SIDE

Often abbreviated to RS in written instructions, this is the perfect side of the fabric. Any pattern should be clear; there may be signs of a finish on the right side, possibly shine. With some plain woven and knitted fabrics it may not be possible to detect any difference between the right side and the reverse. In such cases determine which is to be the outside before cutting out and make sure the entire garment is made up this way.

With few exceptions, the fabric should be arranged right side out for cutting out.

(See also *Selvedge*.)

## RIGILENE

This is the trade mark of a British invention, the word being derived from 'rigid Terylene'. It was produced quite specifically to take the place of whalebone which is now virtually unobtainable. Rigilene is 100 per cent polyester, its lengthwise or warp stiffness being achieved by using a row of strong monofilaments similar to the bristles of a tooth brush but thicker. Rigilene is used for strapless tops and beach garments, theatrical work — i.e. hooped skirts. Also to give shape to soft toys, for instance in rabbit's ears and anywhere including foundation wear where whaleboning was used.

(See also *Boning*.)

## RISE

A measurement on men's trousers from the top of the crutch curve up to waist on the front. This distance varies according to fashion and personal preference. A short rise usually accompanies close-fitting trousers.

(See also *Fork*.)

## ROLL LINE

The roll line is the line on which a collar or lapel rolls into its natural position round the neck.

(See *Tailored Collar*, page 71, for details.)

## ROMANIAN COUCHING

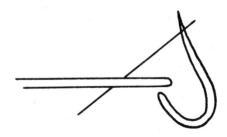

An embroidery filling stitch worked in rows with one thread. The thread is laid by making a long stitch then working from right to left make slanting stitches over it at intervals picking up a little fabric each time. The angle of the stitch will depend on the angle at which the needle is inserted.

## ROMANIAN STITCH

A thick, filling embroidery stitch worked by taking a stitch from left to right with the thread below the needle. Work towards you. Take a small stitch, about half the width of the previous one, from right to left, this time with the thread above the needle, thus forming a stitch across the centre of the straight stitch.

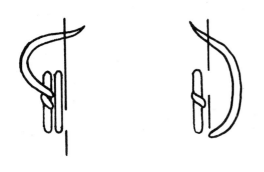

## ROSETTE CHAIN STITCH

A chain embroidery stitch worked in lines literally as rosettes. Work from right to left winding the thread in a loop to the left. Hold the thread down by the thumb and insert the needle a little to the left. Take another stitch downwards and angled inwards. As the needle is pulled through the thread forms a chain stitch. Pass the needle under the top thread to begin the second stitch.

(See *Chain Stitch*.)

Come up to start here

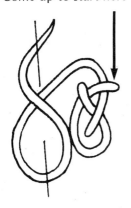

ntf

## ROULEAU

A tube of fabric made as narrow as the fabric permits. If the fabric is cut on the cross a truly rounded roll will result and the seam will not be obtrusive. The seam allowances inside will help to fill the roll, or for a more substantial effect a piping cord can be inserted. If the fabric is cut on the straight grain seam allowances should be trimmed, the join located along one edge and pressed. This is usually referred to as tubing.

Cut pieces of fabric and join if necessary to produce sufficient length. The width of the strips depends on the thickness of the fabric; fine ones can be cut narrow to produce narrow rouleau, heavier ones wider. Experiment with spare fabric to discover the best width because if it is too wide it will be soft and floppy; if too narrow it may be impossible to turn through. Add seam allowances.

### Soft rouleau

Fold the strip wrong side out and machine. Use a slight zig-zag stitch and stitch down the strip at the pre-determined distance from the fold. Note that the strip is not tacked before stitching. Trim the seam allowances evenly but leaving enough to fill out the tubing. If using a stretch or jersey fabric a stretch stitch may be used. In this case the raw edges cannot be trimmed afterwards so make sure the width of the strip is correct before stitching.

Turn the strip by inserting a rouleau turner (a long needle with a ball end) or an elastic threader and sew the eye to the turnings at the end of the tube. Use the ends of machine thread for this. Ease the fabric onto the needle, take hold of the ball end and pull it through, turning the tube right side out. Cut off the needle.

If the fabric was cut on the straight grain, roll the join to one side and press the tubing flat.

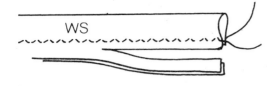

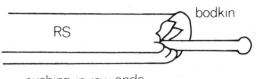

pushing in raw ends

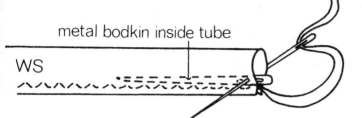

metal bodkin inside tube

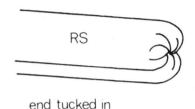

end tucked in

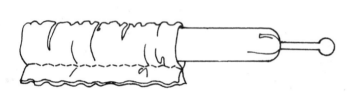

### Finishing ends

Rouleau can be used for belts, drawstrings, ties, etc., and so one or both ends may need to be finished off. The easiest method is to tie a knot and then trim the raw end away. Alternatively push the ends of tubing back inside using a bodkin. The end can be left like this if sufficient fabric is pushed back inside, or run a thread through the fold and gather it up. It may be appropriate to sew a glass or wooden bead or spherical button on the end.

Note that an edge may be bound with a crossway strip leaving long ends, which can be made into rouleau and tied.

### Rouleau with cord

Choose a thickness of piping cord that will be suitable for the weight of fabric being used and for the effect required.

Practise with a piece of cord and a strip of fabric cut on the cross in order to calculate the exact width of fabric required. Cut and join crossway strips to make sufficient length. A piece of cord twice the length of the strip will be needed. Wrap the strip wrong side out round the cord, starting at the middle of the length of cord. Machine across the crossway strip to attach it to the cord, then stitch along the length. Use the zip or piping foot in order to stitch close to the cord. Use a straight machine stitch.

Pull the cord, easing it out and pushing the fabric tube over it. When pulled through cut off the surplus cord and trim the end of the tube. If the end has to be neatened, trim away a little of the cord inside the tube and finish by one of the methods described for soft rouleau.

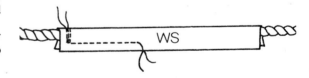

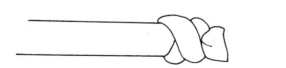

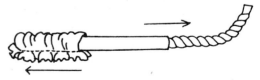

**Decoration with rouleau**

An ornate form of decoration using lengths of rouleau made from fabric. The rouleau is arranged, wound and criss-crossed and then joined with hand stitching, usually fagotting, to hold the design in place.

Any fabric that makes soft, pliable rouleau tubing can be used for this type of decoration. The charm of it is that the intervening areas are transparent.

Draw the design on tissue or soft paper. The design may be a simple motif or a continuous edging. Tack the rouleau to the paper. Work fagotting across the spaces. Remove the paper. It is important to incorporate richelieu work in the original design of yoke, cuff, pocket etc., because it is built up and cannot really be moved or altered.

## ROULEAU TURNER

Sometimes called a bodkin, this is a long thin needle with a ball end that slips easily through fabric. The eye is large for sewing the ends of the fabric tubing to it. The benefit of this tool is that a long piece of rouleau tube can be eased on to it which reduces the risk of thread snapping etc.

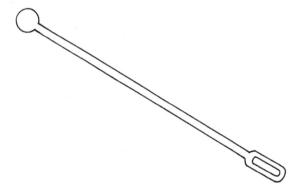

## ROUND NECK

Used at the front or back or both, a round neck can be basic, that is, following the base of the neck on the body or it may be at any position below this. The depth will be governed by the bust position. Anyone with a prominent bust and/or narrow back should fit a low round neck with particular care.

## RUCHE

To gather up.

## RUFFLE

A narrow strip of fabric, gathered or finely pleated on to a garment. A frill is usually wider and attached only to a hem.

## RUNNING STITCH

A simple short stitch used for inserting gathering threads or for seams on fine fabrics in loose fitting garments, in place of machining. Such garments include special lingerie and baby clothes. Not a strong stitch. Work from right to left taking the shortest stitch the fabric will allow. It is difficult to keep a straight line so use an edge as a guide or, if this is not possible, chalk a line before starting.

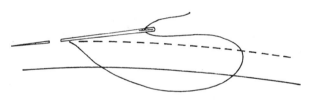

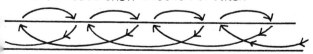

## SADDLE STITCH

Correctly this is worked with two needles which pass back and forth through the same holes producing the same stitch on both sides of the seam. This seam is often used on leather where the edges on the right side form a feature, as on gloves.

A saddle stitch effect on the right side only is created by working machining or a hand back stitch, often in contrasting thread. This is then a decorative stitch worked on a finished garment edge. By machine use normal thread or a bold or buttonhole twist, or fine crochet cotton, and a large machine needle. By hand use top stitching thread, buttonhole twist, fine embroidery cotton or other thick yarn, threaded into a needle with an eye large enough to take the thread. It is fairly easy to saddle stitch a woven fabric, especially a soft woollen one, but it is more difficult to pass the thread through a synthetic knit, and you may have to be satisfied with a smaller needle and therefore a finer thread on some fabrics. Try it out before working directly on the garment.

Work from right to left, if right handed, on the right side of the garment. It is easier to keep even and produces a more raised stitch if you work a back stitch rather than a forward running stitch. Bring the thread out and take the needle just over half-way back to the previous stitch, taking the needle under again and emerging an even distance further on. Keep the stitching small; big stitches look amateurish, and keep the stitches slightly longer than the gaps between. Do not try to take the needle through to the wrong side, or the back of the garment will look untidy.

Do not use saddle stitching as a means of holding an edge or a facing back. This should have been done earlier as part of the construction, either by holding down with fabric adhesive strip (such as Wundaweb), or by working a swelled edge finish. The latter will have the advantage of giving you a line on which to saddle stitch.

If it is essential for the stitching to show on both the right side and the wrong side it would be best to do machine top stitching, but with top stitching thread on the spool as well as on the top of the machine.

## SADDLE YOKE

A style of yoke where the front and back are cut as one piece of pattern, without a shoulder seam. The advantage is that it is quick to attach as the seam is eliminated. A disadvantage is that there is no possibility of fitting the garment at the shoulders, so it should be avoided by those with problems in that area. Most men's shirts are constructed with saddle yokes, but it is also a popular feature on women's clothes.

## SAFARI

A style of jacket worn by men and women based on the type worn by those working on game reserves. It has four patch pockets with button flaps, cuffed sleeves that can be rolled up, a traditional shirt collar and rever and a belt, usually held by belt loops. There may also be shoulder tabs, yokes, a centre back pleat, etc., making it difficult precisely to define the style. Traditionally it is made from dull colours in cotton; polyester and cotton and other blends; sailcloth; poplin, cord. Safari jackets for women first appeared with trousers as an early version of the trouser suit.

## SAILOR

A collar, often in white or contrasting fabric, with a wide square outline at the back. The front may form a narrow rever as in a sailor's collar or fashion may dictate some other style point.

Sailor styles are referred to as any with piping and tabs, or in white with navy or red, or anything reminiscent of a sailor uniform.

arrowheads show direction of stitch

cross-section of stitch used on two layers of fabric to produce saddle-stitch

## SARI

The traditional Hindu dress made from a length of fabric wrapped and draped cleverly round the body. A tight short-sleeved top is usually worn underneath and sometimes one end of the fabric covers the head. The fabrics must inevitably be fine and soft and are often elaborate. Fabric ready cut to the correct length with finished edges can be bought, particularly in specialist Indian shops or where there are a lot of Indian residents or visitors.

## SATIN STITCH

A popular, straight, flat embroidery stitch worked as for single satin stitch, but formed closely together as a filling stitch. Often of irregular length, care should be taken that stitches are not too long or the shape of the design may become uneven. Work from left to right or vertically away from you.

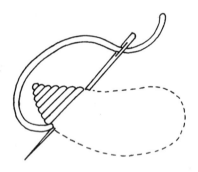

## SCALLOPS

A scalloped edge is one that is finished in a series of semi-circles of matching or varying size. Almost any edge can be finished with scallops provided it is a suitable design feature for the garment and for the fabric. Some fabrics, including lace, broderie anglais and some embroidered cottons may be bought with one edge already scalloped. Care should be taken with these fabrics to adjust the pattern before cutting out to be sure that the finished edge falls in the right position at the hem, sleeve edge, etc. With some designs, particularly with lace fabrics, it may be possible to cut off the scalloped edge and then re-attach it where it is required on the garment.

**Scallops finished with thread**
A fine scalloped edge may be worked over a single edge of fabric. Begin by making a cardboard template with one edge forming several scallops, or find an article such as a coin and use it to mark the shapes on the fabric. Mark the main fabric with small tacking stitches round the template.

A fine fabric should have another piece of fabric (the same fabric is usually suitable), placed underneath before marking. After the scallops have been worked the surplus second layer is carefully trimmed away. Work loop stitches close together round the marked design, having the thread loops at the outer edge of the fabric. The stitches should be deeper towards the centre of each semi-circle. An attractive raised edge can be formed by working a row of chain stitching near the tacking and then working the loop stitch over it. On completion trim away the edge of the fabric close to the loop stitch.

All automatic satin-stitch sewing machines have a scallop stitch and, as with the hand finish, this can be worked on single or double fabric, and over an extra thread for a raised edge. This additional thread is run between the machine foot and the fabric. Surplus fabric is snipped away close to the satin stitch after completion.

If a particularly firm edge is required insert Wundaweb or Bondaweb between two layers of fabric before stitching by hand or machine.

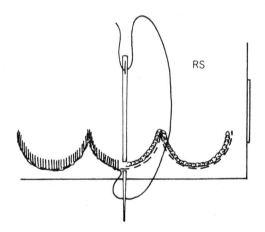

**Scallops finished with a facing**
These are usually quite large, the size being varied according to the position and the type of garment. Find a template of a suitable size, anything from an egg cup to a dinner plate will do, and either mark round it directly onto the fabric or make a paper template. Make sure the scallops are even in size by making marks on the edges of the plate using felt pen or sticky tape.

If the edge of the garment is already established, for example a completed sleeve, skirt, neckline, make sure the scallops are centrally placed and even and that they join up exactly. Do this by searching for the right-sized template. If one seam can be left undone, as it could be on a full skirt, then mark out the scallops first before joining the final seam. Interface the wrong side of the garment if necessary then mark the scallops with tacking stitches or with a tracing wheel and carbon paper, on the wrong side of the garment. If a paper template is used tack through it and then tear off the paper.

Cut a strip of fabric 5 cm (2 in.) wider than the distance from the garment edge the bottom of the scallops. This should be cut on the same grain as the garment.

Place this, the facing, right side down to the right side of the garment and pin. Make seams where necessary to correspond with those on the garment as for a conventional facing. Tack the facing down with a row of diagonal tacking then machine the scalloped pattern. Use a fairly small stitch to minimise fraying and stitch with the wrong side of the garment uppermost. Trim, layer and snip the entire edge. Remove all tackings, roll the facing to the wrong side and roll and tack the edges of the scallops. Press. Trim the outer edge of the facing to a suitable even width and either neaten the raw edge or tack it to the garment and finish with a decorative row of stitching. If it is not stitched down, hem the facing to any seams there may be and also insert pieces of Wundaweb at intervals to hold it in place in wear.

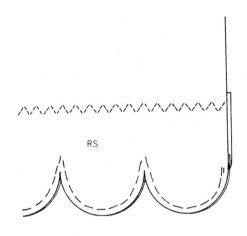

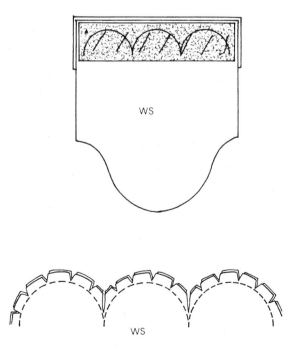

## SCISSORS

Scissors are required mainly for cutting fabric and threads, but paper also has to be cut so use a pair of old or blunt scissors for that to avoid spoiling the sewing scissors.

Scissors for sewing are special tools and should be kept only for that purpose. Also each pair is for a particular purpose, used differently and held differently. Scissors are expensive; it is not worth economising by purchasing cheap scissors even as an interim measure. It is essential for speed as well as enjoyment to be confident that all tools are of good quality and will therefore perform perfectly.

When buying scissors make sure they can be held correctly according to the size. Take a few pieces of various fabrics and try them, cutting with the length of the blades and with the tips. Three pairs of scissors are necessary.

### Small scissors

These have short pointed blades and are used for snipping threads and also for snipping and clipping fabric edges. They should never be used for cutting fabric and only the tips of the blades are used for threads. The best scissors are those with large finger holes which take the thumb in one and the first finger in the other. Finger holes that are too small are not only very uncomfortable to use, but it means the fingers cannot be inserted far enough for correct control. Large holes mean the scissors can be picked up and put down again quickly and there is no need to stop and take off the thimble first.

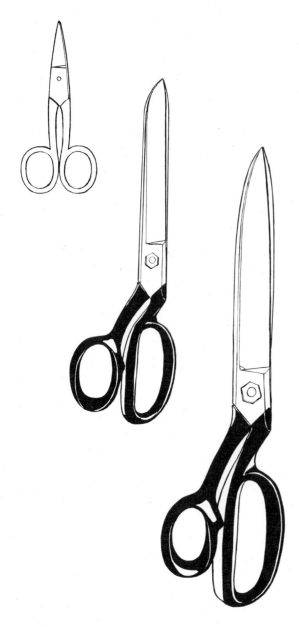

bent. Any scissors with this type of handles are also called shears.

When using them make sure the whole hand is well inside the handles, open the blades only as far as is comfortable for you, and cut right to the tips of the blades.

### Medium scissors
Also with side-bent handles these are a smaller version of the large ones. The thumb fits into the upper handle but only three fingers will fit into the lower one. They are therefore not suitable for cutting out because there is insufficient control and they would be uncomfortable to hold. Use them for small cutting jobs such as trimming seam allowances and surplus fabric. These scissors are often called trimmers. Keep small and medium scissors handy all the time you are sewing to ensure that the correct pair is always used.

Cheap or inferior quality scissors are a waste of money and frustrating to use. Weak blades will bend and refuse to cut through more than one layer of fabric. Poor steel will soon blunt and may be difficult to sharpen. Badly shaped handles cause inaccurate cutting and are very uncomfortable to hold.

### Buttonhole scissors
A fairly old idea. These are very small scissors with short, pointed blades. One side can be adjusted by means of a screw. One blade has a right-angled section cut out so that the cut the scissors make is set. Very useful for eliminating errors in cutting fabric for hand-worked buttonholes.

## SCYE

This is the shape of the armhole at the front and under the arm. The depth and shape of this curve affects the fitting and therefore the comfort of clothes.

## SEAM ALLOWANCE

The margin of fabric left outside the fitting line. The usual width of a seam allowance on a printed pattern is 1.5 cm ($\frac{5}{8}$ in.). Some patterns have no seam allowance included, so it is added when the fabric is cut. It may be desirable to have a wider seam allowance than 1.5 cm ($\frac{5}{8}$ in.) if there is a figure problem to be solved, if the fabric frays easily, or if a particular seam which needs extra fabric is to be used. Occasionally less than 1.5 cm ($\frac{5}{8}$ in.) can be an advantage. For example, when attaching a collar to a neckline and other places where two edges of different shapes are to be joined; where less bulk will make manipulation easier including very full frills and some areas on children's clothes that are difficult to reach. Even if the standard 1.5 cm ($\frac{5}{8}$ in.) has been included when the garment was cut out, it is worth trimming it down before handling processes such as these.

### Large scissors
These should have long blades and very sturdy shaped handles. The lower part of the handle must take all four fingers, the upper one takes the thumb. Buy the biggest pair available. Large scissors not only cut more accurately they are quicker and more comfortable to use than a pair that is too small. These scissors are only used for cutting out and for trimming long edges. They are not heavy to use because when cutting out they rest on the table and when used for other jobs they are only held for a short time.

The shaped handles are often described as side-

## SEAM BINDING

The word 'binding' is misleading as the tape called seam binding is a plainweave tape with a selvedge on both edges. It is usually made from cotton although it can be found made from polyester fibre. It is made in a wide variety of colours. It cannot be used to bind, or enclose, an edge because of its firm edge. It can be used for reinforcing seams, to make skirt loops, and in some instances it is effective as a decoration. However, it should not be used over a raw edge, such as can sometimes be found on hems, because it adds bulk and pressure and the hemline will show.

## SEAM FINISH

The term used to describe the way in which the raw edges inside a garment are neatened. The seam finish chosen should be suitable for the type of fabric, the wear it will get and also care, for example washing.

## SEAM LINE

(See *Fitting Line.*)

## SEAM ROLL

However skilful you are at pressing, there are some fabrics that will leave an imprint of the underlayers. Often this is caused by the use of too cool an iron or too much moisture, but if this is not so, roll up a small hand towel and after pressing the seam or other process initially, press again over the roll. If you want to make a permanent seam roll, wrap a piece of towelling round a length of wooden dowelling and hem the edge in place (as seen in the diagram for *Pressing Block*).

## SEAMS

Seams are the method of making permanent joins in the fabric. Some are purely functional, straight or shaped, and made in order to obtain a particular shape. Other are purely decorative and placed where an obvious line improves the design. Some seams are both functional and decorative.

The method of making the seam will depend on the finished effect required and also on the fabric being used.. If any form of decoration is to be incorporated including even a row of stitching that will be seen on the outside of the garment, it should be tried out before stitching the garment, and if unsuitable, another type of seam adopted.

### Angled seam

A seam may be angled for decorative purposes or as shaping to make a garment fit, or both. If there is more than one angled seam or there are pairs to be matched make sure the pieces are cut exactly on the

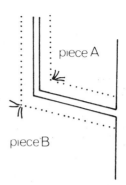

same grain, and that the corners are carefully marked with tailor tacks through both layers to ensure the angles appear even on the body.

The secret of a successful angled seam is to treat it as two straight seams stemming from one point. Work in the same way for both outward and inward pointing angles.

Mark all fitting lines, and place one tailor tack at the corner of the angle. Reinforce the angle with a piece of Bondaweb or soft iron-on interfacing to prevent fraying. Place the two pieces of fabric right side together matching the tailor tacks, especially at the corner. Tack. Machine, starting with the needle precisely at the angle, work forwards a few stitches then reverse to fasten the threads, sew forwards again to the outer edge of the fabric.

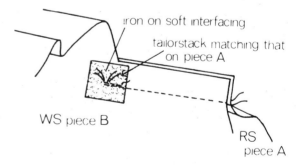

Remove tacks. Press it open as for an open seam and neaten the edges. Snip into the corner exactly to the end of the stitching. Swing the top piece of fabric round until the other two raw edges meet.

If the seam contains body shaping make sure you ease one fabric on to the other correctly and pin at

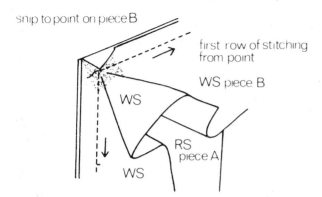

snip to point on piece B

first row of stitching from point

WS piece B

WS

RS piece A

WS

second row of stitching from snipped angle

right angles to hold. Tack. Machine, once more starting at the corner to avoid a pucker. Lower the needle exactly into the first stitch of the previous row, lower the foot, and machine.

Remove tacks, press open, and neaten as for the other side. Turn work right side up and press.

### Check seam

Having cut out so that checks match on every seam there is no worry about placing them but it is essential to make sure that the layers do not move while being stitched.

It may be easy enough to line up large simple checks by placing the two layers right sides together and shifting the top layer until the lines match. Tack and then insert pins across the seam, one pin on each main check. Stitch the seam with the pins in position.

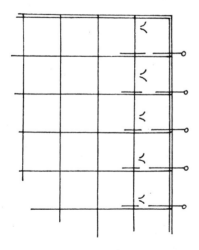

If the design is more complicated turn under one edge on the fitting line and tack. Lay this over the other edge matching checks and fitting line and insert a few pins, both pieces of fabric having right side uppermost. Work slip stitch, using tacking thread, between the fold and the flat piece of fabric. Remove the pins and unfold the top layer. It will fold back and the fabric is lined up ready for stitching. Insert a pin across the seam at the start of each main line of the check and stitch the seam, working over the pins.

If dual feed is available on the machine it is safe to omit the pins but the seam must be tacked accurately.

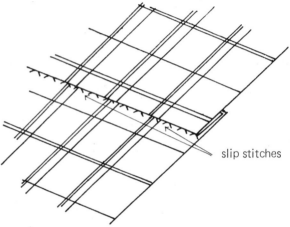

slip stitches

### Corded seam

A raised seam used a great deal in soft furnishing and also on clothes when plain or military styles are in fashion. It is a useful way of breaking up a plain fabric or of emphasising a style feature. On items such as chair covers the cording also prolongs the life of the seams and helps to keep the seams in position.

Piping cord is made of cotton or sometimes with some acrylic fibre and is bought by the metre in a variety of thicknesses. Choose one suitable for the weight of fabric. If it is not clearly labelled pre-shrunk, wash it and let it drip until it is dry.

The cord is covered by a bias strip of fabric before being inserted in the seam. The fabric may be matching or contrasting in colour. In the case of furnishings it should be of similar strength to the main fabric.

For a less bulky effect — for a method of emphasising a style feature without raising the seam — see *Piped Seam*.

To make a corded or piped seam, cut a short piece of fabric on the cross and wrap it round the cord, pin the fabric together close to the cord, trim the edges off at a width of about 5 mm ($\frac{1}{4}$ in.). Remove the pins

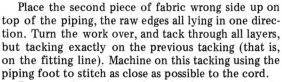

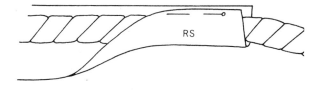

Place the second piece of fabric wrong side up on top of the piping, the raw edges all lying in one direction. Turn the work over, and tack through all layers, but tacking exactly on the previous tacking (that is, on the fitting line). Machine on this tacking using the piping foot to stitch as close as possible to the cord.

Remove the tacks, and grade the raw edges to reduce the bulk before neatening. Press on the right side by running the toe of the iron along on the edge of the fabric beside the piping. Cover the toe of the iron with a cloth to protect the fabric.

If setting piping into a curved seam, snip the raw edges of the piping as you tack to ease it round the curves.

A special braiding can be bought which is in fact a piping attached to a narrow braid. Set the braid between the layers of fabric.

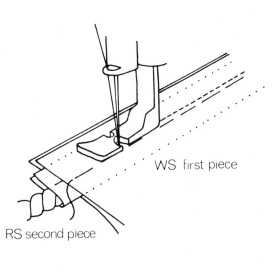

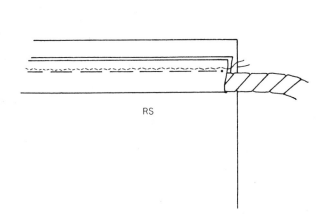

and use this little piece as a guide to the width you need to cut your bias strips. Cut and join the strips until you have a little more than you think you will need. Press the strip but do not stretch the bias binding as you will need all the 'give' to enclose the cord.

Place the piping cord on the wrong side of the strip. Wrap the bias strip round the cord until the two raw edges are together. Tack beside the cord. Attach your piping foot (zip foot) to the machine. adjust and stitch with a slight zig-zag very close to the piping cord.

Remove the tackings and press the stitching, stretching the piping out. Place the piping on the right side of one edge of the garment. Tack in place exactly on the fitting line but with the machining slightly to the outer edge.

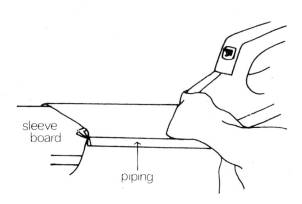

## Crossed seams

Joining two pieces of fabric that are already seamed must be done accurately. Make sure both pieces are well pressed, place right sides together and insert a pin with the head extending to the right to hold the seams together. Make sure the point penetrates the join exactly on both layers. Trim the seam allowances off at an angle to a point just beyond the seam line to reduce bulk. Tack the seam and machine, working slowly over the pin.

When joining french seams press in different

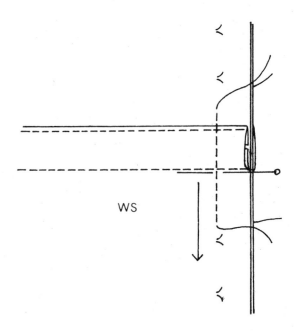

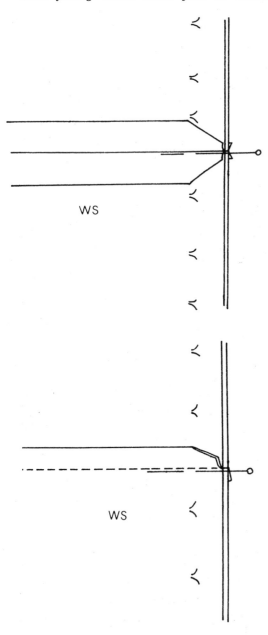

directions to reduce bulk. When joining other bulky seams that are stitched flat, such as machine fell, welt or piped seams, pin as described but to keep the join absolutely accurate start machining on the join and stitch in one direction, then turn the work over and stitch from the join in the other direction.

## Crutch seam

The crutch seam of a pair of trousers has to be shaped to the body and yet allow for movement. In addition, in order to retain its shape in wear, it needs reinforcing in places.

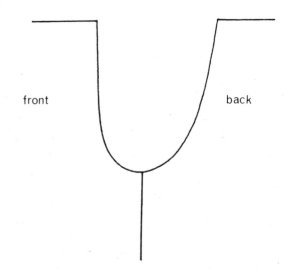

front                                    back

The correct shape of the seam should be that the front follows or nearly follows the straight grain of the fabric from the waist downwards. This line is sometimes slightly altered when fashion changes. If the zip is inserted in this seam it will hold it in shape, but if the zip is to be at the side then reinforce the front seam by stitching a length of tape or straight seam binding to it. Use a straight machine stitch. The front seam then curves, but not deeply, and this part too should be reinforced and should include the first centimetre ($\frac{3}{8}$ in.) or so of the back crutch seam, because there is a lot of strain through movement here. If there is no zip use one piece of tape from the waist to this point.

The back part of the crutch seam should be very sloping so that it is on the bias of the fabric. This not only gives a better fit but allows the seam to 'give' with sitting and walking without splitting. If the seam edges appear to be too straight or if the fit of the trousers at the back does not look good, slope the seam more from just below hip level up to the waist. If this makes the waist tight release the side seams, or in the case of a flat seat, reduce the width of the darts.

In order to retain the vital stretching facility of this seam stitch it with a slight zig-zag stitch or back stitch it by hand using double thread.

The crutch of men's trousers is generally reinforced at the front only, below the zip, with a double triangle of lining or pocketing fabric. One side is stitched in with the crutch seam and the other is included in the inside leg seam.

The back seam is pressed open only as far down as the start of the deepest section of crutch curve, or, only that part of the seam that is visible in wear. The front seam is pressed open to within about 2 cm ($\frac{3}{4}$ in.) of the inside leg. Do not attempt to press the seam open along the section under the crutch or it spoils the close hang of the legs.

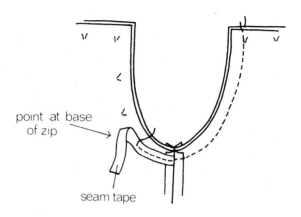

point at base of zip

seam tape

### Draw seam
The method of joining together quite invisibly from the right side two edges folded under and pressed. The particular position where this is found is at the join between a collar and lapel on classic tailored necklines, but it is useful in many other places where the final join is best made from the right side. The draw seam is usually fairly short and often curved, producing a better result than stitching from inside the garment.

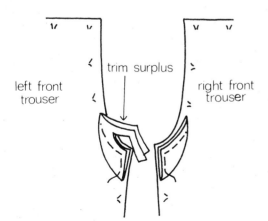

left front trouser

trim surplus

right front trouser

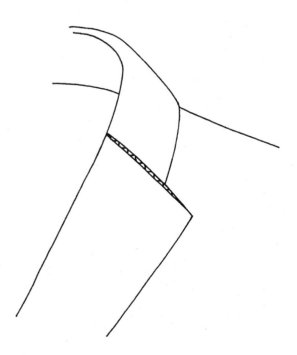

Turn in and tack and press both edges. In all cases there will be a layer beneath to tack to. Use a short piece of perfectly matching thread and join the two folds by taking tiny slip stitches alternately in each fold. Slip stitch used in this way is called draw stitch. Fasten off well. Remove tackings and press, pulling the seam to shape if necessary.

### French seam

A neat, narrow seam best on very lightweight fabrics. The edges are enclosed, so fraying is not possible. It is very suitable for baby clothes, lingerie, fine blouses. Very occasionally something very special might be made by hand and this would be the main seam used, sewn by hand with running stitch. The french seam is not suitable for fitted garments because the bulk of the seam tends to move its position from one direction to another. In addition the first row of stitching is not worked on the fitting line itself and this might lead to small inaccuracies where accurate fit is concerned.

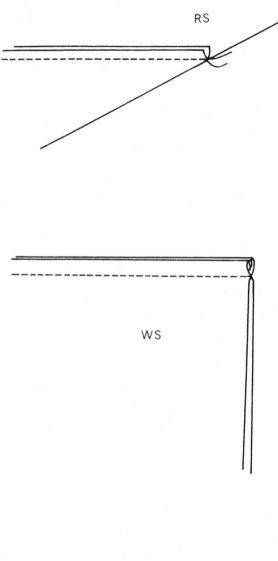

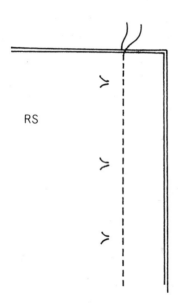

Mark the fitting lines. Place the fabric with wrong sides together and tack. Decide on the best finished width for the fabric and work the first row of stitching that distance outside the seam line. It may be necessary to make a small trial seam to determine the best width.

Press the row of stitching, then trim off the surplus raw edges quite close to it. Open out the fabric and slide it onto the sleeve board. Run the iron along beside the seam edge then press it to one side. Turn the work over and press the seam line. To work the second row of stitching roll the fabrics until they are right sides together and the join is exactly on the edge. Hold it carefully and tack on the fitting line. Make sure the raw edges will be hidden and will not be visible through the seam on the right side. You can clearly see this by holding the fabric up to the light after working a few tacking stitches.

Finally machine on the fitting line, remove tackings and press the seam to one side, towards the back of the garment.

## Fur seam

Real fur should be joined by hand using a small-size, spear-pointed needle and waxed thread. Reinforce both edges of the fur by hemming tape, stay tape or seam binding with one edge close to the edge of the fur. Place the fur pieces right side together and oversew, taking the needle into the tape on both sides. Flatten the seam with the fingers and, if necessary, lift any fur caught in the join, with a pin. The join should then be almost invisible.

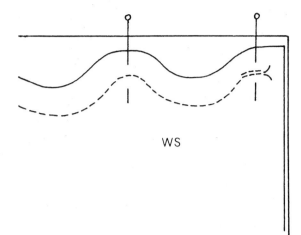

WS

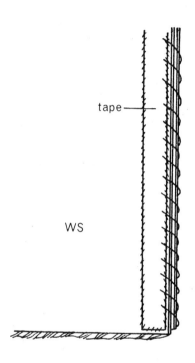

tape

WS

## Gathered seam

The main type of gathered seam is used where one full gathered edge has to be attached to a plain edge. This is used on yoke joins, for attaching frills, etc. The other use is for joining two gathered edges; this may occur where a full skirt is to be gathered on to a slightly gathered bodice.

Insert gathering threads where they are needed, placing them just above the fitting line. Mark balance marks and the central point on both pieces of fabric. If a long section such as a frill is being gathered up, it helps to divide and mark each edge into four equal sections, but if the gathering represents a style feature or shaping area then the section marked on the plain edge must be where it is indicated on the pattern.

Place the two pieces of fabric right sides together and with the piece to be gathered on top, matching the point marked at the centre, and insert a pin vertically. The point of the pin should go under the gathering thread and the smallest possible amount of fabric picked up. Arrange the fabric so that the balance marks also match and insert pins at all of them.

Locate the gathering thread. If it is a single thread or a cord it will be easy to find. If a row of normal machine stitching has been used the thread that came from the spool must be found. If one end of the gathering thread is held by a knot or reverse stitching it is the free end that must be found. Take hold of the end and ease the surplus fabric gently along to wrinkle it up. Use the thumb to do it, with the fingers underneath both fabric edges to support them and provide a base for the pressure of the thumb. The fabric will slide easily over the pins. Continue until each section between pins is pulled up to the same length as the flat fabric underneath. Adjust all the sections and then wind the end of the gathering thread round the pin nearest to it. Re-arrange the gathers in that section so that they are even.

Insert one pin vertically across the gathers in the centre of each section, then divide up that section again with pins and so on until the pins are 1 to 2 cm ($\frac{3}{8}$ to $\frac{3}{4}$ in.) apart. Before inserting each pin use its point to adjust the gathers yet again.

Still holding the gathered side uppermost tack the seam, including any ungathered areas, inserting the needle slightly below the gathering thread. Use very small stitches. Remove all pins. Snip off the ends of the gathering thread and machine the seam. Stitch from the gathered side and work slowly. Hold a bodkin or small scissors in one hand and use the point to flatten the gathers before they pass under the machine foot. This will prevent them being pushed over out of place and forming larger pleats. The

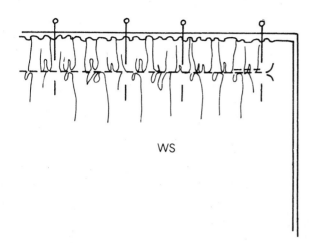

WS

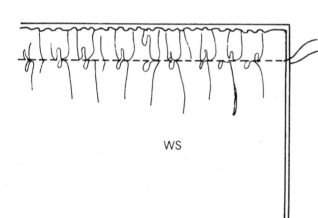

WS

machining should be 1 mm ($\frac{1}{16}$ in.) below the gathering thread.

Remove tacking carefully. Snip the anchored end of the gathering thread and pull it out. The machining will come out easily if the spool thread is pulled first.

The raw edges should be neatened. On light fabrics trim both edges to 5 mm ($\frac{1}{4}$ in.) and zig-zag over them. On heavy fabrics trim the gathered edge only and zig-zag both separately to avoid bulk. Alternatively trim the gathered edge to 2 to 3 mm ($\frac{1}{8}$ in.) and roll the flat edge over it and hem as for a self neatened seam. If the fabric frays the edges may be bound. Bulk can be avoided by using net cut into strips.

When joining two gathered edges, cut a length of tape or the selvedge of the fabric, to exactly the size the seam must be when finished. This may be a waist join in which case it can be measured. If the seam is a style feature the finished length will be given on the pattern. Pin both edges together as shown but pull up one side only to start with and pin the tape to it to establish the size. Pull up the second side to match it. Tack, remove pins, and then machine. After machining neaten the edges together or separately, depending on the thickness of the fabric.
the fabric.

Note that with both seams if a very long area is being handled, such as a waist join, it is easier to insert the main anchoring pins, then pull up the threads but insert the additional pins into one section only and tack that section before moving on. This means fewer pins are in the work as they are removed after tacking; this is less irritating and keeps the work softer. Also it prevents the gathers from moving, stops pins dropping out, and removes the likelihood of threads breaking from the size and weight of the fabric being handled.

### Leather seam

Suede and Nappa leather should be stitched with a fairly large straight machine stitch and with a spear pointed needle in the machine. Choose the size of needle according to the thickness of the leather. Hold the edges together with adhesive tape because pins leave holes. It is possible to buy a special foot with rollers attached for some machines and these make the stitching much easier. With an ordinary machine foot the leather may be inclined to stick to the machine base and to the foot. A light application of talcum powder will help prevent this.

Press seams open with a warm iron over brown paper and then apply a little leather adhesive under the seam allowances. Hammer lightly to flatten. Alternatively seam allowances my be held down with a row of machining worked from the right side an equal distance on either side of the seam line.

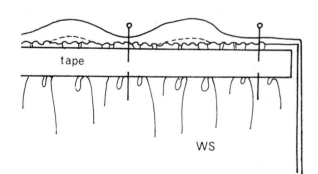

tape

WS

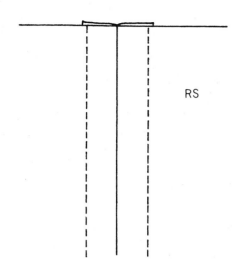

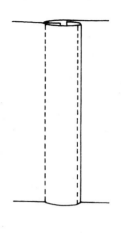

## Machine fell seam

A strong, flat seam that can be used on all fabrics except heavyweight ones. Two rows of stitching, or one row and a seam line, are visible on the right side so this limits its suitability to fairly utilitarian clothes such as shirts, jeans, sports wear, nightwear, children's clothes. No raw edges are visible so it is a good seam to use on clothes that will be washed often.

The usual 1.5 cm ($\frac{5}{8}$ in.) seam allowance is adequate on most fabrics, although on bulky fabrics it might be wise to leave a little more when cutting out.

The seam can be used with either side as the right side. To finish with two rows of stitching on the right side, start with the fabric wrong sides together. If you wish to have the other side outside place them right side together.

Machine the seam on the fitting line. Set the machine to a good-sized stitch, possibly in a contrasting colour, bearing in mind that it will be decorative on the garment. Press the stitching. Press the seam allowances flat towards the back of the garment. Lift the upper one and trim the underneath turning down to 2 to 3 mm ($\frac{1}{8}$ in.). Turn under the upper layer and

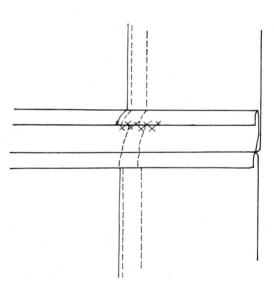

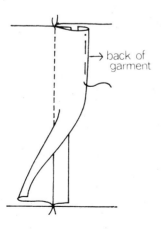

→ back of garment

tack. Press. Machine, having left the machine set to ensure that the stitch is the same. The machining should be very close to the fold. If a narrower finish is desired, trim a little off the top layer before turning it under.

The end of the fell seam is bulky to turn under if another similar seam has to be made. It helps to hem or herringbone the edge down for a short distance in order to avoid a wobbly seam.

## Mock french seam

As the name implies, this seam resembles a french seam when finished. It has the same advantages, namely that it is narrow and the raw edges are completely concealed. It may take a little longer to do.

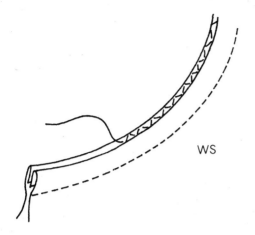

The main uses of this seam are where the fabric is too shaped to make a french seam possible, e.g. armhole; or where the fitting is so precise that it is essential to stitch on the fitting line on the wrong side and not, as in a french seam, apart from it. The mock french seam is not suitable for bulky fabrics.

Stitch the seam on the wrong side and press the stitching. Trim both raw edges down to 13 mm ($\frac{1}{2}$ in.). Turn in these edges to meet each other and tack. Press. Work slip stitch to join the folds, or if the appearance is suitable work a small zig-zag machine stitch. If the fabric is difficult to handle it will be necessary to turn in and tack the first edge only and then turn in the second one.

### Narrow seam
This seam when finished can be as little as 3 mm ($\frac{1}{8}$ in.) in width. It is useful on lightweight fabrics, and transparent ones where the width of an open seam would be too visible.

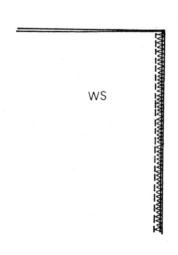

Machine the seam on the fitting line on the wrong side. Press the stitching flat then trim both seam allowances. The width depends on the fabric but trim off as much as possible. Set the machine to a very small zig-zag or any other stitch available that is suitable for the fabric. Machine over both raw edges. Press the seam to the back of the garment.

### Open seam
Sometimes called a plain seam, this is used more than any other because it is suitable for all fabrics and it is flat. One row of stitching is used.

Place one piece of fabric on the table, right side uppermost. Place the second piece of fabric on top, right side down. Raw edges should be nearest to you.

Line up the two seam lines by lifting and respreading, not by dragging. It is easier to do this if you have used tailor tacks because you can feel those on the lower piece of fabric with your forefinger while moving the top fabric into position.

It is best not to use any pins as they lift the material, but if your fabric is particularly obstinate place a few pins down the length of the seam, inserting them across the seam to avoid disturbing the fabric too much.

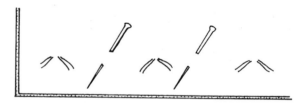

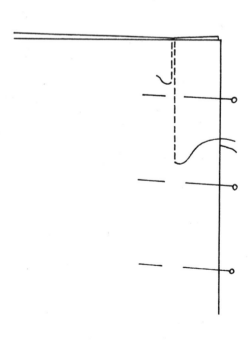

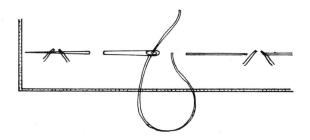

If seams are to be machined without tacking, insert pins across the seam at intervals of about 10 cm (4 in.) but make sure the pin heads are to the right as you stitch. The pins can be removed as you get to them or you can stitch over them provided the speed of machining is not too great.

Use a long piece of tacking thread and a needle one size larger than for hand sewing on the particular type of fabric; put a knot in the end and begin tacking, picking up small amounts of fabric on the needle.

At the end of the seam pull the fabric to loosen the tacking thread slightly, this will help to avoid a puckered seam, and fasten off. On jersey or pile fabrics leave an end of thread, do not fasten off.

On long, straight seams it may help to rule a chalk line before machining, to give you a guide line. Many people remove their tailor tacks at this stage but as they were the first marks to be put in, they are the most accurate, so leave them in and use them as a guide.

Place the work under the machine with raw edges to the right, lower the foot onto the fabric, turn the wheel until the needle is in the work, and machine, reversing for 6 mm ($\frac{1}{4}$ in.) to fasten the thread. Fasten off at the end by reversing.

Remove tacking by grasping the knot, use your bodkin for difficult stitches. Remove tailor tacks, using tweezers (or teeth) for difficult ones.

*Pressing* Press in the same direction as the seam was stitched. Press the stitching flat to remove puckers and to help to embed the thread in the fabric. Use damp muslin and medium-hot iron, or steam iron if that is best for your fabric.

Open the garment out over your sleeve board, arranging one short length of seam in position if it is a long one. Open the end of the seam with your fingers and then, holding a corner of the damp muslin in one hand and the iron in the other, open the seam by pressing on the cloth with the toe of the iron. Work your way along to the end of the sleeveboard in this way, making sharp pressing movements.

Lift the cloth and examine the seam. Correct any wrinkles by pressing again.

Press the whole section again, more boldly this time to set the fabric in its new position. Leave to cool.

Move the work along and press another section in the same way taking care not to leave a mark where the sleeveboard ends.

Turn the work over and press the right side, still using the cloth but with less pressure than you extended on the wrong side. Leave to cool.

Remember that some embossed or pile fabric may be harmed by pressing on the right side, so test a small piece of fabric first.

Using medium scissors, trim back the turnings at an angle to reduce bulk before you proceed to the next seam.

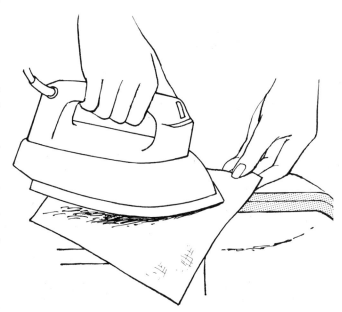

### Overlaid seam

One piece of fabric is laid over the other and stitched from the right side. The advantages of the seam are that the fabric always has its right side uppermost which is useful if checks, for instance, have to be matched. It is often easier, if gathers are included in one of the pieces, to watch the effect being created, moving the gathers if necessary. The edges of the fabric may be shaped in such a way that it would be very difficult and would not produce such good results if another method were used. Or it can simply be to create a top-stitched decorative edge. This type of seam may be used on seams of any shape. It is often used for yoke joins.

Insert any gathers or pleats. Mark the seam line accurately on the piece to be laid on top. If it has a repeating shape to it make a cardboard template, place it on the fabric as often as needed and mark round with tacking stitches or chalk. If the shape is

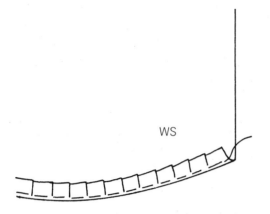

WS

Carefully matching the ends of fabric and balance marks pin this prepared section over the under layer then tack near the edge. Remove the pins. If this is a seam providing shaping it will have to be fitted, so insert another row of tacking 3 mm ($\frac{1}{8}$ in.) away from the first to help take the strain of fitting.

Stitch near the folded edge with a straight stitch or any variation of zig-zag stitch or with machine embroidery. In certain cases hand embroidery can be used. With straight stitching, a top-stitching thread such as Drima Bold may be used for effect or Double Thread Top Stitching, or Twin Needle Stitching.

needed only once or twice, trim the paper pattern on the seam line, lay it on the fabric and mark with tacking or chalk; of if the fabric is folded, with tailor tacks. Also mark any balance marks (notches) on both the pieces of fabric to be joined together.

Prepare the edge of the upper piece by turning under the edge with the fitting line exactly on the fold, tack near the edge with small stitches. Press the fold with the toe of the iron. If the edge is curved it helps to trim the turning down to 5 mm ($\frac{1}{4}$ in.) (or a little more if the fabric frays) before turning under, and then before pressing, snip the raw edge right up to the tacking every 5 mm ($\frac{1}{4}$ in.) to ensure a smooth curve. Infrequent snipping will result in a series of steps or angles.

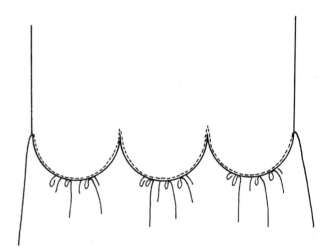

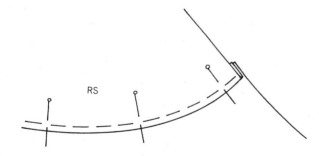

RS

Remove all tackings and press. On the wrong side trim the turnings and neaten with a zig-zag stitch. If a second parallel row of stitching is to be worked on the right side, neaten the raw edges before adding it.

If the fabric is loosely woven or has excessive movement in it, stabilise the upper layer by mounting it if it is a small area, or by cutting a narrow strip of Bondaweb or a fine cotton or lining fabric on the bias and placing it on the wrong side against the fitting line before you begin.

### Oversewing

To distinguish 'oversewing' from 'overcasting', regard 'oversewing' as a permanent joining stitch necessary in many places, but 'overcasting' as the stitch used on single fabric and dispensed with if a machine zig-zag stitch is available.

Oversewing is worked from right to left, inserting the needle straight towards the body. It is often used to join the two finished edges, or at least folded and pressed edges, and it should be as small as the fabric will allow. Take only a little fabric from each edge on the needle, pull the thread tight and work the stitches very close together.

Try to avoid using it on the outside of adults' clothes as it can be seen, use instead slip stitch or ladder stitch although they are not as strong. Oversewing can be used extensively as a strong stitch on children's clothes and on household items.

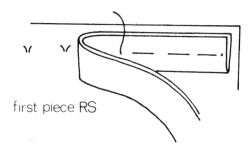

first piece RS

For best results the finished piping is pressed towards the front of the garment which means one seam turning and both piping edges will be pressed towards the back. Remember to attach the bias piping to the front pieces of the garment first and on completion neaten all raw edges.

Cut strips of fabric 2.5 cm (1 in.) wide on the bias. Join them if necessary, and fold in half with the wrong side inside, and press lightly, stretching the strip. Place the piping on the right side of one edge of the garment. Tack in place exactly on the fitting line. The amount the piping extends beyond the fitting line will vary according to the fabric being used, so it is worth working a trial seam first. Machine on the garment fitting line but work with piping uppermost to ensure that the edge is even.

Place the second piece of fabric wrong side up on top of the piping, the raw edges all lying in one direction. Tack through all layers on the fitting line. Turn the seam over and machine precisely beside the first row.

Remove the tacks, and grade the raw edges to reduce bulk before neatening. Press on the right side by running the toe of the iron along the edge of the fabric beside the piping. Cover the toe of the iron with a cloth to protect the fabric.

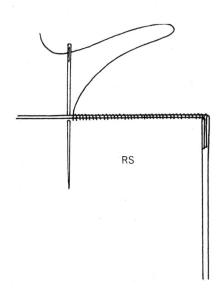

RS

### Piped seam

A decorative effect achieved using bias strips of fabric. The strips may be matching or contrasting in colour, and although the piping should have the same care instructions as the main fabric, it can be of a different weave or texture to add interest. For example, the following all look good in plain jersey or woven fabrics: satin, crêpe, ciré, stretch towelling, suede fabric, bouclé, knit fabrics; and plain-coloured synthetic jersey looks good with a print or plain dark colour.

As the insertion is cut on the cross this seam can be used at any position on a garment; it will easily go round curves but equally it will lie flat on straight seams.

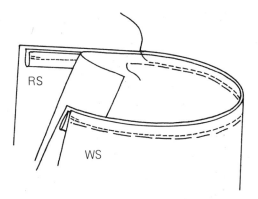

RS

WS

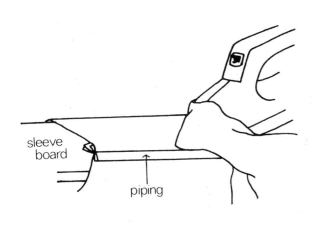

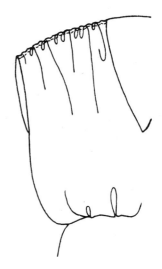

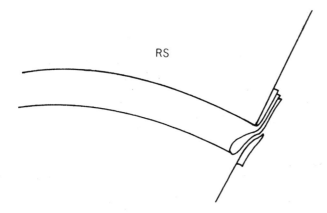

Purchased bias binding or any stretchy plaited braids may be used in place of bias strips; use folded or use flat with one edge extended to form the decorative feature. Piping can be bought in various colours. Attach in the same way by machining close to the filled piping edge to attach it to the first side. On completion press but do not trim the selvedge or 'skirt' edge of the piping, otherwise it will fray.

### Ruched seam

This is a decorative feature added to a normal, open seam. It could be a shoulder seam, even extended into the sleeve where there is no seam, a waist seam, or the side seam of a dress. It can, in some cases, prove a useful way of correcting the fit of a dropped shoulder style. This should only be a last resort as it alters the design of the garment but if the dropped shoulder doesn't suit the individual it is a remedy.

There are two main methods that can be used. In both cases the garment should be complete in that area at least.

For the first method cut a crossway strip of fabric the length of the seam to be drawn up. Make a piece of rouleau tubing the same length, or pieces of tape or seam binding can be used. Tack the crossway strip to the wrong side of the garment, tacking down both

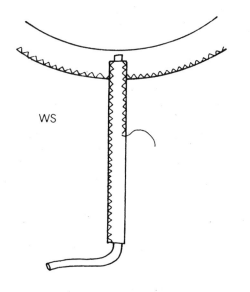

the machine to an attractive open zig-zag stitch or a stretch stitch, and working on the wrong side, centre the elastic over the seam (or chalk a line if there is no seam) and stitch. Stretch the elastic as you stitch to the end. When working on a long seam it helps to mark the centre, and also the centre of the elastic, to give you a half-way mark to work to.

### Seams in pile fabrics

These include velvet, velveteen, panné velvet and corduroy of all types, as well as other fabrics having a pile which lies in one direction. Tack seams working in the direction of the pile and do not fasten off the thread. Machine in the same direction, working slowly, snipping the tacks if bulges of fabric appear on the upper layer. Allow the fabric to move as you stitch. Some machines have a dual-feed facility which enables both fabric layers to move at the same rate and no movement will occur.

### Seams in vynyl, plastic etc.

The fabrics that are made up of a coating of substance on a jersey backing are not too difficult to sew. Use a small machine needle, possibly a leather point, a medium-sized stitch. Tack only within the seam allowance to avoid leaving holes. Welt seams look best as the stitching breaks the plain surface of the fabric. When stitching with the outside of the fabric outwards, prevent it sticking by sprinkling it with talcum powder. It also helps to place a drop of oil on the machine needle.

### Slot seam

A decorative seam giving a pleat effect. The seam is backed with a piece of fabric which is either contrast,

sides. Thread the rouleau through it and out from under the strip at one end. Set the machine to a small zig-zag stitch or even a more decorative one and stitch round three sides of the strip, anchoring the end of the rouleau at the top. On reaching the far end, stop and pull up the rouleau to gather the seam then turn and machine across the end. On the right side even out the gathers. If the end of the rouleau is to be visible, tie it or loop it, if not trim if off.

The second method has a similar finished effect. Cut two pieces of lingerie elastic. This is the open, lacy and soft elastic. The elastic should equal the length you wish the garment to be at that point. Set

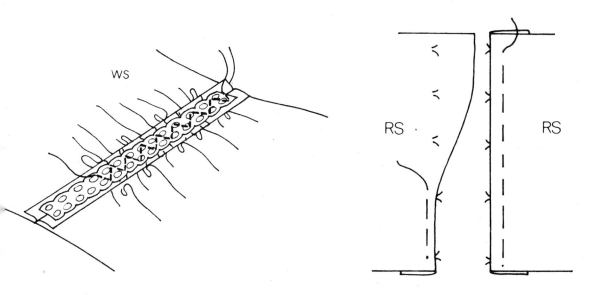

checks cut on the cross, etc., and then top stitched for its entire length. The seam is used both as a style feature emphasising basic seams such as centre front skirt seams and shoulder seams, or as a means of breaking a plain design with additional seams.

To make a slot seam where the fabric edges are straight (or angled) turn in both edges on the fitting line, tack and press well. On a long seam it will help at this stage to put the two pressed edges together and make a couple of chalk marks right across. This will help to prevent any movement when re-joining. If the fabric is checked or striped, there will be no need to mark it.

Cut a backing strip 4 cm ($1\frac{5}{8}$ in.) wide. This can be of self fabric or contrast; cut on the straight or on the cross. Mark the centre of the strip with chalk or tacking.

Place the two folded edges to the chalk line and tack. Catch the folds together with a big herringbone stitch in tacking thread.

Machine beside both folds with normal thread or double thread or top-stitching thread. Either work fairly close to the fold or, using the edge of the foot as a guide, stitch a little further away for a tucked effect. If a wider tucked effect is required attach the measuring bar to the machine.

Remove all tackings and press with a damp cloth over a towel to avoid a ridge. Press both sides. On the wrong side trim the backing and turnings down and neaten together. If the fabric is bulky, trim to varying widths before neatening separately.

To make a slot seam where the edges are curved cut shaped facings exactly to the shape of the edges and on the same grain. These facings may be made

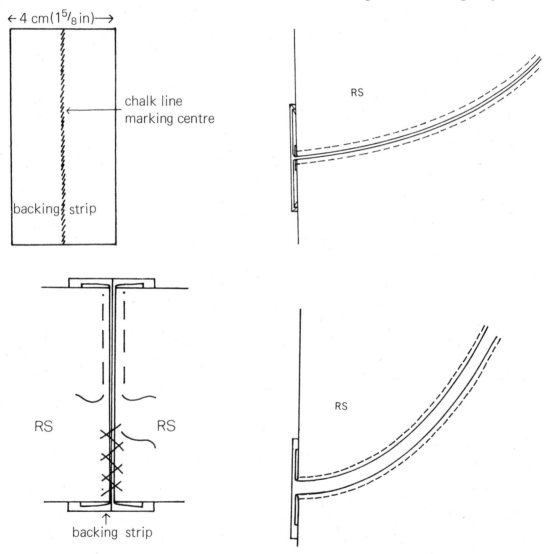

from matching lining or other lightweight fabric if the top stitching is to be near the edge. Alternatively, if the seam backing is being made from a contrasting fabric the facings could also be in contrast and the stitching worked a distance from the edge.

Attach, trim and turn the facings to wrong side. Tack and press the edges and neaten the raw edges of the facings. Cut seam backing strips in a curve to correspond with the edges. Neaten the edges of the backing.

Tack and machine the seam in the same way as for the straight slot seam.

For a more obvious effect a narrow gap may be left between the folded edges when placing them on the backing. If this is to be done either make the seam before cutting out the garment, if it is purely decorative, or, if it is a construction seam the garment edges will have to be turned under a little further to allow for the additional width provided by the backing.

### Welt seam

The feature of this seam is that it forms a ridge and it is decorated with hand or machine top-stitching. It is a well-used way of breaking the surface of plain fabrics particularly the medium and heavyweight ones and is often used as the main construction seam to emphasise such style features as raglan seams, yokes and dropped armholes. If a ridged-effect stitched seam is wanted on lightweight fabrics use a machine fell seam in which the raw edges become completely enclosed.

To make the seam, place the two pieces of fabric with right sides together, matching the fitting lines, and tack. Note that if the garment is to be fitted a second row of tacking should be inserted at this stage, with both turnings held to one side and the stitching penetrating all layers. After fitting remove that row and machine the seam from the wrong side as tacked.

Remove the tacks and press open, then press both turnings to one side (towards the back or upwards). Press both sides of the fabric. Work a row of stitching to form the welt from the right side parallel with the seam line.

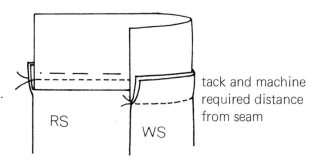

tack and machine required distance from seam

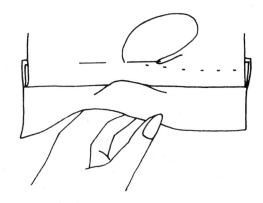

On light or smooth fabrics such as, wool or denim, this can be done by machine, using normal thread or top-stitching thread, but on good quality coatings of any sort the finish can be made to look professional by doing this stitching by hand. Use a small prick stitch, making sure that the needle goes back into the fabric only fractionally behind where it emerged, so that no thread shows at all on the right side. Press the row of stitching with the toe of the iron.

The distance of the stitching from the seam line will depend on the type and thickness of the fabric and on the effect wanted.

If the fabric does not fray or if the garment is to be lined, the raw edges need not be neatened. If the fabric frays trim the edges and neaten them both together before working the welt stitching.

Where welt seams are to meet in another seam, trim away at least one layer of turning at each end of the seam before adding the welt stitching, otherwise the third seam, which may also have to be welt, will be too bulky to handle neatly.

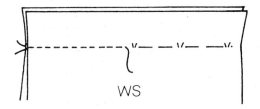

WS

## SEEDING

A simple embroidery space-filling stitch in which small straight stitches are worked at random in the area to be covered. They may also be worked as tiny crosses.

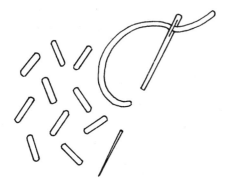

## SELVEDGE

The side edges of fabric. On woven fabric the selvedge is a narrow, closely filled edging that occurs where the weft yarns turn round and proceed back across the warp. The selvedge is often tight and may have a manufacturer's name woven into it. The selvedge should not be incorporated into a seam because its texture is different from the remainder of the fabric.

The edge of knitted fabric is often wider, may be very rough and even wavy. It must be cut off, preferably before laying out the fabric ready to cut out.

The selvedge is where hooks are inserted to hold the fabric flat while weaving. The hooks are usually inserted from the right side so examination of the holes may reveal which is the right side. Sometime small blobs of adhesive are used at the selvedge to hold the fabric flat.

## SEPARATES

A range of 'tops and bottoms' including a jacket, blouse, tunic, waistcoat, skirt, trousers or any variation or selection of these, designed to be put together in any combination. Separates have a point of co-ordination, usually colour, but sometimes also type of fabric, jersey for example.

## SERGING

'Serging' is the tailoring term for overcasting a raw edge to prevent fraying. It is a deep stitch, and can also be used where a raw edge has to be actually caught down onto a layer underneath.

(See *Overcasting*.)

## SETTING IN SLEEVES

This is the method for inserting a conventional sleeve with a smooth seam running over the shoulder bone. The main difficulty lies in the fact that the made-up armhole presents a shape very different from the top of the made-up sleeve. In addition the sleeve has to be inserted so that it hangs correctly and without gathers or folds and yet still allows room for movement.

Make sure the armhole of the garment fits and be sure to check the fit of the sleeve after tacking in and adjust it until it fits correctly. (See *Sleeve Fitting*, page 120.)

The setting in is best tackled in two stages, the underarm, followed by the sleeve head, and if you first appreciate the way in which you are trying to distribute the ease you will find it easier. No ease at all is required at the underarm section, but the sleeve must on no account be stretched. Of the remaining fullness at the sleeve head arrange a little for the 8 cm ($3\frac{1}{8}$ in.) above the underarm section; more than half of what is left should got to the front between shoulder seam and balance mark, while less than half is used at the back because the shoulder is more shallow and there is no protruberance of arm bone as there is at the front.

### Tacking

Turn bodice right side out and have sleeves right side out. Pick up the right sleeve ready to set into the right armhole. Check that you have the correct sleeve by folding it along the seam and smoothing out the head. The raw edges will not be level because the front has been hollowed out and the back extended to allow for movement.

Place sleeve seam to underarm seam and pin. Place together the stitching lines of the underarm for about 7.5 cm (3 in.) on either side of that first pin. Tack with fairly small stitches. Fasten off tacking and remove pins.

Tack in the underarm section of the left sleeve immediately in the same way.

To set in the sleeve head, turn the bodice inside out and roll back the top section of the armhole. Pull the top part of the sleeve through and lay it in position on the bodice with fitting lines matching. Slip your fingers under the two turnings to support them while you pin. Place a pin in the sleeve at right angles to the raw edges. Continue to pin at intervals, dispersing the fullness with each pin you insert. Don't allow a fold of fabric to develop between any two pins. If it does, remove a few pins and spread the ease again. The raw edges will flute as you pin, but at the fitting line itself there should be no folds of fabric. As you pin remember the positions described earlier where more and less fullness is required.

Move to the second sleeve immediately and pin to ensure that they both look the same. Tack the sleeve

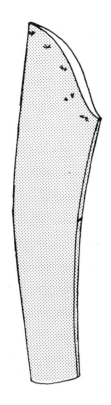

head with very small stitches, removing each pin as you reach it.

If, occasionally, with some twill weave synthetics, you find it impossible to ease in the sleeve in this way, you can run a row of regular machine stitching round the sleeve head on the fitting line. This must not be pulled up but it will help to prevent the sleeve stretching and becoming longer.

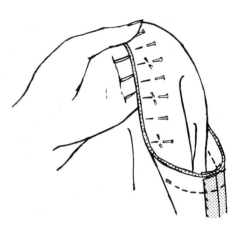

### Sewing

After fitting and adjusting, the sleeves can be sewn in, by one of three ways.

*Sewing by hand* On any soft, fairly thick, material or one with a surface interest, sew the sleeves in by hand. This ensures that the ease will not flatten into pleats as it sometimes does if you machine round the armhole.

If you hold the work with the sleeve uppermost as you did for tacking you will be able to control the ease as you stitch and make sure that you do not form any pleats or tucks in the sleeve head. However, stitching with the bodice towards you ensures a smoother line to the armhole. You may like to compromise by sewing from the armhole side for most of it but turning it over when you start on the sleeve head section.

Use double thread run through beeswax to strengthen and bind it together and back stitch round the armhole close by your tackings. Take the needle half-way back each time, not right back to the previous stitch. This makes a much closer stitch. Pull the thread fairly tight although one of the advantages of hand sewing is that the tension is lower than that of machining and it means with sleeves that you will retain a soft, unpinched line.

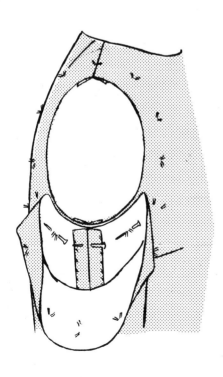

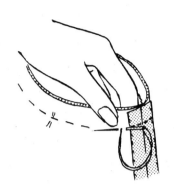

**Trimming and neatening the armhole**
On all except sheer fabrics trim off only the fraying edge of the turnings, leaving 1.3 cm ($\frac{1}{2}$ in.) to be neatened. This wide turning will support the head of the sleeve and keep it a good shape. Neaten the raw edges according to the fabric, using whatever method you have found best on the seams.

On transparent fabrics trim the edges to less than 1.3 cm ($\frac{1}{2}$ in.) and either overcast very neatly or turn the raw edges in towards each other and slip stitch together. The raw edges can be bound provided this dosen't add unsightly bulk.

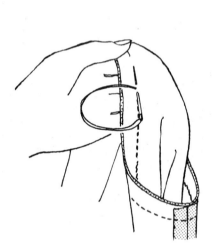

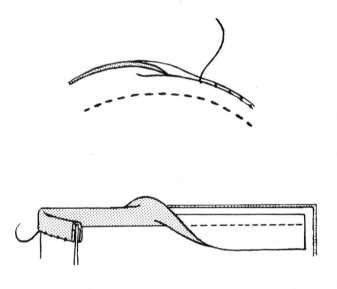

*Sewing by machine*   If you are using cotton or any smooth, thin material that would pull apart to reveal hand sewing, sew the sleeves in by machine. If you have a free arm on your machine, use it. Slip the armhole onto the free arm with the sleeve uppermost so that you can watch the ease. Set the machine to a slightly smaller stitch than for seams and stitch slowly, working only two or three stitches at a time before easing the work round. On jersey or stretch fabric use a slight zig-zag stitch. Fasten off strongly by overlapping the machine stitching.

*Combining hand and machine stitching*   If the fabric is thin and firm but you are worried about coping with the ease when it goes under the machine, back stitch the sleeve head only to anchor the difficult section and then machine round the whole armhole, stitching exactly on top of your hand sewing.

## SEQUINS

Sequins, paillettes and diamanté can be used to create a rich and glittery decoration. Use them densely for best effect. All can be obtained in gold, silver and colours and they can be sew-on or the type that can be stuck on. (These are not usually washable.) There are also some large diamanté with prongs attached. All three can be bought and used singly or in continuous strips. It is usually best to apply this type of decoration to a complete or almost complete article but the decision will vary with the position of the decoration. Strips or strands applied by sewing should be couched down with an over stitch about every three or four sections. Use a thread colour that shows least, this may not be the colour of the sequins or even of the fabric. Use a small size needle. Single sequins are applied by bringing the needle up through the fabric, slipping the sequin on to the needle and inserting the needle again. Pass the needle underneath to emerge at the next point. Do not pull the thread tight. If there is more than one hole, stitch through each.

## SEWING MACHINES

Modern machines have been developed to stitch on all types of modern fabrics. The trusted old straight stitch machine was certainly excellent and, if you have an old one, no doubt it still is if you confine your activities to materials similar to those that were available when the machine was made.

However, dressmaking at home has developed to the degree where nearly everyone wants a modern machine that will do more. This is exactly as it should be. We have accepted gratefully that technology has brought us a deep freeze, a tape recorder, video machine and all sorts of refinements to cars as well as other gadgets used by the family. Women who fear that a new machine will be too complicated to operate should remember that they have mastered other developments without any trouble. Modern machines are not complicated to use, but they do more for us and so there are more knobs and buttons. The problem really lies in making your choice from so many different makes and models. In most cases the main consideration is cost, so decide how much you can pay and go and look at machines in that price range. Then find out what they do. You get only the degree of sophistication you pay for. Also, you don't have the experience of buying a new machine very often, not as often as any other item, so take time to find out what has happened since you last bought one.

The sewing machine was one of the first domestic appliances to be mass-produced using the production line principle, turning what for many housewives must have been a dreary chore into a positive pleasure. And since those early days, sewing machines have become faster, more reliable and more versatile — so that now sewing has developed into a creative craft, limited only by the imagination of the user.

With their infinitely greater penetrating power and various accessories, modern sewing needle machines take materials as diverse as leather and chiffon in their stride. And, of course, they will produce a range of standard stitches which were unheard of even ten years ago. Buttonholing, blind stitch hems, smocking, tailor tacking, basting, shell edging, overcasting — whatever combinations of stitches you need — are available.

The sewing machine has never before been so versatile. Never before has it removed so much of the drudgery and left you so much of the pleasure of being creative.

### Types of machine

It is difficult to classify sewing machines accurately. One manufacturer's range obviously does not correspond precisely to another's. But broadly speaking, machines can be divided into the following groups, in ascending order of facilities and price.

When choosing a machine, it is always best to look for the features you need now — and then select from a group offering more. Most people find that as they 'grow into' their new machine, they become more ambitious — and it is always best to buy the most versatile machine you can afford, so that it can keep pace with your developing skills.

*Straight stitch machines*    Straight line forward and reverse stitching only. This is the only group which still offers the choice of hand operated machine.

*Manual zig-zag machines*    Straight line and zig-zag stitching only, in forward and reverse.

*Zig-zag and blind hem machines*    These machines all offer a blind hem facility, while some offer a stretch stitch and a stretch zig-zag known as ric-rac.

*Utility machines*    These machines will produce all the most commonly used stitches such as buttonholes, blind hems, stretch stitches, seam and overlock, stretch overlock. Each manufacturer offers a slightly different combination.

*Compacts*    Hardly a group in its own right, but one which covers lightweight, portable versions of the machines in the last three groups. These machines come into their own where space is limited, or where they must be frequently carried around.

*Automatics*    This is the term applied to machines which are capable of a variety of automatically produced embroidery patterns. On some the patterns are built-in, on others, cams are inserted to produce the same result. Still others give you a basic range of built-in patterns, plus the opportunity to add to them with extra cams.

All of these machines also give you the widest possible range of practical and decorative stitches which utility machines can't offer. Automatics can also provide a super stretch stitch for sewing reinforced seams in modern man-made materials.

*Electronics*    This is the area of greatest development at present — the sharp end of advancing technology. The most common use of electronics is for speed control, where it gives jerk-free starting, greater penetration power, and stitch-by-stitch control.

Other machines will stop automatically with the needle in or out of the work as you choose.

And finally, there are the fully electronic machines, equipped with micro-processors, which enable you to produce any stitch pattern or combination automatically, at the touch of a button or the turn of a dial.

### Extra attachments

Most modern machines can be fitted with 'optional

extras', either to widen the range of possible stitches, or to improve the machine's performance with certain difficult materials.

Velvet, for example, tends to creep, while thin, sheet fabrics are notorious for slipping. The solution to both problems is the 'walking foot', which effectively feeds both top and bottom layers of material through the machine together. Some more expensive machines have this facility built-in, for others there is an attachment. But even if your machine cannot be adapted in this way, a Teflon-coated foot could still solve your problem.

A similar attachment is the roller foot, particularly useful when sewing leather, or fabrics which are difficult to match.

*Free arm or flat bed?*   All groups except straight stitch machines offer the choice of free-arm or flat-bed models. The former tend to be a little more expensive, but give you much better access to all those difficult corners, such as sleeves, cuffs, collars and trouser legs. It is, however, only a matter of personal preference and there are plenty of flat-bed models on the market for those who prefer the traditional style.

After looking at a group of machines and seeing a demonstration, have a go yourself. Take along some pieces of fabric of the type you use and try the machine. Ask the dealer to leave you alone with it. A final very important point, if you haven't a permanently established sewing area or a cabinet, make sure the machine is light enough for you to lift unaided.

## SHANK

The strong collar of thread left between a button and the surface of the fabric. The shank allows room for the other layer of garment to lie under the button and it should be of sufficient length.

## SHAWL COLLAR

A collar that rolls softly round the neck and over the shoulder to the centre front opening of a coat, dress, jacket. The collar has only one join and it is at the centre back neck. The collar is often cut in one piece with the front of the garment, rolled back into position and joined to the back neck. A shawl collar can be of any width from very narrow to wide (often on dressing gowns and robes). The shawl collar is often used on men's dinner jackets, the facing or part that shows being cut from matching silk taffeta or ottoman or from contrasting fabrics such as satin, tartan or velvet.

## SHEAF STITCH

A popular embroidery spaced filling stitch in which

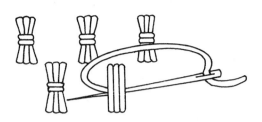

three vertical satin stitches are worked closely together and then tied by horizontal overcasting stitches. Pass the needle under the threads only a couple of times to tie the bundles together.

## SHEARS

(See *Scissors.*)

## SHEER

A transparent or see-through fabric such as georgette, chiffon, voile, made from fine yarns. 'Sheers' is the collective term for them all.

## SHIFT

A straight dress, often sleeveless, and with round or boat neckline. The only shaping is from underarm darts so it is loose at the waist and therefore often worn by those with figure problems. It may be short or full length. The shift first appeared in the late 1950s and enjoyed popularity because of its simplicity; no zips, collars, sleeves, for instance. It is, in fact, an uninteresting garment, similar to the old undergarment it imitates, and is only really successful in very elaborate or rich fabrics that require a simple style.

## SHIRRING

A decorative method of gathering fabric by machine using shirring elastic. It can be used to eliminate an opening, for example the wrist of a long sleeve, or to draw in excess fabric evenly, for example a dress waistline or top of a sun dress or nightdress. It can also be used in place of elastic for a more decorative effect but shirring is not very strong and it may not withstand constant strain when moving or when putting a garment on. It is possible to work shirring on all except heavy fabrics. It is easy to do on fine sheer fabrics but more rows will be needed to pull up heavier ones such as velvet, velveteen or jersey.

The number of rows worked also depends on how tight the area needs to be. The more rows of shirring worked the tighter it becomes. Three or four rows will often be enough on a sleeve, but at least ten or twelve rows will be needed for a bodice or a flat area of shirring.

There are two main methods of shirring although some machine manuals will describe other methods for specific machines.

To work the first method wind the elastic on to the machine spool using the spool-winding mechanism on the machine. This ensures that the elastic is wound under tension; it is not possible to maintain an even tension when winding by hand. Thread the machine with a synthetic thread on top and the elastic underneath. Adjust the machine to the largest straight stitch it will do. Insert fabric right side up. Work a row of stitching, which on some fabrics will barely produce any gathering. Work a second row about 1 cm ($\frac{3}{8}$ in.) or the width of part of the foot away, smoothing out the fabric. Work as many subsequent rows as are necessary.

To work the second method put the embroidery foot on the machine and thread the end of the elastic under the foot or through the hole in the centre and pass it to the back. Thread the machine up with synthetic thread. Set the machine to a medium width zig-zag and a medium length stitch. Put the fabric wrong side up under the foot, making sure the elastic is on top and the ordinary thread zig-zags over it. Work rows of machining, pulling the elastic as you stitch. The more you pull the more it will gather. You may need to practise just to see how much it needs pulling. Use the foot as a guide for keeping the rows parallel and smooth out the fabrics or attach the quilting bar if you wish to space out the rows.

Whichever method you are using, fasten off all ends of thread and elastic on the wrong side by using the thread to hold the elastic down. Where possible work shirring across the whole width of a section so that the ends will be caught in a seam later, otherwise the shirring will be weak and will not last very long. Even when it is caught in a seam it is a wise precaution to double stitch across the shirring when stitching the seam.

When shirring round a completed area such as sleeve hem or waistline, machine round and round, making two or three stitches at right angles, preferably hidden at a side seam, to move on to the next row. This avoids weak joins and leaves only the beginning and end of the elastic to be secured.

On some fabrics and in some positions, for example a waistline, there will now be sufficient grip, but on belts or other positions where the elasticated area needs to be as tight as possible it can be shrunk. Hold the shirring in the steam from a kettle of boiling water and watch it contract. The heat and moisture releases the tension on the elastic causing it to draw up. After some wear it may be necessary to steam it again. Never press over a shirred area.

## SHIRRING ELASTIC

This is a thin rubber core with a covering of yarn, usually cotton. The yarn is would round and round the rubber and can sometimes start to unwind from the cut end. It it does, trim the end off. It is available in black and white and in a limited range of colours.

The use of shirring elastic fluctuates in popularity according to fashion although it is always attractive on lingerie and on children's and baby clothes.

Although it is possible to thread the elastic through the eye of a large needle, it is then difficult to pass it through a fabric, so machining produces the best results. The elastic should be wound on to the machine spool, using the machine to wind it so that the elastic stretches. A few machines will not take elastic in their mechanism, but not many. The instructions with the cone of elastic may state that it should be wound by hand but this gives a loose result and it may not gather up the fabric very much.

An alternative is the wider, open and light elastic, available in several widths. This can be stretched and zig-zagged on to the wrong side, producing an effect similar to conventional shirring.

## SHIRT SLEEVE

This is characterised by the straight armhole and slightly dropped shoulder effect of a man's shirt. The sleeve is usually attached by using a machine fell seam and the shoulder has a yoke, usually double. At the wrist the surplus fabric is reduced to cuff size with two or three pleats. The armhole and sleeve head edges are usually straight enough to allow the sleeve to be attached before the underarm and side seams are joined.

## SHIRT YOKE SEAM

This is the type of seam used on a man's shirt where there is no shoulder seam.

Begin with the back and press into the lower back part any tucks, box pleat, as indicated in the pattern. Place the yoke right side down to the right side of the shirt back. Tack and machine. Remove tacks, press the stitching flat and trim the two raw edges to a level 1 cm ($\frac{3}{8}$ in.). Neaten these two edges with one row of neat zig-zag stitches.

Join the front shirt sections to front edges of the yoke in the same way, although there will be no shaping unless decorative stitched tucks are indicated in the pattern.

Press the seams from both right and wrong side, pressing the neatened edge up towards the yoke. With the right side of the shirt uppermost, work a row of straight stitching as close to the yoke edge as possible, sewing through all layers.

If the yoke is made of double fabric, follow

instructions for a *Double Yoke*.
     Proceed with the shirt, setting in the sleeves next.

## SHIRTWAISTER

Originally this meant quite literally a shirt style with
collar and button front, long sleeves and cuffs exactly
as a conventional shirt as far as the waist, and below
that a matching or contrasting skirt. However, the
shirtwaister dress has become a classic garment never
really out of fashion and looking good on most
women. It may or may not have a waist join and
other fashion elements such as slits, pleats or strap
openings are added as they are appropriate. The shirtwaister may be short or long, even worn over trousers;
it may be made in any fabric from the simplest cotton
print, through woven or jersey fabrics in all fibres
and weights, to pile fabrics, velour, plush, cord, velvet,
and even embroidered and metallic fabrics.

## SHOULDER PADS

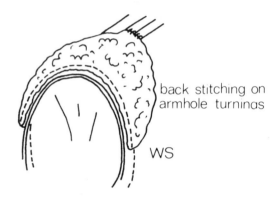

back stitching on
armhole turnings

WS

These come and go in women's clothes according to
fashion requirements but they are always used in
men's clothes. Tailors have always used them almost
as a padded coathanger, believing, rightly, that a coat
will not hang well, and will develop folds and
wrinkles, without them. They are also used in different thicknesses to correct lopsided posture, and can
always be an advantage used in this way in women's
clothes.
     Shoulder pads made from synthetic foam can be
bought in pairs, sometimes in a pack. Some are
covered with a nylon jersey covering; others have
white felt stuck on the outside. The latter are preferable as the surface is softer and since foam against
fabric makes a noise. Tailor's shoulder pads are made
from cotton waste and wadding and often covered
with a layer of soft muslin. To this, tailors add more
wadding as necessary to one or both pads. You can
make your own pads by covering a thin foam one
with wadding; a satisfactory pad because it does not
collapse or become lumpy as the wadding ones often
do.
     For a coat or jacket, whether men's or women's, in
order to create a normal shoulder line, place a thin
layer of wadding on each side of the pad and baste
through all layers with tacking thread. Place in
position in the coat, trim off any surplus along the
armhole edge and back stitch to the armhole turnings.
     For a dress or unlined jacket, shoulder pads should
be covered if they are likely to be seen. A small foam
pad is usually sufficient for a dress but if the figure
needs it, the pad can be built up as before.
     Cover the pads by cutting two pieces of lining for
each, larger than the pad. Wrap one piece round the
pad over the top and pin all raw edges to the under
side of the pad. Place the second piece of lining on

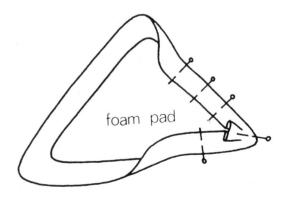

foam pad

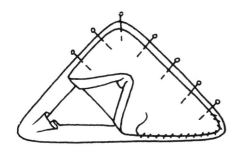

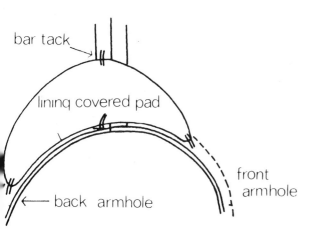

bar tack

lining covered pad

back armhole

front armhole

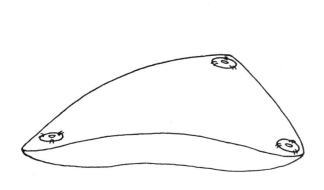

the under side, turn in the edges and pin all round. Hem the folded edge all around the pad.

To insert in the coat, fold the pad not quite in half and have the larger half to the back, with the edge level with the armhole edge. Insert by placing in position and working bar tacks 5 cm (2 in.) long. Place one at each end of the pad, one a little longer at the centre, and one at the outside edge attaching it to the shoulder seam.

Make sure all materials are washable in washable clothes by using polyester wadding. If this is not possible make them detachable. Sew halves of three press studs to the upper side of the covering, and the correspondong pieces to the turnings of the garment, or attach small squares of Velcro. The same pads can be used in several garments in this way.

## SHRINKAGE

All yarns are washed at some stage during fabric manufacture and the finished fabric may be subjected to a shrinking process as well. Most finishing processes now include shrinkage so it is unlikely that you will encounter shrinking on any fabric that has a manufacturer's name on it. However, all fabric is woven or knitted under tension, and sometimes, immersing loosely woven material in water for the first time has the effect of releasing the tension and causing the fibres to close up. A soft fabric plunged for its first wash into an automatic machine on hot wash, and left to spin relentlessly at the end, will suffer this closing up. Avoid this trouble by washing gently by hand and drip-drying, and also pressing, in the early part of the garment's life, especially if you have made it yourself.

If you have bought an unlabelled length from a market stall, if your fabric was abnormally cheap, or if you are at all doubtful about its future behaviour, test it for shrinkage. Measure out a 15 cm (6 in.) square somewhere in the middle of the length and mark it with tacking if it is a fabric you will be

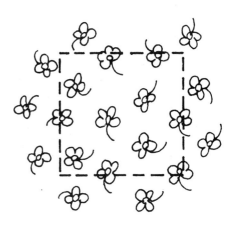

washing, or chalk it if it is to be a garment you will only have cleaned. Then wash this area, or press it with a damp muslin. Allow it to dry, press it and re-measure it both ways. Also, a bubbled effect will be visible if there is any change. Then tack the ends and selvedge together and wash or damp press the whole piece.

If you suffer the effects of a build-up of static electricity, wash the whole length in a fabric softener before cutting out. During the garment's life continue to rinse it in a fabric softener.

## SIDE-BENT

(See *Scissors.*)

## SILESIA

Sometimes referred to as 'pocketing', silesia is a closely-woven strong cotton fabric in basic tailoring colours and white, used for making pocket bags in coats and jackets. (See *Pockets*, for use.)

## SINGLE SATIN STITCH

(See *Straight Stitch.*)

## SHIRT LOOPS

(See *Hanging Loops.*)

## SLEEVE BOARD

This is used for all pressing of sewing processes. It is seldom, if ever, used for pressing sleeves. To press well you work on a very small area at a time and this is one advantage of the sleeve board as it draws your attention immediately to that part only. It also enables you to press shaped areas such as darts and curved seams without flattening them, by using the end of the board. Also the board raises the work to a much better working height.

Stand the sleeve board on the table or on the ironing board to use it.

A tailor's sleeve board is best, although expensive. It is heavy, has two sides to it, and all four ends are rounded at different sizes so you have a choice of two widths and four ends depending on the size and nature of the part you are pressing. It is worth having one made if you can, rather than using the light metal ones sometimes available with your ironing board.

Use a heavy wood, with a finished thickness of 2.5 cm (1 in.). All edges must be rounded for ease of use. The support column should be secured by wood adhesive and two countersunk screws through the top and base.

Covers should be made for the working surfaces. The narrow end of a cover should be sewn closed, and the side end should be left open and elasticated. The cover will form a sleeve into which the board can slide. Thickness can be created by using pieces of old blanket, with elasticated edges, to fit around the board.

Cover the top of the bare wooden board with a single layer of blanket (not foam) cut exactly to size. This may be stuck down with adhesive. Make a fitted cotton cover to fit over the blanket. Place pieces of fabric, cut roughly to shape but with at least 5 cm (2 in.) extra all round with right side to the board, covering the whole of the top and the underneath section as far as the support column.

Pin together accurately round the edges. Machine. Trim the edges. Turn in a wide hem round the remainder of the cover, and insert the elastic. The cover should fit closely to prevent accidental creases making marks on the fabric being pressed. Cover the narrow arm of the board with a fitted cotton cover only, and use this for pressing firm woollens and worsteds.

## SLEEVE HEAD PAD

Also called a sleevehead roll, this is inserted in the sleeves in a tailored coat or jacket. It is an additional fold of soft fabric, such as domette, tailor's felt or lambswool, put in the head of the sleeve to keep it in shape and prevent it from collapsing in wear.

Fold the fabric on the cross, and cut a banana shape about 5 cm (2 in.) wide at the centre and 25 cm (10 in.) long.

After inserting the sleeve and shoulder pad, fold back the top of the sleeve head and back stitch the roll to the turnings of the armhole. Put the fold level with the raw edges, arrange some ease over the head,

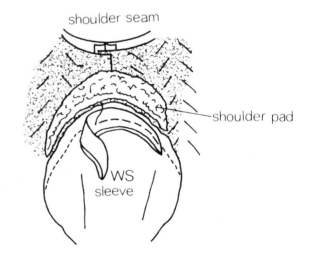

shoulder seam

shoulder pad

WS
sleeve

and back stitch to the turnings. Use double thread and start with a knot. Do not pull the stitches tight. When the sleeve head is pressed, the fabric on both sides of the back stitching is pressed out into the sleeve head to support it.

## SLEEVE LINING

Strong, closely woven silk or rayon taffeta (usually cream with grey stripes) is used for lining men's jacket sleeves. It is generally more durable than the body lining, the latter being chosen to match the colour of the cloth.

## SLIP STITCH

A permanent hand stitch using perfectly matching sewing thread, used for joining two folded edges from the right side. Positions where it may be employed include stitching the gap left after turning through a tube belt or tie, ends of cuffs, waistbands, lapels, etc., and any place where a machine stitching effect is needed, but working from the outside.

Work from right to left taking very small stitches along each fold of fabric alternately. Pull the thread tight enough to close the gap but not tight enough to wrinkle the fabric. The stitches should be 1 to 2 mm ($\frac{1}{16}$ to $\frac{1}{8}$ in.) in length. Press after stitching and the join will be invisible.

## SLIP TACKING

A method of tacking layers of fabric working from the right side. The reason for using it may be accuracy, for example where a fitting alteration has been made from the outside or where the design of the fabric has to be matched accurately. The fabric may be pinned with the two edges folded together, or with one piece of fabric flat. Use tacking thread and slip the needle alternately through each fold of fabric, or through the flat layer and through the fold of fabric on top. Stitches should be about 1 cm ($\frac{3}{8}$ in.) in length. When the fabric is unpinned and opened out the tacks will appear on the wrong side as a normal line of tacking in a seam.

## SLIPPAGE

Movement of yarns out of their true position within woven fabrics. Slippage normally occurs only with cheap fabrics made from shiny yarn, such as satin and taffeta.

## SMOCKING

Like most forms of decoration, not only is smocking an old craft, but in its original form it had deeper meaning in terms of indicating specific areas, types of work, etc. Although now purely ornamental, being used constantly to provide fullness in children's clothes, it also comes into fashion from time to time on women's clothes. It is a very elastic form of decoration.

The area to be smocked should be three times the desired finished width. Apply transfer dots to the wrong side, using a warm iron. Dots can be bought in sheets; the distances between them varying. Each size is known by a number. Generally, the thicker the fabric, the more widely spaced dots should be used.

Also on the wrong side, work gathering stitches, picking up on the needle only each transfer dot. Measure each length of thread before starting and leave a loose thread end to pull up. These threads will be removed later, so tacking thread can be used. When all threads are inserted, take hold of the loose ends and pull up until on the right side all the resulting tubes of fabric are close and parallel. Decorate the right side by working horizontal rows of embroidery stitches pulling up the surface of each tube. Insert the needle from right to left, working the whole from left to right. Stitches can include stem stitch, feather stitch, chain stitch and many others. Use from two to six strands of Anchor stranded thread.

**Mock smocking**

A very effective form of decoration that is extremely quick to do and produces a pleasantly fluffy effect. It is normally worked over a complete area but it can in certain instances be used in addition to provide a little fullness.

It can be worked on the wrong side of the fabric. Widely spaced smocking dots are applied to the wrong side and double back stitches are worked to join pairs of dots together. Alternate dots are joined on every other row to form a honeycomb effect. On the right side of the fabric a pleasantly ruched effect results. Another method is to work in the same way but on the right side. The fabric used is often check gingham. Dots are not used but the corners of the squares are picked up and joined with back stitches, using Anchor stranded embroidery thread. This effect can be created on plain fabric by marking or measuring points to pick up.

## SNIPPING

Fabric edges often need snipping either to make them lie flat or in order to release any strain that might result in puckering. Such edges are usually curved.

Use small scissors, opening the points by the exact amount necessary to make the snip and close the scissors right to the points. Snips should be close together, usually 5 mm ($\frac{1}{4}$ in.) apart, or less on a tight curve. When snipping towards a row of machining such as after attaching a collar or facing, make the

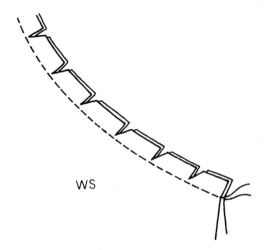

WS

cuts at an angle. This lessens the danger of cutting the stitching because the blades tend to slip beside the stitches but it also produces a longer cut edge which is the part that may be included to fray.

If snips are used to release tension, such as on a neckline when trying to make a collar fit, snip carefully at intervals towards the fitting line but only half-way to it. Complete the process before snipping again, more closely.

## SOAP

(See *Tailor's Soap*.)

## SOUTACHE

A narrow two-cord braid, often silky, although it can now be a stretch braid for sportswear.

(See *Braid*.)

## SPANISH KNOTTED FEATHER STITCH

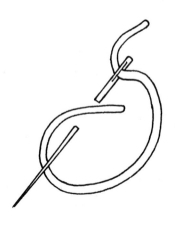

A thick cable-effect stitch. Working towards you make a chain stitch to the left as shown but keep the needle point to the left of the thread. Insert the needle above the initial loop and take a stitch to the right but making sure the thread lies under the needle from right round to left. Take the next stitch to the left and so on.

## SPIDER'S WEB FILLING

An embroidery filling stitch worked in circles. Work straight stitches to form 'points' on a circle, then weave under and over these points to fill the circle. An even number of straight stitches will produce a different effect from an uneven number.

split stitch

ntf

Start with a new thread here

## SPLIT STITCH

A flat embroidery stitch which may be used as an outline, or in close rows as a filling stitch. Work towards you. The first stitch is a small running stitch. The needle is then brought up through the thread to split it and a further running stitch taken.

## SPOOL

The word 'spool' refers to a small reel on which thread can be wound. The feature of a spool is that the ends are wider than the centre section. Also called bobbins and both terms refer to machine spools as well as reels of thread.

## SPRATS' HEADS

These are decorative triangles of buttonhole twist or top stitching thread such as Bold. They are placed at the tops of pleats, ends of jetted pockets etc., and are worked in the same way as arrowheads but they are usually smaller.

(See *Arrowheads*.)

## SQUARE NECK

A neckline that is square in shape at the front or back or both. Often a feature on pinafore dresses and other sleeveless garments. If the neckline is cut wide at the shoulders leaving only a narrow shoulder seam it should be fitted carefully to ensure that it does not slip off the shoulders. Anyone with sloping shoulders should avoid this type of wide, square neck or keep to one that is square at the front but a normal level neckline at the back.

## STAB STITCH

A strong stitch, used mainly where several layers are to be fixed but the total thickness is too great to take the stitch with the usual in-and-out movement. Work with the right side uppermost and stab the needle through to the wrong side. Bring it back on top slightly further on, insert it slightly behind where it emerged, bring it out further on, and so on. On top dents only very small stitches are visible, on the wrong side overlapping stitches are visible. The size of the stitch depends on the fabric and on how much strength is needed. Positions where stab stitch might be used include stitching through double fabric plus

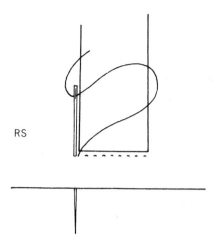

RS

the tape of a zip, the ends of pockets or piped buttonholes and anywhere where a prick stitch effect is desirable but due to the thickness it cannot be worked.

## STAY

A stay is any form of reinforcement or method of stabilising a process or a fabric. The stay must be suitable for the garment and the position in which it is used. The method of application must also be suitable. Examples of types of stay include tape, seam binding, a piece of lining or simply an additional row of stitching. Uses include preventing seams or edges from stretching, adding strength where there will be strain and holding a process, such as pleats or ruching, in shape. In addition interfacing acts as a stay and so does a lining if applied completely to one area such as a yoke. Sometimes the stay is incorporated into the process early and is therefore built, in from the start, sometimes it is added at a later stage, possibly hemmed in place by hand on the back of a process. There are times when it may be realised that a stay is needed only when the garment is nearing completion. An example of this is when a length of petersham is sewn to the inside of a waist join of a dress made from a soft or stretchy fabric, a decision that can safely be decided only at the fitting stage when the full weight of fabric is hanging in posiiton.

## STAY STITCHING

A row of stitching worked within a raw edge to help to stabilise it and prevent stretching.

The value of stay stitching in practice is subject to doubt for the following reasons: the handling involved in doing it will often stretch the fabric anyway; the additional row of stitching makes a hard line on soft fabric; the edge itself has to be seamed, bound, faced, etc., at some stage so while going to the trouble of stay stitching why not simply stitch on the facing? Also, any edge liable to strain in wear will be interfaced, a much more effective way of preventing stretching.

It is better to make sure balance marks are inserted if necessary, then keep doubtful areas flat on the table, without lifting, and begin by attaching interfacing.

If stay stitching is recommended in a pattern before snipping, e.g. an angled seam, it is in fact more effective to prevent fraying by pressing Bondaweb or lightweight Vilene into position.

## STAY TAPE

A narrow cotton tape with a selvedge on both sides can be used at the edge of the canvas on the front edge of a coat from hem to gorge, or it can be used for the bridle. Shrink before use.

## STEM STITCH

A straight, flat embroidery stitch used for outlines, long straight lines, e.g. stems of flowers. Rows can be worked closely together to fill in larger spaces. Work from left to right taking small, even, diagonal stitches.

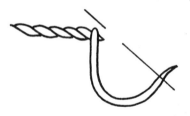

## STEP

The step is the angle between a lapel and a collar in a classic tailored style.

## STILETTO

A pointed steel tool used for forcing a hole in fabric and for re-shaping the round end of a buttonhole after stitching. Insert it only far enough to produce a hole the size required.

## STITCH LENGTH

Hand sewn stitches are not as strong as machining and should be made as small as possible to reduce the gaps of unstitched fabric to the minimum. There may be a handy guide in the form of a row of machining to hem into but otherwise control the stitches to keep them small and even. One extra large stitch will be a weak point. The smaller the needle, the smaller the stitches can be made.

In machine stitching, a guide can be offered, but it is necessary to try a machine stitch on a doubled piece of fabric, adjusting the length until it looks right. On the whole the thicker fabric needs a longer stitch but if, when the seam is pulled, gaps appear then it must be made smaller. Too short a stitch, however, may cause wrinkling especially in spongy fabrics such as crêpe. Too short a stitch in a soft fabric such as silk or viscose may cause wear. Weak fabrics such as lining should be sewn with a stitch that appears fairly long for the weight of fabric because too many close holes will split into a tear quite quickly. On the other hand stitches on all fabrics should be small enough to bed into the fabric and not lie on top.

## STOCK

A wide piece of soft fabric or a long scarf wound round the neck starting at the front, crossing the two ends at the back and bringing them to the front to loop once fairly loosely. Fasten with a cravat pin or brooch, or pass the ends through a scarf ring.

## STRAIGHT STITCH

The term has two meanings. In one, it is used to describe the conventional straight machine stitch of any size. A straight-stitch machine is one that does not perform any other type of stitch.

It is also a straight, flat embroidery stitch which may be regular in length or may vary. Stitches are generally spaced apart, but should never be too long or worked too loosely. It can also be called a single satin stitch.

## STRAP HOLDERS

These are sometimes required in the shoulders of wide-necked dresses, or, with a deep square neck, inside the corners of the neckline.

Choose a very small size press stud, the flat plastic type is excellent for this purpose, and sew the 'well' section in position on a double area of fabric on the garment. When required at the shoulder seam, put on the garment and mark exactly where the shoulder strap crosses the seam. Make a length of rouleau 7 cm ($2\frac{3}{4}$ in.) long and cut it in half. (Straight tape or ribbon has no 'give' and is inclined to cause a bulge of fabric in the garment.) Turn in and hem one end of each piece, turning over just enough to take the knob section of the press stud. Attach the press stud and fasten it. Pin the rouleau flat, turn in the other end and hem to the garment.

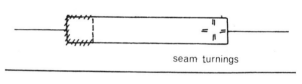

seam turnings

WS

## STRETCH STITCHES

Many zig-zag machines have a stitch that is specifically for use on stretch fabrics. The basis of all these stitches is to introduce a backwards and forwards stitch which puts more thread into the seam. This adds strength but also allows the fabric to stretch in wear without the thread breaking. The type and variety of these stitches varies with each machine. Some machines offer quite a wide range for different purposes. These stitches may also be designed to neaten the seam edges as well as join the two layers. The choice of stitch depends not only on the fabric but also on the position of the seam on the garment. Stitches must always be tried on a piece of fabric.

## STRIPED FABRIC

If stripes are used vertically they are improved by being broken. This can be done quite simply with gathers, with the addition of plain fabrics or by using the stripes the other way in one area, for example a pocket. If the stripes are of almost even width, hold up the length of fabric and look at it in a mirror. You will find that whichever colour is placed at the centre front of the body, then that will appear to be the pre-dominant colour of the garment. Uneven stripes should be made up with a centre seam to ensure a symmetrical effect. Even stripes can be used in any way — on the cross vertically, horizontally, gathered, pleated etc. — and they also look good arranged in several directions on one garment.

Wide stripes should be cut out so that the most prominent line of the design falls in a flattering place on the body. Mark this stripe on the main pattern piece and then put the matching pattern pieces against it and continue the lines. This will ensure that the stripes will fall correctly and also match if the pattern is placed on the fabric on corresponding stripes.

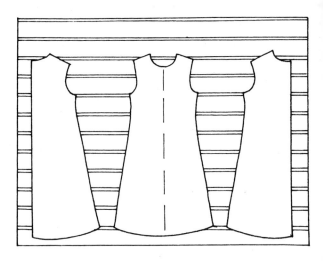

Before cutting out look at any darts and make slight adjustments if necessary to ensure that both the base and the point fall equally on either side of a stripe. If a small dart, as would be found on a back shoulder or neck, is obviously going to spoil the effect or emphasise a figure problem, it may be possible to ease the fabric in rather than darting it.

Stripes can look very effective on the cross and they can also be figure concealing because the lines do not emphasise bulges and hollows. The stripes may be chevroned, which will involve having seams at the centre as well as at the sides. Remember that if the edges of the seams are shaped at different angles the chevron may not remain exact for the entire seam

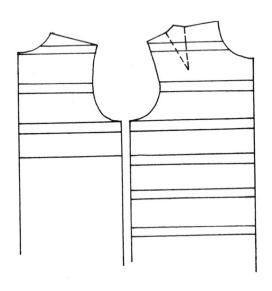

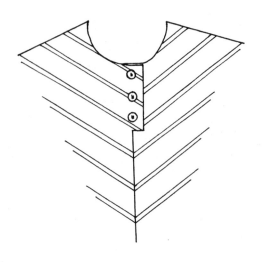

Although for cutting out simple designs striped fabric can be folded and pinned along the fold and edges, with stripes matching, it is safer to cut out with the fabric single, right side up. This is particularly important if the stripes are used horizontally as it enables you to be sure that each stripe is perfectly level under the pattern.

Knit fabrics especially can move imperceptibly and throw out the balance. Either make copies of each pattern piece, labelling each RS to make sure they will be cut out correctly, or cut each pattern piece and then reverse it to cut it again.

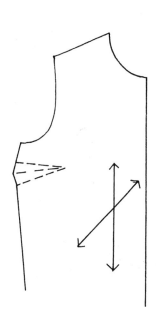

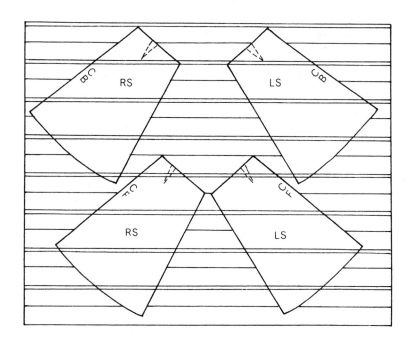

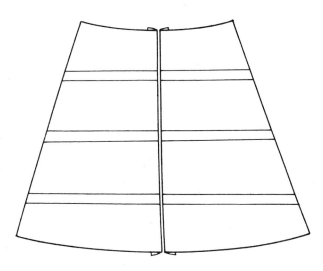

length. This can often be corrected at fitting by adding a little to one edge while subtracting the same amount from the other. Even if the pattern does not indicate cutting on the cross, most fairly simple styles can be adapted. Draw a new straight grain line at 45° to the one on each pattern piece. Make copies of the pattern pieces to be cut on the cross and draw the position of the main part of the stripe on each piece to make sure they will match when cut out. Do not make asymmetric features on cross stripes as they will distort the matching. Cut out on single fabric.

If stripes are to run diagonally across the body, either by turning the fabric on the cross or by using diagonally printed fabric, the traditional direction is from left shoulder down over the body to the right hip and they should maintain this direction on each piece of the garment and right round the body. It is not possible to make the stripes chevron or meet at all positions so it will be the left side seam where they miss. Cut out on single fabric.

Remember to fold seam allowances under on patterns when working out how to make stripes meet, otherwise they will not meet accurately on the fitting line when joined.

## STUD FASTENERS

There are various types of metal stud fasteners available with a variety of attractive metal caps. These are very useful on children's clothes, anoraks, casual clothes etc. Some have to be applied with a special tool which makes them expensive unless they are going to be used regularly.

## SUIT

A combination outfit comprised of jacket with either skirt or trousers. A waistcoat may be part of it in which case it may be called a three-piece suit. The difference between a suit, a jacket and skirt, or jacket and trousers is that they have been designed together, usually contain classic features and are made from the same or closely co-ordinated fabrics.

## SWAGGER

A coat or hip-length jacket hanging full and loose from the fitted shoulder. The fullness is introduced either by flare or sometimes with tucks or pleats into the neck.

## SWEETHEART NECK

This style of front neck curves from the neck point towards the underarm, even almost reaching the side seam sometimes and the base of the neckline is curved down into a low V. This neckline should always be well interfaced and fitted closely. Sometimes the back neck is extended to form a stand collar and the front curve begins at this higher point.

## SWELLED EDGE

The ridge created by stitching round the finished edges of a collar, lapels, front edges, pocket flaps, etc., on tailored clothes. This is done by hand although on anything mass-produced it is always worked by machine. It was once the mark of a hand-made coat although there were always those who sent factory made clothes to a hand tailor to have the stitching added. The stitching serves no utilitarian purpose as the edges are completely pressed and finished before the stitching is added.

Work prick stitch around the finished, pressed edges of collars, lapels and pocket flaps. Work with the right side towards you; on light fabrics the stitches should be 3 mm ($\frac{1}{8}$ in.) from the edge, on heavier fabrics a little more. Use a small needle.

On a lapel, work on the right side of the jacket up to the turn of the lapel, and then change over so that you stitch from the right side on the lapel and collar.

If the cloth is very bulky, work it by stabbing through from side to side.

(See also *Prick Stitch*.)

## SWING-NEEDLE

A term, not in common usage, describing the action of the needle when it works a zig-zag stitch. The term may be used as a description of this type of machine.

## TABARD

This can be a working cover-up or, sometimes, it becomes a fashion accessory. It is composed of a straight front and back often joined only at the shoulders and held at the sides with ties or fastenings. The tabard has a round or boat-shaped neck, slips over the head and may be any length. It can be made in any fabric from plastic and cottons to tweeds edged with braid and worn with matching skirt or trousers.

## TACK

A tack is a small bar of stitches inserted for strength at a point of strain.

## TACKING

Tacking is a temporary stitch used to hold layers of fabric together until the permanent stitch can be inserted. There are a number of reasons for using tacking and there are also times when it is safe to omit it.

(See also *Basting*.)

### When to tack

Shaped pieces of fabric must be tacked together if a garment is to be fitted. There is no point in machining seams and then having to unpick them — tacking is quick to remove and the pulling will not harm the fabric. If further fitting is required tacking is still used right up to the point when machining can be done.

Where style features are an experiment, such as the position of patch pockets, the depth and shape of a yoke or cuffs, these can be tacked in place, examined and moved if necessary. These features need not even be cut in fabric, the experiment can be made using pieces of Vilene initially.

If more than one layer of fabric is to be sewn decoratively, or if the fabric has to be backed with tissue or typing paper, then tacking is used to hold the layers together.

If a patterned fabric is being used, tacking is necessary to hold the matched areas together.

*Creeping*   When machining two layers of fabric, the top layer tends to move forward because the lower layer is gripped and steadied by the feed teeth of the machine. The problem is acute with pile fabric where the additional hazard of interlocking pile makes this 'creeping' worse. It is also a problem when matching checks and stripes, not because the creeping is worse than with plain fabrics, but simply because the movement shows up more. Tacking is vital on these problem fabrics and also horizontal pinning ensures no movement. However, the answer is in the dual feed foot. This, as the name implies, has a toothed feed working on the top layer of the fabric as well as on the under layer, so both layers are fed evenly and no creeping occurs. This may be available as an attachment or on some machines, such as the Pfaf 1222, it is a built-in feature of inestimable value.

Obviously tacking can be omitted if dual feed is available (but not if there is fitting to do) but it can also be left out at other times provided care is taken.

### When not to tack

Tacking is omitted in the following instances. If you are joining long, straight pieces of fabric, perhaps joining to make frills or making curtains.

When using a machine accessory such as a hemming foot which makes it not only unnecessary to tack but the foot would not work if you did.

When using an aid such as Wundaweb in a hem where the edge can be pressed, the Wundaweb inserted, the edge pressed again.

When working very short rows of stitching, for instance joining the ends of facings. In these instances it helps to insert a pin horizontally to keep the layers level.

When edge-stitching the fabric edge can be pressed well first before machining. Remember that if the decorative stitching is to be anywhere other than right on the edge, tacking will be needed or the fabric layers will move and the result will be a wrinkled edge.

### Tacking by hand

Use a larger needle than for permanent hand sewing; no. 5 for heavy fabrics and no. 6 for fine ones. Thread with tacking thread, putting a knot in the end.

Tack all long seams with the work flat on the table; only shaped pieces should be lifted for tacking. Place one piece of fabric right side up with the raw edge towards you and the other, on top right side down. Ease the top piece into position by lifting and jerking rather than by pulling. It may be necessary with clinging fabrics to lift and flap the whole piece several times settling the raw edge down in position first and allowing the remainder of the piece to fall where it will. There must be no pulling or wrinkling or distortion of grain at these edges.

Match up the seam lines carefully and begin to tack. There should be no need to pin except where patterns are to be matched.

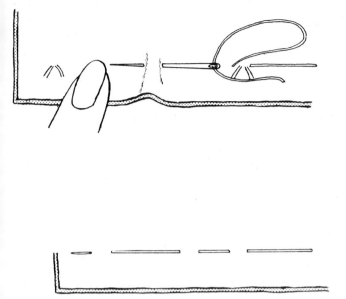

Pick up a small amount, about 6 mm ($\frac{1}{4}$ in.), on the needle, easing the fabric onto the needle with the forefinger of your other hand. The size of the stitch left on the surface should vary according to the position and whether it has to take the strain of fitting.

For example, if tacking up long seams the stitches can be 5 cm (2 in.) long, but shoulder and bodice seams should be no bigger than 1.3 cm ($\frac{1}{2}$in.), and the same on sleeves and on trousers. You can work uneven tacking, which is a compromise between small and large stitches, taking alternately one large and one small. Whatever the size of the surface stitch, never pick up more than 6 mm ($\frac{1}{4}$ in.) on your needle as this is what holds the two layers together.

Fasten off your thread with two back stitches but do not pull the thread tight at this point.

(See also seams of various types.)

### Tacking by machine

Modern machines can be adjusted quickly to tack or baste. A needle with a higher eye than normal is used; adjust the stitch length to medium or large, depending on the fabric. Use sewing thread. Pin the seam first, placing pins across the seam, stitching right up to them before removing.

Use machine tacking for long seams, particularly where you have several to sew. Take extra care on shaped seams. Machine tacking is also very useful where you simply want to see the effect of an idea before you begin to construct it, and also for making up basic patterns in calico, sheeting or Vilene ready for fitting.

### Removing tacking

Snip the back stitch at the end, take hold of the knot at the other end and pull. The thread should come out easily. If it is held by machine stitches anywhere the tacking thread will simply break and will not harm the fabric or the machining. If stitches need removing individually, use a bone or plastic bodkin specially made for this purpose, never the points of scissors.

Tacking threads that pull out in one unbroken length can be re-used.

Remove machine tacking by taking hold of the end of the under spool thread and ease out.

## TAILOR TACKER

There are various tools which purport to make tailor tacking less of a chore. However, some are so complicated to set up and if thread has to be wound it takes time. In addition a sheet of foam or at least the arm of a settee is required but probably the greatest point against them is that they all need a long, sharp needle on them making it a very dangerous-looking tool to have around. If people dislike tailor tacking so much they will probably dislike other forms of hand sewing even more. However, those that use them find they work successfully.

## TAILOR TACKING

The method of transferring any necessary marks to the fabric, usually after cutting out. Both layers of fabric are marked together so it is very accurate and it is quick to do. It is the most satisfactory method of marking because the tacks are easily removed and the fabric is not harmed.

### By hand

Use a larger needle than for normal hand sewing and always use tacking cotton, for example Atlas. When marking very fine fabrics use fine tacking thread; Anchor Machine Embroidery thread is more suitable.

If you have already placed pins in position correctly for cutting out, they are not in the way now that you come to tailor tack, so fold back the pattern on the fitting line and crease firmly. Snip any curves so that it will lie flat. If your pattern is made of Vilene or is pressed on to Vilene, you may have to anchor the corners with a pin. To fold back darts, cut the pattern along one side of the dart. Alternatively, it is more satisfactory to cut off the turnings altogether, and then you can tailor tack much more easily. If you do this remember to write in large letters on each piece that turnings must be allowed every time the pattern is used. It is also easy to tailor tack if you are using a pattern which has no seam allowance.

Thread your needle, no. 5 or 6 Between, with a

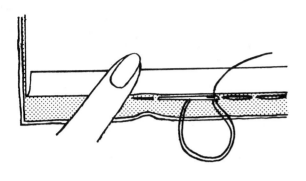

When making darts, you will find it helpful to make one tack right at the point as well as two or three down each side.

Work all round each piece in this way and then, if there are other marks within the pattern that you need, such as centre front line if there is an overlap, fold the pattern back again to this new line and mark it.

At balance marks and other indications such as the depth of the neck slit, position of sleeve opening, sleeve head or zip, make one tailor tack at right angles to the seam line.

Remove the pattern pieces. Snip all the loops of thread. Sit down so that your eye level is lower and carefully part the layers of fabric, snipping each thread as soon as you can see enough of it to do so. Use the points of very sharp scissors.

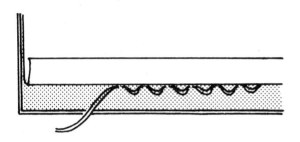

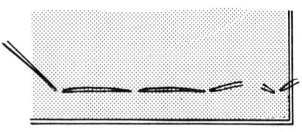

long piece of tacking thread and pull it through double but do not make a knot. Never use ordinary sewing thread for this because the tufts will slip out as you handle the garment. Tacking thread is soft and furry and the pieces will remain in the fabric. Also, it doesn't work to use single thread, the two pieces anchored in the same place will stay firmly in place.

Place the work with raw edges towards you and stitch as close as possible to the edge of the pattern. Take up the smallest amount of fabric that you can, on the needle, helping it on with the forefinger of your other hand, and without lifting the edge of the fabric. Leave stitches on the surface about 2.5 cm (1 in.) long although on long straight seams they can be longer. At the end of the thread simply cut and leave the ends.

On sections where you might need closer marks to guide you, take smaller stitches but leave a small loop of thread on the surface.

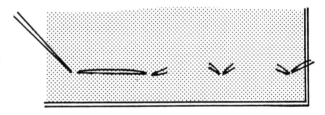

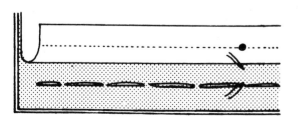

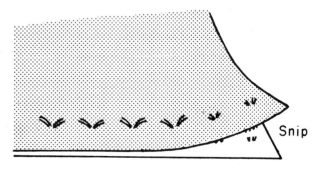

Separate the layers and you can see that the exact shape of the pattern is marked on both pieces and on both sides. However carefully you did the cutting out you can also see that it is vital to transfer these markings for the sake of accuracy. When tailor tacking, a number of long, straight edge marks are not needed very close together, so make short tufts as follows.

Take the first stitch and then two or three more, some distance apart. Pass the needle to the other hand and pick up medium-sized scissors, pull thread slightly taut and cut thread at first stitch on surface, close to where it emerges. Pull thread right through to leave a short end starting the next stitch; cut thread, pull through, cut thread and so on. Work only three or four stitches at a time.

Tailor tacks will not fall out when worked as described but if they do then one of the following things is wrong:
1    Stitches on surface too long, therefore long threads left trailing after snipping; fingers, scissors, etc., catch them and pull them out.
2    Not using correct tacking thread; sewing threads are smooth and shiny and will slip out.
3    Taking too much fabric up on needle so making a wide U stitch which is loose instead of a tight V.
4    Using too big a needle. Needle makes a big hole which thread does not fill and so it falls out.

**By machine**
Most modern machines have a special foot that can be attached so that as you sew loops of thread are made. Use tacking thread on the machine and then set up the stitch according to the instructions in your sewing machine book.

Stitch carefully to ensure that the layers of fabric remain level. Snip the loops between the two layers of fabric.

It is a useful method of marking if there are a lot of pieces or a number of articles to be marked.

## TAILOR'S CHALK

A soft, non-waxy chalk used for marking fabric. It can be bought as square or triangular pieces and also in a plastic container which has a sharpening blade on it. The pieces without a container are more accurate to use as you have a clear view of the marks you are making. Sharpen it frequently by opening out medium or large scissors and shaving both sides of each edge. Hold the chalk so that you use the entire edge of the piece, don't hold it like a pencil using the corner as a point or it will wrinkle the fabric.

Chalk is used for short marks, indicating balance marks, buttonholes, etc; for marking pairs of darts, etc., that must be of equal length; in conjunction with a ruler to provide long, straight lines on which to machine and also for marking fitting alterations.

Make the marks on whichever side of the fabric is necessary.

Use only white chalk as it brushes off easily, and the colours can leave permanent marks on some fabrics. Chalk may be slightly more difficult to remove if you have damp pressed the fabric.

A quick way of transferring marks from a pattern or alteration to both layers is to make the chalk mark on one piece of the fabric, right or wrong side, place the corresponding piece of fabric against it and bang sharply. The mark will now be on both pieces of fabric.

Chalk is only a temporary method of marking, easily removed accidentally while handling the garment and it isn't always very clearly visible on some fabrics. However, it is quick and very accurate.
(See also *Tailor Tacking*.)

## TAILOR'S SOAP

A hard, dry, yellow soap (available in blocks), tailor's soap is rubbed dry on the wrong side of the cloth under seam turnings, pleat and trouser creases, before pressing, to achieve a crisper finish.

## TAILORED COLLAR AND REVER

A term sometimes used by dressmakers to describe the handling involved in shaping and hand-sewing the classic collar and lapel of a coat.

## TAILORED LAPELS

If a coat is interfaced with canvas, a length of stay tape should be placed along the roll line, on top of the canvas.

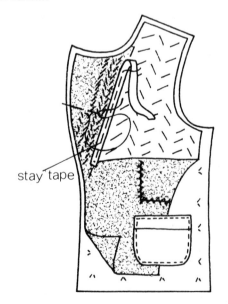

stay tape

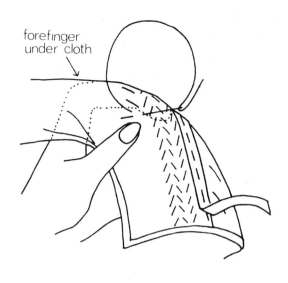

forefinger
under cloth

Cut a length of tape as a bridle at least 10 cm longer than needed. The end is later stitched round the roll of the collar. Attach the bridle: hold it firmly, and baste, then hem down each side.

Fold the lapel on the roll line and work pad stitch in the lapel, moving from the bridle to the outer edge of the lapel. If you hold it properly, the lapel will automatically curl correctly.

## TAPE

Made of soft cotton and loosely woven, tape can be used for reinforcing but it quickly comes apart if cut. Wash it before use to shrink it. Do not use in clothes where it might be seen. Use seam binding instead.

(See also *Stay Tape*.)

## TAPE MEASURE

All tape measures are now marked in centimetres but it is necessary to be able to measure in inches as well. The tape that is quickest to use and read has inches

on one side and centimetres on the other, the latter preferably marked off clearly every 10 centimetres, possibly in colours. A tape should have metal ends and be made of fibreglass for durability and accuracy.

Always use a tape when measuring shapes, e.g. seams and lengths of existing garments, but use a ruler for flat measuring on a table.

## TAPER

To reduce width gradually but still achieve a good fit. The term is most often applied to trouser leg width, skirt width, sleeve width, collar width, etc. Good tapering involves a small amount over as long a distance as possible without visible angles.

## TENT

A dress or coat with sloping side seams, falling from a fitted neck and shoulders. Useful for concealing figure faults and for accommodating a pregnancy, but it is so loose that it is not particularly comfortable.

A pattern with straight sides may have extra sloping width added to cope with the pear-shaped figure but there is always a danger of finishing up with an unwanted tent shape.

## TEXTURE

The word describes the look or feel of fabric. It should be prefixed by a descriptive word such as rough, smooth or shiny.

## THIGHS

Thighs become a problem area only if they are either too big or too small compared with the hips. In making skirts allowance should be made for big thighs when choosing a suitable style and when cutting out. Very thin thighs are not such a problem although it is best to choose a style that will conceal them.

When making trousers the leg seams must be adjusted to the size of the thighs but again without emphasis. This is best done by not making the trousers too tight at thigh level especially if the pads at the inner part of the legs exist as well as outer ones — a common problem with women.

## THIMBLE

The best thimble to use is one made of steel and with an open end. The correct way of sewing, with fingers rather clenched and with the side of the thimble on the needle, means that a top is not used anyway. The advantage of this type of thimble, the type used by tailors and all professional sewers, is that the finger is ventilated and is therefore comfortable for long periods of sewing. Note that if the wrong sort of

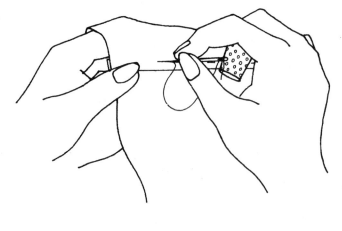

garment lift the thread on the underside and tug at it sharply to pull through the top thread. Both ends should then be threaded into a needle and fastened off with two back stitches. Tying thread ends in a knot is not a good idea as it causes a lump and will also pucker the last stitch of the machining.

All thread ends should be cut off very close to the surface using the points of small sharp scissors, or thread snips. When machining get into the habit of snipping these ends immediately the stitching is done. This is not only for the sake of neatness but it removes the possibility of catching the thread ends and breaking them or at least wrinkling the row of stitching.

## THREAD LOCKS

Small, coloured plastic discs that fit into the end of a reel of thread. The cut end of thread can be wound around between the reel and the disc to stop it becoming unwound in storage. This disc need not be removed when the thread is used.

## THREAD LOOPS

These are used to slip over a button where it is inconvenient or unsuitable to make a buttonhole. It is not a strong fastening, nor even a stable one but it can be used to fasten edge-to-edge openings such as those used on children's and baby clothes, nightwear or neck openings. Usually only one loop and button is used but it can be more.

Use double thread, lightly waxed to prevent it from parting, knot the end and take a stitch through

needle is used for hand sewing this thimble cannot be used properly because the needle is too long. The correct needle is a Between, a short needle.

Anyone who finds a closed thimble uncomfortable should change to the one with an open top and will be converted immediately. The result of this added comfort will be a more relaxed approach to hand sewing, greater enjoyment and smaller, more even stitches.

Thimbles with tops can be used for embroidery because the needle is longer and it is often released in the course of making a stitch. Many thimbles are decorative and not constructed for hard wear. Another disadvantage of using them for good hand sewing is that the top extends far beyond the tip of the finger, old ones are even longer than modern ones, and this long empty top impedes sewing and generally gets in the way.

## THREAD ENDS

When hand sewing, ends of thread should be fastened off with two or more small back stitches placed on the wrong side of the garment out of sight. When machining reverse for two stitches at the end of a seam. If the machining is on the outside of the

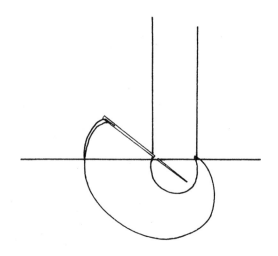

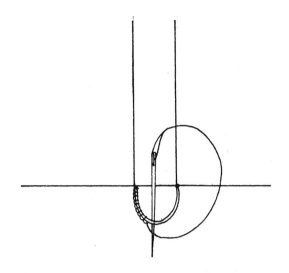

All pins should be well away from the edge of the pattern. Fold back the seam allowances, snipping the paper at curves so that it lies flat. Using a small needle and tacking thread (machine embroidery thread for very delicate silks) work small tacking stitching through the fabric by the edge of the paper. Do not use knots or fastening off stitches, leave ends of thread.

## THREAD SNIPS

A small tool with two short, sharp blades. The handle is held and the blades closed to snip threads. A useful tool for those with manipulative problems.

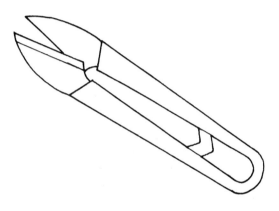

the edge of the opening equal in length to the diameter of the button. Take another stitch back in the opposite direction so that the needle emerges beside the knot. Cut off the knot. Continue to make stitches but working round in the same direction, making the first loop of thread big enough to pass over the button, then check the size again when the second one is added. After four loops stop and complete it in the same way as for a worked loop for a hook, by working close loop stitch over the threads. To do this turn the work round so that the needle is always coming towards you under the loop, working from left to right. Fasten off the thread by taking two or three stitches into the double fabric. Close the opening, pinning the loop flat into position, then sew the button in the loop at the farthest possible point from the opening or the edges will move in wear.

A dome shaped button often stays fastened more easily than a flat one although these would not be used on baby clothes. If the fastening is on the front of a garment is looks better to attach another button on the other side to correspond.

If more than one loop is required, for example on a pair of cuffs, it will help to find something of the correct diameter, such as a pencil, to insert in order to check the size when making the first threads.

## THREAD MARKING

A method of marking seam allowances after cutting out. Only one layer of fabric is marked and the method may be used where fabric has been cut singly, where close marks are needed for extreme accuracy in shape, or where a very soft, slippery fabric is being sewn.

## THREADING A NEEDLE

Like most of the manipulative processes of sewing there are tips which make this essential task less frustrating. If a sight problem exists then a larger needle may be used although as a general rule the needle must be correct for the thickness of thread. There are needle threaders but they work only in large-eyed needles where you probably don't need help anyway.

Pull the thread from the reel, get used to pulling exactly the length you need: long for tacking, short for hand sewing, double the necessary length for double thread. Then, if using tacking thread break it. Cotton and mercerised threads can be bitten off, but cut synthetic threads. The advantage of biting off a thread is that the end is taken out of your mouth, flattening the thread between your teeth, and threaded straight through the eye of the needle. If you cut the thread off put that end in your mouth to moisten and flatten it. Hold the needle in one hand, letting that hand, or at least the elbow, rest, to steady it, then hold the thread very close to the end and thread it through the eye, but rest that hand against the other one to steady it. Finally, if you still find it difficult, hold it against a plain, light background.

## THREADS FOR SEWING

Threads for constructing clothes have been developed alongside the new machinery they are used with. For instance, with the introduction of synthetic fabrics, there came synthetic thread.

Traditionally tailors have used different threads for hand sewing from the machine twist used on the machine, but the home dressmaker demands on thread for the whole garment; a thread that will machine the seams, do the neatening, and also be right for hand sewing, buttonholes and attaching buttons. Sometimes on some fabrics it is advisable to use another thread for a particular purpose, but in the main satisfactory results are achieved on most articles with one type.

### Types of thread

*Polyester*    This is very strong, very fine, has 'give' and beds down well into all types of fabric, whatever their composition. Excellent for jersey and stretch fabrics. Available in a very wide range of colours an example of this type of thread is Drima.

*Mercerised cotton*    Mercerised cotton is available in a wide range of colours; suitable for hand sewing and machining but not as strong as synthetic thread. It should not be used in wholly synthetic fibres as it may be too weak. Also if used on knit fabrics seams may split under strain. Generally available in size 40 which denotes the thickness but is also made in a finer weight which is nice for hand sewing on delicate fabrics, baby clothes etc.

*Cotton*    This is a dull thread used mainly for household sewing, not for clothes. Available in thicker types than mercerised threads.

*Silk*    Pure silk thread can be used on silk fabrics. It is not widely available.

### Special purpose threads

*Button thread*    A thick, strong, shiny thread for hand sewing. Use it for sewing buttons on heavy fabrics used in coats and jackets, and for repairs to thick fabrics. Heavy duty thread can be used for the same purpose on coats.

*Buttonhole twist*    A thick thread for hand-worked buttonholes on heavy fabric. It can also be used for top stitching. It may be of silk of polyester.

*Top-stitching thread*    A thicker thread called Bold that can be used for buttonholes but is mainly for top-stitching work.

*Machine embroidery thread*    Anchor for instance can be successfully used on very fine fabrics provided no direct strain is put on it, as on french seams in a Christening robe. It is also used for tacking on fine fabrics. It is available in two thicknesses, 30 and 50, the finer one normally being used for construction, both being used for machine embroidery.

*Tacking cotton*    A soft cotton thread for temporary stitching. Only in white and black (the latter may leave traces on pale fabrics). It is on large reels and should always be used for tacking as it easily slides into and out of fabric, without harming it. It can be broken with the fingers without the inconvenience of picking up scissors to cut it. It is slightly hairy which means it wedges nicely into fabric for tailor tacking etc. Long lengths removed from seams can be re-used.

## TOILE

An experimental pattern, made in muslin or unbleached cotton. The pattern is made by draping a dummy and cutting the fabric to shape. This is then used as the pattern for cutting in fabric.

## TOP COLLAR

The outer, visible, layer of a fold-over collar when it is in its correct position. When cutting out a collar in any medium or heavy weight fabric the top collar should be cut larger than the under collar. The extra fabric will enable the join round the collar edge to be concealed by rolling it underneath a little.

## TOP STITCHING BY MACHINE

A decorative stitch, larger than used in the construction processes, worked in a matching or contrasting colour. Use it for emphasis at yokes, seams, edges, etc. Whenever feasible use the machine foot as a guide or attach the measuring bar for wider spacing. Tacking as a marker will get in the way and it takes so long to put in evenly that it is hardly worth it. A chalk line drawn with sharp chalk and a ruler is satisfactory but the line will wobble on uneven numbers of layers or near a finished edge.

It is easier to keep it even if worked through only two layers of fabric and not as on a seam by pressing both seam turnings to one side, and therefore stitching through three layers. The more layers of fabric there are, the more inclined the machining will be to wobble or look uneven, so where possible work the top stitching early on in the construction of the garment. If you want a raised effect place a crossway strip of lawn or a length of bias binding on the wrong side under the seam turning.

Insert a number 110 (18) machine needle and thread the top of the machine with a top stitching thread (such as Drima Bold); use a normal thread underneath. Set the machine to a fairly large stitch or one that looks correct on your fabric. Stitch from the right side using the edge or groove in the foot as a guide. Pivot carefully at the corners, and when going round curves turn the wheel of the machine by hand to proceed stitch by stitch.

In places where you have no choice but to work the top stitching last, for example round a collar or front edges, remember that it is very important to trim the turnings right down within the edge to reduce the number of layers you stitch through.

Top stitching can also be worked effectively on modern machines by using two reels of normal thread on the top of the machine (one on each spindle) and then have both threads following the same path to the needle. Use the spool below in the usual way. Machine from the right side with a long stitch.

It is also very effective to use the double needle on the machine and work two close rows of top stitching at once. Use two reels of normal sewing thread on the top of the machine. With all the above make the stitch shorter if any problems arise with thread twisting or breaking.

## TRACING WHEEL

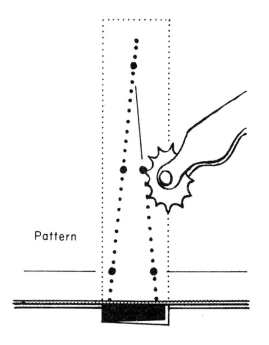

Pattern

A small wheel with handle attached. When pressed on carbon paper with fabric beneath pattern markings and seam lines are transferred to the fabric. Some have a very short handle which is uncomfortable to hold as a fair amount of pressure is exerted. Some have a shaped area for the thumb to rest on, which is fine if the handle is held in a particular way.

The most effective wheel is one that is smooth and therefore transfers an unbroken line to the fabric. The dots produced by a toothed wheel can sometimes be difficult to see. The smooth wheel does not harm the table beneath as much as the toothed wheel.

## TRAILING STITCH

(See *Overcast Stitch*.)

## TRELLIS COUCHING

An open embroidery filling stitch also used in jacobean work. The basic trellis is formed by laid threads either horizontal and vertical, or diagonal. These threads are then held by a couching stitch where they cross, usually a small slanting stitch in a matching or contrasting thread.

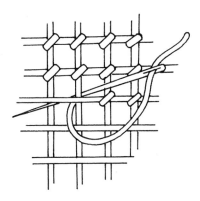

## TRIMMERS

(See *Scissors*.)

## TRIMMING

This word is used in two ways. First it describes any braid, lace, etc., that is used to decorate, and secondly it refers to cutting away excess fabric inside a garment to reduce bulk, prevent a ridge or lump appearing. Also fraying threads should be trimmed before neatening.

## TRIMS

Metal button caps to be covered with fabric, and a metal disc to snap on to the back. Instructions for use are included in the pack and so is a pattern showing exactly what size the circle of fabric should be. Various sizes and shapes are available. Best results are achieved by inserting a gathering thread round the outside of the fabric circles, to pull it up evenly. In transparent fabrics use the fabric double.

## TROUSER CREASES

Apart from correct fit the only other important point in making trousers is pressing in the creases properly. Heat, moisture, steam and pressure will be needed as well as plenty of time. (See *Pressing*, for details of pressing various fabrics.)

Tack and fit one trouser leg as a guide, altering it if necessary (see *Trouser Fitting*, page 121) and altering the other leg to correspond. Stitch, press and neaten the outside and inside leg seams.

Press in the creases before joining the legs together. Even at the next fitting stage the trousers will look better with creases already in. Press them on a table or flat work top, as an ironing board is not wide enough to press legs in one operation. Take care to cover the table with a blanket or cloth to avoid damage to the surface and prevent marks on the trousers.

Arrange one trouser leg on the table with the hem to the right and the inside leg seam uppermost. Move this seam slightly towards the front of the trouser, about 2 cm ($\frac{3}{4}$ in.) so that the inside and outside leg seams are not on top of each other but running parallel this distance apart up to the crutch. Smooth out the fabric so that the leg is lying flat. Arrange the front crease position.

Begin pressing at the hem on the front crease. Use a hot iron and a damp cloth to press in the crease from the hem, up the leg, for about two lengths of the iron, pressing across the leg from front to back — the crease will find its own position at the back. (For the sake of clarity, the damp muslin is not shown under the iron in the illustration.) Remove the cloth and bang in the steam with a pressing block.

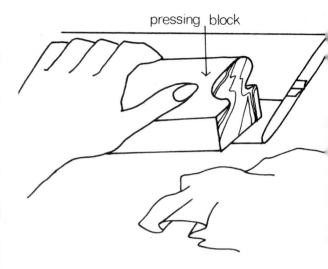

pressing block

Retrurn to the front crease and press another section, then press across the leg to form the back crease. Continue in this way until you are within about 15 cm (6 in.) of the trouser fork or crutch area. From that point there is fullness across the inside leg area, so you cannot press across the leg. Continue pressing the front crease right up to the waist.

On men's trousers the crease runs into the front pleat. On women's trousers the crease runs to a point about 6 cm ($2\frac{3}{8}$ in.) from the centre front, but not necessarily to meet any front dart. The dart may be moved or even removed at fitting, but the crease must still be in its correct position. If there is a pleat at the front the crease must meet it.

Next return to the back crease and complete it. This one must finish exactly at the centre back. You will find that you will have to rearrange and manipulate the trouser in order to achieve this. Turn the leg over and press the lower leg section again. Examine the leg, pressing the seams if necessary and making sure there are no press-marks. Remember that you will not be able to press the garment quite like this again.

## TROUSER CURTAIN

The curtain is the extra piece of lining or silesia extending below the waistband of men's trousers to cover the join and prevent stretching. When a commercial banding is being used it will usually have a wide edge of lining to form the curtain.

## TROUSER HOOKS AND BARS

These are large, flat metal hooks used to fasten the waistband of trousers. The method described below

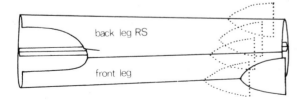

back leg RS

front leg

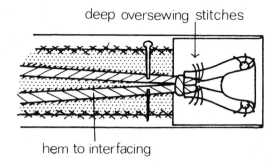

deep oversewing stitches

hem to interfacing

To attach the bar, insert a stiletto into the cloth, and slip each end of the bar through. Tie a length of stay tape to each end of the bar and pin down. Oversew each eye of the bar with plenty of strong oversewing stitches. Draw all ends of the tape together at the base, and hem down all tape edges to the interfacing.

Complete the hook end by cutting a piece of silesia, turning in one end and the top edge, and sliding it under the hook. Baste. Turn in the third side and baste. Hem to the waistband. This piece of silesia should cover the extension only and overlap the faced edge by 3 cm ($1\frac{1}{4}$ in.). Oversew the raw edge to the waistband.

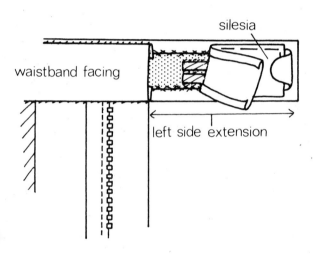

waistband facing

silesia

left side extension

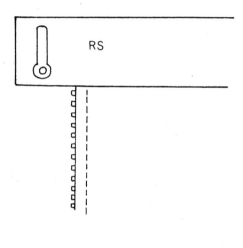

RS

is very strong and durable — the correct method for men's trousers. However, the same hooks can be used on women's waistbands, attaching by working close buttonhole stitch round each hole, and round the holes of the bar.

Establish the exact position for a good fit with one or two hooks and bars. Insert the hook at the end of the extension on the left side. First turn in the end of the band and stitch down firmly. Press. Slip a 5 cm (2 in.) length of stay tape into the end of the hook and knot like a label on a suitcase. Place the hook in position, and pin the tape at the base of the hook. Sew through the two top eyes of the hook using double waxed thread and plenty of deep oversewing stitches. Sew the base of the hook in the same way, then hem all the edges of the ends of the tape firmly to the interfacing.

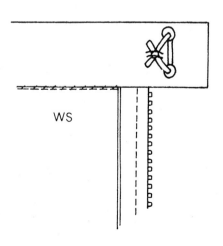

WS

If a second hook is required insert it under the edge of the fly facing, after the left side of the zip has been stitched. This hook will be covered by the waistband backing, which can be of lining or a commercial non-slip variety.

Establish the position of the bar by fastening the hook into it and then wrapping the waistband into the closed position, fastening the zip if there is one. Mark the exact position of the bar ends with dots of chalk. Unfasten the hook, make small holes in the band with a stiletto and force the bar ends through. On the wrong side thread a piece of stay tape through the holes and tie the ends. Trim ends then oversew the centre of the tape firmly to the back of the back, stitching into the interfacing.

On women's clothes the tape may not be necessary, instead work buttonhole stitch round each end of the bar.

## TROUSER POCKETING

This is a strong fabric made in various weights in anything from cotton to nylon for use only in trousers.

## TRUMPET SLEEVE

A sleeve that has a normal fitted sleeve head but from the elbow level flares until at the wrist it is quite wide. The fullness may be introduced into the pattern evenly all round, or it may be added at the seam edges only so that the wide sleeve hangs under the wrist. An effective style in soft fabrics, the sleeve may be double, using different colours; the fabric may be permanently pleated.

## TUBING

(See *Rouleau*.)

## TUCKS

A tuck is a fold of fabric, even in width and usually stitched, appearing as a flat pleat on the right side of the fabric. The width varies from about 1 to 2 mm ($\frac{1}{16}$ in.) upwards, depending on the type of fabric, the amount of fabric available, the type and style of the garment and the effect required.

Tucks can be used singly or there may be several. If an entire section of a garment such as a yoke is to be tucked, the safest thing is to work the tucks on a piece of fabric before laying on the pattern ready to cut out. This ensures that the cut edges are neat and correctly shaped but also it is very difficult to assess how much the actual stitching of the tucks will draw up the fabric. This procedure should also be followed if tucks are being added where they are not allowed for on the pattern, and where tucks that are on the pattern are being altered in width.

Most fabrics can be tucked successfully but it is as well to try them out on spare fabric because sometimes they work well in the warp direction but not on the weft. Also some fabrics such as jersey may need interfacing first. Work tucks of all types in the same direction on the fabric.

### Flat tucks

These may be as narrow as 5 mm ($\frac{1}{4}$ in.) on fine fabrics made into blouses, baby clothes etc. Much wider tucks would be made as a style feature on dresses and jackets. They may be vertical or horizontal. Horizontal flat tucks above a hemline on a child's dress provide an easy method of lengthening as the child grows.

Mark a line on the outside of the fabric representing the folded edge of the tuck. This will often be on the straight grain of the fabric. Do this with tailor's chalk or with tacking. If the width of the tuck has been predetermined, also mark a line showing the width of the tuck. Fold, wrong sides together, and press the fold carefully. Tack on the line marking the width. If there is no line for this, decide on the width and set an adjustable marker or cut a cardboard marker and tack. Decide which way the tucks will be pressed and machine, with a suitable size of stitch, with that side up. Remove tackings and press the tuck flat. Begin by pressing the stitching then push the tuck to one side, finally press on the wrong side.

Mark the position of the centre fold of the next tuck, using a marker and measuring from the completed tuck. Fold the fabric and press, tack the second tuck using a marker, and stitch and press it. Continue in this way until all are complete.

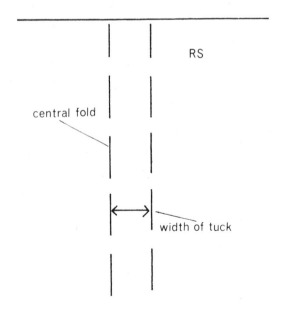

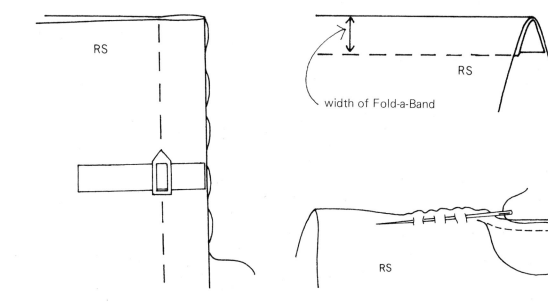

width of Fold-a-Band

Note that although a pattern will indicate the width and position of all tucks it is only necessary to mark the first one and then measure the appropriate distances after that directly onto the fabric.

Fold-a-Band inserted in flat tucks on many weights of fabric produces excellent results. It not only interfaces the fold but provides a crisp edge. It is worth adjusting the width of tucks indicated on a paper pattern in order to include Fold-a-Band which is produced in a standard width. To use it, mark the

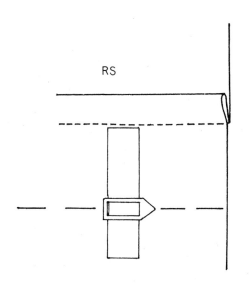

fold line of the tucks on the wrong side of the fabric; this may be a chalk line. Place Fold-a-Band on top, lining up the central perforations over the mark and press in place. Fold the fabric and press. Tack just off the edge of the Fold-a-Band, either feeling it as you tack, or if this is not possible, using a marker.

When narrow tucks are made it is often possible to press a fold on the straight grain of the fabric and, without tacking, machine it, using either the edge of the machine foot as a guide, or one of the lines on the needle plate of the machine. As with wider tucks, press each one before proceeding to the next.

If small tucks are stitched by hand use a running or fly-running stitch and again, it should be possible to simply press a fold and then stitch parallel with the edge but this time following the grain to keep straight.

Decorative flat tucks can be made on transparent fabrics using the double needle with spear which is for hemstitching. Fold and press the fabric as before and machine parallel with the fold.

### Pin tucks

These are tucks that are so narrow they cannot be pressed to one side and so they stand up. No marking of the fabric is necessary but press the first fold. Stitch very close to the fold, the width of a pin from the fold, either by machine or using running stitch. Work all tucks and then press each one still folded. Press the entire area from the wrong side.

Pin tucks are most effective when a number of them are used or when a large area is covered. They should be very close together, or, they can look effective when combined with other fine decoration such as embroidery or lace insertion eyeletting.

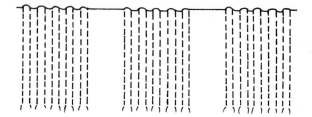

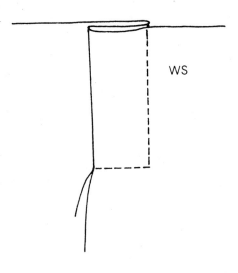

WS

Machine pin tucks can be made using the twin needle and the grooved foot. Do not mark the fabric but take care to do the first row of stitching exactly on the straight grain. This tuck then fits into the first groove in the foot and this guides the second one.

With all pin tucks to be worked in groups it is best to make and press the tucks before cutting out that part of the garment.

### Released tucks

These are often used as decoration and fullness combined and are usually shaped. They may be used on blouses, skirts, maternity clothes and children's clothes. If the folds of fabric are wide the tucks are often made the opposite way from usual, the fold being kept to the wrong side of the garment.

Mark the centre of the tuck and also one side. Fold and press, tack and machine, fastening off the thread securely and neatly. If stitched on the wrong side the machining may be taken out to the fold.

### Shell tucks

A fancy decoration for fine fabrics. The width of the tuck is restricted by the stitch. Fold and press the fabric and either machine with one of the stitches that will form a zig-zag over the fold, or work shell stitch using a running stitch between the over stitches.

## TULIP

This term usually describes a skirt but also sometimes a sleeve, that is narrower at the hem than at the top. The effect is achieved by pleating or gathering fullness at the top and sometimes also incorporating a shaped wrap-over effect.

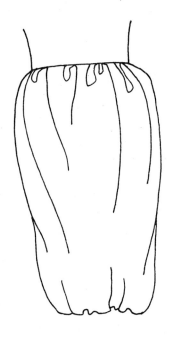

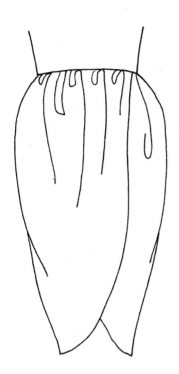

A tulip effect can be created on any straight skirt made from soft jersey by fluting the hem and stretching it so much while stitching that it draws in the hem width.

## TUNIC

A hip- or thigh-length garment without sleeves, often without a collar, and fastened with an open-ended zip or buttons. Worn with a skirt or trousers or over a dress. A very useful garment for adding warmth and often included in 'layered' outfits.

## TURTLE NECK

A stand or rolled-over collar attached to a slightly lowered or widened neckline. The collar stands up but away from the neck.

## TWISTED CHAIN STITCH

An embroidery stitch worked as for chain stitch but the thread crosses at the top of each loop. A stitch is taken just to the left of the previous loop, and not to the right as in chain stitch. The loop is completed in the same way, with a stitch taken under the fabric along the outline to be followed.

(See *Chain Stitch*.)

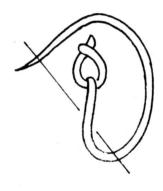

# u

## UNDERCOLLAR

The piece of collar that is attached first to the garment neckline. In a shirt or coat collar it rises then falls and the top collar lies over it. If the collar is of the stand variety and does not fold, the undercollar is still the piece attached to the garment neckline but it becomes the piece that is visible in wear. The undercollar is the piece that must have interfacing attached to it.

In collars that fold over or roll it helps to make the undercollar slightly smaller than the top collar, to ensure that the outer join is not visible. If two pattern pieces are provided it means they have been cut different sizes and can be used as they are. If only one pattern piece is provided, cut out in the usual way but trim 2 to 3 mm ($\frac{1}{8}$ in.) (depending on the thickness of the fabric) from the outer edge of one piece. This will be the under collar.

In stand up collars both pieces are the same size to start with, but adjusted later to prevent the outer seam being visible.

(See also *Collars* for methods of attaching.)

## UNDERLINING

This is a term describing the process of placing all cut pieces of a garment on to another material before making up. It is a slightly misleading term because lining materials are not usually suitable. The process is better known as mounting or backing, and it may be employed to give shape, stability, longer wear or additional warmth and the backing fabric is selected accordingly.

(See *Mounting*.)

## UNEVEN TACKING

The normal tacking stitch is an even stitch of regular size but some slippery fabrics tend to reject each other and the stitches part, especially under the strain of fitting. If a smaller stitch is taken every now and then it helps to prevent this, yet the tacking takes no longer to do. Work to a thythm of one small stitch to every two, or perhaps three, large ones.

## UNPICKER

Although it is also called a 'seam ripper', its purpose is to cut stitches not fabric. It is a small steel blade on a plastic handle. Use it with great care to cut machine-made buttonholes, putting a pin across its path to prevent it slipping too far. It can be used for its original purpose of unpicking stitching but it should be remembered that it can easily cut fabric too.

The tip of the blade is useful for slipping under machine threads to lift a stitch clear ready for unpicking.

## UNPICKING

On fine fabrics machining can be removed safely only by slipping a pin or the end of an unpicker under each stitch or alternate stitches. Once a short length of thread has been withdrawn, cut it off.

On firmer fabrics loosen the thread at the end of a seam or section to be unpicked, until you can hold it. Hold both fabric and thread very firmly and sharply tug the thread back along the stitching to be undone. The thread will break three or four stitches further on. Turn the work over and pick up the thread end, tug it sharply to break it. Return to the first side and so on.

Occasionally it may be necessary to use scissors and cut between layers of fabric but it should be avoided if possible because many small ends of thread have to be picked out afterwards.

Never use an unpicker or seam ripper except possibly where taking apart an entire garment in order to re-cut it. The risk of the unpicker slipping and splitting the fabric is just as great but it perhaps will not matter so much in this instance.

After unpicking press well until dents and holes disappear.

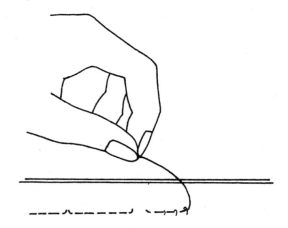

## V-NECK

A neckline shaped at the front or back or both to a V. The neck point is best left in the basic position or the garment is inclined to slip off the shoulders. The depth of the V is governed by the type and position of the bust at the front, although it may be arranged to be lower.

## VANDYKE STITCH

A close looped embroidery stitch worked in any width. The needle is brought to the surface at the outer edge of the area to be worked, then takes a horizontal stitch to the right, a small stitch to the left, and a horizontal stitch to the other outer edge, parallel to where the needle was first brought through. Cross the needle behind the work and bring it through slightly below where it first came out, pass the needle under the crossed threads and insert again just below the stitch on the opposite outer edge.

## VELCRO

This is a trademark made from the words 'Velour' and 'crochet' thus implying hooked velvet. The generic description is usually 'touch and close fastener'. The two other trademarks describing this type of fastener occasionally encountered — Filla-Fix and Scotch-Mate.

Velcro consists of two strips of fabric ranging in width, usually from 15 to 30 mm ($\frac{5}{8}$ to $1\frac{1}{8}$ in.), both components being 100 percent nylon. The strip is covered with hooks and the other with very fine loops. When the two are pressed together the hooks engage in the loops giving a very secure fastening, yet one that can be readily opened by an unpeeling action.

Other slightly similar fasteners of the surface contact type are usually referred to as mushroom fasteners. In these a mushroom shape engages with a loop. The most prominent mushroom fasteners bear the trademark Cric Crac and Brisa.

The hook-and-loop type (Velcro) is suitable for many dressmaking, household and sports applications and has a very long life. The mushroom fasteners are not suitable for clothing applications, in the the main, as the grip is too strong, especially for lightweight fabrics. Moreover, they have a shorter life. Conversely, mushroom fasteners are very suitable for furnishing applications where, inevitably, the number of openings and closings in the life of the product are considerably fewer.

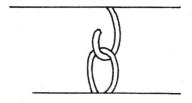

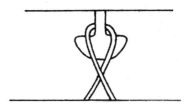

## VELVET BOARD

A piece of thick, slightly pliable, material, usually rectangular or shaped like the top of a sleeve board, which is covered in small vertical steel needles. Its purpose is to prevent the pile of velvet from being flattened when pressed. The velvet is placed pile downwards on the needles for pressing.

The danger in using this aid is that even slight

pressure can press the needles into the backing of the velvet and make holes. These may be visible as spots in wear. The usual method of pressing velvet is much simpler and equally effective.

## VELVET RIBBON

Can readily be called the aristocrat of ribbons. Its quality and wearing qualities have been so improved that it is in much greater use now. It is the advent of nylon which allows a manufacturer to produce qualities that are washable and substantially crush resistant and therefore remain fresh for longer. Velvet ribbons are woven in pairs, one above the other, with the pile between. As weaving progresses a very fast moving knife cuts through the pile revealing the very fine and closely spaced tufts that produce the luxurious surface. The richness of the colour in velvet is due to the depth of the pile which causes a completely different light reflection from that of other fabrics. Usually velvet ribbons can be obtained in widths ranging from 6 to 50 mm ($\frac{1}{4}$ to 2 in.), black being the most popular colour.

## VENT

This is the slit in the back of a jacket. There may be a single one at the centre back, or one in each side-panel seam. Always fit the garment with the vent basted up.

## VICTORIAN

There are still a number of genuine Victorian clothes to be found; the nightwear being probably the only wearable items. Any modern dress referred to as Victorian in style will be one that has at least some of the features associated with that period such as high collars, lace trimming, tight-fitting bodices, full skirts and sleeves.

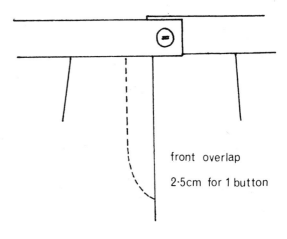

## WADDING

Thick fluffy cotton or blend with a shiny papery surface is used as wadding for shoulder pads and for padding coats out to disguise figure faults. Some wadding can be split to any thickness. Also made from synthetic fibres for quilting, as well as shoulder pads.

front overlap

2·5cm for 1 button

## WAIST FASTENING

The amount of extension for fastening a waistband should be decided according to the type of fastening to be used. The fastening may or may not be visible and the opening, probably a zip, may be at the side or front of a skirt or trousers.

The decision as to whether to arrange the extension as an overlap or underlap also depends largely on the fastening. A long extension is nearly always best as an underlap as it looks unbalanced on the outside. However, if it is to have a decorative fastening it can be an overlap. As a general rule the extension at the side zip should be an underlap unless it is very small and taking only one fastening such as a button. At the front there is some choice. Also the waistband can have some underlap and overlap if the fastening requires a long extension, for example Velcro, and yet it would look unsightly arranged entirely as overlap.

Amounts and positions are shown below.

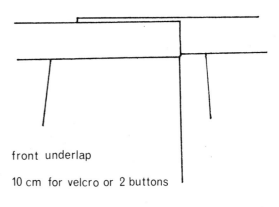

front underlap

10 cm for velcro or 2 buttons

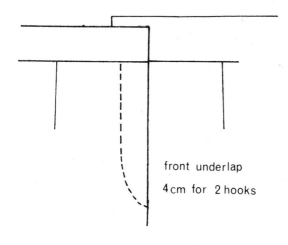

front underlap

4 cm for 2 hooks

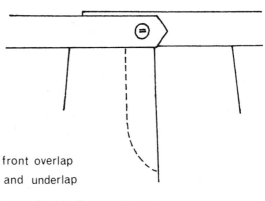

front overlap
and underlap

6 cm for 1 button or 1 hook

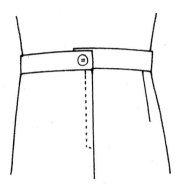

side underlap

2·5 cm  for 1 button

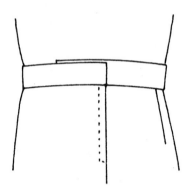

side  underlap

6 cm  for velcro or 2 hooks

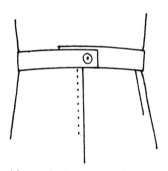

side  underlap or overlap

5 cm  for 1 button or 1 hook or velcro

## WAIST FINISH

The method of completing the waistline of a skirt or trousers. The choice rests between a waistband, straight or curved, consisting of stiffening covered with fabric, or petersham. Conventional petersham may be curved or straight and there is also elastic petersham. For a very soft finish a piece of straight seam binding may be used instead of petersham. Finally a fabric facing may be used although this is usually confined to low-waist or hipster styles, and belt loops are often added to the right side.

The choice of waist finish will depend on the individual figure as well as on the style of the garment.

## WAIST SEAM

Joining a bodice to a skirt is easier if some part of the dress is still open. This may not always be possible but it is worth marking a seam after tacking and fitting and undoing it, in order to make the waist join. If the dress is to have a zip inserted in the side or back leave the skirt seam open; if there is no zip, leave open the centre back seam or a side seam on the bodice and skirt. If none of these is possible leave open the shoulder seams or even, on yoked styles, do not join the yoke to the bodice until after joining the waist. Remember that all fitting should be done, including the waist, before making this join. Mark all necessary fitting lines, centres, etc.

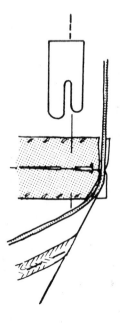

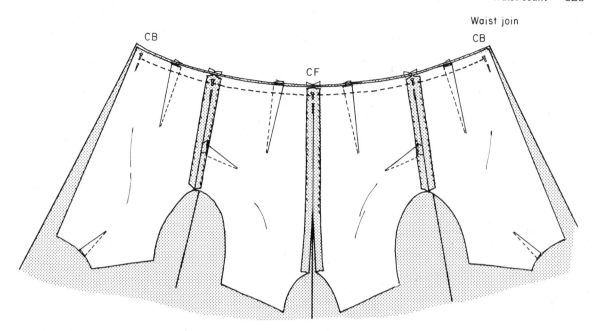

CB  Waist join  CB

CF

### Fitted bodice and skirt

This is probably the most difficult join to make as the bodice and skirt must not only each fit the figure but also fit each other. Mark the fitting line on the bodice and on the skirt. Lay the skirt out right side up and the bodice right side down. Insert pins vertically at the centre front, and back, then at side seams and back, then at side seams and finally at darts. Where seams and darts have to meet insert the pin precisely at the stitching of each. These pins will all be left in while machining. Tack the waist in sections, from centre to side, turn the dress over and tack again from centre to side. Machine with the bodice uppermost. If tackings appear to be tight snip them just in front of the machine foot. Remove pins and tackings.

If the dress is a close fit press both seam allowances up into the bodice and trim and zig-zag them to neaten. With a looser fit trim the seam allowances first then press them open and neaten each edge separately.

### Fitted skirt and gathered bodice

Insert gathering threads at the points to be gathered. Lay skirt out right side up and bodice on top right side down. Match seams and centres and pin. Pull up the gathering threads until the bodice lies flat on the skirt. Begin by tacking the gathered sections then complete the remainder before machining, leaving in the pins holding matching points together. Remove tackings and gathering threads. Trim and neaten both seam allowances together. These should be pressed upwards towards the bodice. If, on springy or bulky fabrics, this is not possible without the ridge being visible on the right side then snip the turnings at each side of the gathered section and allow that part to lie down into the skirt.

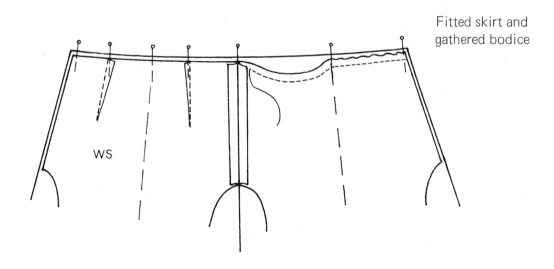

Fitted skirt and gathered bodice

WS

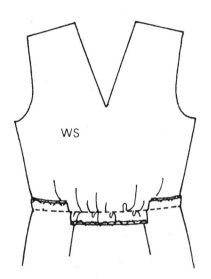

## WAISTBAND JOINS

A waistband often has a seam in it either enforced through economy or to make a shaped waistband. The join must be matched to a garment seam, usually the right side seam but occasionally the back, on trousers that have the zip in the centre front.

Cut the waistband longer than required, but still mark the right size and make the join, attach stiffening and place it to the right side of the garment. Place a pin across the band to hold the two seams together and tack from that point to the end. Machine from just before the pin, over it, to the end. Remove the pin and tack the remaining part of the waistband. Machine it. Complete the waistband. The additional length can be used up at one end if the front of the garment is wider than the back. A corresponding amount will be found to be surplus on reaching the other end.

### Gathered skirt and fitted bodice

Insert gathering threads in the skirt, placing one in front and one across the back. Also mark centres of skirt pieces. Lay the bodice down right side up and place the skirt on top right side down. Match seams and centres and pin. Working on only one section at a time, between the anchor pins, pull up the gathering thread, even out the gathers, insert a few more pins and tack that section. Work on a quarter, or less, of the skirt at a time. Tack close beside the gathering thread with small stitches and fasten off the tacking. Remove the pins in that section and proceed to the next ensuring that there are no ungathered areas where tacking is finished off. Machine with skirt uppermost inserting any matching pins before you start. Machine slowly using the left hand to move the gathered section along to keep the folds at right angles to the raw edges. In the right hand hold a bodkin or small pair of scissors and use the point just in front of the machine foot to flatten and separate the gathers as they disappear. This prevents folds and drags.

Remove the gathering thread, trim both turnings to 4 mm ($\frac{1}{4}$ in.) and neaten together before pressing them upwards into the bodice. If the fabric is bulky or the skirt very full, trim and neaten separately, cutting the skirt to 4 mm ($\frac{1}{4}$ in.) but leaving the bodice turning at full width.

When sewing the waist of jersey fabric, pin and tack the waist join then tack a piece of seam tape over the line of tacking placing it on the underneath. Do not attempt to tack it through both layers but just anchor it to the surface layer. This prevents stretching and as it is underneath it does not obscure your view of the correct line or entail moving the anchor pins.

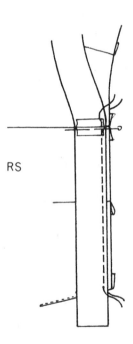

## WAISTBANDING

A commercially produced strip, incorporating a grip of rubber or flocking, used to line the inside of men's trouser waistbands. It is made wide enough to cover the band and also hang below, so eliminating the necessity for added curtain.

(See also *Curtain*.)

# WAISTBANDS

### Curved waistband

Many people find a curved waistband more comfortable to wear than a straight one, because the curve follows the contour of the body as it encircles the waist. In addition if there are fitting problems in the waist area of a skirt or trousers the correct waist level for that figure, often dipped, can easily be found and marked by a curved waistband. The waistband, when worn, will tend to sit lower than a straight one, with the upper, concave, curve at the natural waist while the lower, longer, convex curve spans the start of the hip shape.

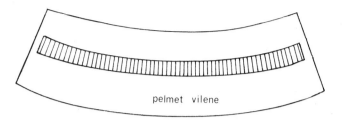

pelmet vilene

using petersham as a guide

Curved petersham provides the shape needed. Occasionally a curved pattern piece will be provided in a pattern but if not proceed as follows.

The curved petersham can be used to stiffen the waistband or, if preferred, it can be used as a template for cutting out stiffening in another material, such as pelment weight Vilene. If a band wider than petersham is required then this method must be used. Remember, when increasing the depth of a curved outline that extending above the concave edge of the petersham in this way makes that edge shorter and therefore a smaller waist size. It is best to outline the new wider shape on the interfacing before measuring off the waist size along it, in order to make sure it is long enough.

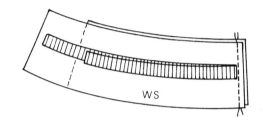

WS

Cut the petersham of interfacing to length, allowing a good overlap for fastening. At least 6 cm ($2\frac{3}{8}$ in.) is needed because on this shape the exact point of strain on the fastening is less defined than with a straight band and therefore the entire length of overlap, or underlap, must be anchored. Use a piece of Velcro cut to length, or use a large book or trouser hook plus another hook, or a press stud on the end underneath. A fastening at one point, such as a button and buttonhole, is not sufficient as the stray end of band beneath will rise and be visible, something that does not happen with a straight waistband.

Establish the length of waistband needed by measuring the figure. (See *Waist Fitting*, page 123.) The curved petersham can be used for this and the size and the overlap marked with chalk. This measuring must be precise. Cut the petersham.

Place the petersham or Vilene on a piece of surplus fabric. If this is medium of lightweight have it double. If it is heavyweight then use one layer of fabric and one layer of a lighter fabric such as lining. Place the petersham on the wrong side and insert a couple of pins. The straight grain of the fabric can be in any direction as the stitching prevents any strain. However, with patterned fabrics such as checks or stripes or others where the grain is noticeable, the fabric must be cut so that the pattern is even. This entails cutting two pieces of curved fabric each with the straight grain at the centre, and joined. This join will

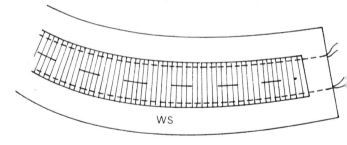

WS

later be matched with either the right side seam or the centre back seam of the garment. The easiest way to cut the fabric is to fold the petersham in half excluding the overlap, and place it on double fabric. The inner or lining piece may still be cut in one piece.

Mark round with tailor's chalk, adding a seam allowance and cut out the fabric. Tack the petersham to one layer of fabric then attach it permanently by working a row of machine stitching inside the edge down both sides. The stitch may be straight, or, it often looks effective to use a more decorative stitch. Re-mark the overlap section.

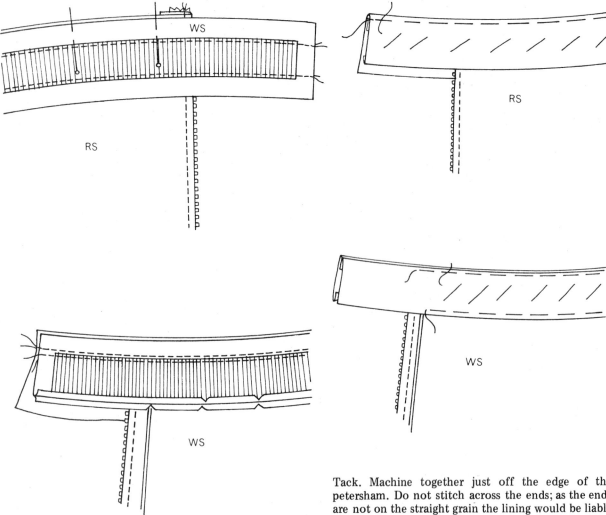

If the skirt or trousers are to be fitted this piece of band can be used tacked to the waist edge. To attach to the garment place it, with the right sides together, matching the garment fitting line to the edge of the petersham and pinning. It is the lower or convex edge that is attached to the skirt and care must be taken that it is attached evenly and the full marked length is used otherwise the waist will be too small. Leave the overlap extending.

Tack the band to the garment and machine just off the edge of the petersham. Snip the turnings at intervals and press the seam open. Trim the turnings to 5 mm ($\frac{1}{4}$ in.).

Attach the inner or lining piece by placing it with the right side against the right side of the waistband.

Tack. Machine together just off the edge of the petersham. Do not stitch across the ends; as the ends are not on the straight grain the lining would be liable to bulge and be visible.

Trim the seam allowances to 3 mm ($\frac{1}{8}$ in.). Do not snip. Press by running the toe of the iron over this join on the right side of the band and pushing the lining over flat. Roll the lining to the inside and tack near the edge. Press. Hold the waistband with the right side outside and allowing the curve to fall over the hand, work a row of tacking down the centre of the band through both layers.

Complete the edges by one of two methods, the first for heavy fabrics, the second for lightweight fabrics.

1    Trim the raw edge of the inner section so that it extends below the waist join by only 5 mm ($\frac{1}{4}$ in.). Neaten this edge. Also neaten the edge of the layer lying flat on the inside of the skirt.

With the inside of the band towards you, tack this edge flat to the skirt, taking care not to allow it to work along out of position as it tends to, due to not being a straight edge. If necessary, tack from the centre along to the end and then return to the centre to tack the other half, in order to keep it flat. Omit the overlap, tacking only where the band is attached to the skirt.

Complete the extension and the end by folding the raw edge of the outer band over the petersham. Tack, trimming the edges afterwards to 3 mm ($\frac{1}{8}$ in.), then press and work herringbone stitch to hold the edges to the petersham. At corners trim away excess bulk before stitching. Remove tacking stitches then turn under the raw edges of the inner piece. Trim them off first then tuck them in so that the edge is 1 mm ($\frac{1}{16}$ in.) back from the waistband edge. Tack. Work slip stitch round the two sides of the overlap and also across the end of the waistband.

Where the skirt edge comes, snip the edge of the inner piece, neaten it with buttonhole stitch and hold it down where it crosses the zip tape, with hemming or very small herringbone stitches. At the other end of the band tuck the inner edge under and hem across the zip tape.

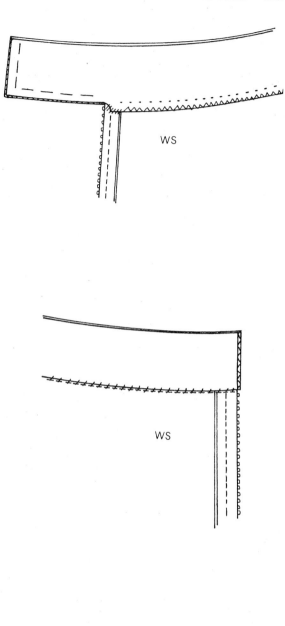

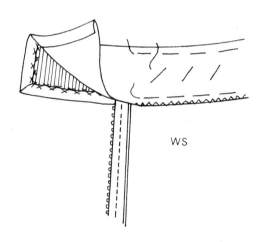

Turn the skirt so that the right side is towards you and work prick stitch in the join between skirt and waistband. On many garments this will be quite strong enough as a curved waistband does not fit quite as tightly as a straight one. However, if preferred a row of straight machining can be worked instead. Remove all tacking and press.

2    Where the band is attached to the skirt, press both seam allowances towards the band. On springy fabrics it may be necessary to hold with tacking. Work it from the right side to maintain the curve of the band but penetrate all layers.

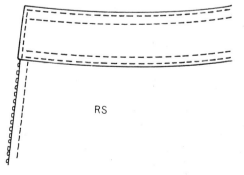

Use the iron and press other raw edges of outer band over the petersham. Trim them down to 5 mm ($\frac{1}{4}$ in.) tack to hold down if necessary. Turn in edges of inner band so that they are slightly to the inside of the edge. Tack Press well. Finish either by slip stitching the ends plus the overlap, and hemming into the machining along the skirt waist, or, from the right side, work a row of machining very close to the edge but taking it round all four sides of the band. Try to match the stitch used to attach the petersham, or perhaps contrast with it. If the effect will be odd the band will have to be completed by hand.

Remove all tacking and press.

### Couture waistband

Cut and stiffen an outer piece of band with an extra 3 cm ($1\frac{1}{4}$ in.) fabric at one end. Attach it to the garment and turn in all fabric edges over it, tack and herringbone including the 3 cm ($1\frac{1}{4}$ in.) at the overlap end. Remember to insert neat bias loops made from lining. Fit the skirt and decide where the fastenings are to be placed. Cut pieces of tape, canvas, or other strong material and hem to the back of the stiffening at those points. If a trouser clip is to be used, attach it now, using a length of stay tape to hold it in place.

Cut a piece of lining fabric, place it to the wrong side of the waistband, wrong side down and tack along the middle. Turn the skirt right side up and trim off surplus lining until only 3 mm ($\frac{1}{8}$ in.) protrudes. From the other side turn in the edge of the lining until it is 2 mm ($\frac{1}{8}$ in.) back from the edge round three sides but just covering the raw edge at the overlap end. Tack, press and fell all round. If the lining bulges on the waistband work a row of shallow prick stitch all round 3 mm ($\frac{1}{8}$ in.) within the edge.

### Petersham waist

A method of finishing the waist of a skirt or trousers without the additional restriction, bulk or extra depth of a waistband of fabric. It results in a softer finish favoured by some people for comfort as the waistline is less defined. It is not possible to achieve a very tight fit with petersham so it is not suitable on some styles such as straight, tight skirts which require a waistband to hold them to the waist, to make them hang properly. Petersham is a useful method of finishing hipster styles and those with yokes that look wrong with an additional band above, and also where there is insufficient fabric for a waistband. Attach petersham before levelling the hem.

Use petersham; straight and of the width required, or curved, or use elastic petersham. This may be quite wide and resembling black eleastic, or it may be the narrow white open kind often also used on knitted clothes and as a stay in a waisted dress.

Measure the petersham round the waist, allow 3 cm ($1\frac{1}{4}$ in.) for hems, and cut. Alternatively allow 6 cm ($2\frac{3}{8}$ in.) if Velcro is to be used to fasten it.

For a hook fastening turn back each end 1.5 cm ($\frac{5}{8}$ in.) and hem or machine turning under the raw edge, if it frays. Attach one or two large hooks and loops. Use a zig-zag stitch if machining. For Velcro turn back each end 1 cm ($\frac{3}{8}$ in.) and zig-zag Velcro in place on top hold down the edges.

The prepared petersham must fit the waist exactly when fastened. The skirt is to be eased onto it.

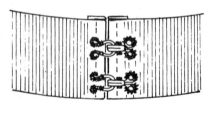

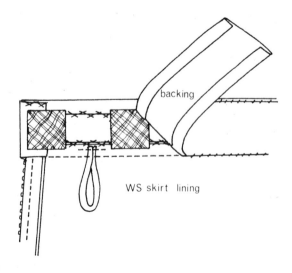

backing

WS skirt lining

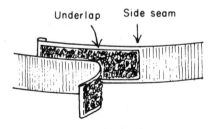

Underlap     Side seam

Insert the zip. Turn in the top edge of the skirt on the fitting line, tack and press, taking care not to stretch it. Neaten the raw edge and where it crosses the main seams of the skirt work a few herringbone stitches to hold it flat. Place the petersham inside the edge of the skirt with its concave edge just below the edge. Fasten the zip and the petersham and locate the fastening behind the zip. Pin at each side, then continue to pin with the petersham even and any ease evenly distributed. The skirt waist will nearly always seem bigger so hold with the skirt outside and pin from that side too. With elastic petersham stretch it between the pins so that it fits.

Tack, remove pins and stitch. Either hem through the skirt edge and petersham, keeping stitches even by using the beaded edge of the petersham as a guide. Work a strong bar tack at each end beside the hook. If Velcro is used the underlap extension will be free but the remainder of the petersham is stitched and the bar tacks worked close to the zip. If sewing by machine use a small zig-zag stitch or a blind hem stitch or another suitable stitch that looks attractive on the outside of the skirt.

Remove tackings, arrange the waist on the sleeve board and press the edge only to prevent stretching and creasing.

Elastic petersham may also be used, joined up to fit the waist, in the waist edge of skirts and trousers in knit fabrics that require no zip. Attach as described or in some light fabrics the top of the garment may have a casing attached through which the petersham is threaded before joining up.

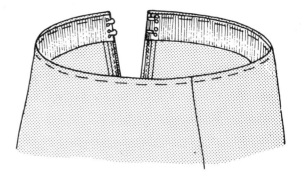

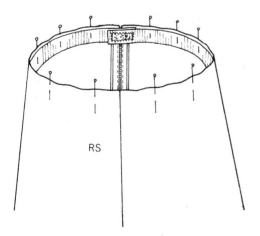

RS

### Straight waistband

A waistband has to be stiffened with a suitable material. The choice is between petersham of various widths, belt backing, interfacing such as pelmet weight Vilene cut to width, Fold-a-Band of waistband quality. If the stiffening selected has been manufactured to a definite width the waistband must be made that width. If you are cutting your own stiffening cut to any width. The choice of stiffening depends on the effect to be created, on the fabric and also on personal preference. Some people feel more comfortable wearing soft waistbands.

Begin by cutting the stiffening to length plus an overlap for fastening the band. Decide on the type of fastening then pass the stiffening round the waist to measure it, cutting it off. This is an accurate measurement as the skirt or trousers will be made to fit the band. If you add a band to the garment and then cut it to length it will in most cases be either too tight or too loose.

Using the stiffening cut a piece of fabric on the straight grain the same length, including the overlap, and twice the width of the stiffening, plus two seam allowances. The straight (warp) grain normally runs the length of the waistband but in the case of patterned fabric such as stripes or uneven checks, cut it in whichever direction looks best.

If using Fold-a-Band place the cut length on the wrong side of a spare piece of fabric, match up the straight grain with the central perforations and press into position. Cut out the fabric, allowing a turning all round.

With the exception of Fold-a-Band and any other self adhesive stiffening, the stiffener must be attached to the waistband fabric. Place one edge along the centre of the fabric and either tack and catch stitch or machine, down each side close to the edge of the stiffening, or, slip a length of Wundaweb between the two layers and press well.

Make sure the overlap mark is visible throughout construction.

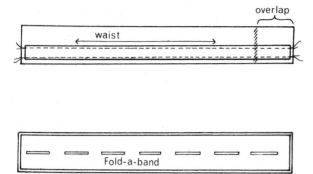

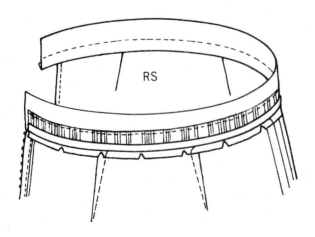

Attach the band to the garment waist edge. Place the band with its right side to the right side of the garment, pin at each end, locating the overlap where it is needed, then insert one or two pins in between. There may be some ease in the band but this is due to the fact that it is straight whereas the garment edge is shaped. Match the fitting lines and tack. Tack from the garment side, feeling the edge of the interfacing beneath, but turn it over and machine from the waist band side, stitching just off the edge of the stiffening.

Remove tackings, snip the skirt edge turnings at intervals and press open the join.

Fold the waistband with the right side inside and pin the ends to hold. Stitch the end and the overlap section by machining just off the edge of the stiffening across the end and, on the extension, along the lower edge too. Have the skirt wrong side up so that you can see the waist seam, also, do not try to stitch right to the end of the stitching in that seam. It is neater and more accurate to stitch it later by hand.

Remove pins. Trim one raw edge to 2 mm ($\frac{1}{16}$ in.) and the other to 4 mm ($\frac{1}{4}$ in.) and, using a bodkin, turn the waistband ends right side out.

Roll the joins and tack, also tack along the top fold of the entire waistband. Press. Work a row of tacking down the middle of the band, holding it right side out to keep it curled the right way for the body.

To finish the waistband use the most suitable method for the fabric. The first is for medium and heavy fabrics, the second for lightweights. In both cases slip stitch the small gaps near the end of the band.

1    Neaten the remaining raw edge of the waistband and, separately, the snipped edge of the top of the skirt. Tack the waistband layer to the skirt. Holding

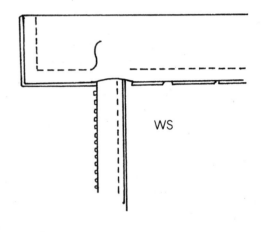

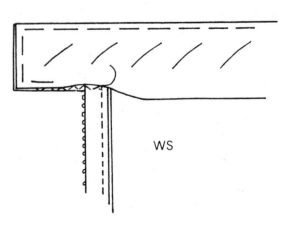

the work right side towards you work prick stitch in the join. Fold the edge under at an angle at the overlap and hem it to the zip tape where it crosses it. Remove all tackings and press.

2    Trim the skirt seam allowance, previously snipped, to 3 mm ($\frac{1}{8}$ in.). Press this up into the waistband. If the fabric is particularly springy tack it in place. Turn under the raw edge of the waistband and tack it in place. If the stiffening used was soft it is as well to tack from each end towards the middle for a little way. Then tack a section at the centre and then fill in the gaps. This will prevent bubbling or movement. Press. Hem into the machining to finish the band, or work a row of machining all round the band close to the edge. Do this from the right side.

### Trouser waistband

One of the main fitting points on trousers is in the centre back seam. Often, after fitting, the waistband has to be set lower on the trousers. Sometimes in doing this the waist becomes larger and the back seam needs adjusting yet again. To make fitting easier, make and interface the waistband in two parts, arranging to have a join at the centre back.

Make only the outer layer of band, cutting the inner one in one piece. Attach each half of the band to the waist of each trouser leg and press. Finish the crutch seam and fitting of the trousers, insert the zip, joining the seam on the waistband too. Press open the join, holding down springy edges with herringbone stitches. Attach the inner piece of waistband and finish in the usual way.

## WAISTLINE STAY

The waist join of a dress may need to have a narrow stay inserted to help to keep the seam in position during wear. Apart from the additional comfort the stay affords, the stay reduces the strain on the shoulder seams — an important point with a stretchy fabric, it also ensures that the seam remains covered by a belt if worn.

Make the join, in the usual way, and neaten the raw edges. Insert the zip. Use petersham — curved for preference for a good fit — or elastic petersham and cut it to fit the waist itself, not the waist of the dress. If the stay is to be fastened under the zip, allow for turning in the ends and also allow ease for movement. Turn in the ends and stitch and attach a large hook and eye. When fastened round the waist it should fit comfortably. Divide its length, marking the stay into four sections. Press the seam turning up towards the bodice, place the stay over it, matching the marks to the seams and garment centre front and centre back.

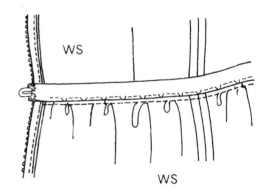

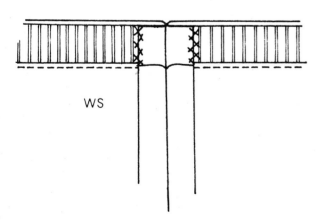

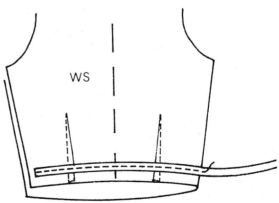

The lower edge of the stay should rest 3 to 5 mm ($\frac{1}{8}$ to $\frac{1}{4}$ in.) above the waist stitching, the remainder of the width of the stay extending up into the bodice. Attach either by working a series of bar tacks over the edge of the stay and into the seam allowance, or by machining. The best stitch to use is the blind hem stitch or any other that combines a straight stitch with one that will traverse the edge at intervals.

If the dress fabric is lightweight a piece of straight tape or seam binding may be sufficient. Tack the binding to the waist seam allowance. Turn in a narrow hem at each end and stitch, then hem or machine the binding to the waist. Note that this will not be fastened but the ends of tape finish just short of the zip tape. Tape may be used on the bodice only as an alternative. This method is effective when joining a

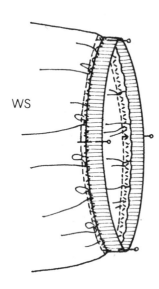

WS

**Less defined waist stay**
Many one-piece dresses, especially those with a belt around the waist, hang better and remain in place in wear if the waist position has elastic attached. This is not tight and is hidden by the belt in wear but it prevents the dress from riding up or looking unevenly bunched.

Put narrow elastic, 6 mm ($\frac{1}{4}$ in.) wide, preferably the soft open variety, around the waist comfortably and cut. Prevent the ends from fraying by button-holing across. Mark elastic evenly into four. Mark the waistline on the dress. Mark four even points on the inside of the dress; side seams and centre seams may act as these points. Set the machine to an elastic zig-zag stitch, or any suitable stretch stitch. Apply the elastic to the wrong side. Do not use pins. Begin by reversing to anchor the end of the elastic beside the zip then stitch forward laying the elastic on the marked waistline and stretching it sufficiently to match the four marks. Work in short bursts, stretching the elastic flat behind the foot and also keeping the fabric flat in front of the foot.

If the dress has no zip, join the elastic first and mark into four sections. Apply in the same way.

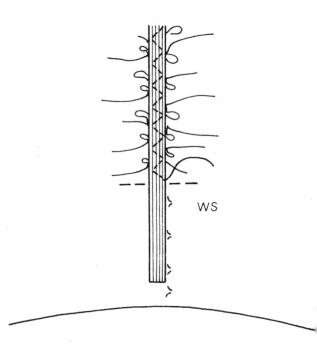

WS

full gathered skirt to a plain bodice, in a fine fabric. After constructing the bodice but before adding the skirt, tack a piece of tape to the wrong side of the bodice on the fitting line at the waist. When the skirt is added later the stitching will penetrate the tape.

If the dress is made of jersey fabric it may be possible to omit a zip. A stay is advisable but it must be made of soft elastic or elastic petersham. Cut a piece and join it so that it fits the waist comfortably. Divide it into four and pin to the waist seam, matching these points to the seams of the dress. Do not tack it in position but machine, using a zig-zag or stretch stitch, holding the elastic uppermost, stretch it onto the fabric so that each section fits.

## WALE

A line of stitches or loops in knitted fabric.

## WARP

The warp yarns are those which run the length of a piece of woven fabric. They are often stronger than the crosswise yarns because they take the strain of weaving. This additional strength is of great importance when deciding which way to have the straight grain on a garment.

## WAXING THREAD

Running beeswax along thread has long been the practice of tailors. The wax coats the thread and makes it smooth and with a doubled thread such as used for sewing on buttons, it helps to stick the two threads together. The wax probably adds strength too.

Dressmakers use thin machine thread for most things which is smooth already but wax is still very useful. If you try to sew with a doubled thread it parts and one get looped on the surface so it helps to wax it first. Also sometimes synthetic thread can twist when hand sewing and beeswax will straighten it.

Wax thread after threading the needle. If it is single, begin sewing and, if necessary, stop and push the needle onto the surface of the fabric, freeing the thread. Place the wax at the base by the needle and run it along the thread once to the end.

Double thread is used for sewing on buttons; it may be a thicker thread for heavy fabric; and setting in sleeves, etc. Thread the needle, double it and knot the ends together, run the wax from knot to needle three times. Keep hold of the knot allowing the thread to lie across the palm and twist it into a cord by rubbing the other palm across it. Still holding the knot wind the twisted section round the thumb so leaving the next length over the palm, twist again and so on.

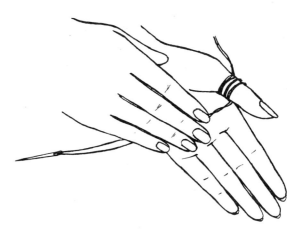

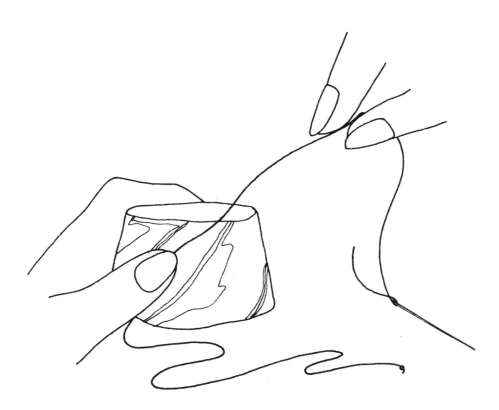

## WEAVE

The weave of a fabric refers to the way in which the yarns are interlaced to form the fabric. Patterns of woven fabrics are recognisable by their weave and the name precedes the word 'weave' as a description. For example plain weave, twill weave, satin weave, herringbone weave.

## WEFT

The weft yarns are those running across the width of fabric, over and under the warp yarns. Often called 'filling' yarns they literally fill the spaces and are often weaker than warp yarns. There may be some 'give' across the width of the fabric because of this — a point to consider when placing a pattern on fabric.

## WEIGHTS

Lead discs of various sizes with two holes in for sewing through. Once regarded as essential, weights are only used now on rare occasions. On items such as wedding and evening gowns their place has been taken by other materials such as heavy Vilene. This has the advantage of stiffening as well as weighting.

However, in coats and jackets there is no doubt that the addition of lead weights will improve the hang. Curtains too should be weighted either with these single weights or by the thin jersey-covered weighting sold by the metre.

When using single weights, cover them with a piece of lining, then stitch through the holes, attaching them to seam allowances or to the hem fabric, not to the garment. Locate them at the bottom of main seams and also at the front corners of a coat.

## WELT

The term refers to a narrow edge of fabric, usually double and therefore with a thick or relief appearance. The welt edge may be formed by adding a strip of material, for example a welt pocket, or it may be created by folding an existing edge and emphasising it with stitching to make it stand up, for example a welt seam.

## WHEATEAR STITCH

A chain embroidery stitch. Work two straight stitches at an angle to each other, then bring the thread through below the point where they join. Pass the needle under the two straight stitches to form the oval of the chain; pull the thread through and take a stitch where the needle was brought through to begin the next straight stitch.

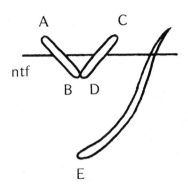

## WOVEN

A woven fabric is produced by establishing a set of lengthwise yarns (warp) and then weaving others (weft) over and under, across them. The pattern may be a plain weave, resulting from the wefts passing alternately over and under a single warp. Other variations result in hopsack, herringbone, twill weaves, for instance. Woven fabrics fray at the cut edges, some more than others.

(See also *Knitted Fabrics*.)

## WRAP-OVER

A dress or skirt with an apron style flap that wraps over the under layer. The wrap may be at the front or back or both, sometimes even at the side. Fastening is kept to a minimum; dresses may rely on a belted waist, skirts on a fastened waistband. Another fastening for all garments is to make and attach ties to wrap and tie at the waist. The disadvantage of front-wrap skirts and dresses is that they often open when you sit down. A second line of defence in addition to the waist fastening can be provided by sewing one or two pieces of Velcro under the wrap.

## WRONG SIDE

Often abbreviated to WS in written instructions, this means the reverse side of the fabric. The wrong side may be less smooth or have a less finished appearance than the right side. With printed fabrics the print may be faint or blurred. With jacquard fabrics the loose threads will be visible. With some fabrics, notably plain knits and plain fine weave cottons, it may be impossible to determine which is the wrong side. In such cases simply make sure that the same side of the fabric is always used as the wrong side.

The selvedge may indicate the wrong side. (See *Selvedge*, page 286.)

## WUNDAWEB

Wundaweb is a web 3 cm ($1\frac{1}{4}$ in.) wide sold in packs containing different amounts. It has a great number of uses because it melts when heat and moisture are applied. Obviously it must first be placed between two layers of fabric, and it must be concealed. After thorough pressing following the instructions, the web hardens again and so the fabrics are bonded in place. It can be used in hems on many fabrics and in small pieces for other things like holding facings in position and it also prevents fraying when inserted in machine-made buttonholes.

line of the body. Examples include yoked trousers where the seam is used to take up excess fabric and achieve a better fit. The yoke line should run over the pelvic bone at the sides and across the hollow or flat part of the back.

The line of a skirt yoke should follow the same lines but there can be more variation for style. A bodice yoke seam can provide bust shaping but the seam must run over the bust point.

Use one of the following seams to make yoke joins: overlaid, angled, welt, gathered, shirt yoke seam, double yoke.

## YARDSTICK

(See *Metre Rule.*)

## YOKES

A small, flat area of a garment from which the remainder hangs. The yoke section is cut to fit that part of the body while the other section may be pleated, gathered, flared or simply straight.

The main reason for a yoke is usually to add a style feature, the main join being in a flattering position and having an attractive shape. The yoke may be plain and matching the garment or it can feature contrasting fabric, embroidery, tucks, appliqué or quilting.

The advantage of being able to join on a fuller piece is that it allows for changing size, for example, on children's and maternity clothes yokes are almost standard features.

However, another valuable use of a yoke join is to provide shaping by the use of curved or angled edges. Whereas with fullness the yoke seam must be positioned slightly above the area requiring the fullness, with a shaped yoke the seam must follow the

## ZIG-ZAG CABLE CHAIN STITCH

A variation of cable chain stitch, each stitch being taken at an angle to the previous one. Work towards you or from right to left.

(See *Chain Stitch* and *Cable Chain Stitch*.)

## ZIG-ZAG STITCH

Strictly speaking a zig-zag stitch is any that is not a straight stitch. The stitches can only be made by a swing-needle machine, or it is possible to buy an attachment that will fit a straight stitch machine. The resulting stitch will be a zig-zag but it is produced as a result of the attachment moving the fabric from side to side.

The maximum width of zig-zag a machine will produce is usually 6 mm ($\frac{1}{4}$ in.) but the width should be adjusted in conjunction with the length to find the most suitable stitch for the fabric. A zig-zag can be used decoratively but its main use is utilitarian. A slight zig-zag stitch of normal length is useful in seams of jersey fabric as the extra give prevents the seams from splitting. The stitch should be only slightly off straight otherwise a good flat seam will not be possible. (See also *Stretch Stitch*.)

A zig-zag stitch is also used for neatening fabric edges. Experiment until a good combination of width and length is achieved. A wide zig-zag does not necessarily prevent fraying more than a narrow one: a long zig-zag stitch will certainly not prevent fraying because there will be spaces between the stitches to allow ends of yarn to come away.

In addition, too wide a zig-zag on a thin fabric may easily compress the edge into a ridge. If, on very fine fabric, it is impossible to eliminate this curling, the answer is to turn under the edge of the fabric and press it and then work the zig-zag over the folded edge. Press the stitching and then trim away the surplus fabric close to the stitching.

On shaped or curved edges or on loosely woven fabrics a zig-zag stitch may stretch the edge, fluting it. Overcome this by laying a length of sewing thread on top of the fabric, zig-zag over it. Pull the thread up until the fabric edge is flat. Press.

For details of variations on zig-zag, such as blind stitch, overlocking, etc., look under the name of the stitch.

## ZIP FASTENERS

The zip is probably the most used fastener in modern clothes. The advantages of speed and reliability in use are obvious, and also the fact that a zip is quick to insert when compared with the old alternatives of placket openings or putting buttons and buttonholes in trouser fly openings. There is a variety of types, lengths and colours made but it is impossible for any shops except large department stores to stock the entire range.

Paper patterns indicate the length of zip needed so it can be bought at the same time as the fabric. Sometimes pattern or fitting adjustments mean the zip is not quite the right length but usually the length of the opening can be adjusted. Sometimes women with small shoulders or short stature find they can use a shorter dress zip than is standard but care must be taken that this does not result in strain on the zip. The same applies to skirts and particularly trousers. The waist measurement plus twice the zip length must equal a little more than the size of the widest part of the body that the garment will go over, hips, thighs, shoulders, etc.

Zip openings can be very simple, just a narrow turning on the fabric, or they can be inserted in a fly opening or a flap opening such as might be found on windproof anoraks. (This type sometimes has Velcro beyond the zip as an added protection.)

Before choosing a type it helps to know something about the zips available. The following sections will help with selection. There is a variety of makes available and although Lightning and Optilon are specifically referred to, the information applies to all makes and types.

**How to measure your zip**

Zip fasteners are always measured over the length of

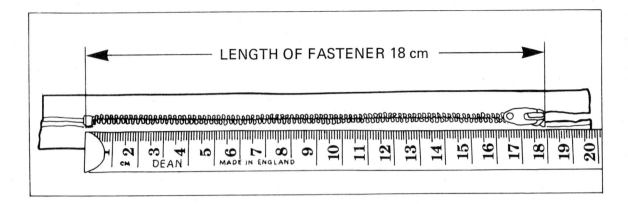

LENGTH OF FASTENER 18 cm

the fastener itself, and not the fabric backing, so lay the tape-measure from the bottom stop to the top of the slider with the zip in the closed position.

### Choose the right type for the job

Conventional zips come in the following types, each designed for a specific purpose. The choice of fastener should be influenced by the weight and type of fabric and by the garment, e.g. sportswear, outer garments and firm fabrics require heavier zips.

Lightweight nylon or polyester zips may be used for all types of openings in dresses, skirts, slacks made from lightweight or jersey fabrics and in knitwear.

Lightweight metallic zips which are slightly stronger are recommended for skirts and slacks in medium but firm fabrics.

Open-ended zips, metallic, polyester or moulded nylon which undo completely into two parts should be used for cardigans, jackets and sportswear. The mediumweight metal zip is for use with heavier fabrics or thick-knit wool. The polyester zip is strong and versatile and is suitable for most applications needing an open-ended zip. The latest addition to the range is the large moulded nylon zip which is suitable for jackets and heavy knitted garments where a decorative effect is wanted.

Featherweight metallic zips can be used for dresses and knitwear in mediumweight and skirts in lightweight fabrics.

Trouser and jean zips are especially made for the purpose. Remember it is important that the zip is long enough for the opening as the bottom stop must be sewn in exactly at the fork. If the zip is slightly longer than it needs to be, the top stops can be sewn in under the waistband.

### Buy the right size for the garment

For perfect results, make sure that the opening in the garment is long enough to allow it to be put on and taken off with ease. Otherwise the zip, when it is fitted, may be subjected to strain. It's wisest to check this before buying the zip!

Remember that even when the zip is fully opened the slider is still above the bottom stop, so that the effective opening is always 13 mm ($\frac{1}{2}$ in.) less than the measured opening. In other words, an 18 cm (7 in.) zip provides only a 16.5 cm ($6\frac{1}{2}$ in.) opening. This is especially important when buying a skirt zip or trouser zip, as the average figure with a 25 to 30 cm (10 to 12 in.) difference between waist and hip measurement requires a 20 cm (8 in.) zip. The same applies to the long back opening in a dress. The length from the waist to the lower end of the opening should be 20 cm (8 in.) if the skirt is slim fitting, or 18 cm (7 in.) if it is flared or pleated.

When buying a zip for the back neck of a hand knitted jumper or the front of a cardigan, the zip should be shorter than the opening so that the wool can be eased onto the zip tape. As a rough guide a 10.5 to 11.5 cm ($4\frac{1}{4}$ to $4\frac{1}{2}$ in.) opening calls for a 10 cm (4 in.) zip and a 53 to 55 cm (21 to 22 in.) opening needs a 50 cm (20 in.) zip.

### Zip failure

Zip failure is comparatively rare. Faults and breakages are nearly always due to some reason other than faulty manufacture. These are some of the points to check.

1 Is the zip the correct weight for the job? Is it too fine or too heavy for the garment?

2 Is the zip long enough? Signs of a zip that's too short are teeth dislodged at the lower end, or in the case of a concealed zip, broken seam stitching.

3 Is the stitching the correct distance from the teeth, according to the fitting instructions? If not, the slider may be unable to move up and down easily.

4 Is the zip wavy because the tape has not been stretched tightly enough, or because the fabric has not been eased gently on to it? This makes it difficult for the slider to run smoothly.

5 Have the edges of the tape curled over and so become caught in the slider?

## Types and lengths available

| APPLICATION | TYPE | PACK | LENGTHS AVAILABLE (CM) | COLOURS AVAILABLE |
|---|---|---|---|---|
| All dressmaking purposes | Lightweight nylon | 'Opti-lon' Clearguard | 10, 15, 18, 20, 23, 25, 30, 35, 40, 45, 50, 55. | 44 |
| Dresses, knitwear | Featherweight coloured metal | Metal Clearguard | 10, 15, 18, 20, 23, 25, 30, 35, 40, 45, 50, 55. | 44 |
| Skirts, slacks | Lightweight coloured metal | Skirt Clearguard | 15, 18, 20. | 24 |
| Dresses, skirts and slacks | Lightweight concealed polyester | 'Opti-lon' Concealed Tabbed | 20, 23, 55. | 14 |
| Jackets | Mediumweight aluminium open end | Clearguard | 30, 35, 40, 45, 50, 55, 60, 65, 70. | 15 |
| Cardigans/jackets | Mediumweight polyester open end | 'Opti-lon' Jacket Clearguard | 30, 35, 40, 45, 50, 55, 60, 65. | 19 |
| Jackets | Heavyweights moulded nylon | 'Opti-lon' Alpine Tabbed | 45, 50, 55, 60, 65, 70, 75. | 10 |
| Trousers | Lightweight nickel silver | Trouser Clearguard | 18, 20, 23, 25. | 13 |
| Jeans | Mediumweight brass | Jeans Clearguard | 15, 18, 20. | 7 |

6 Has the zip been strained in some way? Has the slider been forced over an obstruction, or along teeth in which loose threads or fibres have been caught?

7 Has the zip always been opened fully? In a conventional fastener the bottom stop is intended to take the strain, but if the slider is not fully opened stress is placed on the teeth. In a concealed fastener, it's the seam stitching that takes the strain when the zip is not opened properly.

8 Has the zip been protected from excess strain by additional hooks and eyes, or buttons? Remember, the slider is not designed to take all the stress — its job is merely to close the two halves of the zip once they have been drawn together and held there by other means.

9 Has the slider been knocked by an iron? This could cause the locking mechanism to fail.
or
Has the nylon zip been in contact with a hot iron?

A nylon zip ought to be kept closed when being ironed but if the zip has to be opened, turn the iron down to a low temperature.

10 Has an open ended zip been incorrectly joined at the bottom end? The slider should rest firmly on the end before the other side is inserted and the slider pulled up.

### Points to remember

There are various methods of inserting a zip, the choice depends on the garment, the fabric, the position and the final effect required. However, whatever the method chosen, remember the following.

*Stitching the zip*

1 Tacking: Use a small needle and tacking thread, a large size needle is difficult to force into the tape of the zip.

Work a backstitch occasionally to help prevent the fabric from moving on the tape.

If possible tack straight so that the stitches can be

used as a guide for permanent stitching; if the tacks are not accurate enough draw a dotted chalk line using sharp tailor's chalk and a ruler.

2 Permanent stitching: This may be worked by hand or machine, whichever is most suitable for the fabric, the position on the garment, the type of garment and also depending on how easy it is to reach the zip area, i.e. it may be difficult to arrange the fabric correctly under the machine if the garment is practically complete.

As a general rule stitch fine fabrics by hand because the weight of the fabric is so different from the zip tape that machining may cause wrinkling. Stitch very bulky fabrics by hand to avoid an ugly indentation and a bulky ridge.

Whichever method is used stitch parallel to the teeth and not too close to them. Stitch from the right side whenever possible.

To stitch by machine use an adjustable zip foot if possible and a medium length stitch.

To stitch by hand use single thread and prick stitch, the almost invisible back stitch. If additional strength is required work a row of machining near the edge of the zip tape through tape and turning only.

When inserting the zip, tack and stitch permanently in the same direction on both sides, i.e. either top to bottom or base to top, depending on which end requires the greatest degree of accuracy. Even when stitching by hand the fabric may be inclined to move slightly on the tape.

Ease the fabric onto the zip tape when tacking especially if the fabric edges are shaped, as the tendency is to stretch the fabric unconsciously.

Avoid using pins. They can cause the zip to snake as each pin lifts both zip and fabric out of the flat position.

Avoid a bulky ridge at the top of the opening on skirts, trousers, etc., by placing the slider slightly below the fitting line. The exact distance below depends on the thickness of the fabric, but allow about 2 mm ($\frac{1}{16}$ in.) on fine fabrics and up to 5 mm ($\frac{1}{4}$ in.) on thick ones.

Where pressing is necessary during or after insertion of the zip, cover the toe of the iron with a damp muslin cloth and use the toe of the iron to press the fabric only, running the iron beside the teeth. Never press over the teeth or marks may appear that are impossible to remove.

*Tips*

Make the opening fit the zip, not the other way round. Always prepare the edges of the zip opening by tacking and then pressing. It is not possible to press the fabric adequately once the zip is in position.

When pressing take care not to stretch either edge.

Neaten the raw edges of the seam, including the zip opening, before inserting the zip.

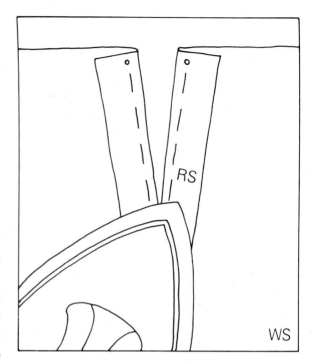

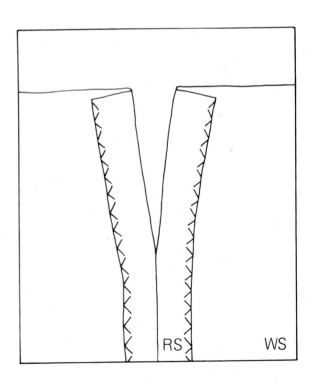

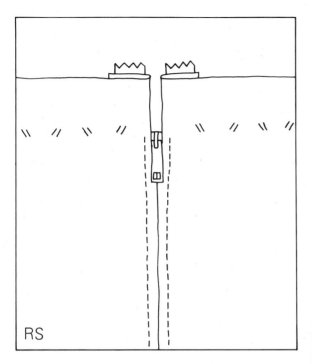

For best results, hem a narrow tape or petersham ribbon to wrong side before inserting zip. This strengthens the edges and prevents either shrinking or stretching during wear and washing.

If neck edge of garment is finished off mitre top tape ends of zip.

Place zip behind opening so that the top of the slider lies at the neck edge, with right side of zip toward you, place zip underneath so that edge of knitting lies down the centre of the teeth. Tack.

Tack second side so that edges of knitting meet.

Oversew knitted edges together with tacking thread. Stitch on the wrong side from the surplus top tape ends and hem these ends.

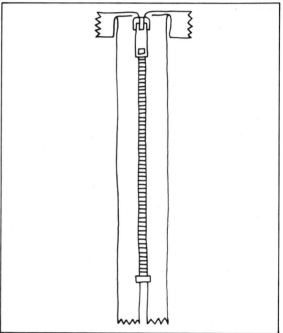

### Replacing zips

This occurs more often in ready-made garments than in hand-made ones and is usually due to inferior inadequate zips being used.

1 Look carefully at the way the zip has been inserted. There are many different methods employed. Make notes if necessary to remind you of how it looks.
2 Detach any facing, waistband, clip, hook, button as necessary, only unpicking sufficient to allow access to the zip.
3 Unpick one side of the zip. Remove thread ends on the garment but leave the stitching holes as a guide for later. Repeat on the second side. If a guard has been used take careful note of how the zip is attached to it. Press both edges of fabric, keeping them folded.
4 Take the zip and buy another of the same length and suitable colour and type.
5 Insert the new zip following the same sequence as on the original, following the stitching lines.
6 Replace facing, waistband etc., following the original lines. Attach any buttons or hooks. Press.

### Zip in knit fabrics

This is suitable for open knits type fabrics and for those resembling hand knitting but not for close knits.

Make the opening about 1.5 cm ($\frac{5}{8}$ in.) longer than the zip.

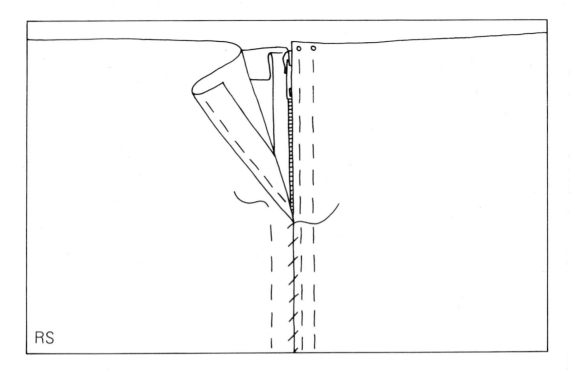

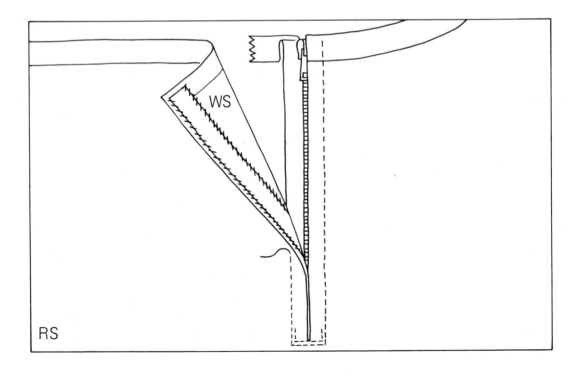

## Open-ended zip in knit fabrics

To ensure that the zip will lie flat when worn it should be from 2.5 to 5 cm (1 to 2 in.) *shorter* than the front opening.

Mitre top ends of tape.

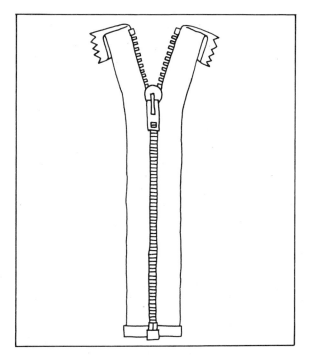

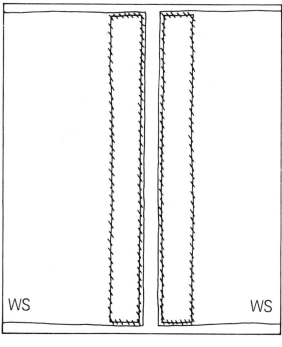

*Sewing — visible method*

With the right side of zip towards you, place zip behind opening with the edge of knitting beside zip teeth. Tack.

At least 3 mm ($\frac{1}{8}$ in.) of zip tape should be visible between metal teeth and edge of fabric. Easing the ribbon and fabric onto the zip tape, tack in position with double row at top and bottom.

Cut two pieces of tape or petersham ribbon equal in length to the opening in the garment allowing extra to turn in at ends — hem to the wrong side of the knitted edges.

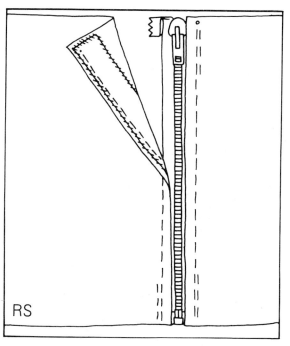

Tack second side in the same way. Stitch zip Remove tacking.

### Semi-concealed method

With right side of zip towards you place zip behind opening but with the faced edges meeting over the centre of the teeth.

Oversew edges of knitting with tacking thread. Stitch and remove tacking.

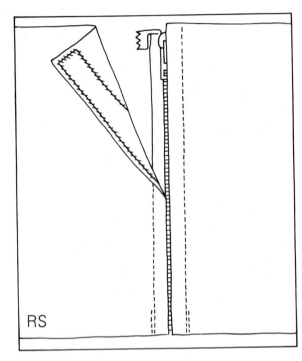

RS

### Concealed zip

A specially made zip that is inserted in a slightly different way from other zips. It is easy to insert because no stitching is done through the garment. An excellent method for beginners and also good for pile fabrics and those which stitching might spoil. Stitch in by hand or with the zip foot adjusted. Some special zip feet, for example the one included with some Pfaff machines, there is a central bridge specially for use with concealed zips, making insertion very easy and accurate.

Stitch up the garment seam leaving an opening for the zip at least 1.5 cm ($\frac{5}{8}$ in.) shorter than the length of the zip teeth.

Stitch up the gap left for the zip, preferably with a large machine stitch, or with small tacking stitches.

Press the whole seam open firmly — it cannot be pressed again.

With the prepared seam wrong side up place the zip over the seam with the slider in position below the fitting line. Tack the tape to the seam turning, sliding your fingers under the turning to prevent the stitches penetrating the garment. Tack to the bottom of the tape. Tack both sides in this way.

Remove the large machine stitches from the zip opening. Undo the zip.

Roll the zip teeth over until they are flat and stitch the tape to the seam turning as close to the teeth as possible. This may be done by hand using a back stitch, or by machine using the adjustable zip foot. Fasten off the stitching.

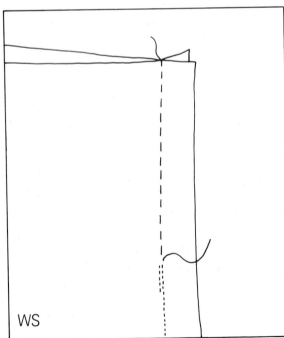

WS

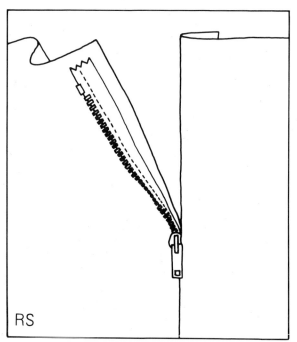

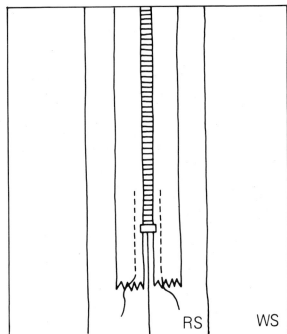

Close the zip gently to roll the teeth into the closed position.

Complete the stitching at the base of the zip from the end of the stitching to the bottom of the tape ends. Do this either by hand using the ends of the machining if possible, or machine these ends only. Stitch the tape to the turning as before, keeping as close to the teeth as possible. Remove tackings. Do not press.

### Uneven edges zip
This is a popular method because the wider edge covers the zip completely. However, care must be taken with steps one and two to make sure this is done correctly.

Stitch seam leaving correct length opening. Press.

Turn the outer edge under on the fitting line, tack and press.

On the underside or hidden edge turn under, 3 mm ($\frac{1}{8}$ in.) away from the fitting line, tack and press.

Place this folded edge close to the zip teeth and tack. Tacking right to the bottom of the zip tape. Stitch.

Remove tackings.

Bring first side over zip matching folded edge to fitting line of underside.

Attach folded edge to garment using tacking thread and oversewing or catch stitch.

Stitch beside teeth.

Turn work to wrong side, snip turning at base of tape to release the narrow edge. Remove tacking.

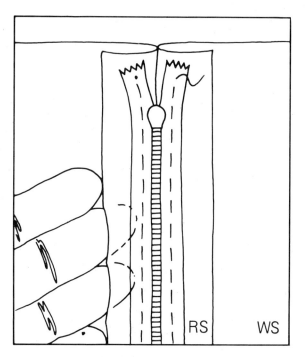

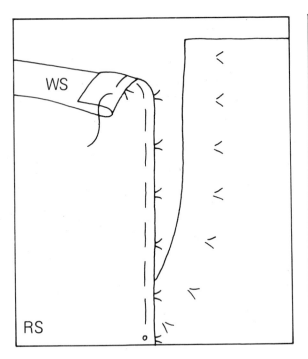

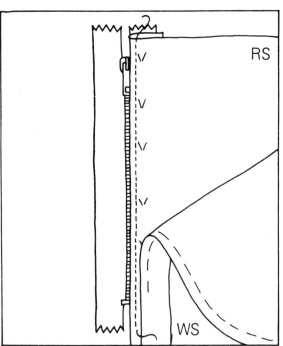

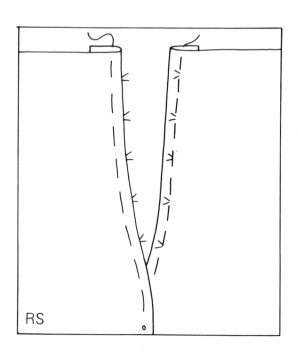

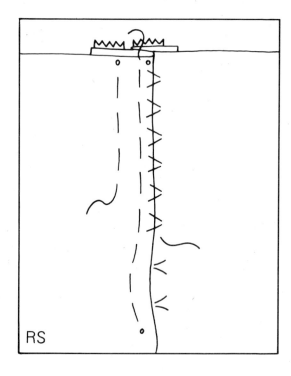

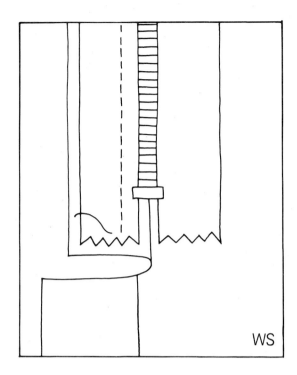

### Even edges

This method where the folds of fabric meet evenly down the centre of the teeth can be used almost anywhere. The illustrations show the top ends of the tape mitred but they need not be treated like this if a collar, facing, etc., is to be attached.

Measure correct length of opening by placing top of slider slightly below neck fitting line and easing fabric on to zip tape.

Stitch up centre back seam making sure the opening is long enough to allow the dress to be put on without strain, usually 55 cm (22 in.) and at least 18/20 cm (7/8 in.) of this should be below the waistline.

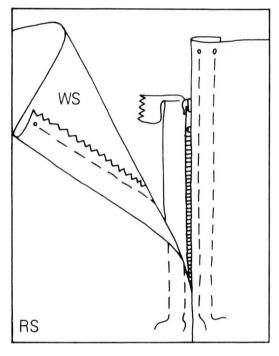

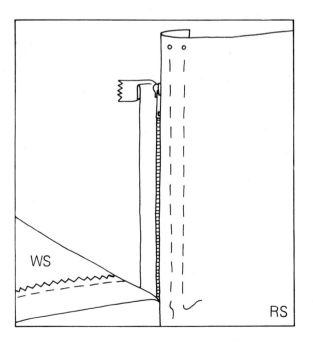

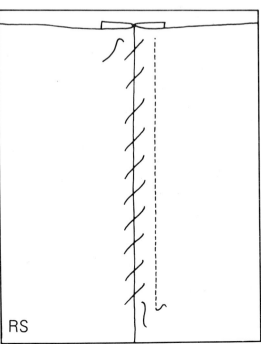

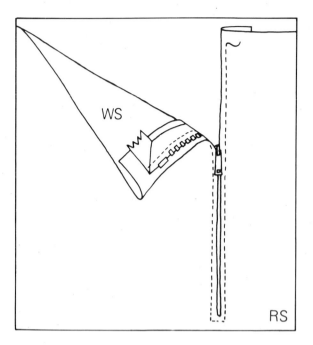

Snip a triangle at the base and press back all edges. If the fabric frays press a small piece of Bondaweb in place at the base of the opening. The size of the resulting rectangle must be exactly equal to the width of the zip teeth so care must be taken with snipping the base.

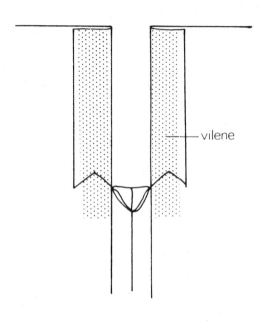

Press and neaten seam and turnings up to the neck line.

Mitre top tape ends of zip if neckline is already finished with collar or facing.

Turn edges under, tack and press on fitting line.

With right side of zip towards you place zip underneath, so that the bottom stop lies exactly at the end of the seam, and the slider below neck fitting line. The folded edge should be centrally along the zip teeth.

Tack beside the teeth easing the fabric on to the zip tape rather than stretching.

Place the other edge of fabric so that the two folds meet centrally over the teeth. Tack beside the teeth working in the same direction as the first side. Oversew the two folds together with tacking thread. Stitch the zip.

Remove tacking.

### Decorative zip

An easy way to put in a zip is to allow the teeth to be visible rather than worry about covering them. This method lends itself to the large Alpine zip and to metal zips. The colour can be matching or contrast. It is also a useful method to use on fabrics with surface interest fibres that easily get caught in the teeth but the method should be confined to front openings. There may or may not be a seam at this point on the garment. If the fabric is lightweight attach a narrow strip of iron-on Supershape Vilene to the wrong side of each edge of the fabric. Stitch the garment seam if there is one, leaving the gap for the zip. If there is no seam cut the fabric.

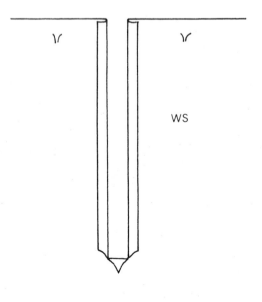

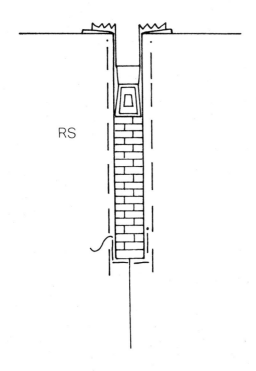

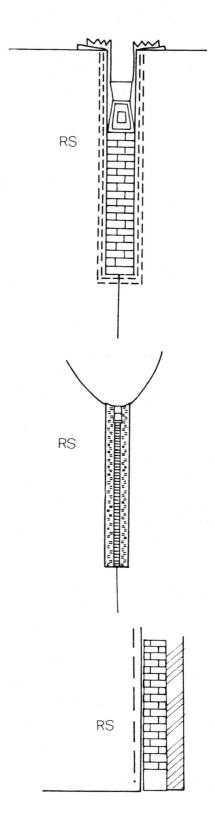

Place the zip underneath and tack the fabric to the tape on both sides. Stitch the zip. As this is decorative it is probably best to machine the zip. Use the zip foot. Work two rows if desired. The second row could be more decorative than straight stitching. Another alternative is to sew braid on top of the stitching as decoration. This has the advantage, for beginners, of covering the stitching.

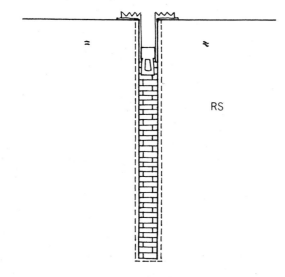

If an open-ended zip is inserted by this method, finish the hemline of the garment then put in the zip, lining it up from the bottom. The neck, collar etc., are then completed afterwards. If an open-ended zip of exactly the right length is not available, a slit opening can be left below the bottom of the zip. This is quite usually done on robes and coats.

### Zip in bias seam

If a zip is inserted into a bias seam it will almost certainly bulge because the zip tape has no 'give' in it to match the 'give' in the fabric.

First, look carefully at the zip position and make sure it is in the least conspicuous position, moving the opening if necessary. For instance, if a dress is cut on the cross avoid putting a long zip at the centre front or centre back. Instead, insert a shorter one in the left side seam and put only a short zip at the centre position — it is easier to control the buckling and will not show as much. Another alternative is to make an opening in the shoulder seam in combination with a side seam zip.

With a bias cut skirt, avoid inserting the zip in the centre back — it will bulge outwards — always put it in the left seam where it will show less and it will curve over the hip bone.

If after these considerations the zip has to be put in a bias seam in a conspicuous position, stabilise the fabric edges first. Either cut narrow strips of Bondaweb the exact length of the opening and press them to the wrong side of the fabric before inserting the zip, or cut pieces of tape or even the selvedges of a fine fabric.

Cut the strips accurately taking the length from the paper pattern, tack in position on the wrong side of the fabric edges, centred over the fitting line, then machine down the tape slightly off-centre. Take care not to stretch the fabric. Machine slowly to prevent movement.

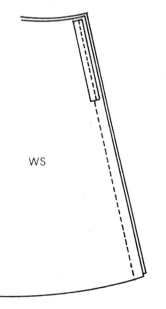

WS

### Men's trouser waistband and fly zip

The order of working zip and waistband on men's trousers is different from women's in order that a full fly extension and guard can be used, and also to enable the zip to be taken partly into the waistband if desired. The effect of this being to eliminate the diagonal crease that invariably develops below the waistband on the fly. In addition men's waistbands are not usually worn as tight as women's, nor is there such an easily defined waistline on the figure.

*Waistband backing*

Waistband backing on men's trousers can be a soft backing such as a piece of lining or sleeve lining, or a stiff, strong Terylene backing bought by the metre. A special band backing made of cream knitted nylon with rubber gripping thread running through it is also available; this latter backing eliminates the necessity for a trouser curtain or flap below the band.

*Guard*

The guard is made from a piece of fabric and a piece of silesia or from two pieces of cloth. The fly facing is one piece of cloth. Both should be 10 cm (4 in.) wide and 10 cm (4 in.) longer than the zip and curved at the bottom. It is easiest to cut this curve after attaching.

*Curtain*

A fold of fabric is inserted to hang below the waistband on the inside. This prevents stretching and also gives a smoother appearance to the outside of the trouser in wear.

*Waistband*

The waistband is made in two pieces and attached to the trouser legs before the crutch seam is sewn. Insert the zip and attach the waistband as follows.

A 25 cm (10 in.) curved metal zip is normally used. This is designed to fit the crutch seam to include part of the curved part of the seam. In well-fitting trousers this distance varies with the individual and it is usual to trim off any surplus zip teeth at the top. This is firmly held and concealed by the waistband. If a curved zip is not available, shorten the opening so that the bottom of the zip comes before the curve of the seam.

*Right side and fly extension*

Place the zip right side down to the seam line on the right side of the cloth. Tack and machine 5 mm ($\frac{1}{4}$ in.) from the teeth; fasten off well at the base of the teeth. Place the fly extension, or guard, right side down on top of the zip, then tack and machine.

To enable this second row to fall on the first row as near as possible, turn the work over and stitch from underneath.

Fold over the guard so that it forms an extension, fold the trouser leg back with right side uppermost, and tack through all the layers beside the teeth.

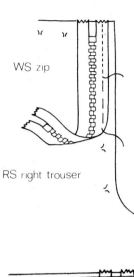

WS zip

RS right trouser

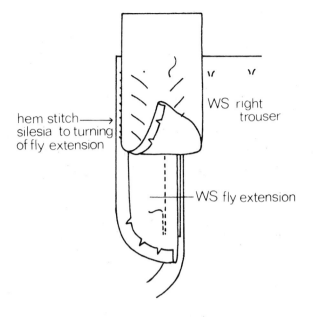

hem stitch
silesia to turning
of fly extension

WS right
trouser

WS fly extension

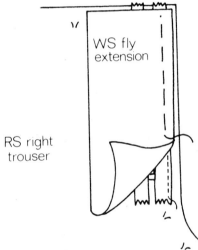

WS fly
extension

RS right
trouser

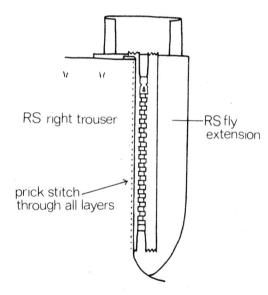

RS right trouser

RS fly
extension

prick stitch
through all layers

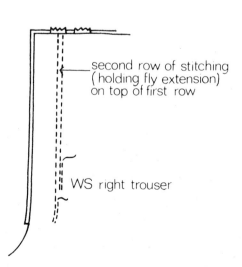

second row of stitching
(holding fly extension)
on top of first row

WS right trouser

Cut a piece of silesia or lining to back the guard; make it wider than the guard and long enough to cover the depth of the waistband later. Place this against the fly guard extension wrong sides together, and baste. Turn in, tack, and press the edge of the extension. Turn in and hem it to the edge of the silesia, leaving the top edge loose to allow the waistband to be attached.

Turn in the other edge of the silesia just beyond the zip and tack down. From the right side, prick stitch beside the zip teeth through all the layers of cloth including the silesia.

*Band*

Cut two strips of cloth on the straight grain 6 cm ($2\frac{3}{8}$ in.) wide and long enough to fit the waist of the trousers. On the right end of the trouser side it must be long enough to include the fly extension plus turnings. On the left end it should include 8 cm ($3\frac{1}{8}$ in.) for overlap plus turnings. Cut firm interfacing (collar canvas or Vilene) slightly narrower, and attach. Baste canvas and cloth together.

Fold over the top edge of the cloth and tack, then herringbone the edge to the interfacing, or with the wrong side of the band uppermost place the interfacing with one edge just overlapping the cloth and machine. Fold in the top edge including the interfacing, so that the machine stitching cannot be seen from the right side of the band. Baste the top edge, and press.

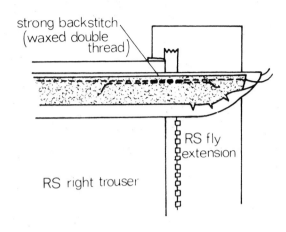

strong backstitch
(waxed double thread)

RS fly extension

RS right trouser

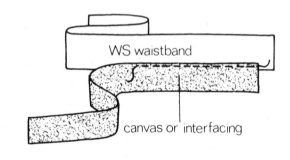

WS waistband

canvas or interfacing

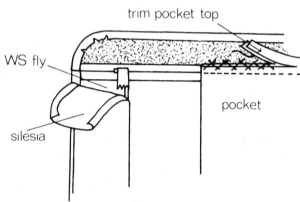

trim pocket top

WS fly

silesia

pocket

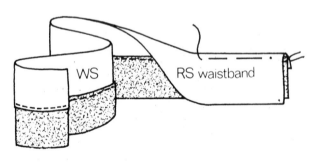

WS        RS waistband

Replace the top of the pockets so that they lie flat over the waistband. Trim off the suplus pocket. Back stitch through the pocket and into the waistband join, and then herringbone over the raw edge, picking up only the interfacing.

*Attaching the curtain*

Omit this stage if backing has curtain on it. Cut pieces of lining on the lengthwise grain 12 cm ($4\frac{3}{4}$ in.) wide and long enough to fit the waistband. Fold in half, right side out, and press in the crease. Place inside the trouser with the raw edge just overlapping the waist join. Baste in position.

On the left side of the trouser, the end of the curtain will tuck under the fly facing. (For strength this can be done before the final prick stitching beside the zip.) At the right side, the trouser curtain tucks under the piece of silesia backing the extension piece.

*Attaching bands*

Fold pocket tops down to prevent them from being caught up in the waistbands. Place the right side of the waistband pieces to the right side of the trouser, tack and machine. The stitching across the top of the zip must be very close to the teeth, so this section may have to be stitched by hand, using double waxed thread and a strong back stitch. Press the waist join open.

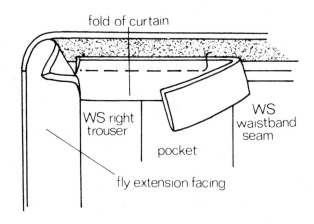

fold of curtain

WS right trouser

pocket

WS waistband seam

fly extension facing

*Left side and fly facing*

Cut the fly facing piece in cloth and also in linen or cotton. Baste the linen to the wrong side of the cloth facing. Place the facing to the trouser, with straight edges and right sides together. Machine from the end of the crutch seam stitching up to the waistband. Finish off the stitching firmly at each end. Trim the raw edges, roll the facing to the wrong side, and baste the edge; press.

Back stitch the curtain to the waistband along the join. Back stitch across each end of the curtain to the turnings beside the zip. Herringbone over the raw edge of the curtain, taking the stitches through the interfacing only.

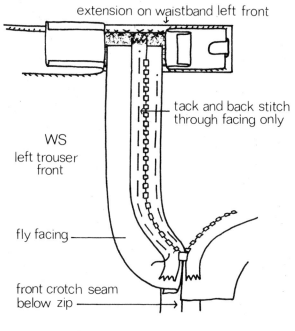

extension on waistband left front

WS left trouser front

fly facing

front crotch seam below zip

tack and back stitch through facing only

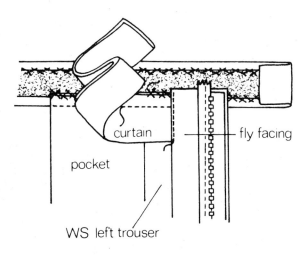

curtain

pocket

fly facing

WS left trouser

*Joining the legs*

Place the inside leg seams with right sides together; place the waistbands exactly together; tack. Stitch this seam with a strong back stitch using double waxed thread, to allow this seam, which is on the cross to 'give' in wear. It can be machined if a slight zig-zag stitch is used.

Stitch through the waistbands, down the seam, under the crutch through the reinforcement and to the base of the zip. Fasten off very firmly.

Press the seam open. Do not snip the seam as it weakens it. The seam is not on the straight grain so it should press open easily. Neaten the raw edges by overcasting.

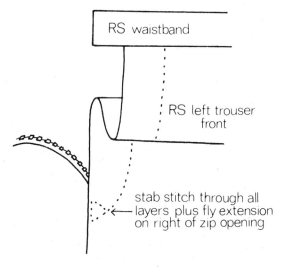

RS waistband

RS left trouser front

stab stitch through all layers plus fly extension on right of zip opening

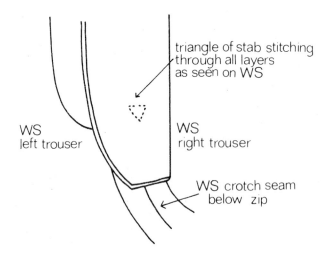

triangle of stab stitching
through all layers
as seen on WS

WS
left trouser

WS
right trouser

WS crotch seam
below zip

On the right side of left trouser, chalk a line about 3.5 cm ($1\frac{3}{8}$ in.) from the finished edge and parallel with it. Curve the line round at the base of the zip to meet the crutch seam. Working with right side up, prick stitch or machine on the line, starting at the waist join.

At the base of the zip, work a small triangle of back stitches right through all the layers, including the guard. Use stab stitch as the area is bulky.

Pass the needle through to the wrong side and stitch through the guard to the turnings at the same point, making a strong bar tack. Finally stitch the base of the guard to the opened seam turnings.

position about 1 cm ($\frac{3}{8}$ in.) back from the edge of the trouser, or place it so that when the zip is fastened the edge of the fly on the left side covers not only the teeth but also the stitching on the right half of the trouser.

Back stitch or machine the zip to the facing, close to the teeth, then hem along the edge of the tape.

Bring the top edge of the facing and zip over the inside of the waistband. Back stitch across the facing, and hem down the raw edges.

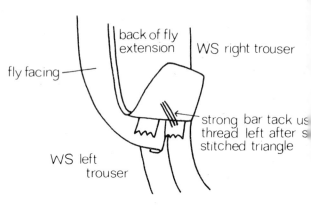

back of fly
extension

WS right trouser

fly facing

strong bar tack us
thread left after s
stitched triangle

WS left
trouser